INNOVATION AND THE STATE

From social media to subprime mortgage-backed securities, innovation carries both risk and opportunity. It also throws up profound regulatory challenges. As it evolves, innovation continually undermines, circumvents, and sidelines regulatory structures designed to accommodate it. Here, Cristie Ford investigates the relationships between contemporary regulatory approaches and private-sector innovation, and considers the implications of both for broader social welfare priorities including equality and voice.

Regulation is at the leading edge of politics and policy in ways not yet fully grasped. Seemingly innocuous regulatory design choices have clear and profound practical ramifications for many of our most cherished social commitments. Innovation is a complex phenomenon that needs to be understood not only in technical terms but also in human ones. Ford argues for a fresh approach to regulation that recognizes innovation for the regulatory challenge it is, and that binds our social values and our regulatory tools ever more tightly together.

Cristie Ford is Associate Professor and Director of the Centre for Business Law, Peter A. Allard School of Law, University of British Columbia. She is an internationally recognized scholar in the fields of financial regulation and regulatory theory. She has written, lectured, and consulted extensively on financial regulation and was previously editor of the journal *Regulation & Governance*. She is also a coauthor of the leading securities regulation text in Canada.

Innovation and the State

FINANCE, REGULATION, AND JUSTICE

CRISTIE FORD

Peter A. Allard School of Law,
University of British Columbia

CAMBRIDGE
UNIVERSITY PRESS

CAMBRIDGE
UNIVERSITY PRESS

One Liberty Plaza, 20th Floor, New York, NY 10006, USA

Cambridge University Press is part of the University of Cambridge.

It furthers the University's mission by disseminating knowledge in the pursuit of education, learning, and research at the highest international levels of excellence.

www.cambridge.org
Information on this title: www.cambridge.org/9781107644892
DOI: 10.1017/9781139583473

First published 2017

Printed in the United States by Sheridan Books, Inc.

A catalogue record for this publication is available from the British Library.

Library of Congress Cataloging-in-Publication Data
Names: Ford, Cristie, author.
Title: Innovation and the state: finance, regulation, and justice / Cristie Ford.
Description: New York: Cambridge University Press, 2017. |
Includes bibliographical references and index.
Identifiers: LCCN 2017023475 | ISBN 9781107037076 (hardback) |
ISBN 9781107644892 (paperback)
Subjects: LCSH: Technological innovations – Economic aspects. | Industrial policy.
Classification: LCC HC79.T4 F648 2017 | DDC 338/.064–dc23
LC record available at https://lccn.loc.gov/2017023475

ISBN 978-1-107-03707-6 Hardback
ISBN 978-1-107-64489-2 Paperback

Dedicated with immeasurable love and gratitude to my family

The bourgeoisie cannot exist without constantly revolutionizing the instruments of production, and thereby the relations of production, and with them the whole relations of society.... All fixed, fast-frozen relations, with their train of ancient and venerable prejudices and opinions are swept away, all new-formed ones become antiquated before they can ossify. All that is solid melts into air, all that is holy is profaned, and man is at last compelled to face with sober senses, his real conditions of life, and his relations with his kind.

Karl Marx and Friedrich Engels, *The Communist Manifesto*

The major impulses to successful financial innovations over the last twenty years have come, I am saddened to have to say, from regulations and taxes.

Merton Miller, 'Financial Innovation: The Last Twenty Years and the Next', *Journal of Financial and Quantitative Analysis*, 1986

Contents

Figures

Tables

Acknowledgments

No book can be produced without enormous help from many quarters. A book such as this one, which aims to link legal sub-disciplines that do not always speak directly to each other, and which also aims for some level of interdisciplinarity, has perhaps drawn on (and drawn on the patience of) a wider group of readers than most. For their encouragement, engagement, and insightful feedback on previous drafts and portions of this book, I am very much indebted to Dan Awrey, Lawrence Baxter, Julia Black, John Braithwaite, Alex Burton, Cary Coglianese, Onnig Dombalagian, Adam Feibelman, Stavros Gadinis, Erik Gerding, Benjamin Goold, Fiona Haines, Douglas C. Harris, Carol Heimer, Camden Hutchison, Rony Kahan, Don Langevoort, David Levi-Faur, Emilio Marti, Saule Omarova, Christine Parker, Frank Partnoy, Nancy Reichman, Tanina Rostain, Chuck Sabel, Dan Schwarcz, Jodi Short, Susan Silbey, Steve Davidoff Solomon, Elen Stokes, Judith van Erp, Bill Wilhelm, and David Zaring.

This project has also benefited greatly from feedback from participants at faculty lectures and workshops from 2014 through 2016 at the Bar Ilan, Berkeley, Cornell, Georgetown, Hebrew University, Tulane, University of British Columbia, and Utrecht Faculties of Law; and the Centre for Corporate Reputation at Oxford University. An earlier version of Chapter 1 was published as Cristie Ford, "Innovation-framing regulation" (2013) 649 *Annals Am Acad Polit & Soc Sci* 76–97, on which I received helpful feedback from participants at the volume's associated workshop at the Faculty of Anthropology at MIT. I also appreciate the helpful feedback received at annual meetings of the Law and Society Association and the Society for the Advancement of Socio-Economics, and the fifth and sixth Regulation & Governance biennial conferences of the European Consortium for Political Research. Errors and omissions of course remain my own.

I have enlisted the help of several research assistants from my home institution, the Peter A. Allard School of Law at UBC, over the long course of this project. Each of them demonstrated exceptional commitment and thoughtfulness, and each contributed in unique and valuable ways. My sincere thanks go to Andrew Burgess, Dustin Chelen, Stephanie Dickson, Sebastian Ennis, Emilie Feil-Fraser, Hardeep Gill, Kelly Kan, Vera Mirhady, Carly Peddle, Kendra Shupe, and David Wu for their engagement, their curiosity, and their dedication. I could not have hoped for a more talented or pleasant set of interlocutors. Their contributions, and this book, would not have come to pass without the support of research grants from TMX Group Capital Markets Initiative, the Law Foundation of British Columbia, and the Allard School of Law, which I very much appreciate. My thanks, as well, to Lisa Gourd for insightful copyediting on the first three chapters, and to my editor, John Berger.

Above all, I am grateful to my family for supporting this project, and me, in more ways than I could possibly say. This book is for my beloveds – Sasha, Moss, and Nina Liv – and is in honor of the two fierce, loving, and remarkable women who raised me to imagine that writing academic books might be a reasonable thing for me to do: Liv Kulterstad Oyen (1909–2009), and Donna Oyen Ford.

Abbreviations

ACBC	Asset-Backed Commercial Paper
CDO	collateralized debt obligation
CDS	credit default swap
CFPB	Consumer Financial Protection Bureau
CSE	Consolidated Supervised Entities
EMT	Efficient Market Theory
FASB	Financial Accounting Standards Board
FDA	Federal Drug Administration
FSA	Financial Services Authority (UK)
FSB	Financial Stability Board
FSOC	Financial Stability Oversight Council
GAAP	generally accepted accounting principles
HFT	high-frequency trading
IFRS	International Financial Reporting Standards
IOSCO	International Organization of Securities Commissions
ISDA	International Swaps and Derivatives Association
LTCM	Long-Term Capital Management
MMS	Minerals Management Service
NPM	New Public Management
NPR	National Program Review
OFR	Office of Financial Research
OMB	Office of Management and Budget
OTC	over-the-counter
PIG	public interest group
SEC	Securities and Exchange Commission
SPV	special-purpose vehicles
VaR	Value at Risk
WEF	World Economic Forum

Introduction: Why Innovation Is Not (Just) Romantic, and Regulation Is Not Dull

INNOVATION AND REGULATION

This book is being written during an ideological "cusp time," in the wake of an unexpected rise in political populism across the United States, the United Kingdom, and Europe. The year 2016 was politically an extraordinary one, which saw the election of a President Donald Trump in the United States (after the unexpected political rise and then fall of a socialist senator from Vermont, Bernie Sanders, as a potential Democratic Party candidate), along with a British popular vote in favor of leaving the European Union, rising populism in Europe, and a generally palpable sense of popular anger. Clearly, this is not business as usual. The target of the anger varies – big banks, off-shore workers, undocumented immigrants, refugees, people with any range of minority characteristics, elites. Some versions of this early twenty-first-century version of populism carry alarming strains of racist and anti-democratic sentiment, which must be resisted. A more common theme, though – and perhaps one we might be sympathetic to – seems to be deep popular dissatisfaction with the political status quo, with globalization and its dislocations, and a sense of increasing inequality, loss of opportunity, and a sense that the benefits of globalization have been concentrated among a small few. At least one public intellectual has blamed the recent rise of populist anger on a thing called "neoliberalism."[1]

By the time this book is published, the current political moment will be passing and we will be confronting a newer iteration of these challenges. Yet the wheels of policy, as opposed to politics, will grind forward in their slow way, and it is at this level that fundamental change will be embedded, institutionalized, and made real. As a scholar of regulation, my contribution lies in drawing the long arc of policy over the last few decades.

Though it takes different forms, one of the key questions before us is really how we intend to deal with the effects of innovation in our societies. We love innovation – crowdsourcing, the sharing economy, communications technology, the hive mind, and the extraordinary medical advances. But several distinct voices today also channel a degree of inchoate anger and confusion about the dark side of innovation. For innovation, of course, also produces globalization, financialization, complexity, surveillance, and insecurity. Groups of people win, and lose, when innovation changes the ground rules. Innovativeness begets power, and influence. To some extent, at least in regulatory terms, the fight from here will be about what kinds of policies we want to put in place to deal with these innovations and their consequences.

Some would say that our romance with innovation, and the thrall in which innovators sometimes hold the rest of us, have profoundly influenced the trajectory of public policy and regulation in the last three decades or more. Whether this is true is one of the questions this book tries to consider. Even if it is not so stark as all that, there is no doubt that private sector innovation and public sector regulation these past few decades have been engaged in a close and complex dance. Moreover, though a great deal has been said about "regulatory innovations," sometimes we are left with the sense that those innovations have been aimed primarily at making regulation more flexible, less burdensome, cheaper, and more efficient, not for everyone's sake but the sake of certain private sector actors and their innovative efforts.

Our collective romance with innovation presents powerful framing opportunities, including for those who describe their own work as part of a grand innovation narrative. This group can include not only those seeking a cure for a particular cancer, but those seeking to protect the statutory monopoly that patent law provides; not only those trying to get credit and insurance into the hands of poor women in the Global South, but also those trying to develop financial products that are more lucrative for their firms, and more illegible to regulation; not only those trying to build a sharing economy, with all its promise and peril, but also those burrowing ever more deeply and insidiously into once-private aspects of our lives.

Yet, of course, there is no easy separating "good" innovation from "bad," even if we could agree on what fell into each category. Nor can we, except at great cost, turn back the clock. The postwar Welfare State ceased to exist for reasons beyond ideology, though of course ideology mattered too. As much as we may now romanticize the postwar economic era, the path forward will have to look different from the path we have trod so far. Charting that path requires that we know where we have come from and where, exactly, we are now. Real work is needed at the level of policy and regulation. In the service of trying to generate a more decent, democratic, and effective kind of financial regulation, this book aims to highlight the relationship between innovation and regulation.

I argue that it is time for regulation, and regulatory scholars like me, to turn our gaze toward innovation as a phenomenon. What if, instead of seeing *regulation* as the flawed structure that we should be tinkering with, we turned our attention toward the problems that *innovation* itself presents – both for public policy, and for regulation itself? Thinking of innovation as a regulatory challenge (or a nested set of regulatory challenges) puts regulation on firmer and more independent footing. It makes it possible for regulators to articulate an autonomous, coherent set of regulatory priorities and practices, in the service of the public good, that amount to more than simply trying not to get in the way of private sector innovation, or trying not to fall too far behind its practitioners. This book tries to begin this project.

However, thinking of innovation in this way requires a more nuanced and granular understanding of private sector innovation than we have developed thus far. Innovation is not a monolithic phenomenon, and it interacts with regulation in a variety of different ways. For instance, sometimes innovations are specifically designed to circumvent regulatory restrictions. Sometimes, private sector innovations can be incorporated into regulation, thereby improving it. Sometimes, innovation proceeds quite oblivious to regulation, even while it has the effect of undermining regulatory goals. Thinking more carefully about these interactions also requires us to understand how regulation has ended up being so apparently change-loving, innovation-focused, and sometimes deferential to private actors. It requires embedding more, and more careful learning about innovation into our regulatory structures. Indeed, we need to ask a fresh set of questions before we can even *see* innovation happening clearly. Finally, and most fundamentally, thinking about innovation as a regulatory challenge should push us to think more deeply about why, as a matter of public policy, we value innovation as highly as we do and what tradeoffs we make when we give it priority of place. These are the challenges this book undertakes.

This book advances the idea that financial regulation will be more effective if it substantially redirects its attention toward a different regulatory object: toward financial innovation itself.[2] This is not because financial innovation is invariably bad; it is not. It is not because I am opposed to innovation, financial or otherwise. I am not. It is because focusing on regulating innovation can serve as an Occam's razor for cutting through the otherwise-almost crippling sets of overlapping, multiscalar, interconnected considerations and concerns that animate regulation in the very complicated, complex spaces in which financial regulation must operate.

The project was spurred by some of the hard questions raised by the 2007–2008 financial crisis about the ways in which regulation, particularly the regulation of innovative financial products, has been structured over the last two decades. More about that later. But it was a line in the UK Financial Services Authority's (FSA's) Turner Review from March 2009 that provoked its precise shape. In his analysis of the origins of and responses to the financial crisis, Lord Adair Turner makes this observation:

> An underlying assumption of financial regulation in the US, the UK and across the world, has been that financial innovation is by definition beneficial, since market discipline will winnow out any unnecessary or value destructive innovations. As a result, regulators have not considered it their role to judge the value of different financial products, and they have in general avoided direct product regulation, certainly in wholesale markets with sophisticated investors.[3]

This is a provocative statement. Breaking the quote down, Lord Turner is making three separate points, each of which is potentially controversial. His first claim is that financial regulation across the world assumed that financial innovation is by definition beneficial. I cannot speak for transnational financial regulation as a whole, though I have my doubts that the assumptions underlying financial regulation "in the US, the UK and across the world" were quite so wholesale or monolithic as all that. The Turner Review does not pretend to have done the empirical work needed to support that assertion.

Second, Lord Turner is saying that the *reason* financial innovation was thought to be beneficial was because market discipline – that is, an efficient and rational market – could be counted on to winnow out unproductive ideas. In other words, according to Lord Turner, financial regulators across the world had accepted, wholeheartedly if not explicitly, what is known as the Efficient Market Theory (EMT). The EMT posits that the collective behavior of rational, self-interested actors in a frictionless market will lead to the most efficient possible allocation of resources. Few working in economics believe that such a market actually exists outside the realm of theory. However, Lord Turner suggests that financial regulators believed it, at least in the wholesale markets, where ostensibly sophisticated investors like global financial institutions manufacture and market new financial products.

Lord Turner's third claim follows from the second. If the market is the most efficient way to allocate resources, then financial regulators can only mess things up by intervening in the market, whether to judge the value of different financial products or to regulate them. In other words, according to Lord Turner, in the highly innovative and fast-moving world in which wholesale-level financial institutions operate, even regulators saw themselves as having virtually no active role at the regulatory "front end" (though presumably they could still enforce the anti-fraud and other laws at the enforcement "back end").

I am a legal scholar who writes about financial regulation. Among other things, I write about the speed and complexity that characterize financial markets, and I think about what this means for regulation. I have even written favorably about the main target of Lord Turner's critique, the (now abolished) FSA in the UK. Yet, reading Lord Turner's analysis, I can say that embracing private sector innovation and celebrating market discipline was not what I thought I was doing in my work. Nor did his words resonate as an accurate account of what I thought my colleagues in regulation and governance studies were doing. On the contrary, I would wager that most of my academic colleagues in the field would have celebrated the idea of a tough, independent-minded, well-resourced regulator, as I did, and celebrated the renewed sense of regulatory mission that Lord Turner's review helped generate.

Certainly, financial regulatory scholarship, like regulatory scholarship generally, has changed a great deal over the past two or three decades. There is a sort of superficial, at-first-glance correspondence between the innovation-loving model Lord Turner describes and the receptiveness to innovation in the regulatory work that I know. But very little of this work has had much to do with unmitigated faith in market discipline or the kind of chastened regulatory role the Turner Review described.

If asked to define the goals of regulation and governance scholarship generally, of most financial regulation scholarship, or of my own work, I would have said they were to strengthen and deepen public regulation in order to help it better meet the challenges of contemporary society, not to cede the field to private actors based on some sweeping confidence in market forces (or, indeed, in self-interested market actors). The scholars whose work I know best are overwhelmingly concerned with what in North America are understood as progressive priorities: they want to deploy innovative regulatory strategies in the service of equality and human dignity, environmental regulation, workplace safety, employment discrimination, and the like. They are not blind to the ways in which market behavior can advance self-interested and even predatory behavior. While some may be skeptical of old-style, rigid formulations of "rights" and argue that they should be opened up to debate, they do so not out of a desire to roll back hard-won successes of equality-seeking groups but rather to make them even more meaningful. If they find rights-based analysis unsatisfactory, it is because it does not go far enough in promoting priorities such as equality and human flourishing.[4] While some scholars may adopt locally driven (including private sector) innovations as a basis for regulatory change, they do not imagine that self-regulation on its own is a prescription for greater social welfare. Rather, they seek to link private, local learning with a public – and publicly enforced – set of goals and to embed public-mindedness, compliance, and responsibility into private institutions.

In the wake of the financial crisis and in the midst of a populist political moment, marked by widespread anger and a perception that the dislocations and losses associated with innovation and globalization have been concentrated while its benefits have not been shared, the path forward for progressive priorities is not yet clear. A great deal of important work is being done to understand the origins and nature of inequality and its relationship to political and economic choices. There is work to be done at the level of "high politics" – those high salience moments, like elections, when everyone is paying attention.[5] At the same time, "high politics" are always only part of the picture, and they can be unpredictable. The "low politics" of regulatory structure and policy are where a lot of real work gets done.

Regulation is at the leading edge of politics and policy in ways that we do not always fully grasp. Seemingly innocuous regulatory design choices have clear and profound practical ramifications for many of our most cherished social commitments. This book examines the somewhat wonkish, unglamorous, and yet highly consequential world of regulation as it relates to the phenomenon of innovation: it asks how regulation should understand innovation, and how it should respond to it. For regulation affects innovation, but the converse is also true.

This is this book's essential point: that as much as progressive-minded and equality-seeking people may celebrate initiatives geared toward, say, enhancing normal peoples' access to and voice within financial regulation policy, or exerting more effective regulatory oversight over the financial institutions that affect everyone's financial wellbeing,[6] those initiatives and others like them will not be certain to succeed if we do not also start to think of innovation (and in that context, financial innovation) as a *first-order concern* for regulation. Without losing sight of its broader normative goals, regulatory attention – in securities, in banking, in insurance, and in systemic risk regulation – needs to shift more of its operational focus toward innovation itself, and the ways that it undermines and circumvents the best-laid regulatory structures. This involves understanding innovation as a technological phenomenon, but also as a very human, almost sociological phenomenon. By looking closely at both contemporary regulatory approaches, and the nature of innovation, this book begins the work of developing the vocabulary and approach required to understand how to design regulation that is better able to withstand innovation's corrosive effects.

INNOVATION, PROGRESS, HOPE

To say that we live in an age of innovation and rapid change is such a trite and eye-rollingly tired observation – and such a true one – that most of the time we can hardly bear to make it. We have been grappling with profound change for centuries now. In some parts of some societies, hardly any generation since the Renaissance has been spared momentous change over its life span. But still, these days, change – particularly human-generated change, and particularly spurred by innovations in computing and communications technology – is clearly moving very quickly. Hot innovation topics over the last year have included communications and social media technology, artificial intelligence, big data, driverless cars, functional MRI and brain mapping, DNA mapping and CRISPR, the rise of the sharing economy and new financial technology ("fintech"), and cyberterrorism.[7] Even by the time this book goes to press, new topics will have been added to that list.

The idea that human innovation is a central driver of positive social change and greater human flourishing is not new. Nor is resistance to it, which dates at least as far back as the Luddites' famous crusade against the mechanical loom.[8] Yet most of us today would probably prefer a world that is constantly being remade by human innovation to one that is shackled to the eternal wheel of unchanging fate. Westerners today can barely conceive of their lives in the static, resource-poor, and generally zero-sum terms that characterized (and for many people in the world, continue to characterize) most of human existence.

Our dominant cultural story continues to be pro-innovation (and pro-growth).[9] Innovation is the product of that most cherished good, human creativity. It carries with it the prospect of problems solved and diseases eradicated, of fresh adventures and a larger pie. For most people to be anti-innovation is still to be unenlightened, fearful, backward, and blind to possibility. Change-resisters – individuals, corporations, states, even *species* specialists like migratory songbirds and polar bears – are doomed, often tragically, to the wrong side of history. Our public policy choices and our public dialogue endlessly reflect this, often speaking of innovativeness as if there could be no higher compliment.

Certainly there are times when the debate is more nuanced, and we seem more aware of both the pros and the cons of innovation.[10] In particular, we understand that we rarely know exactly where our innovations will lead us. We may be convinced that innovation is generally a good thing – sometimes, a great thing – but we also recognize that it brings with it new risks and new anxieties. Our concerns today focus around the ways in which an increasingly integrated global economy, communications technology, financial engineering, and anthropogenic climate change and environmental degradation – all products of human innovation – could affect our standards of living, our privacy and personal security, our physical communities, and our interpersonal connections.[11] Financial innovation in particular is sometimes treated almost as a traitor to the otherwise-virtuous innovative cause, or some malign, outlier form that needs to be eradicated without disturbing the broader innovative effort.

Our current post-crisis political moment is marked by greater than usual concern about the effects of innovation. Yet this moment is analogous to the weather event – the particularly cold winter – that seemingly gives the lie to the claim that the climate is changing. In fact, climate reflects the broader pattern, and weather is variation along the way. Fundamentally, our modern Western social and economic climate still cannot imagine a future without innovation. Or, perhaps it is more accurate to say that we resist confronting the real costs associated with our affluent, convenient, miraculous modern age. Where we can, we prefer to embrace have-our-cake-and-eat-it-too solutions: "sustainable" growth, "green" energy, silver-bullet new innovative solutions. When the challenges innovation has generated seem too closely connected to benefits we cannot stand to part with (like our fossil fuel-reliant homes and vehicles, the Green Revolution in agriculture, incredibly cheap consumer goods), we may lapse into paralysis. Ours is an era of persistent hope about what human ingenuity may produce, coupled sometimes with denial and inchoate apprehension about its potential consequences.

Contemporary word use illustrates where the balance sits. Through linguistic analysis of popular and academic English language word use – itself a "big data" innovation – we can see which words we use most commonly and how we use them. It turns out that the word "innovation" figures prominently. In late 2012, "innovation" ranked 3684 within the 60,000 most commonly used English words, placing it near the top 6 percent, which is high given that the top scorers were words like "the," "be," and "and."[12] Interestingly, "innovation" is used more frequently than "liberty" and "equality," and much more frequently than "globalization." And although it ranks well below words used in a wide variety of contexts, like "risk" and "growth," it is not actually that far behind "democracy" or "freedom."[13]

The academic sector uses the word "innovation" more – just under half of its use is in academic sources[14] – but close to another third of its frequency among most commonly used English words comes from popular magazines. As well, innovation is associated with very positive normative language. We can discern this by looking at "collocates" – the words that tend to appear next to or close to a root word.[15] The top collocates for "innovation" include words such as: "important," "key," "successful," "encourage," "introduce," "leadership," "promote," "progress," "educational," "adopt," "improvement," "invest," "creative," "initiative," "discovery," "inspire," "embrace," and "exciting."[16] This means the top hits for "innovation" in the corpus include phrases like "we should embrace innovation" or "an exciting innovation." Overall, our collective conversation around innovation tends to be highly normative, and highly positive.

Comparing the top collocates for "innovation" with those for words like "growth," "globalization," and "regulation" only reinforces this point. These words carried far less explicit normative content. Most commonly, their collocates were indicators of the pace, type, or nature of the root word. For example, "globalization trend" and "command regulation" were common phrases. Even related words like "freedom" had slightly less normative content than "innovation," perhaps because the normative goodness of freedom is so accepted as no longer to merit discussion.[17]

Based on their collocates, the normative content of the word "liberty" slightly outstripped "innovation," and words like "equality" and "democracy" outstripped it further.[18] These words tended to be associated with highly normative collocates, such as "protection," "respect," "privilege," "ideal," "blessing," and "happiness." It is no surprise that "innovation" is less normatively laden than "liberty," "equality," and "democracy," words of a far stronger and deeper vintage. The fact that "innovation" is even comparable to those words, in terms of normative load and frequency of use, illustrates how deeply it has become embedded in our collective imagination. What is more, the collocates for "innovation" tend to be more energetic and forward-looking. We may "protect" or "respect" well-established principles like democracy, but we want to "embrace" innovation, which is "exciting."

Our romantic associations with innovation cannot help but influence our response to it, including our public response in the form of regulation.

WHAT DOES CONTEMPORARY REGULATION LOOK LIKE?

The idea of innovation pops up everywhere in contemporary life. By contrast, regulation – this book's other main concern – operates in a hard-to-see, seemingly technocratic layer, insulated from the realm of easy sloganeering and popular engagement. And yet it is crucial legal architecture: it touches virtually every facet of modern life. What is more, *how* it structures aspects of modern life – the tools it uses, the points at which it enters – fundamentally shapes the options available to private sector actors and affects their conduct in subtle but highly consequential ways.

What is regulation? The Oxford English Dictionary defines it as "a rule or directive made and maintained by an authority."[19] When used in this way, regulation can be understood as a subspecies of the broader category of law. Yet other definitions would actually make law a subspecies of regulation. Particularly when it is linked to the broader notion of "governance," regulation can be understood as incorporating not only formal, traditional state activity but also a broad range of influential non-state forces.[20]

For our purposes, two other definitions of "regulation" are especially useful. The first is Philip Selznick's, who defines it as the "sustained and focused control exercised by a public agency over activities that are valued by a community."[21] Selznick's definition emphasizes the public nature of regulation and its connection to policy priorities. Describing regulation as "sustained" distinguishes it from ad hoc enforcement activity or specific deterrence. However, it may bring to mind a direct, top-down, agency-driven effort at control, something that not all contemporary regulatory structures necessarily do. (Selznick's definition dates from 1985, eons ago in regulatory time.) It also implies that the public agency will inevitably succeed in its efforts to control the designated activities, which, of course, is not always true.

A second definition is Julia Black's: she defines regulation as "the intentional activity of attempting to control, order or influence the behaviour of others."[22] As Black notes, intentionality is an important element that distinguishes regulation from non-intentional forces – like the market, social norms, or technologies – that may also control, order or influence behavior. As chapters 3 and 4 show, flexible regulatory structures often seek to harness and steer these other forces, directly or indirectly, even while they maintain a public character that is distinct from them. Black's definition allows for any agent, not just the state, to be attempting to regulate. While non-state action certainly can control, order, or influence behavior, my interest is primarily in state action (whether acting directly, for example, through legal sanction, or when intentionally trying to influence other phenomena, like the market or social pressure, through the use of its legal and structuring tools). For our purposes, then, regulation should be defined as *sustained and intentional activity by the state in attempting, through direct or indirect methods, to control, order, or influence the behaviour of others in the service of public policy priorities.*

Contemporary regulation may attempt to control, order, or influence the behaviour of others in a variety of direct or indirect ways. As Christopher Hood and his coauthors have pointed out, regulation requires three fundamental things: there must be "some capacity for *standard-setting* to allow a distinction to be made between more and less preferred states of the system ... some capacity for *information-gathering* or monitoring to produce knowledge about current or changing states of the system … [and] some capacity for *behaviour-modification* to change the state of the system."[23] Each of these components can be structured in several different ways. For example, the standard-setting component can be rules-based or principles-based, detailed or "bright-line," static or dynamic. The mechanisms for information gathering are many too, but include formal state compliance and investigatory mechanisms, third-party input, and mandatory disclosure or information-forcing requirements. Behaviour modification strategies are equally varied: they may include various different kinds of formal sanctions (e.g., fines, incarceration, license revocation), as well as more indirect strategies, still built into the regulatory regime, that assume that regulation can be used to channel and control social norms, public pressure, market forces, or other behaviour modifiers.[24]

These choices matter. Regulation is literally constitutive of its environment – it forms it in important ways – and is in a reflexive, two-way relationship with that environment. Regulation helps set background conditions for regulated actors, and profoundly affects individual private lives in the process. Regulation has its official objectives: e.g., to ensure good telephone access in rural areas of sparsely populated country, to ensure that airlines abide by consistent safety rules, or to maintain the stability and integrity of the capital markets. Yet the means through which regulation tries to advance these objectives will have their consequences too: they can either promote competition or protect cartels;[25] they can encourage consumption, or conservation;[26] they can restructure business processes, sometimes introducing new conflicts of interest or regulatory problems in the process.[27] Precisely *how* regulation goes about trying to achieve its official objectives can have enormous and sometimes unforeseen consequences for other values that we collectively hold dear.

When people think about innovation, they usually imagine the innovator to be a private sector entity. In fact, the notion of innovativeness, as something to strive toward, has also diffused into the tissues of our laws and our state apparatus, often in unrealized and unappreciated ways. The public sector has also been innovating, and rapidly so, over the past quarter-century. And while regulatory innovation – that is, regulators developing and applying novel techniques and forms – may be a subtle phenomenon, its effect has been considerable. We cannot understand the contemporary era, or the policy choices facing us now, without a clearer sense of what recent regulatory innovation has looked like, how flexible regulation came to be, and how it is related to private sector innovation – and influence.

Across subject areas, one of the truly significant shifts in regulatory theory over the last few decades has been a move to a new, more variable and interactive kind of state regulatory apparatus. Let us call this project "flexible regulation."

Regulatory scholarship has moved beyond the rigid rules and binary choices of traditional mechanisms to deploy a fuller and more richly stocked regulatory toolkit. While there are differences between them, the several versions of flexible regulation share a common feature: they seek to tailor regulatory tools to the specific needs of the situation at hand – to move away from one-size-fits-all prescriptions to a more context-sensitive and dynamic approach.

Flexible regulation, as it developed from the 1990s onward, aimed to be outcome-oriented, pragmatic, and data-driven. It used empirical performance measures to assess its own performance as well as that of regulated actors, transcending conceptual boundaries (national, federal, public/private) where evidence suggested that those boundaries were overdrawn or counterproductive. It aimed to better recognize and leverage compliance-enhancing non-legal forces – including community norms, individual morality, and market forces – both by themselves and as leveraged by legal mechanisms. Perhaps above all, flexible regulation sought to be iterative: to register change in its environment, to develop contingent strategies and provisional responses, and to adjust its behavior based on context and its own experience. As Orly Lobel has said, "the idea of dynamic [regulatory] innovation is intrinsic to the theory."[28]

Regulation scholarship over the last three decades has both reflected and helped to create real-life regulatory transformation. Since the 1990s, regulation scholarship has emerged as a distinct and important field that cuts across social science disciplines including law, political science, psychology, sociology, history, and economics. Focusing on this scholarship is illuminating in an era marked by globalization, the fracturing of the Welfare State, populist discontent, and the subtle trickling-down of some very large normative questions into what a Canadian Supreme Court judge once colorfully called "the bowels and recesses of government departments."[29] Regulatory studies examine not only this subtle but enormously consequential shift of state action downward to agency regulation, but also the lateral shift toward novel "beyond the state" strategies for achieving public ends, as well as the "upward" shift to the transnational and network-based realms of action. Perhaps more than any other group, regulation scholars work on the pressing and difficult problems that sit at the three-way intersection between high-level public priorities, on-the-ground implementation, and the challenge of ongoing human-generated change.

A THOUGHT EXPERIMENT: INNOVATION-FOSTERING REGULATION

How are innovation and regulation even connected? The hoariest old observation, dating from the anti-bureaucratic late 1970s, if not earlier, is that regulation, with its red tape and sclerotic processes, stifles innovation. Contemporary regulation scholars might counter that that has not been an accurate image for some time. Evaluating these claims requires looking at the details of regulatory design, and trying to think about how its structural features might either inhibit or foster private sector innovation. We can all perhaps imagine a regulatory regime that, successfully or otherwise, tries to shut down innovation. So let us begin with the contrary thought experiment: what would it look like if we were to design regulation that really, truly *fostered* innovation? (In the current post-financial crisis, populist era, it may be worthwhile to try to hold two different images in mind while engaging in the experiment: the celebrated cancer research innovator on one side; and the reportedly conscience-free Wall Street financial innovator, or the global corporate job-outsourcer, on the other.)

What is innovation? The Oxford English Dictionary defines it as the act or process of making "changes in something established, especially by introducing new methods, ideas, or products."[30] As opposed to an invention, which is the first creation of an idea or good, innovation is the process of applying an idea in practice. In other words, invention becomes innovation when it enters the world of action. For financial innovation, I adopt Peter Tufano's definition: "financial innovation is the act of creating and then popularizing new financial instruments as well as new financial technologies, institutions and markets."[31] Crucially, for our purposes, financial innovation includes not only the new financial instruments that mathematicians or finance scholars or economists may help to create, and bankers to market. It also includes the work that lawyers do in creatively deploying old instruments in new contexts, reimagining market and regulatory structures, and identifying and helping their clients to take advantage of new opportunities. Legal innovation is a central, inextricable part of financial innovation.

The first step to developing truly innovation-fostering regulation would be to understand what private sector innovation looked like and how it developed, so that regulation could work with and enhance innovation's own natural tendencies.[32] What does private sector innovation look like? We now understand that it tends to be a social, not individual, phenomenon. The idea of the lone inventor toiling away in basement solitude does not actually reflect how innovation usually arises. Most of the time, innovation is the product of incremental steps made by many people, generally within particular social or industry spaces that become hubs of innovation. Innovations may be diffused across different organizations and through networks, but within industries there tend to be "nodes" of particular productivity. Diffusion of innovations, close imitations, and small modifications affect the path of innovation too, and often contribute to a new and unanticipated round of innovation.

Innovation is also often undertaken for self-interested reasons. People are more likely to innovate in ways that offer them potential rewards of a kind they value. Particularly in capitalist systems, innovation is very often undertaken by for-profit entities, which innovate in ways that tend to be aligned with their own business models and their bottom lines. A private entity's structural characteristics, including its self-described mandate and its organizational posture, affect whether it is likely to innovate, and what kind of innovation be it is likely to foster. So does its position relative to its peers: geographic clustering and network effects (including whether an organization shares weak or strong network ties with others, and its proximity or status as a network hub) will influence how innovative it is, and how influential its innovations are. The regulatory structure, including the strength of property rights regimes, can create new opportunities for innovation or affect the speed and trajectory its diffusion. Reportedly, there is also such a thing as an "innovative personality profile," describing the out-of-the-box individual who has a greater-than-average willingness to question assumptions and boundaries. At the same time, such nonconformity notwithstanding, most of the time norm-driven compliance acts as a brake on the boldest and most boundary-pushing innovative instincts.[33]

With all of this in mind, the starting point for this thought experiment in developing innovation-fostering regulation would be to notice that a regulator, from its central position, really could not have that much control over the direction of innovation at all. Having made the assumption that innovation was, on balance, beneficial – which we have already done by this point, without really even noticing it – we must conclude that innovation can be counted on to build on its own momentum and carve its own course. The regulatory structure could establish other priorities – innovation for its own sake would not be its goal – but subject to such limits on scope, the mechanisms by which innovation proceeded would be left up to the innovative process itself.

Because private innovators tend to be self-interested (and here our hypothetical regulator, innovation-loving though it is, would have to make a small concession and recognize that completely unfettered private sector innovation may not be totally beneficial for the rest of us), the regulatory regime would want to establish outer perimeters for permissible private innovation, and it would want to establish its own set of regulatory goals and expectations that were distinct from those of private innovators. Because innovators as individual personalities may be willing to push the boundaries not only of established ways of thinking but also of regulation, law, and even morality, the outer boundaries of permissible conduct would have to be policed and their breach sanctioned. Beyond that, however, the *means* that innovative private actors used to reach those regulatory goals would really be best left to the private actors themselves, and to the collective energy of their networks. Because innovation is such a mutable and fundamentally unpredictable phenomenon, it would not make sense to try to distinguish in the abstract, or *ex ante*, between "good" and "bad" forms of innovation. The regulator should not imagine that it could predict the potential future value of an innovation.

What our hypothetical regulator would hope is that, freed from the fetters of overly rigid regulation, private innovators would be in a position to improve not only their own welfare but others' too, along with the regulatory regime writ large. If innovators could bring the same creative energy they have around, say, new product development to the question of how they comply with regulation, even regulation itself could be radically improved. Because most regulated entities comply with regulation most of the time, it is in regulated entities' interest to have a low-burden regulatory regime that can be flexible and fosters trust with good actors, while still credibly punishing misfeasors.[34] A regulatory jurisdiction that fosters innovation and that is attractive to innovative actors would offer a competitive advantage over other jurisdictions. Its economy would reap the benefits. And beyond that, a regulatory regime that allows innovative actors to contribute to regulatory design, by determining in their own enlightened self-interest how best to meet regulatory goals, is a regulatory regime that could be expected to produce better results overall, both in terms of regulatory outcomes and regulatory efficiency. Even better, if the regulator in our thought experiment could incorporate some form of comparative, iterative "best practices" learning into its regulatory structure, then the competitive, social, cumulative nature of innovation could be harnessed in the service of ever more efficient and effective regulatory design.

Now, notice what is left out of this narrative. It has proceeded on the assumption that innovation is a sort of productive force that can be harnessed, but we have not developed a particularly filled-out image of what innovation looks like – how it develops, who develops it, to what ends, or what it looks like as a geographic, sociological, economic, or normative phenomenon. The depiction of innovation is inspiring, like an organic outpouring of creativity and progress, but it is also stylized, more evocative than actually elucidated. Note also the casual way in which control, or agency, has been ceded to innovators. The assumption turns out to be that innovators, though self-interested, are still in a better position to chart a course forward than regulators would be. There is no positive, affirmative account of a public role in this narrative, apart from a sort of general boundary-setting one. Note, finally, the apparent absence of struggles over hard choices. On the contrary, there is a sense that innovation will lift all boats – that valuing and enabling innovation can ease or perhaps even resolve difficult tradeoffs among priorities or interests. The narrative holds out the possibility of improvement across the board – of regulation that, by fostering innovation, regulates effectively, almost effortlessly, even while being easier to comply with and attractive to high-performing industry actors.

Stepping further back, we should also consider innovation's unpredictable effects on the regulatory landscape it occupies. Sometimes we fail to see the effects of innovations until they collect, as if suddenly, in unexpected locations (much as risk collected in over-the-counter derivatives markets in 2007–2008). In fact, those innovations may have built up over time but only registered with us after they had reached a certain critical volume. In this way, innovation is like water: a single droplet is rarely remarkable on its own, but many droplets together matter quite a lot. Moreover, innovation runs down avenues of opportunity, whether or not those outside the innovative process recognize those avenues. Innovation will run under, around, and over obstacles (including seemingly-clear regulatory requirements). If we extend the water metaphor further, we can say that innovation, like a watched pot, cannot be made to boil through force of will; it will boil (and sometimes boil over) when conditions suit, and according to its own properties. In modern societies that place social value on innovation and reward it in economic terms, states cannot and would not choose to stop the flow of private sector innovation, though they may try to channel it in particular directions.

However, innovation is also like water in its potentially corrosive effect. In the language of the business scholars, it is "disruptive." Decentralized, private sector innovation creates its own opportunities. It can open up novel and unexpected ways of working that challenge existing divisions of responsibility between regulators. It can destabilize or swamp regulatory structures, sometimes in obvious ways but sometimes in latent or inconspicuous ones. Even innovation that undermines and disrupts core components of regulation can sometimes be hard to track until it is very far along, by which point it will have gained momentum, interests and defenses will have coalesced around it, and it may have become hard to contain.

We are not used to thinking this way about the relationship between innovation and regulation. In the late 1970s, in what we might call the baroque phase of the Western Welfare State, we had a regulatory system that many thought was stifling innovation. Assume for the moment that that account is accurate: the system was the way it was, *not* because regulators were actively concerned about the risks associated with private sector innovation. They were not. The impact on innovation was at most a side effect of a heavy, traditional regulatory approach, which prioritized other things (stable wages and prices, collective security in illness or old age, high employment, and the like). Innovation was simply not regulation's main concern.

The regulatory approaches of the 1990s and 2000s seemingly became more innovation-fostering. Yet, again, this was not because regulators suddenly fully appreciated the water-like nature of private innovation and made a conscious, empirically informed, normatively careful decision that the benefits of embedding innovation into regulation outweighed the risks. They did not. Rather, regulation in this period was to some extent a reaction to the more rigid, earlier styles of regulation, and it operated sometimes based on a stylized conception of innovation.

Failures in financial regulation in the early years of this millennium contributed to the recent financial crisis. That crisis is still fairly fresh in our memory but, as Erik Gerding has pointed out, we have been here before: across the centuries, over and over, we seem to perform variations on a dance involving first innovation and deregulation (or deregulation and innovation – they are intertwined), followed by crisis, and then reactive reregulation.[35] If that is so, then the specific regulatory and political responses needed to respond to current problems are only part of a solution. The other part of the solution must depend on our acquiring a better understanding of the persistent subterranean streams of action and inclination that not only drove our most recent bubble-crash-crisis, and the weak and inequality-riven recovery that has followed it, but other crises in the past as well. Those streams of action and inclination are centrally concerned with ongoing human-generated change – that is, with innovation.

The idea of *innovation as a key challenge to regulation itself* has not been explored as part of any modern regulatory model. In fact, innovation – not specific instances of it, but private sector innovation itself as a phenomenon – is exactly the kind of risk that regulation should be concerned with. Innovation carries enormous potential, and the point is not to discourage it in some sweeping manner. All the same, it is time to consider how innovation is a challenge to regulation, and how regulation can engage more intentionally with it.

While some regulatory sectors are more buffeted by human innovation than others, in many sectors and across regulation generally, one of the great challenges facing regulation is learning to engage with innovation in a more systematic and conscious way. Instead of following through on the thought experiment above, the real question for socially minded scholars of regulation must be: what would it look like if we were to design regulation that genuinely understood not only the promise – which is considerable – but also the challenge that innovation presents?

ON REGULATION: THE WAY FORWARD

In seeking to chart a path forward for progressive-minded regulation in the wake of the financial crisis, my starting point is the intellectual space between the poles of Great Society-era regulation and Reagan-era deregulation – in the productive, novel work on the theory and practices of regulation and governance that emerged from the 1990s onward. The scholarly work that forms the core of this project was both witness to and progenitor of a meaningful shift in regulation, which tried to find footing, on uncertain and shifting new ground, for the social welfare-oriented impulses of the traditional state. These are scholars for whom humility about existing tools' capacity gave rise to greater interest in beyond-state forces, including both markets and engaged, deliberative communities.

Historically speaking, the various strands of flexible regulation emerged as alternatives to the so-called "bureaucratic" and "command-and-control" regulatory apparatus, which had lost credibility and support by the end of the 1970s. Relative to what came before it, flexible regulation was more concerned with how to develop regulatory strategies that were nimbler, more plastic, and capable of nuance and context-sensitivity (while still achieving regulatory objectives). Flexible regulatory strategies were a response not only to the discrediting of the old "Welfare State" at the time but also to factual uncertainty, increased complexity, and environmental heterogeneity. They were tools of law reform.

Regulatory scholarship also captured the zeitgeist in important ways. By the mid-1990s, the dominant schools in contemporary regulatory scholarship were advocating for a regulatory stance that was flexible, pragmatic, collaborative, *innovative*. In other words, their vision was, and in fact remains, intimately bound up with the particular concerns and assumptions of the late modern era in which we live. In particular, recent approaches to regulation have sought to link with and embed themselves into private sector innovation (and vice versa – to embed innovation into regulation) to a degree that would have been completely foreign to a regulator from an earlier generation. Studying this work also helps to unearth the reasons why some (not all) pro-government, progressive-minded scholarship adopted a number of regulatory stances that, with the benefit of hindsight, seem unacceptably blasé about the bona fides of private innovators or the urgency of independent-minded, energetic regulation.

It seems clear that there was something about the zeitgeist circa 1980 through 2007 that underpinned the recent financial crisis, as well as the regulatory inadequacies that contributed to it. Market fundamentalism of the Alan

Greenspan variety and deregulatory programs of the Reagan/Thatcher variety undeniably influenced regulatory priorities, regulatory scope, and regulatory structure. At the same time, these are too convenient as scapegoats. Blaming market fundamentalism for our woes allows us to see some of the specific errors of our ways, but it also oversimplifies the historical narrative. Most of us these days can abandon market fundamentalism without hesitation, if indeed we ever subscribed to it. It is much harder to grapple with the double-edged impact of innovation itself – something with which we are still romantically involved, even after the financial crisis, which is central to our modern selves, and which has contributed greatly to the Western standard of living. In crucial ways, understanding our commitment to innovation, including to developing regulatory structures that can work with it, is the key to understanding not only our current regulatory straits, but the path of financial innovation and regulation across time and into the future. Understanding our stance toward innovation, particularly financial innovation, in turn is key to understanding the phenomena underpinning globalization and, separately, inequality.

This book investigates the ways in which regulatory scholarship in the two decades leading up to the financial crisis proceeded on the basis of a partial and sometimes mistaken understanding of innovation. The promise and the risk associated with innovation turned out to be central to the regulatory project in areas like the oversight of new financial products. Yet while the word "innovation" was and continues to be bandied about, the literature, like society as a whole, seemingly failed to register that innovation was not, and is not, a monolithic phenomenon in terms of its trajectory or purposes. Nor is it an isolated phenomenon, hermetically sealed from related phenomena like the diffusion of innovations across a broader set of players. Perhaps more than anything, flexible regulation underestimated private innovation's potential to profoundly destabilize its environment, including the carefully designed contemporary regulatory structures established to harness or limit it.

This book is not an argument against flexible regulation. We will not have more success in grappling with innovation by trying to return to a world of over-bright and/or over-detailed, static, traditional regulation. While innovation presents difficult problems for flexible regulation, the solution is not to try to paper over a moving object or to suggest that facts on the ground are either more stable or more knowable than they actually are. Many aspects of modern societies *are* far too complex, diverse, and dynamic to be regulated in a centralized, command-and-control fashion.[36] Enlightened regulatory choices *should* sometimes (though not indiscriminately) seek ways to work with, harness, and even celebrate the creativity and the boundary-bursting fluidity of contemporary society, in the service of greater human flourishing. There is no putting the genie of innovation back into her bottle, and nor would most of us actually want to.

To be extra clear: this book also does not claim that flexible regulation (let alone flexible regulation scholarship) caused phenomena as multifactorial as the financial crisis or the rise of populist politics. It almost claims the opposite. Also, the fact that this book focuses on regulation does not signify that regulatory failure was what primarily caused the financial crisis. Emphatically, private sector conduct drove the financial system to the brink of collapse in 2007–2008. The forms of private sector financial innovation that have emerged in the years since – in fintech, in crowdfunding, in high-frequency trading, in dark pools and the sale of order flow – with all their considerable promise, and their considerable risks, will continue to drive disruption and present regulatory challenges.

The reason I focus on flexible regulation is not that it is the problem. On the contrary, it is within this body of work that we will find the potential solutions to the regulatory challenge that innovation continues to present. Regulation's relationship to private sector innovation was two things in the post-Reagan, pre-crisis era: it was largely underappreciated, and it was hugely consequential. Without having had a genuine policy conversation about innovation and without investigating closely how it operates, regulation over the last quarter-century has been deeply enmeshed with it. We have made progress in understanding financial innovation, but the links between innovation and regulation remain under-examined. Moreover, the relationship between innovation and regulation implicates important normative questions that sometimes – whether or not by design – were pushed aside. Arguably, the consequences have been most pronounced in that most innovative (and most unapologetically capitalist) industry: global finance. The challenge now for flexible regulation, as for all regulation, is to learn how to see private sector innovation as the regulatory challenge that it very much is. The challenge for legal scholars is to better embed fundamental legal values and structures – the rule of law, human dignity, accountability and reason-giving, "justice" – into financial regulation.

This book's first chapter presents four innovation stories. It describes how several different forms of financial regulation, though for different reasons, created regulatory structures that turned out to be porous to private sector innovation, the full consequences of which went unappreciated. Using examples drawn from accounting rules, the regulation of commercial paper, global capital adequacy requirements for financial institutions, and the unregulated over-the-counter derivatives market, these narratives illustrate how innovation manages to seep around regulatory structures, no matter how sophisticated their form. The point is not that trying to manage innovation through regulation is pointless; it is that innovation interacts with regulation in specific ways, and we can learn from these experiences. For example, the easiest rules to circumvent through innovation are the traditional, old-style, bright-line rigid rules like those that characterized American accounting principles in the Enron era. More nuanced and flexible regulatory strategies, when appropriately developed, are an improvement in that regard. However, designing effective flexible regulation is no easy task, and flexible regulation can highlight and even amplify complexity and feedback effects that then go on to cause their own challenges. Chapter 1 closes with three insights about how assumptions about regulation and innovation undercut the ability to see innovations' impacts, including on the regulatory regime in question, in real time.

From there, in order to better understand those regulatory takeaways and the alternatives to flexible regulation that may exist, the next chapters explain how we have gotten to where we are. Chapters 2 through 4 put flexible regulation scholarship in broader historical, intellectual, and political context, identifying both its real contributions and its practical limits. They trace the origins and development of "flexible regulation" as theory and practice, identify the main conceptual buildings blocks on which flexible regulation is built, and describe four key perspectives (responsive regulation, reflexive law, smart regulation, and new governance and experimentalism) that have significantly influenced the scholarship. Each of these perspectives also takes a particular stance toward innovation, and to some degree that stance evolves chronologically through them. Considering those four approaches, reinforced by a qualitative empirical review of the 198 United States law review articles most cited in the field, helps us to understand what the various proponents of flexible regulation sought and what they assumed in generating regulatory models that advanced contingency and fluidity, accepted the inevitability of continual innovation-driven change, and to different degrees (intentionally or not) located non-state innovation at the core of regulatory functioning.

Chapter 5 then tries to take the measure of flexible regulation as a progressive political project. Flexible regulation is not a "neoliberal," market fundamentalist, or Hayekian perspective. It is a progressive, though not revolutionary, one. It is a pragmatic approach that aims to respond adequately, not perfectly, to contemporary regulatory challenges that are recognized to be complex and difficult, and to learn from experience. Crucially, in its best forms it is deeply deliberative and committed to a meaningful, engaged, civic republican notion of governance. At the same time, flexible regulation in the years before the financial crisis sometimes misapprehended the nature and significance of private sector innovation, or underestimated its enormous capacity to destabilize and undermine regulation. Scholarly work was also abused and misapplied in practice, and the strong civic republican, anti-domination ethos that underpinned it was lost in translation. The subtle and multilayered notions of regulatory "flexibility" that scholars developed some-times were deployed, simplistically and instrumentally, by regulators seeking an advantage in a competitive regulatory environment, or a persuasive claim in a political contest. At least as importantly – and there were historical reasons for this – flexible regulation scholarship spent rather too much time on regulatory design and technocratic analysis, and too little time explicitly calling attention to its own progressive ideals and normative commitments.

The next puzzle piece we must put in place in charting a path forward for progressive regulation requires a sense of what private sector innovation, stripped of all the hype and romance, actually looks like. While this is not an anti-innovation book, my interest is not in how, for example, to foster a "culture of innovation."[37] It is in trying to tease apart the links between innovation and regulation in order to generate a principled stance from which to assess innovation, both as a public good and a direct regulatory challenge. Thinking clearly about our choices requires a better sense of what innovation is and how it develops and diffuses, as well as who exactly these private innovators are, that we should accord them so much autonomy in their creative endeavors. For example, does financial innovation look different from the most familiar stories recounted by innovation scholars? Can we identify particular innovation trajectories, and develop provisional proposals for responding to those ideal types? Above all, what would regulation have looked like over the last decade or more if regulation and regulatory scholarship had begun from a very different perspective – namely from the position that private sector regulation is a regulatory challenge, not just some generalized and abstracted social boon? The book's second broad section (Chapters 6 through 8) seeks to enrich and expand the flexible regulation scholarship by examining what innovation actually looks like, in order to develop a clearer and better-informed understanding of what corresponding responses from regulators and scholars it ought to generate.

Ultimately, these are epistemological questions. There is a great deal we do not know about how innovation develops in particular contexts, and developing a better sense of what we do and do not know is the beginning of responding to innovation as the regulatory challenge that it is. A more nuanced understanding of the phenomenon of innovation – which must appreciate innovation not only as a technological process but as a profoundly human, socially embedded one – suggests fresh sets of regulatory choices. The book's final chapter introduces a set of epistemological questions for innovation-ready regulation, which incorporate the insights on innovation that were developed in Chapters 6 through 8. Chapter 9 also returns to the concerns about inequality and domination that the flexible regulation scholarship introduced. Financial innovation is neither an unmitigated good nor an unmitigated evil, in egalitarian terms, but there can be no question that it has profound effects on society, social ordering, and individual lives. Moving beyond technical responses, the chapter argues that the absence of a robust public voice in regulatory policy is the key piece that is lacking in contemporary financial regulatory approaches to innovation.

Looking at innovation through the lens of law requires us to consider larger questions about social welfare and policy tradeoffs. Conceptually linking innovation and flexible regulation forces us to confront some very difficult political and normative choices about social welfare, equality, and justice – the very ones that have sometimes lain buried under flexible regulation's preoccupation with technique, and that are now confronting in several countries in the political arena. At the same time, this book also mounts an argument against nostalgia, romance, and oversimplification – against nostalgia for a Keynesian Welfare State that was far less perfect than it may sometimes seem now, against an uncomplicated romance with innovation, against oversimplified accounts of what has gone wrong and who is to blame. Managing the continual challenge that financial innovation presents is central to good governance. It will require that we actually understand financial innovation as a phenomenon, and bring all of the intellectual, experiential, and moral resources we have to bear on it. We can perhaps hope that the current popular discontent, combined with careful learning from experience, will become a catalyst for a new generation of regulatory strategies – one that sees innovation for the regulatory challenge it is, and that binds together our progressive ideals and our regulatory tools ever more tightly in the service of greater human flourishing.

1

Innovation as a Regulatory Challenge: Four Stories

We know that regulation can stimulate innovation in intentional and unintentional ways.[1] Deregulation can generate innovation and, ironically perhaps, regulation can also generate innovation, prominently including innovation geared toward getting around an inconvenient piece of regulation.

To some degree, the converse is also true: innovations generate regulation designed to address them. But a central problem for regulation in responding to innovation is that political legitimacy and the rule of law require public, state-sanctioned rules to have and maintain a degree of certainty, constancy, transparency, and public accountability.[2] Because regulation-makers must take these considerations into account, regulation is legally and structurally encumbered, in responding to change, in a way that private sector innovation is not. Particularly in fast-moving or complex environments, private sector innovation can present real challenges for the regulatory project.

It is not that regulatory structures cannot contemplate change. All legal structures anticipate a level of change in their environments. No legal system – even one built around a centuries-old Justinian Code or one built around originalist, constitutionally entrenched concepts – expects to hold itself completely static. Even if the written law remains unchanged, as Ronald Dworkin has pointed out, at its base, law is *interpretation* and so is inextricably bound up with its social and political context.[3] Even the most detailed, seemingly rigid rules one could conceive of will still be subject to interpretation.[4]

So, it is one thing – surely a common and important thing – to build the formal capacity to manage change into any regulatory infrastructure. We can hardly conceive of law without its change-managing processes, like the statutory amendment process or the "living tree" of case-by-case common law evolution.[5] Both civilian and common law systems appreciate that change is inevitable, and both contain mechanisms for responding and adapting to exogenous change. Regulation, like law generally, contains these mechanisms.

Along with being statutorily created and therefore capable of statutory amendment, regulatory mechanisms like notice-and-comment rulemaking in the United States,[6] and similar mechanisms elsewhere, establish structures for modifying enforceable rules in (more or less) transparent and (more or less) accountable ways.

It is another thing to *embrace* change as inevitable, and to try to build regulatory structures that are capable of reacting and adapting to constant exogenous change. This would be a more direct strategy for responding to the challenge that innovation presents. As alluded to in the Introduction and described further in the next two chapters, this is essentially what flexible regulation seeks to do. Weaving dynamic, non-regulatory mechanisms, like the market or deliberative dialogue, directly into regulatory architecture gives those dynamic forces the capacity to propel the regulatory project along, while still operating within the bounds imposed by the rule of law. Since it is concerned with social welfare and not just bureaucratic efficiency, flexible regulation, like the law generally, must also be concerned with weaving rule of law necessities like equality and non-arbitrariness into its fabric.

Now, it is still another thing to do what the 2009 Turner Review charged UK financial regulators with doing, as discussed in this book's Introduction: to embrace a particular kind of change – private sector-generated human innovation – as positively desirable and effectively capable of self-regulation within an efficient market, and to locate that innovation at the very center of the regulatory project by, for example, allowing private actors to develop their own innovative systems for policing their business innovations.

So, what have interactions between regulation and innovation, particularly financial innovation, actually looked like? How well does regulation generally deal with the promises and perils that financial innovation introduces?

This chapter links four signal regulatory moments since the turn of the millennium, each of which can be seen as the effect of a particular and powerful phenomenon: private sector financial innovation (which includes legal innovation) in the creation and marketing of securitized financial products. The first case study looks at the Enron debacle, and in particular at how the innovation of derivatives undermined bright-line, detailed accounting principles.[7] The second considers the 2007 Asset-Backed Commercial Paper (ABCP) Crisis in Canada, in which the innovation of derivatives undermined assumptions about how the market could be counted on to keep commercial paper relatively risk-free. The third case study is of the more innovation-framing capital adequacy regime developed under the Basel II Capital Accords, a highly influential transnational agreement concerning how countries would regulate the safety and soundness of banks operating in their jurisdictions. Here, a series of beliefs about how innovation worked, grounded on the presumed reliability, capacity, and bona fides of private sector innovators as regulatory partners, created a regulatory regime that actually encouraged gamesmanship, excessive risk-taking, and collective irresponsibility. The fourth case study points to the public comment process surrounding the so-called Volcker Rule in the United States as an example of how complex innovations, like securitization and derivatives, can privilege technical expertise and esoteric knowledge even more than usual, and squeeze public input out of policy-making spaces.

Each of these brief, inevitably partial, and very different case studies considers how private sector financial innovation intersected with regulatory structures designed – to greater and lesser degrees – to accommodate change. The Enron example is based on traditional, bright-line rule-based regulation; the ABCP regime in Canada was essentially market-based; the Basel II capital adequacy regime incorporated private standards and, though terribly flawed and disastrously implemented, arguably is the example that most resembles a version of flexible regulation;[8] and the Volcker Rule example considers administrative rulemaking as a participatory mechanism. And yet, while each example is different in its particulars, in each case the regulatory strategy failed to perform as intended, in part because it did not take seriously enough the swamping effect that private sector innovation would have on regulatory structures designed to channel it.

Here is the difficulty: innovation seeps under, through, and around regulation, no matter its structure. Bright-line rules are the easiest to game and the hardest to tailor properly to any given situation. Flexible regulation offers a richer, more varied and more sensitive set of tools with which to respond to innovation. However, innovation still seeps under, through, and around all regulatory structures, including the most sophisticated ones. Regulatory technique on its own does not address the persistent regulatory challenge that innovation presents. Nor is this a problem that is unique to securitization and derivatives, or the pre-crisis era: today's financial innovations in high-frequency trading, blockchain technology, and other emerging financial technology (fintech) bring their own significant regulatory challenges.

Within each of the stories below, we should notice how background assumptions about how innovation operates, and what can be achieved through regulation, influenced how regulatory structures themselves are designed. The more sophisticated and flexible regulatory strategies, like Basel II, while still far from perfect, at least are more consciously attuned toward helping regulation keep up with constant private sector innovation. Across the board, though, what goes unnoticed until it is too late is how, at a technical level, private sector innovation also opens up unexpected interstitial spaces *within* the very tissues of regulatory conduct.[9]

Regulation can never anticipate every eventuality or provide explicitly for every contingency. For this reason, spaces exist *within* definitions and assumptions, in the structural spaces *around* regulation and in the temporal spaces *before* and *after* regulation. Innovation has the capacity to move through these spaces and, in the process, to fundamentally alter how regulation functions. Taken together, the case studies also demonstrate the reflexive and change-accelerating properties that regulation can have – the opportunities it generates – and the clear influence of well-connected private actors in shaping regulatory architecture and assumptions to suit their own interests. Thus, the challenge that innovation presents for regulation is not just about regulation "keeping up". It is about regulation maintaining its bearings and its capacity to pursue its mandate even as innovation alters the terrain around it, and denatures its subject matter.

THE INNOVATIONS: SECURITIZATION AND DERIVATIVES

The financial crisis is too multifaceted to describe here, but it is possible to talk about financial innovation based on a general understanding of two related innovations that contributed directly to the subprime mortgage crisis and credit crunch in the United States and ultimately to the global financial crisis. Those innovations were securitization – the turning-into-securities – of assets that could produce an income stream; and the explosive deployment of financial derivatives. Neither securitization nor derivatives were particularly new inventions at the time of the financial crisis. Both used decades-old tools, such as options, swaps, and special-purpose vehicles (SPVs), except more extensively or in new arenas in response to new opportunities.[10] It was their multiplication and diffusion that raised challenges.

In the run-up to the financial crisis, one of the primary things to be turned into sellable securities through securitization was consumer debt. Individual consumers' debt obligations (mortgages, credit card or student loan debt, auto loans and the like) could be collected together, or "bundled," to be held by SPVs or entities. These are collateralized debt obligations, or CDOs. The SPVs were often trusts, but sometimes corporate structures, and they in turn issued units or securities for sale. The units' or securities' value was derived from the income flow from the securitized assets. Some underlying consumer debt – such as mortgages issued in the "subprime" market in the United States, to individuals who would not have been approved for a mainstream mortgage – carried a higher risk of default. This made their income streams less reliable and therefore made securitized assets based on them less valuable. However, after being boosted and tweaked by the addition of other financial instruments, side deals and guarantees, even risk-heavy units from these SPVs could be packaged into risk-rated layers called "tranches" and sold. Along with transforming a financial institution's consumer debt into a sellable product, securitization also made "maturity transformation" possible. That is, it made it possible to transform fixed-rate, long-term assets such as thirty-year residential mortgages into immediately realizable and marketable assets. This unleashed the present value of these assets and, through aggregation and actuarial risk analysis, aimed to quantify, disperse, and manage (or mismanage) certain kinds of risk.

While some derivative products are based on securitized assets, they can *derive* their value (hence the name) from any underlying asset or variable or agreement. The most familiar kinds of derivatives – options and swaps – operate essentially like side bets on the anticipated value or risk associated with a particular asset or variable or agreement. For example, a certain kind of derivative side bet, the credit default swap (CDS), was a side bet that operated somewhat like an insurance policy against default: for a fee, a third party would purchase the risk that a certain proportion of credit card holders, student loan holders, or mortgagors, for example, would default on their debts. As part of making securitized assets less risky and more marketable, CDSs were baked into many subprime mortgage-backed securitized products. (As we all know, ultimately this caused vast difficulties for one of the main sellers of CDSs, insurance company AIG Ltd., as well as for American taxpayers, when those subprime mortgages began to default at unexpectedly high rates.) However, CDSs are only one kind of derivative. The number and variety of possible over-the-counter (OTC) derivatives that could be created is practically infinite, since they are bespoke products.

The noteworthy thing about these two innovations is that, in combination, they had the effect of essentially "shattering the atom" of property well beyond anything that twentieth-century corporate law envisioned.[11] Through securitization and derivatives, we can play with time horizons, we can disentangle risks from the products that generate them, and we can separate an income stream from its source. Non-bank financial institutions can produce products that from the consumer's perspective operate in functionally identical ways to banking products. Among its effects, this radical de-lumping produced far greater complexity in terms of the varieties and shapes of engineered financial products that could be sold, financial institutions' exposure to them, and the interconnected markets within which they were bought and sold.[12] The increased complexity and product variability had consequences not only for regulation, as we discuss below, but also for the institutions dealing in the new instruments.

For example, in order to sell these securitized instruments (which involved obtaining a credit rating from an approved credit rating agency and taking other steps to make the products attractive to the market), financial institutions had to evaluate the risks associated with them. By the turn of the millennium, this risk assessment had become the responsibility of highly sophisticated and complex modeling and analytical software, developed in-house by those financial institutions. The risks associated with these products had become simply too complex for humans to model themselves. Financial institutions used their proprietary risk-modeling software to allocate, shift, and spread the risks associated with the products they were marketing. At the same time, the widespread use of computer-based risk modeling allowed financial institutions to develop and market increasingly complex financial products to consumers. It was a competitive business, and a lucrative one, in which, for a time, financial institutions profited virtually whenever they brought a new structured product to market. Profitability was front-loaded, meaning that there was a large first-mover advantage for those bringing a new product to market for the first time. A financial product's profitability fell off dramatically once it had been imitated, which it was in short order. The pace of financial innovation soared as a result, as did the largely unregulated OTC derivatives market on which these products and their component parts traded.

As it turned out, the software that many financial institutions used to assess such things as the default risk on subprime mortgages was often badly flawed.[13] Moreover, the increasing reliance on code to manage risk – or, as Erik Gerding has described it, the "outsourcing" of risk analysis to "the new financial code" – also obscured questionable assumptions about the nature of the products being sold, in the process removing those assumptions from the purview of human judgment.[14] Gatekeepers, like credit rating agencies, who were supposed to vouch for the products' quality, fared no better in their analyses. In hindsight, it is clear that in the run-up to the financial crisis, in part as a function of the automation of many risk and compliance processes, human beings actually had considerably less conscious, concrete knowledge about how they measured their own risk levels and compliance than was generally realized. To make matters worse, financial institutions and consumer debt originators, like mortgage lenders and credit card companies, had little incentive to be prudent in their investments, either in entering into underlying loan agreements (because under the originate-to-distribute model, they no longer held those underlying assets) or in devising new derivative products for sale (because there was a high international demand for any investment that could offer good returns, as these products did).[15]

We should remember that financial innovation, including securitization, can produce important social benefits. The fact that lenders such as banks and community credit unions can securitize long-term assets and trade in the derivatives markets means that it is far easier, even after the crisis, than it was a generation ago for small business owners to obtain loans, for individuals to obtain credit, and for the "real" Main Street economy to grow[16] – even while it also disproportionately enriches the "virtual" Wall Street world of finance. Derivatives make it possible to slice risk more finely, leading to more efficient use of capital.[17] They can be used to hedge and offset virtually any risk, including those associated with changing costs of supplies, commodity prices, foreign exchange rates, contractual counterparty default, and even crop failure. As such, they have become essential tools not only for sophisticated international financial institutions, but also for many small businesses engaged in contractual relationships, for commodity sellers (including farmers and resource companies), and for entities doing cross-border work.

At the same time, however, derivatives and securitization have undermined the means by which finance has traditionally been made accountable – to regulation, to the public and the political process, to economic forces, and to corporate law mechanisms. They have dramatically increased systemic risk and engendered a level of technical complexity that pushes the limits of our regulatory capacity, at least based on current tools. They have tied the same small business owners above, who use these tools to hedge their business risks, to powerful, poorly understood global systemic forces far beyond their control. Ultimately, financial innovation has allowed businesses and financial institutions to hedge risk and increase their own short-term certainty – right up to the point at which it turns out that the risk was never eliminated, but only shifted, and that in times of systemic crisis it ends up being shifted all the way to taxpayers and nations.

Not long ago, business scholars Josh Lerner and Peter Tufano attempted to set out a series of "counterfactuals" that imagined, as hypotheticals, that particular financial innovations had not been invented or widely adopted.[18] They went on to identify possible alternatives to those innovations and, essentially, to try to determine whether we would have been better off had they never been developed. They conclude that determining the social welfare implications of an innovation like securitization, given how multiple and interrelated the consequences of securitization are, is almost impossibly difficult.

The separate and narrower question I address here is the relationship between financial innovation and our efforts to manage it. If, after taking into account our best estimates of the value of financial innovation, we decide that we should regulate some of its versions or aspects, then it is a good thing to be able to do so effectively. The point here is to examine the ways in which financial innovation *itself* – whether in the form of securitization, or high-frequency trading, or some other as-yet-unrecognized financial innovation heading toward us now – by its very nature presents challenges for regulating financial innovation. The narratives below consider four separate moments at which regulation, in different forms, intersected with that innovation.[19]

FOUR REGULATORY MOMENTS

Enron and Derivatives: Gameable Bright-Line Rules

In contrast to the standard image of administrative action, modern financial regulation, and especially securities regulation, has never been a traditional, top-down, command-and-control system. Since the inception of modern securities regulation in the Depression era, it has been a disclosure-oriented, rather than merit-based, system, reflecting deep support for market mechanisms and for the basic autonomy of the public companies that raise capital in those markets. On the other hand, generally accepted accounting principles in the United States, or "US GAAP," have historically been much more prescriptive and detailed. The Enron debacle demonstrated the ways in which derivatives – in that case, energy derivatives – undermined those rules.

People generally remember Enron as having used SPVs to hide debt "off balance sheet," thereby making its financial statements look healthier than they were. While this is true, the use of SPVs on their own was neither new then nor unusual even today. If Enron had been operating a viable energy business while incidentally cooking its books, it could have restated its financials, taken a temporary "hit" to its share price, and continued on its way. The reason it could not was that by the time it ran into trouble, Enron's derivative trading operations far outweighed any actual energy-related work it was doing.[20]

For example, using derivatives called "options," Enron basically loaned its temporarily unsellable dot-com shares to an SPV it created called Raptor I. Raptor I then sold units to the public. This securitization had the effect of transforming Enron's temporarily unsellable dot-com shares into immediately available cash. However, Enron guaranteed Raptor I's value in order to make its units attractive to buyers. Therefore, when the dot-com company shares lost value during the dot-com bust, Enron was forced to shore up Raptor I's value at the expense of its own balance sheets and its own shareholder value. Since it had effectively just *loaned* its dot-com shares to Raptor I, however, the accounting rules did not require Enron to reflect a loss in its own financial statements.

Enron used derivatives to circumvent other accounting rules as well. For example, a "bright-line" GAAP rule stated that if Enron owned 51 percent of an SPV, then it would have to include that SPV's financial performance in Enron's own financial statements. One such SPV was called the Joint Energy Development Investments Limited Partnership (JEDI). Enron owned only 50 percent of JEDI, which meant that JEDI could issue its own financial statements and its performance did not have to count toward Enron's. Enron created many other SPVs as well, including one named Chewco Investments, L.P. (Chewco), whose assets were almost entirely debt-based derivatives. As it had done with Raptor I, Enron guaranteed repayment to Chewco's investor. It then made Chewco a 50-percent owner of JEDI, so that it did not have to count JEDI's financial losses as part of Enron's own balance sheet. Although Enron had all the real economic exposure associated with both Chewco and JEDI, its financial statements did not reflect that reality.

These are not the only examples. Enron appears to have repeatedly created SPVs, securitized otherwise-unsellable assets, and engaged in derivatives transactions specifically in order to game detailed, bright-line accounting rules. Moreover, Enron was far from the only public company engaging in this kind of accounting gamesmanship. Among other fallout following Enron's ultimate collapse, the primary US accounting standard-setter, the Financial Accounting Standards Board (FASB), was criticized for relying too much on detailed rules to determine appropriate accounting treatment with respect to accounting standards.[21] Thereafter, considerable work went into the possibility of drafting more principles-based GAAP that might have forced Enron to produce more realistic financial statements,[22] and an international debate ensued on the relative merits of different national GAAP approaches, and of principles-based versus rules-based accounting standards generally.[23]

Much of the fight has gone out of this specific conversation in recent years as most countries converged around an alternative, more principles-based approach called International Financial Reporting Standards (IFRS). To be clear, though, rigid rules – whether of the "bright-line" or the detailed variety – continue to exist in many contexts, to be gameable, and to be gamed.[24]

ABCP in Canada: Outdated Assumptions about the Market

A second moment, less consequential in global terms but illuminating in regulatory ones, was the September 2007 ABCP Crisis in Canada. The crisis is historically interesting because it foreshadowed the larger credit crunch that followed in 2008, but also because the way in which ABCP was distributed in Canada demonstrates the corrosive behind-the-scenes effect that financial engineering can have on discrete regulatory provisions. Canadian securities regulations gave commercial paper blanket exemptions from certain securities law disclosure requirements on the basis that any kind of commercial paper that could possibly be devised would still have to operate within well-understood practical limits. Specifically, the ABCP regime was premised on the assumption that commercial paper was inherently safe because of its short-term nature and the limits of its marketability. Yet, through innovation, the market for commercial paper was fundamentally transformed in ways that completely undermined that assumption.[25]

"Commercial paper" by itself is a promissory note used to secure short-term loans (that is, loans due in less than 270 days). It is like an "IOU". The loan is not secured by underlying collateral. Investors are willing to buy it on the strength of the issuer's reputation, buttressed by a good credit rating from a recognized credit rating agency. For this reason, commercial paper has historically been issued by banks or large financial institutions that have a very low risk of default. "Asset-Backed Commercial Paper" (ABCP) is a similar promissory note, but one that is also secured by collateral. In the event that an ABCP issuer cannot honor the ABCP when it comes due, the investor may lay claim to the underlying assets. In the years leading up to the 2007 crisis, ABCP was issued by banks and other large financial institutions, as well as some non-bank parties.

Under Canadian securities laws, ABCP was exempt from the costly and somewhat burdensome disclosure and regulatory requirements that otherwise would have applied to securities distributions to the public.[26] This made ABCP a cheap means for raising capital, and the amount of ABCP issued grew. The rationale for the exemption was that ABCP was a very safe investment with a very low risk of default. Therefore, the cost of disclosure outweighed its benefits. That view in turn was based on a series of assumptions that would have been entirely reasonable in an earlier era: first, that the only issuers who would be able to market commercial paper successfully would be very sound and reputable institutions, because no one would buy unsecured IOUs from anyone else. (For some, the fact that ABCP was secured by assets might have made it look even safer.) Second, the risks associated with commercial paper were lower because the paper would mature and the investor would be paid back in 270 days or less. (Often, commercial paper actually had much shorter maturation periods than that.) The likelihood that a reputable institution would suffer a default event within such a narrow window was very small. Third, as a condition of the exemption, the commercial paper had to have received an acceptable rating from an approved, arm's-length credit rating agency. Finally, like the rest of the so-called "exempt market," product sold under the commercial paper exemption would only be marketed to sophisticated institutional investors. Individual "retail" investors, who needed the protection that a prospectus (the mandatory disclosure document associated with distributions of securities) would have offered because they could not do their own research, would not even be buying ABCP.

In fact, each of these assumptions was flawed and reflected expectations about the financial markets that were no longer accurate.[27] First, the fact that ABCP was *marketable* did not mean that it was *safe*. There was no relationship between the soundness of the financial institution offering the ABCP and the assets underlying the ABCP, which could often be of very poor quality. In particular, ABCP assets included high-risk CDSs, including those on securitized American subprime mortgages. Moreover, financial institutions used ABCP to avoid capital adequacy requirements designed to ensure the institutions' solvency: they moved long-term credit obligations, such as mortgages, off their own balance sheets and into an ABCP conduit (like Enron's, another SPV). Nevertheless, ABCP was highly marketable, especially internationally, because it offered higher returns during an era of low interest rates.[28] Second, the short 270-day window for the commercial paper was irrelevant. ABCP functioned more like a highly leveraged liquidity fund than like old-fashioned commercial paper. ABCP issuers had to obtain a continuing stream of investors in ABCP in order to pay off the holders of maturing ABCP, in a never-ending cycle of "rollovers". The ABCP issuer's liquidity completely depended on there always being an active market for ABCP. Third, the credit rating agencies were not the zealous independent assessors they were thought to be, at least in the United States. Fourth, purchasers of ABCP were not always sophisticated investors, because purchasers did not always purchase on their own behalves. Thousands of retail investors also found themselves invested in ABCP. (Individuals' pensions and savings were also affected when their pension and investment funds participated, although those funds were professionally managed.)

The market for ABCP in Canada froze completely in September 2007, after it had become clear that some ABCP (no one knew quite how much) was exposed to the increasingly toxic US subprime mortgage market. Once worried investors stopped buying ABCP, ABCP issuers could no longer pay investors whose maturing ABCP notes were coming due. Since savvier institutional investors had been rushing to dispose of their holdings over the summer, retail investors held disproportionate amounts of ABCP assets by the time the market actually froze.[29] By that point the gap between the opportunities perceived and seized upon by sophisticated actors, and the expectations of the regulators and retail investors around them, was clear.

The ABCP story suggests that a regulatory regime that rests heavily on market discipline to police the boundaries of a regulatory provision, underestimates private innovation's capacity to push those boundaries, and fails to continually recheck its own assumptions for validity, will fail.

Basel Capital Adequacy Rules: Evolving into and Out of Innovation-Framing Regulation

Since the OTC derivatives market was largely unregulated (itself a crucial and mistaken policy choice, but not something we cover in this chapter), one of the first regulatory engagements with financial innovation occurred at the point at which financial institutions' capital adequacy was assessed, initially based on the 1988 Basel I Capital Accord, and later based on the Basel II capital adequacy standards and the somewhat-equivalent Consolidated Supervised Entities[30] (CSE) Program in the United States. The first Basel Capital Accord (Basel I) was introduced in 1988 and implemented by Basel Committee member states by the end of 1992 and nearly globally by 1999.[31] By establishing an international standard, it sought to bolster capital adequacy, strengthen the stability of the international banking system, and remove competitive inequality arising from different national capital requirements.[32] By 2004, however, when Basel II was introduced, securitized and derivative assets had become an enormous part of the assets being held by global financial institutions, meaning that an important regulatory interaction with these products took place in the context of examining whether they were being properly accounted for, for prudential regulatory purposes.

The purpose of capital adequacy standards is "prudential regulation" – that is, to ensure that financial institutions keep adequate capital reserves on hand to cover their liabilities and the risks they run in the course of their business. Prudential standards aim to protect depositors, and also to ensure financial system stability as a whole. The transition from Basel I to Basel II standards illustrates an effort to manage the challenges presented by financial innovation.[33] It also reflects an evolution in regulatory technique from the bright-line, rule-based requirements that also typified accounting rules in the years leading up to the Enron debacle, to a more flexible and collaborative strategy in the early years of the new millennium.

Assessing capital adequacy under the 1998 Basel I Capital Accord was quite straightforward, at least on the surface.[34] Unfortunately, it was also blunt and underinclusive in terms of how it described both capital and risk, and this made it highly gameable. For example, Basel I did not adequately account for variations in risk between and within categories.[35] All mortgages, whether prime or subprime, were assigned the same risk weight even though subprime mortgages were far riskier.[36] All residential mortgages, and the securities based on them, were considered less risky than other financial assets, such as corporate loans. Basel I's rigid risk categories incentivized banks to pursue the higher returns associated with riskier assets because they were not required to hold any additional capital to compensate for the greater risk.[37] As well, Basel I focused on one type of risk – credit risk – while failing to consider other types of risk that could affect the bank's assets, including operational risk (the risk of loss resulting from inadequate or failed internal processes, people or systems, or from external events),[38] market risk (the risk of loss due to adverse market conditions),[39] or liquidity risk (the risk of not being able to meet financial obligations as they came due and payable).[40] Just as Enron was able to game the bright-line US GAAP accounting rules, international banks gamed the gaps in Basel I to reduce their capital requirements.

The opportunities for regulatory arbitrage and circumvention under Basel I were widely recognized by the early years of this millennium.[41] A revised accord agreed to in 2004, the Basel II standards,[42] tried to address some of Basel I's shortcomings. The Basel II Capital Accord standards are an example of the more principles-based, outcome-oriented, innovation-framing turn that financial regulation took in the years between Enron's collapse in 2002 and the credit crunch in the fall of 2008. The forms of financial assets that had been created through financial engineering, even before 2004, had become of such a varied and mutable nature that risk assessment had become a complex undertaking. The Accord aimed to develop a more risk-sensitive metric for capital allocation relative to Basel I, with the goal of better quantifying categories of risk, responding to the impacts of innovation, and reducing the scope for regulatory arbitrage.[43]

In an effort to both permit and reflect the impact of financial sector innovation, while not forcing regulators to try vainly to keep up with the details of that innovation, Basel II developed a "three pillars" approach to capital adequacy. Pillar I established minimum capital requirements for financial institutions, while also according substantial discretion to what were thought to be the most high-functioning financial institutions. Pillar II established a supervisory review program overseen by national regulators. To supplement regulation and offset the greater discretion that certain financial institutions had under Pillar I, Pillar III required financial institutions to make extensive disclosure of their capital reserves. The idea here – familiar from disclosure-based securities regulation and information-forcing regulatory scholarship – was that greater disclosure would enhance transparency and make those institutions more answerable to disciplinary market forces.

What is especially relevant here is that, under Pillar I, the largest global financial institutions were able to use their own internal risk assessments to evaluate the risks they were running. While a "standardized approach" and a "foundation approach" were available to less sophisticated institutions, Basel II incorporated an "advanced approach" that gave a financial institution more freedom to use its own systems to weigh the risks associated with its business lines. So long as the financial institution met the minimum organizational and risk-modeling standards set by the Basel Committee and maintained what was thought to be a strong control environment, it could use its own risk models to determine how much capital it needed to keep in reserve.

Two key assumptions underlay the Pillar I approach: first, that financial institutions were in a better position to assess the risks they were running than were regulators; and second, that sophisticated institutions with strong control environments could be counted on to behave responsibly in regard to risk and leverage, because it was in their own self-interest. As well, there was limited awareness that the innovation being undertaken could be generating large-scale, systemic risk.

In the end, in response to strong competitive pressures and (correlated) flawed risk-modeling, financial institutions' own internal risk analytics under Basel II's "advanced approach" generated much lower risk assessments than the "standardized" or "foundation" approaches did. Since lower capital reserves and greater leverage generate larger profits, the financial institutions that could use the "advanced approach" generally did so. Of course, greater leverage also entails greater risks, and the shift to more risk-taking was exacerbated by uneven supervisory review under Pillar II. As the collapse of the toxic asset-laden Northern Rock bank in the United Kingdom demonstrated, not all bank supervisors supervised effectively.[44] In addition, while the disclosure requirements under Pillar III were expected to allow market participants to gauge for themselves the capital adequacy of an institution, the complexity and opacity of the assets in question made real market discipline ineffective. In fact, in many cases equity investors actually *favored* more risk-taking financial institutions because those financial institutions posted higher returns.[45]

As well, while Basel II provided a more fine-tuned approach to risk modeling than Basel I, it did not eliminate the incentives to hold riskier assets.[46] An OECD study from December 2010 found that financial institution regulation based on Basel II encouraged risk-taking and unconventional business practices, and contributed to the systemic shocks underlying the recent financial crisis.[47] The study found that capital regulation based on risk-weighted assets encouraged innovation that was designed to circumvent regulatory requirements, and to shift riskier assets off the balance sheet to subsidiaries or third parties. Persistent ambiguities in the definitions of Tier 1 and Tier 2 capital, which remained largely intact from Basel I, meant that banks could still restructure assets in order to classify them as Tier 1 capital.[48] This allowed banks to technically comply with Basel II's capital requirements while not actually reducing the magnitude of risks they were running.[49] Basel II also allowed banks to calculate risk using a model based on the inaccurate assumption that there would always be a certain degree of liquidity in the markets for assets like derivatives and securitized products. As it turned out, those markets became illiquid in times of market stress.[50] As well, as with Basel I, the capital accord risk-weighting system incentivized financial institutions to hold more securitized assets, and particularly more seemingly low-risk mortgage-backed securities.[51]

Thus, Basel II did not completely correct the problems that existed under Basel I, and the Accord's assumptions about the relative safety and desirability of mortgages and securitized products in particular proved to be flawed. At least as flawed, however, was the particular image of how innovation operated – as a benign and even productive force, if and when undertaken by sophisticated, rationally self-interested and prudent parties, within an efficient market. In other words, the value of financial innovation and securitization was taken as a given – notwithstanding the problems that complexity was posing for regulators – and the goal was to require banks to establish adequate capital reserves, without in any way questioning the actual content or implications of the financial innovations they were engaged in.

This may have changed. In a move that may help define the post-financial crisis relationship between innovation and financial regulation, the Basel III regulatory framework essentially aims to establish simply thicker capital and liquidity buffers around banks in general, and particularly around the kinds of risky business lines that produced so much trauma during the financial crisis. It aims to increase the quantity and quality of capital that banks must keep on hand to offset their risks; to add important new minimum liquidity standards alongside those capital standards; to strengthen supervisory mechanisms and make them more forward-looking; and to improve the transparency of the internal model-based approaches that banks use to calculate minimum regulatory requirements.[52] In some ways, these represent reintroduced bright-line requirements. Yet Basel III has been criticized for shifting even more power to banks and actually increasing the risk of regulatory arbitrage due to its increasingly complex rules and continued reliance on banks' internal measures of risk.[53] Now, as before, regulators are forced to rely on banks to design and explain details of compliance programs, because banks, by virtue of their position, possess more intimate knowledge of their compliance risks.[54]

Arguably, the Basel III strategy for dealing with the pernicious informational asymmetry and temporal imbalance between financial innovators and financial regulators has been not to try to compete on that score, but rather to build higher protective walls against the risks to the public associated with financial innovation, and greater disincentives to engage in that financial innovation at all. Pessimists might interpret this as a concession of regulatory defeat, while the more hopeful may see in these steps a recognition that innovation remains a problematic phenomenon in finance, and one whose scope should be limited and its effects walled off to the extent possible.

The Volcker Rule: Innovation as Silencing to Non-Experts

The Dodd-Frank Act[55] was passed in 2010, but its full implementation has required US financial regulators to draft and pass the detailed content of many hundreds of regulatory rules. As of Dodd-Frank's sixth anniversary, in July 2016, 274 (about 70 percent) of the 390 total rulemaking requirements had been passed as final rules; 36 (about 9 percent) more rules had been proposed, and 80 (about 21 percent) of rules had not yet been proposed.[56] Rules concerning derivatives and mortgage reforms were disproportionately among those where rulemaking deadlines had been missed without a final rule having been passed.[57]

On its surface this is a different kind of regulatory moment from the ones discussed above, since it concerns administrative rulemaking procedures that are both formal and longstanding. Notice-and-comment rulemaking is not innovation-framing at the level of regulatory design, though it is change-oriented in the sense that it provides a mechanism for incorporating public input into anticipated regulatory changes. But the rulemaking process under Dodd-Frank brings with it a broader cautionary tale about the effect of innovation on regulation, and its role in framing a topic as a complex one that demands highly technical treatment. Unlike the examples above, administrative notice-and-comment rulemaking procedures are not about the content of a particular regulatory provision; they are about the means through which that content – in the United States, really the content of virtually all regulatory rules – is settled.[58]

The rules promulgated under Dodd-Frank implicate the same difficult questions about the choice of mechanisms through which to regulate financial innovation that we see elsewhere – should rules be cast in bright-line terms? How much can market forces be counted on to impose limits? Should proprietary financial firm software be permitted to contribute to regulatory standards? Yet the fact that these consequential choices are left to after-the-fact administrative rulemaking also suggests that private sector financial innovation influences the rulemaking process at two distinct levels: at the political level, in restricting the options available to politicians and contributing to a decision to "punt" the problem to regulators; and at the regulatory level, where the highly technical nature of the discussion limits both the range of possible outcomes and the possibility of meaningful public input. The Dodd-Frank Act is structured (and it has been criticized for this) to leave a great deal of important definitional work to regulatory agencies to develop. Even during times of overt political anger and anti-bank sentiment, the power of innovation as an idea, and the cognitive sway that financial industry actors seemingly have within the regulatory process, effectively insulates key regulatory decisions from democratic input. At the same time, the regulation of financial innovation in those arenas has turned out to be highly porous, in both intentional and unintentional ways, to the benefit of the financial industry actors involved.[59]

The Dodd-Frank Act contains a number of important provisions addressed to responding to the financial crisis, including creating a new regulatory framework for OTC derivative products. For our purposes, concerned as we are with the impact of innovation in particular on regulation, one illuminating account concerns the notice-and-comment rulemaking process around what has come to be known as the Volcker Rule, the final version of which was passed in January 2014.[60] The rule's purpose, as originally envisioned by former Federal Reserve Chairman Paul Volcker, is effectively to insulate financial institutions' consumer banking businesses – which take federally insured deposits from depositors – from the institutions' own for-profit risk-taking. Whether or not the Volcker Rule will effectively insulate banks' depository function from speculative risks will depend a great deal on the details of what is now a very detailed regulatory rule.[61] As with Basel III, it will be some time before we can take its measure.

Regardless of the Volcker Rule's ultimate effectiveness, the decision by lawmakers to "punt" the crucial questions to the regulatory level is a significant one, and the Volcker Rule is only one of many for which this choice has been made. As a particularly high-profile and well-documented exercise in regulatory rulemaking, the Volcker Rule example offers a window into the rulemaking process generally.

Rulemaking around the Volcker Rule initially fell to the new Financial Stability Oversight Council (FSOC), which, as it was required to, used a notice-and-comment rulemaking procedure as part of developing the detailed content of the rule. During this time, the Volcker Rule attracted more public comment than any administrative rule in history.[62] The issue of bank risk-taking, which normally garners little public notice, was suddenly salient in the wake of the financial crisis.

The difficulty was that lay citizens, while engaged and often angry, did not generally have the necessary technical financial expertise to make persuasive arguments about the specifics of financial regulation. As Kim Krawiec has demonstrated,[63] the notice-and-comment procedure around the Volcker Rule generated huge numbers of letters from citizens, but the overwhelming majority of them were not detailed enough or specific enough to actually affect the final form of the rule. The vast majority of letters from members of the public (and 91 percent of all 8000 letters received) were based on form letters generated by a public interest group. Most of the remaining letters from private individuals were very short – the average word count was eighty-six words – and not substantive.

By contrast, financial industry comment letters were far longer and, in Krawiec's assessment, "contain[ed] cogent arguments in support of a generally narrow interpretation of the Volcker Rule's scope of prohibited activity. Overall, they advance[d] detailed legal arguments relying on numerous statutes and cases, reference[d] the Dodd–Frank legislative history, and often contain[ed] thorough empirical data. Most [were] meticulously argued and carefully drafted."[64] Moreover, public attention to the issue slid steadily downward as the topic of the Volcker Rule moved from the high-profile legislature, to the regulators' initial call for public comments, to low-profile in-depth meetings with regulators. By contrast, regulators' meeting logs showed that financial sector actors maintained the pressure across all deliberative stages. Financial institutions, their lawyers, financial industry trade associations, lobbyists, and policy advisors met with federal agencies to discuss the Volcker Rule fifteen times as often as all other public interest groups and research or advocacy organizations outside the financial sector combined.[65] Heads of financial institutions also had more one-on-one access to the heads of agencies.

What emerges from this account of rulemaking around the Volcker Rule is that the content of the regulatory subject – efforts to regulate private sector innovation – can operate as a brake on the scope of possible options considered, and the technical regulatory outcomes achieved. The choice to allocate so much consequential decision-making to the regulatory level virtually guaranteed that deliberation about the final form of the Volcker Rule would take place in highly technocratic terms, amplifying existing inequalities in participation and voice between financial industry players and others. The experience of notice-and-comment rulemaking around the Volcker Rule reflects the age-old problem of the limits of public deliberation in rulemaking, but that problem is also exacerbated by the same barriers to entry – the need for esoteric technical expertise and access to private information – that makes regulating financial innovation so difficult in the first place.

Making important policy choices through administrative rulemaking rather than in the Dodd-Frank statute itself may also imply that continued support for private sector financial innovation has seeped so fully into political dialogue that, really, only the details are left to be worked out. Rulemaking under Dodd-Frank left no space for a fundamental challenge to the idea that fast-moving financial innovation could itself be subject to hard, public questions about whether it is in the public interest at all. Thus, the contemporary fixation on innovation – pushed along by the influence of financial sector actors – can paralyze even the consultative mechanisms designed to ensure the public-regarding nature of regulations.

INNOVATION AND REGULATION: THREE MISPERCEPTIONS

Private sector innovation presents a significant challenge to regulators. Brightline rules like those at issue in the Enron debacle are very easily gamed. Regulatory regimes like the ABCP regime in Canada – which establish highlevel principles and that imagine, without building in verifying mechanisms, that they can predict the limits of those principles' use by highly innovative and self-interested private actors – will also be gamed. Regulatory regimes that are designed to embrace innovation and step out of the way, as Basel II did, must assume too much about the bona fides and capacity of industry actors and the beneficial impact of market and social forces. Moreover, as the Dodd-Frank Act rulemaking account demonstrates, the private actors involved in financial innovation are in a better position to advocate for it than is the general public, especially when the conversation is cast on a technical regulatory plane. Popular forces that might have argued for more extensive limits on financial institutions' abilities to expose consumer banking funds to proprietary trading risks were effectively shut out.

While each case study is different, in each one the regulatory regime demonstrates a lack of understanding about the phenomenon of innovation it is grappling with. It is crucial to develop a better understanding of how innovation intersects with regulatory strategies. As a starting point, the three sections below highlight some of the assumptions or sets of assumptions that innovation-framing regulation makes about innovation. The problem here is more than a pacing one; it is not simply that, as a technical matter, innovation moves faster than regulation can.[66] This is an *epistemological* problem. It is about how we construct knowledge about financial innovation – what we see and, by virtue of our interpretive lenses, cannot see; how we interpret it; and the implications this knowledge has for how we in turn construct regulation.[67] If we want to do better on this front, we will need to see not only innovation's technical attributes (something we do not always do enough of) but also its social and political ones. We will want to draw on insights from law, sociology, financial geography, psychology and behavioral economics, even biography if we hope to appreciate the nuances that determine so much about how innovation develops, and how it challenges regulation.

Complexity and Dynamism: The Reality and the Narrative

Our definition of the "success" of regulation will depend on our definition of the problem to be addressed through regulation. What we imagine financial regulation to be primarily concerned with – whether that be the efficient allocation of capital, or protecting investors, or safeguarding the integrity of the capital markets, or about some other version of fairness – will inform what we aim to achieve. Different branches of financial regulation – securities, banking, insurance, systemic risk – will have their own definitions of success. So, as it turns out, will the powerful actors they seek to regulate.

Back in 1962, political scientists Peter Bachrach and Morton Baratz coined the term "agenda-setting power."[68] Agenda-setting power is the ability to decide what will be discussed.[69] It determines what assumptions will be made, and what questions it is even possible to ask. In periods of "low politics," such as during the pre-crisis 1990s and 2000s, when the public at large was not terribly engaged with how the financial sector operated, policy choices were often left in the hands of a semi-closed epistemic community of bankers, their lawyers, and their regulators.[70] (Of course, Enron received attention, and public pressure helped produce a new statute, but then Enron was a public company. It and its accountants got a lot of attention, but financial institutions did not.[71]) Institutionalized norms and assumptions went largely unquestioned from outside.

We see financial firms' agenda-setting power on the topic of derivatives operating in the background across the narratives discussed above. To begin with, there was the decision not to regulate the over-the-counter derivatives market essentially at all. Brooksley Born's ultimately futile battles against Lawrence Summers and Alan Greenspan on this front are well documented.[72] More insidiously, we see the level of agenda-setting power that financial institutions themselves accorded to their own "quants" (quantitative risk analysts) and to technical code.[73] If Michael Lewis's popular analysis of high-frequency trading (HFT) is to be believed, even stock exchanges have accorded agenda-setting power to HFT firms: they have established their fee structures and even their physical architecture so as to court those firms' business.[74] The point is not that this kind of power is unstoppable, and it is not helpful to understand these challenges in overdrawn, conspiracy theory terms. The point is simply that if regulation is to be effective, it must be capable of registering these kinds of forces and their influence on regulatory design, and of responding to them.

In financial regulation before the crisis, the regulatory agenda was substantially framed around the sense that modern financial markets moved too fast and were too complex to be regulated in a top-down, traditional way. As the Enron and ABCP examples show (and our upcoming discussion of innovation in Chapters 6 through 8 reinforces), the problem is not that this assumption was necessarily false. Global financial markets are indeed fast-moving and intricate, and complexity raises genuine and considerable problems for regulation. One thoughtful observer even considers complexity to be "the greatest financial market challenge of the future."[75] Consequently, the prevailing view that was top-down regulatory tools were too blunt and too slow to deal with this kind of environment.

Though there is a lot of truth to it, the difficulty with this assumption is that by framing the agenda around the inevitability of speed and complexity in global financial markets, innovation-framing regulators lost the ability to articulate a regulatory agenda independent from some panicked attempt to keep up with industry developments. Some years ago, Malcolm Sparrow argued that the trick to effective regulation was, in his deceptively simple terms, to "pick important problems and fix them."[76] Regulators came to understand that their most essential challenge – their most important problem – was staying abreast of industry-driven developments.

In the middle two case studies above, regulatory design was based on expectations about the other forces that would provide "backstops" to keep what was essentially self-regulation robust, while permitting change and innovation. In the case of ABCP in Canada, the marketability of commercial paper was expected to set a built-in limit on its riskiness, and the regulatory design substantially underestimated the potential impact of innovation to erode that backstop. In the case of Basel II, market discipline and rational self-interested action on the part of industry were expected to keep leverage and risk-taking within reasonable bounds. The fact that financial innovation was undertaken at least as much for rent-seeking and avoiding regulation as it was for any socially beneficial purpose[77] was not appreciated.

This mindset also affected the operative definitions of expertise. Bankers' quantitative analytical skills were seen to be more (or even uniquely) valuable. These were the skills that drove change, while more policy-oriented or process-oriented analytical skills were held in comparatively low regard. This left social questions about the nature and implications of the speed and complexity of global financial markets – the reasons for it, the concerns it might raise, and the broader regulatory reorientation it might demand – insulated from interrogation. In the end it affected even the political system's openness to contestation and inquiry.

The Assumption That the Regulatory Moment Is the Important One

Innovation-framing strategies like Basel II are based on an appreciation for how hard it is to regulate a chimeric object like financial innovation through a time-bound, formal tool like regulation. To be clear, and as the Enron study demonstrates, we should not expect to have more success by papering over factual uncertainty, variability, or dynamism with artificially clear legal constructs, so long as the regulatory object continues to shape-shift. Yet we should not imagine that this is all that can be done. A flawed assumption behind the Basel II design but even more so the ABCP instance is that the regulatory moment is the crucial one.

In fact, the spaces *before and behind* formal regulation were at least as important to the regulatory outcomes described above. In the ABCP Crisis, asset-backed instruments created by bankers were pushed through a disclosure exemption in securities regulation – a space that was never intended to make risky products available to retail investors. The technical work that underpinned ABCP was both consequential and antecedent to the regulatory moment, but the regulatory structure was effectively oblivious to it. It contained no capacity to register the changed nature of commercial paper, let alone to evaluate it in any meaningful fashion.

In this regard, the explicitly innovation-framing Basel II structure fares better. At least it registers the fact of innovation and innovation's effect on its predecessor accord, Basel I. It tries to put in place regulatory scaffolding based on "strong internal control systems," regulatory supervision, and enhanced disclosure. Its difficulty is that it incorporates by reference proprietary industry risk-modeling as some form of best practice, based on assumptions about how it will function, without having put in place the kind of robust regulatory infrastructure needed to critically evaluate it. Seemingly "strong" systems turned out to be profoundly inadequate.

Just as consequential is the space *after* formal lawmaking, and after public attention has died down.[78] As the story of ongoing rulemaking efforts under Dodd-Frank demonstrates, it matters very much which parties are (or are still) in the room when important details get determined. Years ago, Louis Kaplow observed that rules-based regulation imposes costs *ex ante* (up front) on regulators, while principles-based regulation imposes costs *ex post* (after the fact), and on a more extensive set of actors.[79] But principles also present opportunities *ex post* for well-resourced actors to help shape the detailed content of regulation. Lay people do not generally have the expertise to speak to the kinds of significant technocratic details that underlie things like the implementation of detailed financial rules. Therefore, once the choice is made to treat the question of how to regulate financial innovation as a technocratic one rather than a policy one, it is possible to engage in a ritual of lawmaking that takes care of the "optics" for political reasons, without necessarily having much real impact on influential players' interests. The Dodd-Frank Act persists as a highly visible symbol of law reform even while, in practical terms, important pieces of it can be hollowed out after the fact.[80] The point is not that lawmakers or regulators are necessarily captured, but rather that the decision to cast a conversation about financial innovation in detailed terms, in a technocratic arena, has consequences – for the kind of input that will be considered, and potentially for regulatory outcomes too.

Moving the detailed decision-making process to a later stage can be a wise choice, if one can design a process beyond the political moment that permits a more thorough, meaningful analysis of the issues at hand. But agreement on principles (as opposed to rules) can also just defer hard choices, pushing normative or power battles underground. This may well be part of the Volcker Rule story. Establishing formal consultation processes such as notice-and-comment rulemaking around politically charged and consequential issues like the Volcker Rule has its merits. However, where skeletal statutory language is used effectively to punt what are fundamentally political questions into inaccessible arenas focused on technocratic details beyond most peoples' expertise, public consultation will be cosmetic at best. It matters very much what back-end processes are in place to resolve any indeterminacy that remains after the public regulatory moment has passed. The formal regulatory moment is not the only, or perhaps even the most important, one.

The Assumption That Regulation Sits Outside Innovation and Is Not Directly Implicated by It

Collectively, regulatory standards, domestic laws and other forms of rules build up interconnected *layers* of rules that together govern behavior. It is instructive to look at gaps between these layered rules, and facts on the ground, when looking at the financial crisis and the definition of regulatory success.[81]

Structural gaps can be the product of a misfit between a regulatory tool and its environment. Weak spots, ambiguity, and competitive opportunities are embedded in the regulatory structure, and financial innovation can exploit them.[82] The gaps can be a product of the porous nature of innovation-framing regulation. Just one example is the gap around regulatory risk analysis, which is left to be filled by financial institutions' proprietary risk-modeling software. On the other hand, in the Enron scenario, the gaps were the product of the opposite problem – of overly rigid rules being gamed in unanticipated ways through the use of derivatives. The securities law exemption for safe investments that opened the path for the ABCP Crisis in Canada, for example, were the product of yet another shortcoming – an insufficiently context-sensitive and market-aware regulatory form that missed the sea change in its environment.[83]

For flexible regulation scholars, whose work we discuss further in the next two chapters, a key underlying assumption has been that it was possible to erect regulatory scaffolding of carefully designed incentives and principles that, in combination with the other forces it leveraged, would be adequate to channel private sector action to align with public priorities. In fact, innovation circumvented flexible regulatory forms just as it circumvented other forms of rules, albeit in different ways. Additionally, what may have been unappreciated before the financial crisis is that the regulatory choice to acknowledge private sector financial innovation, for example by incorporating proprietary risk-modeling into Basel II, may actually have helped constitute and enlarge the very market for more and different innovative financial products, along with the complexity of the global financial system and the attendant risks and uncertainties. The relationship between innovation and regulation is reciprocal. As Donald MacKenzie has compellingly argued, financial modeling is "an engine, not a camera," meaning that financial models that are supposedly just describing the world actually, in describing it, influence and shape it too.[84] The same is true of financial regulation, to the extent that it defines, and then influences and shapes and makes room for, what it defines as the inevitably fast-moving, innovative, and complex world it must contend with. In other words, innovation-framing regulation may itself beget more innovation, and further accelerate the pace of change.

The fact that we simply cannot seem to "solve" the problem of innovation, no matter what flexible, bright-line, or innovation-framing regulatory strategy we take, suggests that we may need to reframe the problem itself. Developing viable regulatory responses to extensive and continuous private sector innovation requires an appreciation for just how much regulatory structure interacts with and is affected by private sector innovation within its bounds. It demands a better understanding of innovation itself, as a challenge for regulation full stop.

CONCLUSION

As measured by the fact that a catastrophic financial crisis occurred, financial regulation must be deemed to have failed generally in this time period. The reasons for failure were multiple and affected both more flexible and more prescriptive regimes, but we can learn something abidingly relevant by examining the particular epistemological limits, described above, that were baked into these regulatory assumptions and structures.

Just as importantly, the rulemaking process under Dodd-Frank reminds us that politics, including politically acceptable accounts of innovation, shape and limit the scope of regulatory conversations about how to handle innovation. It also reminds us that there is no such thing as value-neutral, objective, purely technocratic regulation. Regulatory choices inevitably require trade-offs between policy priorities, in ways that differentially affect different constituencies. Developing functional regulation in environments characterized by rapid and continual private sector innovation requires careful examination of contemporary assumptions about innovation, the regulatory moment, and the relationship between innovation and regulation.

This does not mean that we cannot say "no" to innovation. We can. We can keep oil in the ground.[85] We can stop financial innovation, implications be damned, as the United States stopped stem cell research under the George W. Bush Administration.[86] We could equally choose to ban all nanomaterials, or genetic mapping, or emerging fintech, each of which certainly carries risks and costs. We should not be Pollyannaish about the real costs of doing so, but we can choose to ban certain kinds of activities, including certain kinds of research or materials or new techniques. Under some circumstances this may be the right choice, and we discuss it further in the context of so-called "seismic" innovations in Chapter 7.

Even if outright bans will be rare, bright-line rules will continue to be essential regulatory tools. Rigid, one-size-fits-all rules backed by meaningful enforcement can establish a "floor" of permissible behavior, and can help snap private behavior into line more effectively and comprehensively than softer tools.[87] For example, when the US Congress imposed fuel efficiency standards for automobiles following the 1973–1974 Arab oil embargoes, the automobile manufacturing sector was forced to innovate to meet them.[88] Just as importantly, non-negotiable, context-insensitive, bright-line legal rules – think not only of consumer financial protection but also workplace rights, environmental protection and anti-discrimination – are in some sense legal victories, the equivalent of planting a flag on a hill won in battle. Holding onto traditional, static provisions is a strategy for maintaining those gains as long as possible – right up to the point where the degree to which they are being gamed or circumvented outweighs any value they may still retain.

We would be mistaken, though, if we thought that – notwithstanding their other virtues – more bright-line rules would actually do much to stop innovation. Consider Bitcoin. When the crypto-currency was first introduced, its legal status was widely questioned.[89] Efforts to ban it were largely futile,[90] however, and their main effect was to spark the proliferation of the many other species of crypto-currency now available. Efforts to shut down the Silk Road "dark web" site, on which transactions were conducted in bitcoins, had a similar effect. The website had been used to trade all manner of illicit items – particularly illegal drugs, in which it represented about 70 percent of the online market. The United States FBI shut the site down in October 2013 but only months later, a successor site sprang up. When that site in turn was shut down, two more took its place. And since one of those sites ceased operating, a whole slew of similar new websites has emerged.[91] The blockchain technology on which cryptocurrencies rest also looks poised to have a far more disruptive effect on financial services than the cryptocurrencies themselves. The "smart contract" technology it arguably makes possible could further disrupt professional practices in law and accounting.

Moreover, the more we try to shut down particular kinds of innovation, the more private actors may innovate around our bright-line rules themselves. For example, the same standards that improved automobile fuel efficiency in the 1970s also generated the huge market for "Sport Utility Vehicles", or SUVs, which, because they are mounted on truck chassis rather than car chassis, are not subject to those standards.[92] Or consider the fact that shadow banking (lending and other bank-like activities undertaken by non-bank financial institutions) seems to be growing again, following efforts to tighten *bank* regulation in the wake of the financial crisis. Shadow banks, which in the US were often the broker-dealer arms of global financial institutions, ran into trouble in the financial crisis. Their parent financial institutions, many of which were subject to regulation as banks, were required to prop them up. Some of those parent banks in turn needed bailouts themselves. Now the stricter regulation of banking following the crisis is causing banks to turn increasingly to shadow banking, particularly in emerging markets like China, where the sector grew by 42 percent in 2012 alone.[93] We may be seeing a similar flight out of regulated spaces in Canada, where new securities regulations will require investment fund managers to provide extensive additional information about their investments, including the mutual funds that so many ordinary investors own. The obligations will not apply to insurance vehicles, which can offer functionally identical investment products, often through the same firms, without the new disclosure obligations – potentially prompting those firms to simply categorize their investment products as segregated insurance funds instead.[94]

Trying to use bright-line regulation to respond to such problems can feel like a game of whack-a-mole. Regulatory limits are essential but at least in highly complex and dynamic environments, establishing a new bright-line rule cannot be the end of our task. It will take a range of strategies, including non-legal ones, and it will take keen detection systems and the wise use of resources to manage these kinds of problems. Financial innovation and its attendant complexity make for challenging background conditions for any regulatory regime. In this regard, flexible regulation is a guide to thinking about a broader and more varied set of regulatory tools to manage the regulatory problem.

Flexible regulation and better regulatory techniques do not mean that we can create simply "better regulation"[95] that can make everyone happy at once. The large policy choices at stake, and the attendant deep disagreements and conflicting interests, will not be resolved through some magical step change in technical regulatory (or financial) expertise. Moreover, financial expertise, while celebrated in programs like Basel II, is clearly not the only kind of expertise required to chart a path forward for financial regulation. Nor is technocratic regulatory expertise enough. The regulation of financial sector innovation in recent years in no way counts as successful if what we care about is transparency, accountability, or bending the arc of private innovation toward greater social benefit than the market will produce on its own. Effective financial regulation still demands that a public-minded, longer-term policy perspective be represented. Whether or not we understand the technical intricacies of a particular financial innovation, we should be prepared to engage in a debate about the policy implications associated with finance. As part of this, we may need to consider whether the democratic processes we have in place now are even notionally sufficient to give citizens a stake in the issues that so directly affect their material and social wellbeing – particularly when the mechanics of those processes are buried in highly technical and ultimately inaccessible regulatory conversations, or else in transnational spaces marked by real democratic deficits.

Thinking about these questions requires us to have a clear and historically informed understanding of regulatory design, including regulatory scholarship – of how regulation has evolved over the past several decades, what regulatory tools we now have at our disposal, and what we can reasonably expect of regulation. The next chapters begin this project.

2

How We Got Here: The History and Roots
of Flexible Regulation

If, as this book claims, we in the West are in an ongoing romantic relationship with innovation, then our relationship with financial innovation in particular may sometimes feel more like a dysfunctional, even abusive, one. We may be inclined to think of financial innovation as if it were some different species from the innovation that produces almost magical new immunotherapeutic treatments for cancer patients, or gives us fingertip, mobile access to inconceivable quantities of information through our smartphones. Indeed, in the wake of the financial crisis, it is appealing to think that we could somehow distinguish "good," socially beneficial innovation from "bad," rent-seeking or rule-avoiding regulation, and to foster the first while stamping out the second – in one former UK cabinet member's words, to promote "less financial engineering and a lot more real engineering."[1] If financial innovation is in fact so adept at undermining, circumventing, and gaming regulation, as this book claims, it may be tempting to try to turn the clock back, to put the genie of financial innovation back in the bottle, to re-simplify and de-intensify our financial arrangements.

The next question would be how to do so. The answer would be regulation. In spite of its importance, we have a far less emotional relationship with regulation, and where it has emotional content that content tends to be sour. For some, the word "regulation" connotes bureaucratic red tape that imposes a drag on the economy and on human creativity while providing little corresponding benefit. For others, regulation is disappointing because it is ineffective or, worse, captured by powerful interests.[2] Expectations of what regulation could conceivably accomplish, if only it worked better, remain perennially high but few seem satisfied with actual outcomes achieved. Dissatisfaction and anger toward financial regulators is understandably running high these days across much of the West, but other regulators too – remember the 2010 Deepwater Horizon blowout in the Gulf of Mexico, or the 2011 Fukushima

nuclear disaster, both of which are now considered to have been preventable –
seem only to confirm that contemporary regulation has not been tough
enough, well-enough resourced or independent-minded enough to protect
us from corporate short-sightedness and financial rapaciousness.[3] Enormous,
preventable disasters such as these can feel like an indictment of regulation
overall, and of the so-called "regulatory state" structure that has characterized
state action since the 1990s.

One contemporary instinct has been to try to recapture the hopefulness
and rising prosperity levels of what is sometimes called the Golden Age of
Capitalism, or the Welfare State era – those economically glorious decades
after the Second World War, during which the state also played a more direct
and visible role in many Western countries. With this in mind, the notion of
creating a twenty-first-century Glass-Steagall Act is appealing, not only for its
content but also for its allusion to the energetic controls over the financial sector that characterized the New Deal era when the first Glass-Steagall Act was
passed.[4] Evoking a similar sentiment, 2016 candidate for US Democratic presidential nominee Bernie Sanders was famous for not having changed his position on issues such as income inequality across four decades of speeches.[5] For
some of his supporters, his message was appealing in part because it held out
the possibility that one need not accept the precariousness and hyper-com-
petitiveness that seems to have accompanied a globalized economy. Though
their specific messages were radically different from Senator Sanders', both
the UK's 2016 vote to leave the European Union (the "Brexit" vote) and the
election of President Trump in the United States can also at some level be
understood as a vote for the past over the present.

Is this the path forward? What *did* happen to the Welfare State, and to
our mid-twentieth-century aspirations for public action? Were things actually better then? Why is regulation necessarily so flexible now, and should it
continue to be?

We cannot simply turn back the clock, but it takes a history lesson to explain
why. We can celebrate the progressive instincts that underpin contemporary
efforts at reregulation, and that seek to reassert a more forceful and progressive
public voice in the economy, without assuming that we had things completely
right the first time. We have learned a great deal in the last several decades
about the limits of state action, and the real potential of non-state regulatory forces. We also now live in a more complex, interconnected, globalized
world. Regulation today operates differently – more pervasively, but perhaps
also less obviously – than it did in the times when the state's default tactic was
to impose bright-line rules and then oversee compliance with them, or when
it intervened directly in economic affairs though such tools as wage and price

controls. And still, on many fronts, regulation today is more effective than it was four decades ago. Making regulation, including financial regulation, work in the service of progressive goals will depend on tailoring our responses to these times, and not to earlier ones.

Consider the Consumer Financial Protection Bureau (CFPB) in the United States, thus far one of the more successful post-financial crisis pieces of regulatory architecture. The CFPB's mission is to "make consumer finance rules more effective, to consistently and fairly enforce those rules, and to empower consumers to take more control over their economic lives."[6] However, it aims to do so not by imposing an extensive formal compliance-and-enforcement structure, or by intervening directly to provide financial services to consumers – both tactics that a postwar Welfare State agency might have adopted. Instead, the CFPB emphasizes public education, publishing complaints and data about compliance, coordinating with other agencies, and anticipating and discussing future trends, like the impact of financial technology and crowdfunding. It seeks restitution for wronged consumers as well, and successfully so, but this is perhaps only the most visible, and not the most significant, piece of its work. Sabeel Rahman has argued that both the Dodd-Frank Act (including its CFPB-enabling provisions), and the Carbon Limits and Energy for America's Renewal (CLEAR Act) (which sought to overhaul oil drilling regulation in the Gulf of Mexico following the Deepwater Horizon disaster) in the United States show signs of greater attentiveness to democratic accountability and meaningful public input, as well, relative to more traditional technocratic approaches.[7] The concern for democratic participation as a basis for regulatory legitimacy is a hallmark of our more recent regulatory state, not the older Welfare State, structures.

The US Affordable Care Act ("Obamacare") is another example of a regulatory state approach to establishing a new public service. Certainly, from its inception Obamacare was the imperfect product of political compromises as much as ideal design, but it was also a product of the twenty-first century, not the twentieth. When Canada instituted its comprehensive, universal health care system, "Medicare," in 1966, it established a not-for-profit state monopoly over core health care services provision. Almost five decades later, the Obamacare model (as it existed at the end of the Obama Administration) employed a different and more varied set of tools including a rating system for different health care plans, to provide information to the public; tax credits and subsidies; and new marketplaces, including both licensed private channels and government exchanges, on which to purchase insurance.[8]

This chapter and the next one put new regulatory structures such as these in historical and theoretical context, and explain how flexible regulation – which inevitably has a more porous interface with private sector innovation,

but more about that later – became the dominant stream of regulatory practice, and regulatory scholarship.

THE REGULATORY STATE AS AN IDEA

Tracing the development of the modern regulatory state – and, therefore, of
flexible regulation as an approach – can be a contentious business. Scholars
differ in how much they see contemporary regulatory mechanisms as a con-
tinuation of the postwar New Deal/Welfare State, or its replacement. Views
differ as to how much of a neoliberal or, alternatively, a progressive project it
has been; about how much we can generalize across borders and subject matters; and about whether the "regulatory state" itself has gone through various
stages of evolution and, if so, what those stages are. Sometimes the modern
regulatory state is evaluated by reference to the high water mark of state action
in the 1960s. Yet an open question is whether it even makes sense to start our
historical narrative of modern regulation in the postwar era, or perhaps even
the Progressive Era before it. Arguably, the merits and demerits of modern
regulation need to be understood in the context of the great sweep of Western
history over the last few centuries.[9]

What is clear is that regulation is now pervasive. To a layperson, topics like
food safety standards, the regulation of Wall Street, and cellphone plan rates
may not seem to have much in common. In fact, they are all part of what
Giandomenico Majone has called the regulatory state.[10] Even though we have
recently lived through an era of what we have been told is "privatization"
and "deregulation," our lives are probably more pervasively regulated now
than they have been at any other point in history. As noted earlier, the word
"regulation" in this book refers to sustained and intentional activity by the
state in attempting to control, order, or influence the behavior of others in
the service of public policy priorities. The state can act directly or indirectly,
for example by leveraging other social forces.[11] Regulation – including formal
state rulemaking on its own, and when used to leverage other social forces[12]
– is the dominant mechanism of state action today.

In important ways, regulation helps constitute its environment. Regulation
in its various guises is a necessary precondition to a functioning market: among
other things it legitimizes markets themselves, facilitates transactions by
engendering trust, and sets background rules that enhance certainty and
allow parties to contract with each other. As David Levi-Faur puts it, building on Karl Polanyi's work, "efficient markets do not exist outside the state."[13]
Therefore if we want to understand the social, economic, and technological
milieu in which we operate, we need to examine exactly what contemporary

regulation seeks to accomplish – and, just as importantly, what it emphasizes and what it ignores.

Regulation is far more complex now than it was thirty years ago. The "regulatory toolbox" is fuller, the tools in it more varied.[14] The classic mid-twentieth-century Welfare State has been transformed. For example, while state-owned utilities and direct state intervention in the economy were once routinely adopted as solutions to a range of socioeconomic challenges, states now act far more often through regulation.[15] Relative to Welfare State direct intervention strategies, regulation opens up a broader range of possibilities: whom to regulate, when, and how? And within that range of regulatory possibilities, a subset of options, which I would collectively call flexible regulation, have explicitly sought to develop regulatory strategies that can be more flexible, context-sensitive, and nuanced than Welfare State methods could be.

"Flexible regulation" is the term I have coined for a group of related scholarly perspectives that have comprised the core of active research on regulation in North America, the United Kingdom, Europe, and the Antipodes over the past few decades.[16] It is not a term that these scholars generally use to describe their own work, but it serves to highlight an underappreciated commonality within the scholarship. Flexible regulatory approaches include responsive regulation,[17] reflexive law or regulation,[18] outcome-oriented regulation,[19] risk-based regulation,[20] management-based regulation,[21] principles-based regulation,[22] experimentalist or new governance regulation,[23] and meta-regulation.[24] Though each is distinct and the boundaries between them contested, there are considerable areas of overlap.[25] Forms of flexible regulation have been applied in areas as diverse as international and domestic labor and employment law,[26] EU governance,[27] and environmental regulation,[28] as well as securities and financial regulation.[29] As the next chapter describes, environmental regulation and administrative law writ large are the fields where the most work has been done. However, it is in certain technically complex or esoteric fields – like deepwater oil drilling, or the creation and marketing of complex synthetic financial products, or perhaps nanotechnology – that the private sector *innovation* that flexible regulation frames seems most clearly to take on a life and momentum of its own.

I discuss flexible regulation's core elements below, but first we must put it in context. Flexible regulation's preoccupations with nuance, context-specificity, and responsiveness are a function of history, of circumstance, and of the regulatory status quo against which flexible regulation defined itself from its early days. If we want to understand the contemporary state, we must first understand the shift in thinking about regulation over the last few decades. What happened?

FROM WELFARE STATE TO REGULATORY STATE

In the beginning – or so goes one celebrated account – there was the Welfare State. Europe is the context for Majone's influential work, which described a move from what he called the "Welfare State" – a top-down, control state that engaged directly in the economy as well as in social affairs – to a modern "regulatory state" defined by its use of rules to intervene less directly in the economy and society. This shift is conceptually important, even if it has the greatest resonance on the European continent, where it is easier to identify an historical Welfare State in the terms Majone describes.[30]

Following the devastations of war and economic depression, many states in Europe (including Great Britain), North America, and the Commonwealth were concerned with building a strong, positive state presence. The state assumed a level of responsibility for securing "some basic modicum of welfare for its citizens."[31] In Western Europe in particular, the social democratic postwar states' mandates extended to redistribution and macroeconomic management. The state could be planner, producer, and employer as needed. Several states owned stakes in key industries, especially utilities, and asserted centralized discretionary authority over extensive parts of their national economies.[32] Taxes were raised and public spending increased.[33] The precise shape and nature of state engagement in the economy and society varied based on the each state's political philosophy and underlying values, but Welfare State regimes typically used methods based on then-standard Keynesian economics.[34] What emerged after World War II was not just the "Welfare State," but the "Keynesian Welfare State," which legitimized the state's stabilization functions and its redistributive ones, along with the tools of direct intervention and demand management.[35]

Even in the United States, where distrust of the state has historically run deeper and where the devastations of war were less immediate, the size and presence of the state increased from the New Deal era through the late 1960s.[36] The idea that social rights should stand on equivalent footing to traditional property rights was not seriously contemplated in the United States until Charles Reich's important argument for it in the 1960s.[37] Nevertheless, between the late 1940s and the early 1970s, muscular state action fundamentally transformed the social and economic landscape in the US, as it did in much of the Western world. The result was a more or less hierarchically organized, centralized bureaucratic apparatus with a Keynesian understanding of its mandate and with formidable, direct economic and social levers at its disposal. Growth of the formal US federal civil service peaked in the late 1960s, with slightly over 3 million federal civilian employees in each of the last two

years of the decade.[38] (These formal employment numbers can be misleading as indicators of state size or presence, as we discuss below, but they say
something important about the way in which the Welfare State government
apparatus was structured.)

During the Welfare State years, government was involved in economic
regulation to a degree, and in a centralized fashion, that is completely foreign to us now. In a country like mine, so-called Crown Corporations were
(and occasionally still are) major, often the only, players in key regional industries including rail, airlines, ports, oil and gas, utilities and power generation,
telecommunications, even liquor sales. But even in the United States, international trade barriers protected domestic industry, and regulatory barriers
protected incumbent industry actors in many sectors. For long though not
always overlapping periods of time, regulatory agencies centrally established
many different rates and prices – local telephone rates, interest rates, oil and
natural gas and other commodity prices, stock exchange trading commission
rates, and more. Strict regulatory boundaries separated the common carrier industries – ocean shipping from rail from trucking from airlines from
buses; long-distance telephone from local telephone from cable – imposing
requirements and corresponding protections on each of them regardless of
their relatively rising or falling fortunes, changing technology, or the potential
inefficiencies produced by this particular form of regulation. Within these
protected regulatory spaces, competition was often mild, because muffled.
Protected industries engaged in rent seeking. Stability, security and widespread accessibility to services – not efficiency – were the aims.[39] In many
sectors, unions were strong and labor enjoyed steady, well-paid employment.[40]
Standards of living increased, for several decades in a row.

We cannot forget that some allocative choices were easier during the Welfare
State era. Effectively, the pie became bigger during the postwar years thanks
to historically exceptional levels of growth.[41] Thomas Piketty has argued that
it may also have been that, exceptionally, return on capital in Europe (not so
much the US) grew more slowly than overall growth during this period thanks
to the devastations of two World Wars and a Depression in the first half of the
twentieth century, which decimated capital and reduced income inequality.[42]
During this postwar Golden Age of managed capitalism, "prosperity, equality,
and full employment seemed in perfect harmony" and the Keynesian consensus perceived no trade-off between social security and economic growth, or
between equality and efficiency.[43] As subsequent decades show, this was not
because Keynesianism had perfected state economic regulation. As effective
as the Keynesian Welfare State may have been in smoothing out business
cycles and supporting peoples' income security, it was also operating in an era

of American hegemony, and enormous growth in Western economies generally. Economies could afford to absorb the new social costs while still producing high levels of growth in GDP. In the background, however, foreshadowing
future challenges, US manufacturing performance was becoming less competitive relative to some other nations, notably Japan.[44]

Then, according to Majone, something (or some series of things) happened
to foreshorten regulatory ambition and to alter the nature of the state. By the
late 1970s, the very concept of the Keynesian Welfare State was under attack
from both the left and the right.[45]

The regulatory landscape in the United States began to shift in the 1970s.
Despite the very real successes it had achieved in responding to natural risk
and increasing citizens' standards of living, by this point some of the costs
associated with the postwar model had begun to show. Growth was also slowing, and government circumstances were straitening. In the United States,
where anti-government sentiment was already high because of the Vietnam
War, rising inflation, and social unrest, it seemed that Lyndon Johnson's Great
Society initiative, which strove to build on the New Deal, was doomed to fail.[46]
Keynesian economics' apparent inability to deal with the macroeconomic
forces producing stagflation and unemployment, as well as resource shortages
like the Oil Crisis of 1973, helped establish the conditions leading to the rise of
supply-side economics and financial market deregulation.[47] Newsworthy stories about other apparent regulatory failures – awareness of acid rain and pollution after the Cuyahoga River "caught fire" in 1969; the financial collapse
of the railroads' artificial economy, culminating in Penn Central's bankruptcy
in 1970; the Love Canal emergency in 1978; the Three Mile Island nuclear
meltdown in 1979 – only fueled increased frustration with and distrust for what
seemed like regulatory ineptness, or corruption, or both.

A view of government bureaucracy as cumbersome and counterproductive
was on the rise. In the United States, along with concerns about regulatory
costs[48] and capture,[49] bureaucracy was criticized for having become inaccessible, over-proceduralized, and either (or both) non-transparent and unaccountable in its decision-making and/or pathologically observant of rigid rules
and procedures.[50]

Meanwhile offstage, state restructuring and deregulation, including the
end of the Bretton Woods regime in 1971, helped catalyze the emergence of
the modern financial industry.[51] Silicon Valley venture capital funds Kleiner
Perkins and Sequoia Capital were founded in 1972. In 1973, Fischer Black
and Myron Scholes published the Black-Scholes equation for the first time.
The equation made it possible to model securities price movements with a
greater degree of confidence. The model led to a boom in options trading and

the creation of the Chicago Board Options Exchange, and ultimately to the development of the broader market for financial derivatives. In 1974, Robert Merton developed the Merton Model for Credit Risk, which came to be used to break down an entity's risky debt into its risk-free component and a sellable option, similar to what later become CDSs.

Also in 1971 – the same year that Bruce Brent and Henry Brown established the first money market mutual fund in the US[52] – President Richard Nixon's administration established a Quality of Life review process, overseen by the Office of Management and Budget (OMB). It required all federal agencies to consider regulatory alternatives and costs when promulgating "significant" regulations. However, if concerns about the cost of government were initially associated with US Republican Party small government advocates, public opinion soon made bureaucratic reform initiatives difficult for either party to oppose. Both Republican President Gerald Ford and Democratic President Jimmy Carter took significant steps to encourage independent government agencies to use economic impact statements and comparative analysis.

Political and regulatory change were in the air. In 1976, President Gerald Ford vetoed legislation allowing common situs picketing, one of the top items on the American Federation of Labor and Congress of Industrial Organizations' wish list. The legislation was defeated in the House the next year. Carter's 1977 energy package deregulated new oil and natural gas prices.[53] The Civil Aeronautics Board, which controlled market entry and airline fares, was dismantled in 1978 due to a perception that overregulation was impeding economic performance.[54] Ralph Nader's consumer protection agency bill was also defeated in 1978 despite having had strong Democratic support just a few years earlier. In 1980, the Depository Institutions Deregulation and Monetary Control Act effectively eliminated interest rate ceilings for home mortgages.[55] Near the end of his term, President Carter directed government agencies to begin experimenting with "more flexible modes of regulation". He directed independent agencies to begin experimenting with eight general categories of innovative regulatory techniques – fascinating to consider in retrospect – ranging from a sort of proto cap-and-trade regime to enhanced disclosure regimes.[56]

By the end of Carter's presidency the view was widespread that the professional bureaucracy had acquired too much control over the management of the state, that bureaucratic organizational design excessively restricted both bureaucrats and elected officials, and that the bureaucracy had become inefficient, bloated, ineffective, and beholden to interest groups.[57] A sizable portion of the US public also perceived the state to be bungling, ineffective, costly, and corrupt. In the United States, by 1980, more than 60 percent of those

surveyed in a Gallup Poll felt that "quite a few of the people running government did not seem to know what they were doing."[58] As Eugene Bardach and
Robert Kagan described it,

> Ronald Reagan campaigned successfully for the presidency on a platform
> that, among other things, called for much less government intervention gen-
> erally and much less regulation specifically. Many other Republican candi-
> dates – and Democrats – did the same. Hardly a voice was raised during the
> 1980 campaign to defend the federal record on regulation.[59]

The adjective "bureaucratic" was becoming an epithet. Scholars, even those
who valued state action as a political matter, criticized bureaucratic entities
for their intractability and unreasonableness.[60] As Jodi Short has demonstrated, legal scholars' use of "command-and-control" as a pejorative term
to describe traditional bureaucratic methods also rose dramatically from the
1980s through the 1990s.[61]

Interestingly – and for the progressively minded, subsequent events make
this a bittersweet anecdote – even while government was being associated with
waste and inefficiency, public support for public benefit programs remained
intact. As Ladd Jr and Lipset describe it, writing in 1980, public dissatisfaction
with government and regulation

> Do[es] not involve opposition to liberal policies – to those designed to aid the
> underprivileged; to control aspects of the economy; or to improve the leisure,
> home, and work environments. Rather, what seems to disturb many people
> is a sense of government incompetence and waste, as well as, in recent years,
> the inability of government to handle the number one problem, inflation.[62]

Public support for the state and its services remained stronger in Western
Europe. But even there the public sector, which had expanded steadily from
1945 through to about 1975, began to halt its expansion and in some cases even
to reverse it.[63] Majone tells us that in Europe, publicly owned firms were exco-
riated for being unaccountable, incompetent, inefficient, and beholden to
political interests.[64] The crucial component of the new continental model was
a shift from strategies of direct, "positive" state intervention in the market, such
as public ownership of utilities and a clear, sanction-oriented state enforcement
model, toward the development of a richer regulatory tool kit with rule-making
powers and the administrative state at its core. The growth of the European
Community and later, the European Union, as novel regulatory forms also
shifted the continental rule-making project in unique and significant ways.[65]

Meanwhile, in 1981, the US investment bank Salomon Brothers created
and brokered the first major currency swap, between IBM and the World

Bank. By 1986, many new financial markets, including those for Eurobonds, zero coupon bonds, and financial futures were in regular operation.[66]

The newly ascendant conservative governments of the 1980s, including Margaret Thatcher's in the UK and Ronald Reagan's in the US, capitalized on public dissatisfaction with government and undertook large-scale reforms. In this first wave of change, these governments set about privatizing publicly owned industries (including virtually all major utilities in the United Kingdom), liberalizing the regulations governing them, or even actively deregulating them (as with airlines and telecommunications in the United States). They sought to increase competition within formerly protected industries, to focus on the supply-side of their economies, and to limit aspects of social service provision.[67]

The United Kingdom endured massive strikes, and the United States was thrown into a recession marked by exceptionally high unemployment and interest rates; but the governments of Margaret Thatcher and Ronald Reagan (and their respective successors, John Major and George H.W. Bush) nevertheless succeeded in putting in train a fundamental reorientation of the public landscape. The leaders of the New Right – Thatcher, Reagan, and others, including Brian Mulroney in Canada – were elected on promises to eliminate "big government" and to reform the civil service. Thatcher cut the civil service by 22 percent and attempted to increase efficiency by introducing performance-related pay schemes and hiring business executives into government.[68] Reagan and Mulroney adopted similar measures. Their stated goal was to shrink the civil service and privatize public functions where possible, to empower "bottom-up decision-making" as opposed to "bureaucratic top-down commanding", and to replace "administrators" and policy advisors with "managers."[69]

Meanwhile, in 1987, bankers at Drexel Burnham Lambert issued the first CDO. Like the CDOs that held subprime mortgages and wreaked such havoc two decades later, it pooled debt instruments together into a special-purpose entity, which then sold securities that issued payouts based on the underlying debtors' payments on their debt. Starting in 1987, the Value at Risk (VaR) model was developed. It depicted everyday market risk associated with a given financial product, like a CDO, in simple whole numbers.[70]

In the 1990s (and we should not forget the invigorating effect of the Soviet Union's collapse in 1989), political parties more toward the center or near-left of the political spectrum, including Bill Clinton's in the US and Tony Blair's in the UK, adopted and modified the regulatory reform project for their own.[71] The reforms shifted from the deregulation-focused agendas of the 1980s toward strategies that aimed to make more effective and efficient use of public resources. They were often modeled on private sector strategies. Their reforms went by different names, including National Program Review (NPR) in the United States and New Public Management (NPM) in Australia, New Zealand, Great Britain, and Canada.[72] The NPM/NPR movement, like the New Right-driven initiatives that preceded them – though this time without the revolutionary, deregulatory zeal – sought to transfer private sector markets and managerial systems into the public sector in order to improve efficiency. A distinct set of drivers within the European Union generated a similar fracturing of the traditional state there.[73] A new post-Welfare State model, often referred to as the regulatory state, began to take shape.

These initiatives advocated government decentralization and "streamlining." NPM and NPR initiatives provoked deep cuts to the service sector – something that some observers have never forgiven. The goal was to develop effective, efficient, less costly government infrastructure that could partner with and learn from the private sector. For example, the Clinton Administration's National Performance Review sought to benchmark government service standards alongside private business standards, and also advocated for increased contracting-out to private business of the delivery of public goods and services.[74]

NPM and NPR implementers were willing to break up existing institutional structures in the name of greater responsiveness, nimbleness, and accountability. In many cases, the result was a new public management structure that allocated the authority for developing high-level strategic priorities to centralized government institutions, but devolved operations and implementation to dedicated local departments or even to private (for-profit or not-for-profit) actors. The term "government by proxy" was coined.[75] In David Osborne and Ted Gaebler's famous phrase, government's job in the new model was to "steer, not row."[76]

With decentralization came the need to assess the performance of service providers. Responsibility for the day-to-day operation of public services was devolved generally through arm's-length contracts (even between government departments) and tendered competitively. Performance under the contracts was then assessed based on incremental efficiency gains. Particularly under US Vice President Al Gore's NPR regime, a "customer service" ethic framed the reforms in the US.[77] Government departments, acting as purchasers, sought value from their contractors, to the greater benefit of the public in terms of cost savings and more effective service provision.[78]

Throughout, the new national programs sought to use empirical methods to evaluate the public sector's performance. Their use is telling. As Michael Power has suggested, data collection, analysis, and management – collectively, auditing – "is not simply a solution to a technical problem; it also makes possible ways of redesigning the practice of government"[79] in situations where stable, widespread trust in the state is lacking. Governments rely on auditing "as they grapple with the production of risks, the erosion of social trust, fiscal crisis and the need for control."[80] For Power, intensive, formal, detailed auditing across a broad range of topics became institutionalized in this era precisely because auditing served an important *legitimizing* function within the new decentralized regulatory state.[81]

Third Way advocates shared with their deregulatory predecessors the conviction that promising means of achieving public service provision could sometimes be found in private action,[82] but in theory at least they sought to harness private action in the service of recognizably progressive public policy goals. For example, during the Clinton Administration, civil service jobs were downsized by 191,000. However, the same period also saw an increase of 600,000 non-defense contract and grant jobs for carrying out government services.[83] As Tony Blair wrote in 1998,

> The Third Way stands for a modernized social democracy, passionate in its commitment to social justice and the goals of the centre-left, but innovative and forward-thinking in the means to achieve them. It is founded on the values that have guided progressive politics for more than a century – democracy, liberty, justice, mutual obligation and internationalism. But it is a third way because it moves decisively beyond an Old Left preoccupied by state control, high taxation and producer interests; and a New Right treating public investment, and often the very notions of "society" and collective endeavor, as evils to be undone.[84]

The same year, Bill Clinton said,

> We have moved past the sterile debate between those who say Government is the enemy and those who say Government is the answer. My fellow Americans, we have found a Third Way. We have the smallest Government in 35 years, but a more progressive one. We have a smaller Government but a stronger nation.[85]

These were important years for regulatory scholarship as well. A new conversation had begun to emerge. In 1992, Ian Ayres and John Braithwaite published their influential book, *Responsive Regulation*.[86] It was a significant step relative to the work that preceded it, and simultaneously reflective and emblematic of the larger ideological and strategic shift taking place. The book represents a convergence between law and economics-based game theory analysis, which was perhaps then at its apogée, and a more sociological (one might say progressive) account being developed by people like John Braithwaite and Peter

Grabosky. David Osborne's and Ted Gaebler's book *Reinventing Government* had come out the month before – the same month that the Maastricht Treaty was signed, creating the European Union. Mary Ann Glendon's *Rights Talk* and Robert Ellickson's *Order Without Law* – both acclaimed ruminations on the relationship between law and the broader regulatory forces produced by norms and civic responsibility – had been published the year before. Together, these books laid the foundation for a richer and more theoretically robust understanding of regulation, not only as social ordering but also as a multifaceted, deliberative, flexible embodiment of democracy and public will.

In many Western nations by the mid-1990s, the state, including the "regulatory toolbox" it had at its disposal, was radically different than it had been two decades earlier. The new regulatory state model had moved the state off the perch of authority and power it held during the postwar era. But what emerged was not nineteenth-century-style laissez-faire capitalism reborn. Both state and society, and the relationship between them, had changed. Al Gore-style client-centered initiatives came to be supplanted by more elaborate and sophisticated regulatory methods, which in the UK went by the self-confident program moniker, "better regulation."[87] Regulatory strategies began to employ a mix of instruments tailored to the unique complexities of different problems. "Smart regulation" theory advocated reaching out to a broader range of actors, including business interests, NGOs, and third parties, and not only through traditional regulation but also through economic instruments (e.g., taxes, cap-and-trade regimes), disclosure-based and verification instruments (e.g., labeling and certification schemes, audits, community right-to-know legislation), and legal instruments (e.g., liability laws, enforceable self-regulation).[88]

Meanwhile offstage, on August 6, 1991, the World Wide Web went public, and the first website was put online. JP Morgan is credited with creating the first modern CDS in 1994 when its client, Exxon, needed a line of credit to cover potential damages from the 1989 *Exxon Valdez* oil spill. Venture capital, particularly around the tech industry, boomed through the 1990s. By the late 1990s, when the use of derivatives was exploding, US securities regulators and an international rulemaking body, the Basel Committee on Banking Supervision (they of the Basel Capital Accords discussed in Chapter 1), had come to endorse the VaR model as a basis on which financial firms could both disclose the levels of risk their products contained, and determine how much capital they had to have on hand to protect against those risks.[89]

Regulation and governance scholarship continued to develop through the 1990s and early 2000s. Julia Black advanced a "conversational model" of regulation in which regulators and regulatees could come together and address the over-inclusiveness and under-inclusiveness of traditional rulemaking, emphasizing individualized approaches to regulation and compliance rather than deterrence.[90] Christine Parker, pointing to Australia's Competition and Consumer Commission as a regulator that was taking learning seriously, anticipated regulators' growing ability to respond to changes and revise regulatory goals and strategies, in a system of "triple loop learning."[91] Other scholars identified a new model at work within international, transnational, and regional regimes (like the EU), in which regional flexibility is what allows states to agree to broad principles, while still maintaining the notion of sovereignty and while tailoring schemes to fit their domestic institutional and legal regimes.[92] Still others struggled with the difficult question of how to ensure accountability on the part of a state that aimed to "steer" while private entities "rowed," and where private and public spheres had blurred.[93]

The regulatory state did not restructure all aspects of the Welfare State. Scholars disagree about how significant the break between Welfare State and regulatory state really was.[94] Indeed, statistics show that welfare spending in most OECD nations – a form of direct state intervention into the economy – has nevertheless grown steadily since the 1970s, if at a somewhat slower rate than before.[95] What is more, taken as a whole, the changes did not deregulate: instead, they altered the nature of regulation. Certain industries were deregulated at one level, only to be re-regulated through different mechanisms at another. For example, as Majone has pointed out, public utilities in Europe were privatized, but in the process they lost their immunity from European competition law.[96] In Canada, the United States, and other Anglo-American countries the state devolved the responsibility for implementing its policies to private sector contractors, but then subjected those contractors to demanding performance reviews.[97] Tax-and-spend power shrank, and markets were liberalized; but the scope for rule making increased.[98] Thus while the discourse was often framed around deregulation, especially in the 1980s, what had actually occurred by the mid-1990s was that regulation and governance had been reinvented by "an increase in delegation, proliferation of new technologies of regulation, formalization of inter-institutional and intra-institutional relations, and the proliferation of mechanisms of self-regulation in the shadow of the state."[99] The new methods were not necessarily equivalent in terms of goals, outcomes, or transparency, but nor were they fundamentally *de*regulatory.

In trying to tell a transnational narrative like this, we should also be careful not to oversell the similarities across nations. There were significant differences. Most fundamentally, regulatory technique attracted more attention in Europe and within the Westminster systems, while American scholars focused to a greater extent on state architecture, legitimacy, and power struggles.[100] Some states, like Japan, resisted delegating powers to autonomous agencies while others, like Britain, created a number of semi-autonomous regulators.[101] Michael Moran has observed that, in the UK, the regulatory state replaced an elite, discretion-heavy, closed "club government" model with that of a modern, transparent, empirics-based – and panoptic – state.[102] (While Moran is no fan of club government, nor is he a fan of what he sees as the threatening and oppressive modern regulatory state.) The new UK model was also a response to the intellectual challenge that public choice theory presented to the legitimacy, even credibility, of the Westminster parliamentary ideas of responsible government and the independent public service.[103]

Meanwhile, offstage, in 1997, Robert Merton and Myron Scholes received the Nobel Prize in Economics for their work on options pricing (Fischer Black had passed away). Even so, in 1998, Long Term Capital Management, the highly leveraged hedge fund on whose board they sat and which specialized in derivatives trading on their model, faced collapse and had to be bailed out to avoid potentially catastrophic consequences for its financial industry counterparties. Clayton Christensen published *The Innovator's Dilemma* in 1997, coining the now-ubiquitous term, "disruptive innovation."[104] In 1999, HFT was developed. This is a highly technical form of algorithmic trading that today accounts for up to 70 percent of trade volume and continues to present regulatory challenges. In 2000, the Commodity Futures Modernization Act was passed in the US, which exempted most of the OTC derivatives market from regulation.[105] The same year, David X. Li developed the so-called Gaussian cupola, a mathematical method for pricing risks like those in the bundles of debt instruments underpinning CDOs. Based on an oversimplified form of the cupola, financial innovation exploded. In the wake of the dot-com bust, money moved into new asset-backed financial products, which were generating exceptional returns with seemingly minimal risk in an era of otherwise low returns on investment.

Thus, even as regulatory innovators were relinquishing the blunt instruments of traditional, control-based, top-down regulation in favor of a more varied and flexible set of regulatory strategies, private sector innovators were shattering the atoms of property, debt, and risk through a vastly varied and complex new set of financial products and strategies.

SHIFTING IDEOLOGIES IN THE MOVE TO THE REGULATORY STATE

Scholars tell us that the regulatory state that developed across these decades was more flexible, nimble, and collaborative than what preceded it. Arguably, in the pursuit of greater effectiveness it also relinquished its place of authority, with a corresponding effect on the direct presence of a public voice in regulation. According to the late Peter Aucoin, 1980s- and 1990s-era pressure on government to reimagine itself came from three circumstances that were common to all Western democracies at the time: the political and economic need to reduce public spending, the widespread decline of public confidence in the effectiveness and quality of public programs, and the need for states to compete in a new, global economic order.[106] While these factors were present, they are themselves consequences of deeper geopolitical and intellectual shifts. Those forces both undermined the legitimacy and perceived capacity of the state, and enhanced the perceived promise of other, non-legal forces. The result was a strange and, for some, perhaps unexpectedly palatable new brew of economic analysis, norms scholarship, civic republicanism, and procedural justice. Some of these forces are identified below.

The Influence of Economics in the New Innovation-Framing Regulation

Perhaps the key thing that "happened" to the state, beginning in the 1970s, was the rise of economics as a disciplinary and evaluative tool for assessing government effectiveness.[107] Economic modeling was fairly well developed by the mid-1960s, and so-called "Chicago School" economic thought had gathered considerable momentum by the 1970s.[108] Applying efficiency-based analyses to public/regulatory state functions gave scholars and policymakers the tools to assess state performance relative to other means of channeling and determining conduct.[109] Straitened circumstances meant they were already developing the incentive to do so.

Such assessments led to a more efficiency-based and efficiency-valuing approach to regulation, which demanded accountability and pushed for continual improvement. As the global economic order shifted in the 1970s, conventional Keynesian solutions struggled to explain the problems of stagflation and economic insecurity, and failed to provide solutions. The monolithic Welfare State was conceived in a less complex and interconnected world and, following fast-moving events like the 1973 Oil Crisis, it seemed ill-adapted to the more fluid, decentralized, globalized environment in which it was newly embedded.

A history of federal regulation written in 1986 stated that "[t]raditional administrative rulemaking – so called command and control rulemaking – came under general attack for its economic efficiency in failing to discriminate between low-cost and high-cost compliance activity."[110] This new critique decisively moved the needle of policy discourse and changed the range of permissible options. Government programs were expected to demonstrate that they operated efficiently, not only relative to alternative formal regulatory strategies but also relative to alternatives like market-based regulation or self-regulation. By the 1990s, it had been broadly accepted that regulation had to be accountable for its efficiency.

Economics introduced a question that had not been particularly salient in the postwar years: under precisely what conditions does it make sense to engage active, public regulatory tools, as opposed to letting the market "regulate?" For economists, the increasingly convincing answer was that regulation only made sense when markets failed. Even where regulation was appropriate to control so-called "externalities" – pollution, monopoly, the inadequate provision of public goods, etc. – it did not follow that an entire industry should be comprehensively regulated, let alone nationalized and run by the state. Regulation made sense only to the degree necessary to manage the externality.[111] The concept of market failure as the prototypical case for regulatory intervention was so analytically forceful that in the United States, even civil rights issues – like the question of how to protect "discrete and insular minorities" – sometimes came to be framed in terms of using judicial intervention to correct (political) market failure.[112]

The rise of economics changed more than the standards to which regulation was held accountable. Economics also changed the content of regulation, not least by introducing a new set of tools and assumptions. The predictive, model-ready set of conceptual framing devices that economics offered, and its considerable explanatory force, meant that regulatory scholarship virtually across the spectrum had to contend with it. Along with learning to think of regulation writ large as, most essentially, a response to market failure, regulatory theory learned to talk about regulatory challenges and prescriptions using the language of incentives, efficiencies, market failures, performance, and games.[113] Indeed, background assumptions deriving from economics, including the efficient market hypothesis – the notion of an efficient market, within which rational self-interested players act in their own self-interest and thereby generate outcomes that optimize allocative efficiency and maximize overall welfare – came to be invoked in more regulatory conversations than Great Society-era progressive scholars might ever have anticipated. In Elinor Ostrom's formulation, the economic model of the prisoner's dilemma became a familiar hammer in the possession of which much of the world, ultimately, started to look like a nail.[114]

As the next chapter argues, these economic ideas were not generally driving policy or scholarship on their own. They were more terminological conventions or credibility boosters, marshaled in support of positions already arrived at through other means. Nevertheless, framing devices are powerful. Market-oriented logic and market-oriented values, such as efficiency and economic utility, would at one time have been seen as being of limited relevance to public state functions like ensuring environmental protection or social service provision. Distinctly public-realm values, such as justice or equality, had previously been seen as either being beyond-market, or else purposefully entrenched to counterbalance the market's strong influence.[115] The regulatory state era saw the logic of economics imported into public service provision, albeit in the name of advancing public values. The widespread adoption of economics-influenced language in debates about public service provision and government showed the degree to which economic analysis had put the Welfare State on the defensive. If by adopting the language of economics, regulation and governance scholarship implicitly accepted that government might be "the problem," as Ronald Reagan once charged,[116] then greater efficiency and responsiveness were the paths to its redemption.

Risk as Regulatory Touchstone

A natural outflow of the new focus on economics was a new regulatory interest in risk. Risk-based analysis makes sense in efficiency terms, because it aims to allocate regulatory resources to the most serious risks. Yet risk's centrality to regulation is also illuminating because it helps illustrate the changing nature of regulatory theory over the last several decades. As the late Peter Bernstein so engagingly demonstrated, the concept of risk has a rich history, and humans have used it through time to wrest from the universe (or the gods) a degree of control over their lives and futures.[117] Risk and probability are mathematical concepts, developed over the years as much by gamblers and business people as by philosophers and mathematicians. For contemporary regulators, they are fundamental analytical tools.

As Anthony Giddens has described it, natural risk was the Welfare State's primary concern.[118] Many of the changes made to state action during the postwar era were driven by a desire to increase citizens' security and to mitigate the misery of economic crisis, war, illness, and aging. The aim was to establish fundamental baselines for human material wellbeing, safety, and dignity. In an era "before economics" and before intense transnational competition, in systems with little prior experience with modern public administration, bureaucratic efficiency was not top-of-mind; effecting change was. Positive social change through regulation was the new frontier of progressive advancement.

Giddens has suggested natural risks were largely and (in the West) quite successfully addressed through mechanisms like private insurance and public social safety nets.[119] While actuarial science has been around since at least 1693, the twentieth-century insurance industry professionalized actuarial analysis and collectivized shared risks to a previously unknown degree.[120] Actuarial methods and assumptions co-developed alongside the Welfare State and modern social insurance.[121] As a form of public insurance, the Welfare State ushered in a new era of freedom from the natural risks that had terrorized individuals and societies in the past.

Concerns about natural risk in the mid-twentieth century gave way to concerns about what Giddens calls "manufactured risk" – risk "created by the very progression of human development," producing uncertainty within "new risk environments for which history provides us with very little previous experience."[122] Giddens has argued that we now live in a "risk society" that exists "after nature" – meaning that "we [have] stopped worrying so much about what nature could do to us, and we [have] started worrying more about what we have done to nature." The risk society also exists "after tradition:" our destinies are individualized, in a world "where life is no longer lived as fate."[123] And as society and the state became more fluid and contingent, the concerns underlying regulation shifted too.

Giddens provocatively argued that we are now living "at the barbaric outer edge of modern technology," in an era of "reflexive modernisation" in which society is running into its own limits.[124] Without having to adopt this somewhat apocalyptic vision, we can probably agree that manufactured risks are the most salient risks we run today. (Manufactured risk may of course produce a whole new round of natural risk in the form of environmental disasters associated with, for example, anthropogenic climate change. Based on their provenance it still makes sense to think of such consequences as manufactured risks.) Of course, risk is not always something to be avoided. In finance and investing, there is no profit without risk. The two are correlated: high risk and high return, low risk and low return. In other ways as well, risk is the flipside of opportunity. Modern manufactured risk, like innovation itself, carries with it hope and not only apprehension.

However, in contrast to natural risk, the consequences and boundaries of manufactured risk are highly uncertain. Almost a century ago, Frank Knight used the terms "uncertainty" and "risk" to denote different kinds of "unknowns" in a way that helps us understand what manufactured risk really entails.[125] What Knight described as "risks" are those events that, though we do not know for certain will happen, nevertheless are known to us as risks and are to some degree quantifiable. As Knight wrote, anything that "can by any method be reduced to an objective, quantitatively determinate probability, can be reduced to complete certainty by grouping cases." These are risks.

True uncertainty, on the other hand, is "not susceptible to measurement and hence to elimination."[126] In Giddens's terms, manufactured risk is "risk" as the term is commonly used, certainly, but it also awakens actual Knightian uncertainty.

These days, the popular shorthand used to describe uncertainty comes from former US Secretary of Defense Donald Rumsfeld, who in a different context once said that there the "known unknowns," and the "unknown unknowns."[127] The unknown unknowns are possibilities of which we are not even aware, which are marked by profound indeterminacy. As catchy as the term is, it does not fully capture what Knight was describing. The risk-versus-uncertainty dichotomy is richer than just a statistical assessment. The term "risk" assumes that we can be quite certain about the likely distribution of possible outcomes. This is a circumstance that only exists in theoretical models. In market terms, any profit would be impossible in such a world because all possibilities would be accounted for.

By contrast, the real world inevitably involves a degree of irreducible uncertainty that partly comes down to the need for humans to exercise subjective judgment. A central and important component of Knight's work is that decision-makers have real difficulty in even classifying possible outcomes into useful categories in the face of uncertainty. Beyond just lacking data or awareness, we will not always exercise judgment adequately, for example in defining the right "groups" of comparator cases. Expectations about the future are based on subjective assessments, which cannot be publicly or objectively verified except after the fact – and worse, we are blinkered by our own biases and imperfect reasoning.[128]

What has all of this got to do with regulation? The awareness that risks can be dynamic and radically unpredictable was another catalyst for change in the nature of the state. Well before the financial crisis, thanks to technological advances, macroeconomic shifts in global trade, and other world-shrinking and pace-accelerating phenomena, the monolithic, slow-moving, stability-oriented postwar state came to seem about as out of step with the times as Soviet Five-Year plans, thirty-year fixed-rate mortgages, defined benefit pensions, or rotary telephones. The regulatory state is perhaps more accurately called the "risk regulatory state," in which risk not only defines the mandate of regulation but also has changed the procedure, organization, and evaluative processes for regulation itself.[129]

If we look at the frequency with which the terms "welfare state" and "risk management" appear in books published between 1900 and 2008, as Figure 2.1 does, we can see the relative rise of the idea of risk management:[130]

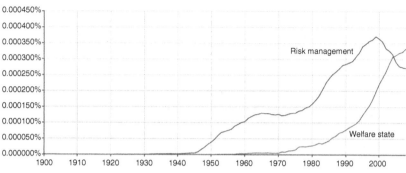

FIGURE 2.1. Frequency of terms in books from 1900 to 2008.

Risk-based analysis is now a first-order regulatory tool in part because it is able to function under conditions of imperfect information and uncertainty.[131] Risk-based analysis as an approach tries to make things measurable and apparently objective, based on the careful dissection of phenomena into their component and causative parts. Modern regulation too aims to be empirically grounded, dispassionate, and analytically robust. It aims to compensate for the impossibility of certainty by relying on data as much as possible. But even where clarity is elusive, risk-based analysis is appealing as a response to uncertainty. Risk-based approaches use empirical analysis and probabilities to try to wrest knowable bits out of contexts that indisputably will never be completely known. Such an approach does not deal in certainties. As the UK FSA was fond of pointing out, the goal was not to run a "zero failure" regime[132] but rather to generate an informed estimate about where problems are most likely to lie and thereby determine how to allocate inevitably scarce regulatory resources. Moreover, the move toward risk analysis is a move from sweeping conviction to the specific, fine-grained, contextual knowledge about individual and collective action that only became possible as our own knowledge and capacity to manage information increased. In this way, perhaps, our certainties fell away even as actual understanding grew.

Flexibility in regulation attempts to respond to the profound dynamism, uncertainty, and complexity that characterize contemporary society. A changed global and economic landscape, and the Keynesian Welfare State's loss of credibility, spurred the need to imagine more flexible forms of regulation – regulation that was, crucially, more porous to and engaged with the fast-moving social and economic forces operating beyond its grasp. Orly Lobel, speaking of what she calls the "Renew Deal," has said that "the idea of dynamic [regulatory] innovation is intrinsic to the theory."[133] In other words, regulatory theory from the 1990s onward, including its risk-based aspects, have embraced *change* as inevitable – in particular, it embraced human-generated change.

The relationship between risk-based regulatory thinking and progressive social policy is complex. Risk-based regulation may have made regulation more effective and certainly seems to have helped make better use of public resources, which is all to the good. At the same time, in embracing risk not only as a useful conceptual framework but as a matter of individual, choice-oriented social policy, actuarial science and risk-based accountability standards may have eroded the common protections – even perhaps the sense of common fate and shared human vulnerability – that once characterized the Welfare State.[134] As well, the pervasive regulatory preoccupation with risk management may have generated its own organizational logic, sometimes more as performance, ritual, and an ongoing legitimation exercise in an age of uncertainty.[135] Finally, the turn toward contingency, specificity, and contextuality has entailed more consultation, more collaboration with private actors, and greater openness to information and expertise from outside the regulatory apparatus itself. This opens the door to further change and more innovation, even if that was rarely part of any explicit rationale for regulatory reform. One of this book's aims is to understand how innovation, particularly financial innovation, has affected regulation, including its capacity and its ambition. Part of its effect can be seen in the development of flexible regulation as a more flexible, dynamic, adaptable approach, built to keep pace with private innovation. In the process, another part of its effect has been in creating a regulatory structure that proved ultimately, even if not always consciously or explicitly, to actually be porous to innovation itself.

The Philosophical Dimension in Flexible Regulation

Another blow to the Welfare State came in the form of a deep philosophical critique of state action that developed from post-modernism, post-structuralism, and associated critical approaches to social and legal thought, particularly from the 1970s onwards.

Much of post-structuralism is concerned with power, authority, and control. For Michel Foucault, the "micro-mechanisms" of power were what structure "regulatory spaces" – that is, the multiple fields of action in which individuals operate. Foucault located power both everywhere and nowhere, not only in the formal sphere of politics but inescapably in all social relations.[136] This power constitutes the individual. It shapes preferences (in Pierre Bourdieu's terms, enabling individuals to develop a socially-acquired *habitus*, or "feel for the game")[137] in subtle but profound ways. The post-structuralist account implies that a positivist, institutionally focused image of the state or regulation not only oversimplifies, but actually misconceives, how and where authority and control are exercised. In academic circles, Foucault's work provoked considerable rethinking about politics, institutional relations and regulation studies. The concept of government was broadened to include Foucault's broader ideas of "governmentality," which included not just explicit government action but the ways in which the state insidiously controls individuals' conduct, teaching them to police themselves.

Separately but not unrelatedly, in 1992, political scientists James Rosenau and Ernst Czempiel described the concept of "governance without government."[138] The concept of governance, in optimistic contrast to Foucault, captured the idea of transition from centralized government authority, which operates through traditional regulatory tools such as bright-line rules and top-down commands, to a much more diffused set of forces exercising influence on private actors. In this conceptual framework, "government" is associated with "activities backed by formal authority," while "governance" refers to "activities backed by shared goals that may or may not derive from legal or formally prescribed responsibilities."[139] Within the emerging study of regulation, as well, a distinct idea of "governance" was identified.[140] Conventional state instruments were recognized as not the only – and sometimes only the clumsiest and least consequential – available systems of control.[141] Power in fact is distributed among many institutions and relations, both public and private, and those functioning within regulatory spaces are often as much subjects of regulation as they are objects of it.[142]

Over the same time period, prominent critical legal scholars,[143] feminists,[144] critical race scholars,[145] and others revealed how traditional conceptions of rights and norms, and the institutions that existed to advance them, could in fact be used to reinforce existing inequalities. Some highlighted law's capacity to be reductive and essentializing, including within theoretically well-intentioned state initiatives aimed at advancing the interests of marginalized populations. Liberal legalisms such as "rights" may be instrumentally useful sometimes, but critics questioned how normatively defensible they actually were given how rarely such concepts take into account the pervasive sexism, racism, and inequality that structure modern society, including within those liberal legalisms themselves. These critiques to some degree helped confirm the demise of any collective faith in universal solutions, including (liberal, non-revolutionary) "Great Society" initiatives.

Today, when our concerns are more about the potentially totalizing effect of economic analysis and the hollowing out of the state (not to mention potentially linked phenomena like increasing economic inequality and corporate domination of public space), we may yearn for a more forceful, interventionist, clear-voiced public presence in our social conversations. But as David Lodge suggested, "we can never go back to a state of pre-Theory innocence about the transparency of language or the ideological neutrality of interpretation."[146] Nor can we go back to a state of unalloyed idealism about the possibilities of traditional state action. To suggest that critical legal scholars – in many ways, the fellow travelers of today's progressive thinkers – could have been part of a shift that undermined the authority of the Welfare State may seem ungenerous. It is certainly not intended to be. Rather, it is worth remembering that our choices are not binary.

We do not have to choose only between the Welfare State and the regulatory state, as we know them today. We are entitled to criticize a hierarchical, certainty-laden Welfare State structure if it is insensitive to diversity, for example, and also to criticize a regulatory state structure to the extent that too many of its outcomes are determined by economic priorities and economic influence. The Welfare State may indeed have been imperfect in social justice terms, and we need to look beyond it in seeking to build a richer, more inclusive and more satisfying model for the state. As explored more fully at the end of this book, our social account of innovation is bound up with this task.

As scathing as they could be about the limits of traditional state action, neither post-structuralism nor critical legal scholarship was devoid of hope. Hope lay in recognizing that rights, like preferences and social relations, are socially constructed, not natural and immutable. This means it is possible that better, more just, more democratic or sensitive social constructions can still produce real, transformative change.[147] In other words, if postmodernism undermined the apparent solidity of artifacts like laws-as-written, then the trick must be to pivot to consider the nature of the "interpretive community" that filled in the spaces in the law.[148] This brings us back to the historical account of where the regulatory state came from: a new perspective began to emerge from the wreckage.

GOVERNANCE, REGULATION, AND THE SHATTERING OF AUTHORITY: THE PHOENIX RISES

By the late 1990s, observers on both the right and the left of the conventional political spectrum seemed to agree, though for different reasons, that traditional floors-and-ceilings regulation was dysfunctional. Whether the situation was as dire as all that, especially as measured by the priorities of its time, is less obvious now. Regulation is not inevitably the failure it is sometimes portrayed to be. Neither the image of regulation-as-red-tape nor the image of regulation-as-ineffective-and-captured reflects the very significant successes that regulation has achieved thus far.[149] We know now, for example, that traditional, mandatory, state-imposed legal requirements do a great deal of work in setting minimum compliance standards and in forcing clear, immediate, and generally sustained shifts in industry conduct.[150] The fact that we have clean tap water to drink, safe buildings in which to live and work, and some degree of security in the event of natural disaster, employment-related injury, or plain old age should not be taken lightly. Measurable, material, outcome-oriented successes such as these are more common than we sometimes imagine and less appreciated than they deserve to be. Many of these strides are the product of postwar regulation, somewhat tweaked in the years since.

In some regulatory arenas, more flexible forms of regulation even emerged in the 1980s and 1990s in response to the *success* of what we now think of as traditional forms of regulation. By that time, many Western societies had made real progress in protecting people from some of the natural risks that had provoked the rise of the Welfare State. Memories of economic depression and war were fading. Having then made advances in areas such as civil rights, employment and housing discrimination, anti-poverty initiatives, corporate accountability, and environmental protection using traditional methods, equality-seeking groups and progressive scholars ran into the limits of law to accomplish more.[151] While the most egregious "first generation" problems had been dealt with, what persisted were subtler, more contested "second generation" problems – problems that seemed to be baked right into organizational hierarchies, corporate and institutional practices, and tacit assumptions.[152] Some sought ways to go beyond law and beyond the limited compliance-oriented mindset that accompanied it, to use more sophisticated regulatory design to address persistent problems.

Engaged in this pursuit, some scholars began to investigate other sources of normative authority. Emerging strands of flexible regulation saw promise in the norms literature of the 1980s and 1990s – Robert Ellickson on Shasta County ranchers, Lisa Bernstein on the New York Diamond Dealers Club, Robert Cover's celebrated article on nomos and narrative[153] – which pointed to robust and respected non-legal rules that seemed to play a central role in social ordering. It was a certain humility about the state, not just a sense of possibility around "civil society," which provoked a new focus on community norms as forces to be harnessed by regulation.

Starting from a different vantage point, Tom Tyler's important work looked at why people obey the law, when they do. He found that people will obey laws that they perceive to be procedurally legitimate and fairly enforced.[154] Tyler's work contributed a positivist, proceduralist, and practical basis of legitimacy for law that did not depend on some deeper shared commitment to the order that gave rise to it. This, just as much as the norms work above, helped shape the new regulatory sensibility.

Perhaps just as influential for scholars was the revival, particularly in the US, of civic republican thinking, which emphasized dialogue, mutual respect, and the constitutive power of the social realm in full personhood.[155] Civic republican theorists suggest that one of the state's key roles is to foster respectful, inclusive discourse based on non-domination, which affirms a richer, more empowering and emancipatory sense of citizenship and individual identity.[156] Through discourse, citizens come to a consensus about what is best for the community and in the process generate a legal order with a basis of legitimacy derived from the shared dialogic experience.[157] While traditional rulemaking approaches do not permit this kind of dialogic, evolutionary method, more flexible regulatory strategies possibly could.

Works like *Responsive Regulation*[158] braided these insights together with the nascent regulation scholarship. Ian Ayres and John Braithwaite pointed out that, most of the time, most regulatory actors behave responsibly not because of a fear of sanctions but because they perceive the law to be legitimate, fair, and consistent with their own moral and ethical codes. In keeping with civic republican priorities and the power of shared norms, interpersonal trust within the regulator–regulatee relationship is indispensable. In good postmodern fashion, Ayres and Braithwaite recognized that both organizations and individuals have "multiple selves" that emerge and operate differently, depending on both our situation within a regulatory space and the forces acting upon us. One of the priorities for regulation therefore is to be supple enough to react to the behavior of regulated entities in ways that encourage compliance – that is, in ways that accord respect and trust to regulated actors that are complying on their own – and, in allocative efficiency and risk-based regulatory terms, to dedicate regulatory resources in proportion to the need for them. Ayres's and Braithwaite's famous enforcement and regulatory pyramids, discussed further in the next chapter, embody this perspective.

Later works built on the responsive regulatory foundation in ways that were more collaborative, more porous, and even less state-centered. As we examine in the next chapter, very often flexible regulatory approaches aim to transcend the public/private divide through public/private collaborative initiatives that involve a multiplicity of diverse stakeholders. Non-state actors participate more in shaping public policy. Informal, non-governmental forces and actors are incorporated into the regulatory project itself. In the process, flexible regulation shifts, reallocates, and shares authority beyond the traditional state itself.[159]

Today, it may be tempting to tar the 1990s reforms with the scarlet label of neoliberalism, to consider NPR and NPM as wolves in sheep's clothing, hollowing out the state and betraying the progressive cause (if indeed they were ever part of it).[160] It is also easy to deride Tony Blair's "Third Way" and Bill Clinton's "Reinventing Government" initiatives as cynical political tactics designed to entice a middle ground of voters and to distance themselves from the still-reviled tax-and-spend-liberal policies of an earlier era. Such political calculations were almost certainly real, and operating. Bill Clinton, Tony Blair, and others oversaw extensive public sector cuts and were accused of undercutting the social progress and economic programs for which their political parties had fought for decades, if not generations. However, we should still be cautious in adjudicating on the overall sincerity or public-mindedness of the NPM/NPR initiatives in the hands of their implementers or their observers. They emerged, after all, during a time when the earlier Welfare State's credibility and public support was in tatters. The label of a "Third Way" aptly describes what felt to many at the time as a fresh, promising, less ideologically doctrinaire but still hopeful path between a discredited "old school" state apparatus and the distasteful deregulation projects of the Reagan and Thatcher era.[161]

The era in which flexible regulation developed was characterized by both a sense of limitation and a sense of possibility. Flexible regulation emerged at a time when the traditional state's legitimacy and capacity were more in doubt than they had been during the New Deal or Welfare State eras. To this day, we operate with a more chastened sense than the postwar generation had of the state's capacity to produce lasting, meaningful change using directive, top-down methods. Flexible regulation was the tip of an iceberg of more fundamental social, political and philosophical change. Yet at the same time, buoyed by sociolegal and civic republican scholarship, flexible regulation held out hope for the possibilities inherent in a new, more dynamic and potentially richer, state-transcending form of governance.[162] One of the fascinating things about flexible regulation is the creative and energetic ways in which it helped reformulate an authentic vision of the regulatory task, even as the state's traditional footing in authority and control was slipping away.

3

Four Key Perspectives: Flexible Regulation and the Link to Innovation

Notwithstanding the transformations wrought by politics, terror, war, and communications technology since the turn of the millennium, so-called "regulatory failures," like the Deepwater Horizon Disaster in 2010 and the Fukushima Nuclear Plant disaster in 2011, still rate as salient events in our recent collective history. Each has colored our era and our notion of the regulatory state, but perhaps none so much as the financial crisis.

Even thinking about these events as "regulatory failures" is problematic and politically laden. Both the financial crisis and the Deepwater Horizon blowout were the product, first and foremost, of private actors' failures rather than regulators'. According to the Deepwater Horizon commission, the "clear root cause" of the disaster was "a failure of industry management."[1] It was also private sector conduct that drove the financial system to the brink of collapse in 2007–2008. Causal factors there included self-interested and public-disregarding industry conduct driven by short-term performance indicators, bounded rationality, and a behavioral cascade within the industry (particularly the "shadow banking" industry) toward excessive risk-taking. This in turn drove transnational regulatory arbitrage, as private actors exploited unevenness in regulatory coverage. This book's focus on regulatory failure should not obscure the crucial point that many of the so-called regulatory failures of our era can be traced back to private sector behavior. We can say that regulation and regulators ought to have done better, without letting private actors off the hook for errors and misconduct that ultimately originated with them.

With enough failure to examine all around, intellectual discourse in the years since the start of the financial crisis has shifted toward scrutinizing capitalism and globalization; the seemingly disproportionate influence, size, and reach of the financial sector; and income and wealth inequality.

79

The shift crystallized in the post-Obama, post-Brexit era. These powerful new (or renewed) critical winds are swirling too around the sometimes mundane-seeming worlds of regulation and governance. In the wake of a focusing event like a financial crisis or environmental disaster, public/private partnerships, self-regulation, and similar notions may look like abdications of public space to private actors.

As noted at the outset, this book was initially prompted by an assertion that Lord Adair Turner made in 2009 about the relationship between innovation and financial regulation. In the UK FSA's review of the causes of and proposed regulatory responses to the financial crisis, Lord Turner charged that US, UK, and worldwide financial regulators had proceeded on the assumption that financial innovation was beneficial by definition, because the market would winnow out any unproductive innovations.[2] If Lord Turner was right, then in retrospect (and notwithstanding any policy or legislative assertions to the contrary that may be made in the coming years) this perspective seems clearly to have been mistaken.

At one level, it no longer matters much. The FSA, the main target of his critique, has been abolished, itself a victim of the financial crisis and perhaps also of the political imperative to be seen to be doing something to respond to it. The crisis and its political and regulatory fallout have surely burned away any residual faith that agency personnel might have had in the across-the-board benefits of financial innovation. More importantly, we now know that enormous under-resourcing was a central problem at the FSA, as it was within those Divisions of the US Securities and Exchange Commission (SEC) where regulation proved during the financial crisis to have been completely inadequate.[3] Lack of focus was another problem: prudential regulation, at least at the FSA, was simply not a priority.[4] To the extent that regulatory (in)action was implicated in the crisis, the key lessons have more to do with political economy and resources than with regulatory theory. Proper resourcing and capacity are essential to regulatory state structures, just as they were to Welfare State structures.

Yet the FSA was also, on paper if not in practice, the model of a modern regulatory state institution. It was a thought leader, not only among UK regulators but among financial regulators internationally: it was risk-based and principles-based. It relied heavily on empirical data. It consulted and collaborated with private sector actors. It thought about its mandate in terms of regulatory efficiency, market failures, and the need to keep up with industry-driven change. Its methods were highly transparent. At least on the market conduct front, its Treating Customers Fairly program was widely considered to be very demanding.[5] Under-resourcing aside for now, if Lord Turner was even partially right about the FSA's philosophical stance toward innovation, what might this mean for other modern regulatory state institutions? Is it possible that Lord Turner's critique applies more broadly? Should we be concerned that flexible, dynamic regulatory state structures generally are over-reliant on the Efficient Market Theory, or on the unexamined assumption that innovation is by definition beneficial? Is there something more fundamental going on, something wrong with how we, and how regulators, have conceived of regulation in highly innovative contexts? These questions are still very relevant, to financial regulation generally (whose basic premises remain unchanged since the crisis); to the emerging challenge of regulating new fintech innovations; and to regulation generally across many economic, social, and environmental sectors. The economic and social legacies of the last quarter-century are very much under scrutiny in countries like the UK and the US, but we do not yet have a clear sense of what better balance between innovation and regulation can be struck from here.

Trying to draw links between regulators' behavior across different statutory regimes and different administrative bodies, with different histories and staffed by different individuals, is an almost impossibly challenging task. Every regulatory failure is the product of its own unique set of conditions. Getting access to any one regulator and engaging in careful investigation of a complex event within it is the kind of thing that can be a lifework. And yet for all the agency-specific particularities and unanticipated factual wrinkles, regulators operating across industries share a common era, and the assumptions of that era shape (albeit in different ways) how regulators operate and how regulatory regimes are structured. In this sense, there is a forest as well as just trees.

This chapter and the next two look at regulation and governance scholarship, by academics, as a way to understand the zeitgeist within which the regulatory state emerged over these last decades. Scholarship is not a perfect proxy for practice. Nevertheless, the links between academia and policymakers, though sometimes subtle, are real. Both individual work and broader scholarly trends can influence regulatory and industry practice in positive ways;[6] they can also be misunderstood, misapplied, or used for instrumental or political purposes by regulators, policymakers, and private entities. Moreover, because academics have the ability to take a "big picture" view, sometimes they have the capacity to distill and give voice to broader themes or trends that are not obvious from within any single regulatory institution. Looking at the scholarship can help us see broader patterns in ways that even tracking the explicit links between theory and practice cannot. For these reasons, understanding regulation and governance scholarship as it has evolved over the last thirty years is a useful route to understanding the modern regulatory state, the challenges facing it, and the ways in which it needs to continue to evolve.

Nothing in regulation scholarship caused the disasters mentioned above. Nevertheless, as this chapter and the next two argue, the scholarship is illuminating for three main reasons: first, regulation and governance scholarship from the 1990s onward has been characterized by a preference for flexible regulation. It has identified and largely advocated a "scaffolding-style" regulatory structure that makes formal state regulatory requirements porous to a range of non-state forces that include the market, private expertise, and community norms. The result has been a more flexible, context-specific, and collaborative regulatory architecture that is also reflexive. Just as state action (regulation) influences non-state action (including regulated actors' conduct, but others' too), so non-state action in turn influences state action. Flexible regulation therefore sets up a new and noteworthy kind of relationship with private sector forces, including the forces that catalyze and register private sector innovation. In looking at the development of flexible regulation scholarship through an account of four key perspectives, below, an image emerges of regulatory scholarship opening itself up over time, by degrees, to embrace greater flexibility and contingency in response to situational uncertainty.

Second – and this will matter quite a lot as we chart a path forward from here – it turns out that Lord Turner's charge in regard to the FSA is not accurate vis-à-vis this scholarship. Though different scholars have different perspectives, overall there is no general view within the scholarship that innovation will be "by definition beneficial." Nor do flexible regulation scholars share some bedrock commitment to the Efficient Market Theory, or take the position that the market can be relied on to winnow out all unproductive ideas. As a description of regulation scholarship overall, the Turner Review vastly overplays the emphasis on market forces and oversimplifies how they are depicted; moreover, it underplays the importance of the other mechanisms and priorities that underpin flexible regulation scholarship, including democracy-enhancing and equality-oriented ones.

Third, while regulation scholars appreciate the importance of flexibility, particularly in complex and dynamic environments, and they appreciate the reflexive regulator–environment relationship that flexible regulation produces, the conversation is still primarily a regulatory and legal one. In other words, regulation scholars (predictably) are more interested in *regulatory* innovations than in the corresponding non-regulatory environments in which those innovations are located. That is, as we shall see in more detail in the next chapter, regulation and governance scholars discuss regulatory innovation, but being scholars of regulation rather than of environmental engineering or the like, they spend less time discussing the origins and development of the underlying technology and innovation that they often seek to foster. What this means is that *what* flexible regulation is meant to be porous *to* has generally not been closely investigated. Thus, a review of the scholarship serves to identify not only what the collective conversations about regulation and innovation, including financial innovation, have focused on, but also – just as importantly – what they have not focused on. The understudied assumptions that lurk in the shadows of these conversations can be as consequential as the dialogue itself.

THE CONCERN WITH FLEXIBILITY

Notwithstanding the considerable variation within the literature, regulation and governance scholarship over the twenty-odd years leading up to the financial crisis was primarily characterized by a preference for *flexibility* in regulation. The flexible regulation literature distinguishes itself from what it depicted as the rigid, top-down, blunt instruments of traditional Welfare State regulation. It aimed to develop regulatory structures that could be tailored to the needs of a particular situation (and, importantly, tailored by the regulated firms themselves). Where regulatory structures could be made more flexible, it followed (or so went the assumption) that they would also be a better and more effective fit for a regulatory problem, much in the way that a tailored suit keeps one warmer on a cold day than a drafty cardboard box would. Potentially, even, the more flexible and context-specific the regulatory scheme, the better.

For many, old-style Welfare State regulation of the kind described in the last chapter was seen as a clumsy, blunt instrument for achieving regulatory objectives. The only tools it had at its disposal were one-size-fits-all mandates, prohibitions, and penalties, meaning that a regulator was forced either to respond to small problems with disproportionately large sanctions, or to exercise its discretion not to act in non-transparent ways. Bright-line regulatory boundaries – like those between local and long-distance telephone companies, trucking and shipping lines, and banking and securities firms – along with trade barriers and wage, price, and interest rate controls were perceived to produce and then entrench significant inefficiencies, to the public's disadvantage. Not only that, but bright-line rules could be actively counterproductive, because rules that seemed sensible in the abstract could be unreasonable when applied to discrete situations.[7] Flexible regulation scholars pointed to the pathologies, including the influence of interest groups, seemingly inherent in developing detailed regulatory rules.[8]

The flexible regulation scholarship was thus full of the claim that regulation could be improved simply by making it more adaptable, and less one-size-fits-all. To take one example among many, in analyzing the failures of traditional, top-down regulation, Cass Sunstein claimed back in 1991 that traditional regulation's "main problem is structural."[9] He argued that traditional floors-and-ceilings regulation generates poor incentives, focuses on symptoms over root causes, and is insensitive or unresponsive to context. (All of this is probably true.) The fundamental problem, for Sunstein, was rigidity and poor tailoring, which imposed unnecessary costs. By extension, he argued that "flexible, market-oriented, incentive-based regulatory strategies" were more likely to "increase efficiency and promote [regulation's] own purposes."[10] Similarly, Richard Stewart claimed in 1993 that the United States should "seek to reduce excessive costs and burdens imposed by its exceptionally rigid, legalistic system of environmental law and administration."[11] Expressing a worry that pops up repeatedly in American scholarship, all the way through to the debates around the Sarbanes-Oxley and Dodd-Frank Acts,[12] he explained that it is the "rigidity" of environmental law and administration that causes excessive costs and burdens. He explored how to "achieve greater [regulatory] flexibility,"[13] drawing on now-familiar mechanisms such as the decentralization of decision-making, the contracting out of aspects of public service provision, and the use of market-based approaches. (We return in the next chapter to consider the emphases on markets, costs, incentives, and efficiency.)

Looking at the regulatory scholarship from the 1990s onward, we see a consistent preference for more flexible, context-specific, and collaborative regulatory architecture. For example, flexible regulation focuses on instruments, not actors. As Lester Salamon has observed, one of the key components in the shift to flexible regulation has been "a shift in the 'unit of analysis' in policy analysis and administration from the public agency or the individual public program to the distinctive tools and instruments through which public purposes are pursued."[14] The bright-line regulatory "floors" and "ceilings" that characterized traditional regulation give way, in flexible regulation, to an instrument-oriented assessment of the "regulatory toolkit" and appropriate "instrument choice."[15]

Opening Up and Accepting Contingency, by Degrees

It would be inaccurate to suggest that flexible regulation has developed in some linear fashion over the last three decades, or to suggest that there is a particular canon of scholarship that comprehensively defines it. That said, the story of regulatory scholarship since the early 1990s can be seen as one in which scholars, and the regulators they studied, progressively became more receptive to input from non-regulatory sources. As the last chapter discussed, this was partly a response to a keen awareness that earlier state models were suffering from a crisis of credibility, and to some extent of effectiveness. The other part of the puzzle, however, was that society itself was continuing to change and regulatory problems to become more complex. Regulatory scholarship evolved alongside the regulatory challenges it aimed to meet, and reflected those challenges in its structures. In the process of thinking more deeply about what regulation could and could not accomplish, it was perhaps inevitable that scholars would eventually run into the problems of complexity and uncertainty that characterized the thorniest regulatory challenges.

Assessing the overall wisdom of the regulatory state project and charting a path forward requires understanding what has come before. To this end, below are four key perspectives that have shaped the field: responsive regulation; reflexive law; smart regulation; and new governance and experimentalism.

Responsive Regulation

In his important 1982 book *Regulation and its Reform,*[16] future US Supreme Court Justice Stephen Breyer laid out a comprehensive analysis of regulation that was informed by economics scholarship and looked in particular at how to match regulatory strategies more effectively with problems to be addressed.[17] A decade later, nascent flexible regulation scholarship experienced its true watershed moment when Ayres and Braithwaite published their book *Responsive Regulation: Transcending the Deregulation Debate.*[18] Its promise was explicit: to move beyond a stalemated deregulation-or-reregulation debate that in the authors' view excessively had preoccupied both the academy and policy-makers thus far. Responsive regulation presented itself as a way of using regulation more effectively so as to leverage outside forces, allocate regulatory resources efficiently, and remain "responsive" to its context. Ayres's and Braithwaite's book remains one of the most cited works on regulation today.

As Ayres and Braithwaite describe it, a vociferous debate was taking place at the time between advocates of deregulation and advocates of regulation. Much of the argument centered around the question of to what degree regulatory goals could actually be accomplished by *self*-regulation, buttressed in various ways by state intervention. Crucially, responsive regulation's answer to this question began with John Braithwaite's conviction that most regulated actors are in fact compliant most of the time.[19] Regulators that treat good actors as if they were Holmesian "bad men,"[20] motivated only by the fear of sanctions, undermine the goodwill and essential trust of regulated actors.[21]

However, Ayres and Braithwaite emphasized that the presence of a "benign big gun" – the "shotgun behind the door," in the words of former US SEC Chairman and later Supreme Court Justice William O. Douglas – along with a credible impression that the regulator will use it, was essential to motivate even well-intentioned actors to remain compliant. Wielding a credible "big gun" makes it less likely that it will actually have to be used, but its credibility requires that it be used sometimes, and that its aim be true. Therefore, under responsive regulation, regulators should seek to work with cooperative actors where possible and to respond aggressively and punitively toward only the most intransigent actors, calibrating the response to the offence. To this, one of Ian Ayres's important contributions was to incorporate Robert Axelrod's game theory-based argument in favor of a tit-for-tat repeat-player interaction.[22]

The book claims that regulators can allocate their resources wisely to the most intransigent players by ratcheting their enforcement activities and regulatory oversight up and down as appropriate across regulatory interactions. At the same time, regulated actors have a built-in incentive to comply with regulation because the consequences of not doing so are predictable and negative, taking the forms of both closer oversight and the imposition of increasingly strong sanctions. Notice the variability and context-specificity that result: rather than basing regulatory interactions on a set of predefined, legislatively-prescribed, and non-discretionary engagements, regulators tailor their behavior to the behavior of the regulated entity. Responsive regulatory approaches give regulators and enforcement staffers a more nuanced set of decision-making tools than a non-negotiable, statutorily defined, centrally enforced, bright-line, floors-and-ceilings approach can provide.[23]

Embedded in *Responsive Regulation*'s enforcement and regulatory structures are two mechanisms that are especially relevant to this book's innovation-oriented story. The first is "enforced self-regulation," the mechanism that operates at the hard-working intermediate layer of regulatory enforcement. Under enforced self-regulation, regulated actors are required to endogenously develop their own sets of internal conduct rules. These rules can then be ratified by public regulators, just like standards promulgated by regulators themselves.[24] The public regulator can also enforce them. At the same time, the privately developed rules have the perceived benefit of having been tailored to a very particular context and of having forced a mostly-trusted regulated actor to turn its mind to its own compliance, thereby ideally (and by comparison to blunt sanctioning tools) fostering and strengthening a compliance culture within. The concept of enforced self-regulation has influenced subsequent scholarship, not least because of its ideologically transcendent promise: it offers a non-deregulatory, compliance-fostering argument for greater autonomy for regulated actors on which, for a separate set of reasons, efficiency-minded law-and-economics scholars can also agree.

The second mechanism is Ayres's and Braithwaite's prescription for tripartism. Tripartism involves broadening the circle of participation in regulation from a dyadic, regulator/regulated relationship to one that brings third parties into the formal regulatory process. Ayres and Braithwaite argue that bringing public interest groups (PIGs) into the regulatory conversation serves to prevent harmful regulatory capture by putting third parties in a position to punish regulators who fail to penalize non-compliant firms.[25] The presence of PIGs also increases the parties' incentives to cooperate, thereby indirectly helping build dialogue and eventually trust. PIGs' expressions of disapproval of an uncooperative firm's behavior – for example, through shaming – can be a powerful tool to ensure regulatory compliance. PIGs can also assist in monitoring and information gathering, especially where regulatory agencies have weak capacity to do so. In the authors' words,

> PIG involvement can strengthen the acceptability of deregulatory shifts by injecting public accountability and resistance to supine enforcement under the softer options. PIG involvement can also provide the data on noncompliance that justifies escalation of state regulatory intervention.[26]

Ayres and Braithwaite also defend tripartism in democratic empowerment terms deriving from civic republican thinking. Citing Sunstein, they endorse a description of civic republicanism that involves "four basic commitments: (1) deliberation in government that shapes as well as balances interests (as opposed to simply doing deals between prepolitical interests); (2) political equality (which [they] read as requiring the organizational empowerment of disorganized constituencies); (3) universality, or debate to reconcile competing views, as a regulative ideal; and (4) citizenship, community participation in public life."[27] An ethos of non-domination, as a positive form of liberty that amounts to more than just non-interference, was central to their approach. Its significance to Braithwaite's thinking in particular should not be underemphasized.[28] Like enforced self-regulation, tripartism has been an influential concept,[29] and became a building block for the more expansive network-based analysis that others later developed. Thus, tripartism provides stakeholders with the ability to participate in decision-making that affects them and ensures the "democratic good" by having "risk-takers and risk-bearers ... both be involved in decision making about the distribution of risk."[30]

Empowering PIGs also prevents regulatory agreements from becoming horse-trading exercises, whereby the bargaining outcome simply lands at some suboptimal halfway point below what the law requires and above what the regulated actor in question wants. Where PIGs advocate for a position above what the law requires, countering the demands by industry, they can push outcomes closer to the legal standard that was settled through the democratic process.[31] (If this sounds unsatisfactory, in the sense that it makes legal standards sound so negotiable and irresolute, we should remember that even now we have concerns about industry actors and corporate interests pushing regulators off a legal standard settled through a democratic process – through lobbying, input in administrative rulemaking, and the like.)[32] At the same time, because responsive regulation sees tripartism as a formal device that takes place within the bounds of an existing regulatory process, it is not utopian in its aspirations for civic engagement. For Ayres and Braithwaite, tripartism is "a route to a more participatory democracy, a more genuine democracy, but a practical democracy that does not make unrealistic demands of mass participation in all institutional arenas."[33]

Responsive Regulation may not be explicitly innovation-framing – that is, it may not be preoccupied by the regulatory need to manage a highly dynamic or uncertain subject matter area – in the way that some later flexible regulation strategies were. It locates interpersonal relationships, not the phenomenon of dispersed and fast-moving learning itself, at the center of its model. That said, it is very much a product of the age of the "end of certainty."[34] It makes efficiency-based arguments, aspires to civic republican-style, engaged citizenship, and puts its faith in interpersonal trust and ongoing, broadly participatory dialogue as a basis for regulatory legitimacy – not least because by 1992, there is hardly any firmer ideological ground on which it can stand. Moreover, some of the essential features that made later, more innovation-centric versions of flexible regulation plausible were already in place within the responsive regulation model: tailoring regulation to the situations of particular regulated actors, using economic-derived incentives to channel private behavior, collaborating with private regulated actors as well as other stakeholders, and demonstrating a commitment to pragmatism.

Reflexive Law
Shortly after *Responsive Regulation* made its high-impact entrance, environmental law scholar Eric Orts imported the notion of reflexive law into the American regulatory conversation.[35]

Many scholars have worked with and around the concept of reflexivity, though the notion of reflexive law in particular is most closely associated with German sociologist Gunther Teubner.[36] Reflexive law seems to have developed entirely independently from responsive regulation, and also quite independently from the American pragmatist strains of new governance, discussed below.[37] However, it very much emerges from its era's disenchantment with formal state action, and especially from critical and postmodern challenges to the legitimacy of law and formal legal orders.

As discussed above, responsive regulation linked its faith in civic republican dialogue and respectful deliberation with a particular understanding of the reciprocal interpersonal relationship between a regulator and a regulated entity. It scaled up from the specific relationship to a more general principle about non-domination and citizenship. Reflexive law gets to a compatible end point – to an argument for procedural legitimacy and democratic autonomy among and between different actors in society – but by way of a separate, more theoretical route.

Teubner starts from the position that translating norms across boundaries of different social systems, organizations, and institutions is virtually impossible, without doing violence to those different systems, organizations, or institutions.[38] Specifically, law is one such system. It develops according to its own internal dynamics, which are the product of basic legal norms, principles, and concepts; and also of social forces, institutional constraints, organizational structures and procedures, and conceptual range. It is semi-autonomous, mostly internally coherent, and self-referential. It possesses its own institutional logic. However, the legal system also responds to stimuli from "outside," though these are only selectively filtered into legal structures in ways that make sense to the legal subsystem itself. The legal mode of thinking mediates the stimuli, and the stimuli modulate the legal mode of thinking, in a reflexive relationship. Like the legal system, other social systems are also dynamic and they interact with and are influenced by their environments. They do so through their boundaries, which can be more or less porous, interpreting and responding to their environments through the lens of their own internal logics. It appears that Teubner's units of analysis can be as wide as the market as a whole, or community norms, or as narrow as a particular firm or group of people.

Teubner argues that given the postmodern crisis of faith about law's formal rationality, we can no longer credibly claim that law itself is, or especially will be perceived to be, more legitimate in its content than other forms of ordering. Moreover, mismatches occur when the substantive and normative content of law's system conflicts with other content. In this sense, substantive law itself is limited. As Teubner describes it,

> Reflexive legal rationality requires the legal system to view itself as a system-in-an-environment and to take account of the limits of its own capacity

as it attempts to regulate the functions and performances of other social subsystems.[39]

For these reasons, law's legitimate role must no longer be to dictate the appropriate substantive content of another institution's decision-making outcomes. It can only set parameters for democratic, self-regulatory decision-making (such as procedural norms, institutional competency requirements, and a requirement for internal discourse) within other social institutions, with the goal of producing self-reflective processes within those different social institutions themselves. This is the particular form of regulatory "scaffolding" that reflexive law adopts.

Where Teubner wrote in theoretical terms, Orts spoke in more concrete ones. He described the European Eco-Management and Audit Scheme (EMAS), developed in 1993, as one of the first instances of reflexive environmental law. EMAS standardized procedures for environmental auditing, reporting, and management. Unlike traditional regulation, which focused on adhering to specific and static bright-line requirements, EMAS – doing what Teubner would have described as setting parameters for good self-regulatory decision-making within the firms themselves – focused on procedural and decision-making processes. It encouraged firms to be critically self-reflective about their procedures, and to incorporate environmental considerations into their decision-making in a systematic way.

In addition, alongside EMAS's disclosure-based mechanisms, Orts identified an additional, morality-based motive for firms to comply.[40] The disclosure requirements at the core of EMAS aimed to promote transparency with respect to firms operating within the system, and to publicly signal the environmental commitments (or not) of firms that opt to participate (or not), but this aimed to trigger both the self-regulatory compliance and tripartism mechanisms that responsive regulation also identified.

What is most important about reflexive law in the context of flexible regulation as a whole is that reflexive law is reflexive in two respects. First, it recognizes the limits (real and perceived) of law, especially in the face of complex social problems and legitimacy disputes. Second, by emphasizing certain procedural minima, it can help to enhance the capacities of actors outside the legal system. For example, by requiring firms to publicly disclose results of their internal decision-making, reflexive law modifies firm behavior because it gives firms reason to ensure that such reports are accurate, thereby avoiding public criticism.[41]

Considered another way, reflexive law sets out an alternative philosophical justification for flexible regulation – for regulation that is procedurally oriented, tailored to context, that assumes that regulated entities are dynamic and respond to their environment, that engages regulated entities as actors and not just passive objects of regulation, and that incorporates forces beyond formal state action to try to effect desired change. Julia Black's important work on how regulatory rules actually function in interactions within and between "interpretive communities" is probably best understood as an outgrowth of the reflexive law approach. Black's work investigates regulatory rules in an almost anthropological way, as tools deployed by both sides in the process of negotiating what formal rules mean and how they will be applied.[42]

Reflexive law starts from a different set of premises than does responsive regulation, which centered on tit-for-tat enforcement, regulatory spectrums, and tripartism as formal regulatory devices. Yet, each for its own reasons, reflexive law and responsive regulation ultimately arrive at the claim that regulation will be more effective where it either acknowledges or engenders some degree of "enforced self-regulation," which in turn conscripts a dynamic and contextually situated industry actor into the work of its own regulation.

Smart Regulation

Neil Gunningham and Peter Grabosky coined the term "smart regulation" in 1998 to describe the use of a mixture of regulatory instruments, with the goal of mobilizing new regulatory forces and third parties and thereby harnessing the enlightened self-interest of regulated actors themselves.[43] They argued that regulators need to become adept at deploying a larger regulatory "toolkit" of policy instruments and actors, and not just the rules-and-state-enforcement tools that typically characterized Welfare State action.[44] They argued that every regulatory instrument has strengths and weaknesses depending on the situation, but that additional and complementary instruments can help mitigate the weaknesses. Employing more instruments also means that a more diverse set of actors must be involved to implement them effectively.

Smart Regulation builds on the work of the authors' fellow Australian, John Braithwaite, but it modifies and extrapolates on it too, and incorporates more of the economic regulatory tools familiar from Stephen Breyer's initial work in the field. Smart regulation is a more polycentric project, which would replace responsive regulation's single pyramid of escalating sanctions with a new three-sided pyramid, with state regulators on one side; quasi-regulators, or "regulatory surrogates" including trade associations, insurers, or professionals on a second; and private industry actors themselves on the third. The book identifies a comprehensive range of different regulatory instruments – traditional regulation, self-regulation, voluntarism, education and information, economic instruments (such as taxes and subsidies), and market-based instruments (including private property-based regimes, such as cap-and-trade pollution regimes). Then, based on a detailed analysis of the chemical and agricultural industries, the authors assess the success of the various regulatory approaches advocated. *Smart Regulation* investigated new sets of questions around precisely when it makes sense to use top-down regulatory rules, and when it might be safe to leave matters to market forces or other non-state forces (still created or buttressed by regulatory structures);[45] when *ex ante* standards, like licensing regimes, make sense and when *ex post* enforcement sanctions make sense;[46] when private sector actors can be conscripted into public service, for what purposes, and when they cannot;[47] and under what circumstances people are likely to obey the law on their own, and when they are not.[48] Neil Gunningham's subsequent work with his collaborators has continued in this vein and considers, for example, how to tackle difficult compliance problems presented by both very small and very large industry players,[49] and how to assess the relative effectiveness, under different conditions, of the so-called "regulatory license" vis-à-vis an industry actor's "social license" and "economic license" to operate.[50]

Part of the book's value is simply taxonomical, in setting out the broad range of tools contained within the contemporary regulatory toolkit. Just as importantly, however, it develops an approach to regulation that is polycentric, flexible, and deeply pragmatic. In a fashion reminiscent of reflexive law (though perhaps more remarkable today), the authors do not automatically assume that publicly developed standards are necessarily more effective or normatively weightier than privately developed standards. Their work can be seen as part of a larger wave of scholarship that had begun to consider the technical aspects of regulatory design in a more fine-grained way and, influenced by the norms scholarship and a strong concern for practical effectiveness, to situate conventional regulatory tools within the broader context of possible mechanisms that might influence and channel behavior. Along with developing generalizable insights about how flexible regulation might be made effective in different circumstances, smart regulation began the project of investigating how networks of public and private actors could, sometimes and under particular circumstances, productively work together.[51]

New Governance and Experimentalism
By the early years of the new millennium, a new overarching moniker had emerged to describe several additional varieties of flexible regulation: "new

governance." At some point the concept grew beyond the useful boundaries of a single term, though a meaningful core of common assumptions persists.[52]

In 2004, in what remains the most cited article within the new governance cohort, Orly Lobel argued that a new paradigm in regulatory thought was emerging, amounting to the greatest such shift since Franklin Delano Roosevelt's New Deal in the United States.[53] In her view, the various "renew deal" approaches – generally coterminous with new governance approaches – have in common the following organizing principles: participation and partnership; collaboration; diversity and competition; decentralization and subsidiarity; integration of policy domains; flexibility and non-coerciveness (or softness-in-law – and on this principle there is disagreement[54]); and fallibility, adaptability, and dynamic learning. Lobel's description of new governance distinguished it from an old, discredited Welfare State model and demonstrates how much new governance shares with, and owes to, the antecedent approaches of responsive, reflexive, and smart regulation:

> The new governance model supports the replacement of the New Deal's hierarchy and control with a more participatory and collaborative model, in which government, industry, and society share responsibility for achieving policy goals ... Highlighting the increasing significance of norm-generating nongovernmental actors, the model promotes a movement downward and outward, transferring responsibilities to states, localities, and the private sector – including private businesses and nonprofit organizations ... At the same time, by linking together geographically and materially dispersed law reform efforts, the model provides innovative ways to coordinate local efforts and to prevent the isolation of problems. Scaling up, facilitating innovation, standardizing good practices, and encouraging the replication of success stories from local or private levels become central goals of government. Legal orchestration is achieved through interpenetration of policy boundaries, new public/private partnerships, and next-generation policy strategies such as negotiated rulemaking, audited self-regulation, performance-based rules, decentralized and dynamic problem solving, disclosure regimes, and coordinated information collection.[55]

In a similar vein, Cary Coglianese and David Lazer coined the term "management-based regulation" in 2003.[56] Management-based regulation designs process specifications around acceptable planning and implementation of systems and controls. It aims to address situations in which regulators do not have a reasonable understanding of what good outcomes look like, but they and regulated actors do at least have a reasonable understanding of what good control systems look like. Management-based regulation sets out detailed, robust internal processes around internal controls.[57]

Meta-regulation, as Christine Parker defined the term in 2002, also takes a process-oriented stance.[58] Principles-based securities regulation, as I and Julia Black have (separately) discussed it, shares considerable features.[59] However unlike management-based regulation, in which the regulator is understood to have a relatively good understanding of what kind of control system an industry actor should adopt, and therefore has the ability to assess the control system it has put in place, meta-regulation can operate in high-uncertainty conditions where the regulator knows even less: it only needs to have a degree of comfort that risks are being managed and that the firm is following through on its commitments. As Neil Gunningham has stated, describing what he calls "meta-regulation" or "meta-risk management,"

> The role of regulation ceases to be primarily about inspectors or auditors checking compliance with rules, and becomes more about encouraging the industry or facility to put in place processes and management systems which are then scrutinized by regulators or corporate auditors. Rather than regulating prescriptively, meta-regulation seeks to stimulate modes of self-organization within the firm in such a way as to encourage internal self-critical reflection ... Thus under meta-regulation, the primary role of the inspectorate becomes that of "regulating at a distance", relying upon the organization itself to put in place appropriate systems and oversight mechanisms, but taking the necessary action to ensure that these mechanisms are working effectively.[60]

Parker described meta-regulation – this "regulation of self-regulation" – as a core regulatory state strategy, in which "the state attempts to withdraw as direct agent of command and control public management, in favor of being an indirect regulator of internal control systems in public and private agencies."[61] Internal corporate compliance mechanisms are a key part of the arrangement: private entities self-regulate through internal compliance mechanisms, and state regulators then assess the adequacy of their self-regulation. Like responsive regulation, smart regulation, and new governance regulation, meta-regulation also deploys incentives to try to channel private action toward voluntary compliance. Like reflexive law, meta-regulation imagines corporations whose boundaries are permeable to external values and stakeholders. Parker envisioned corporations that were open to deliberative democratic action both internally and involving external stakeholders; a learning regulator, which developed its own new methods in parallel with the corporations' and so was not in a position to dictate best practices to those corporations; and a "leading edge" of institutional practice that ratcheted up industry practice through enlightened self-regulatory methods and best-practices-based leadership.

Meta-regulation, like management-based regulation and new governance in general, asserts that there are things that the regulator does not know or should not take the lead on – whether because building accountability norms and a culture of compliance must be an endogenous process; or because regulated actors are too heterogeneous to be regulated in a one-size-fits-all way; or because background conditions are simply too uncertain and the right path forward too unknown – that is, because there is too much uncertainty to allow anyone, regulator or otherwise, to act confidently on its own. In its recognition of the uncertainty and contingency that can exist within the regulatory project itself, it resonates as strongly after the financial crisis as it did before (and perhaps more so, even if our patience for uncertainty and deference to private actors is shorter now). Deep contingency – the sense of trying to generate regulatory strategies capable of "building the boat in the middle of the river" – characterizes each of these models. The models accept that neither regulators nor regulated actors can have more than a time-bound, context-specific understanding of what a good outcome or a good control system might look like. Both actors are conscious of working in a highly changeable environment. The various new governance approaches therefore focus in somewhat different ways on developing systems geared toward learning and adapting, rather than knowing and directing. They focus on determining whether the systems and controls being used are designed to both generate and respond to ongoing learning, thereby improving outcomes as measured by reference to a high-level set of principles.

Under the broad new governance umbrella, Charles Sabel and his collaborators have developed a distinct approach, which they call "experimentalism." Experimentalism assumes change, and it assumes that knowledge is decentralized (more about decentralization in Chapter 5) such that on its own, a central regulator cannot be expected to produce sufficiently informed or flexible responses to local problems. For these reasons, experimentalism emphasizes decision making through a broadly participatory, non-hierarchical process; working from only broadly agreed-upon common problems toward open-ended goals; established processes for ensuring continuous feedback, reporting and monitoring as a means of continually revising and improving practice and results; and ensuring that lower-level actors who have better local, contextual knowledge are the ones that implement agreed-upon practices.[62] One thing that makes experimentalism unique is how fully it imagines a centralized "learning-by-monitoring" clearinghouse mechanism at the regulatory level, which is designed to aggregate data from local learning experiments into an overarching set of regulatory requirements. Experimentalist governance describes a set of practices involving open participation by a variety of entities (public or private), lack of formal hierarchy within governance arrangements, and extensive deliberation throughout the process of decision making and implementation.[63] Information and communication are key.

As Edward Rubin puts it, new governance devises open-ended learning systems, which are preferable to prescriptive, command-oriented regulatory systems under conditions where the regulator "knows the result it is trying to achieve but does not know the means for achieving it, when circumstances are likely to change in ways that the [regulator] cannot predict, or when the [regulator] does not even know the precise result that she desires."[64]

Let us step back to notice how far the scholarship has moved, now, from traditional Welfare State ideas – and even from *Responsive Regulation's* focus on tripartism and tit-for-tat engagements within the context of discrete regulatory interactions. New governance assumes as a background condition that fundamental uncertainty exists about both means and ends. Experimentalism in particular is explicit about the idea that its initial normative goals should be revisable in light of experience. Intentional, systematic, ongoing destabilization therefore plays an important role. This does not mean free-for-all plasticity. New governance is not anarchist, nor radically democratic in Roberto Unger's pure style.[65] It situates its destabilization mechanism within a matrix of abiding institutions.[66] At the same time, it proposes that conditions of deep instability are sometimes the moments when new governance approaches stand the best chance of emerging – moments when no one knows what the solution to a problem might be or how to get there, though everyone also knows that the status quo is no longer an option.[67]

ABIDING INSIGHTS FROM FLEXIBLE REGULATION

Flexible regulation rolls a wider and more varied range of tools into the regulatory project. Its models weave in insights about incentives, efficiency, and tit-for-tat enforcement from economics and game theory, but these are not its only ingredients. Flexible regulation has also incorporated nuanced understandings of governance, legitimacy, and compliance through its cross-pollination with civic republicanism, the norms scholarship, and procedural justice, all underpinned by more complex image of the state, the citizen, and the polity.

As a response to the specific challenge of innovation, flexible regulation makes an important contribution. While it sounds trite, the simple fact that flexible regulation acknowledges that innovation is happening makes it a more realistic and promising response to that innovation. Recall the ABCP Crisis discussed in Chapter 1, and the way in which the regulatory regime's blindness to changes in the relevant product and market made it oblivious to problems until the regime had been utterly undermined. A regulatory regime that assumes a static subject matter – whether based on bright-line requirements, like the accounting rules that Enron gamed, or based on a static set of assumptions about a market's attributes, like the Canadian ABCP regime – is in no shape to adapt nimbly to change. For all its limitations, deploying risk as an overarching metric for thinking about modern regulation has produced significant benefits in terms of resource allocation. Since risk is a fluid thing, risk-based regulation is also better designed than object-based regulation if the goal is to try to project regulatory force forward in time, or to anticipate future possibilities. Developing systems that are capable of learning from experience is also essential.

While regulators would probably prefer to operate in environments not characterized by pervasive uncertainty, this is not always the environment they inhabit. The financial markets in particular have been and continue to be characterized by substantial, often genuinely Knightian uncertainty. In the financial crisis, it was not the known that was the problem but rather the unknown. A regulatory approach that focuses on what is known may not do an especially good job in that environment. In uncertain and dynamic contexts, it may actually make more sense to assess regulatory approaches not in terms of the information they work with, but in terms of the strategies they possess to grapple with uncertainty and the lack of information. Flexible regulation presents a suite of potential tools – risk-based regulation, enforced self-regulation, management-based and meta-regulation and the like – that build a degree of provisionality and learning into their operation.

Another important insight, which comes from flexible regulation's philosophical connection to civic republicanism and procedural justice, is an understanding of what it means to regulate, in a world marked by a lack of consensus around basic things. Flexible regulation emphasizes pragmatism and structured problem solving – a preference that is at least as important to regulation as a process as it is to politics and public deliberation. As this relates to innovation, the lack of consensus is profound: there will be no political consensus on what constitutes "good" versus "bad" innovation.

Consider the ongoing debate about fracking, which is the process of extracting natural gas from shale by hydraulically fracturing the rock, as an example of how fraught conversations about innovation can be. Even assuming the impossible – that we all shared identical political priorities, and that we all weighed energy independence and "clean(er)" fossil fuel energy as having the exact same value when weighed against the particular kind of environmental damage that fracking produces – and assuming we could measure exactly how much energy independence and (short- and long-term, local and global) environmental damage we were trading in – it would still be nearly impossible to identify "good" or "bad" innovations in real time. Would a more effective fracking technique be a good thing, if it reduced site-specific environmental damage but also increased the absolute amount of fracking going on?

This is not very different with respect to financial innovation: the innovation of securitization generates real benefits in some contexts, as do derivative markets, though there is no consensus on when, how, and under what circumstances those benefits (to whom?) exceed their costs (to whom?), or along what measures (increased wealth, greater systemic resilience, etc.) one should measure such things. Even if we could have agreed on the relative benefits of securitization at a particular moment, technology and markets, and costs and benefits all change over time. With securitization, the benefits generally came earlier and increases in rent-seeking and systemic risk came later. Other innovations seem to work in the opposite direction: they lay fallow or impose costs in the short term, but have the potential to measurably improve social welfare over the long term and as conditions change.

The civic republican instinct plays out in another way here too, in that the flexible regulation literature imposes a degree of information-forcing, reason-giving and transparency that is crucial to genuine citizen empowerment. One way to think about this point would be as a choice between structuring regulation around "rules" on one hand, or "principles" (or "standards") on the other. Rules – with their clarity and their apparent non-negotiability – can be thought of as a proxy for the traditional Welfare State approach, with its bright-line floors and ceilings and its non-negotiable sanctions. Principles stand in for the more flexible, context-sensitive regulatory state approach. The conventional example used to illustrate the difference between rules and principles relates to speed limits in driving: a rule will say, "Thou shalt not drive faster than 55 mph," while a principle will say, "Thou shalt not drive faster than is reasonable and prudent in all the circumstances."

Bright-line rules and top-down directives can produce real benefits, and any effective regime, including a flexible regulatory one, will need a good number of them.[68] At the same time, what we think of as rules have always been more modulated and variable phenomena than they have sometimes been caricatured to be. Discretion at every level – individual, organizational, regulatory – helps determine how rules will be interpreted, by whom, and based on what sets of priorities. Particular provisions can be read "up" into more sweeping principles or "down" into more limited ones, depending on context. Systems, assumptions, conventions, practices, and tacit knowledge all shape perceptions of an organization's behavior, and a rule system's expectations.[69]

Think of speeding: does a posted limit of 55 mph, which is a bright-line rule, *always* set a non-negotiable upper limit for driving speed, or can you sometimes go a little bit faster without getting a ticket? How much faster, exactly, can you go – in other words, what unwritten rules about acceptable margins of excess speed do you apply? In deciding whether or not to stop you, will the nearby traffic officer (consciously or unconsciously) consider other factors, such as what kind of car you drive, what the weather is like, what time of day or night it is, what neighborhood you are in, or whether your community has recently seen speed-related accidents? Once the traffic officer actually approaches your car – here, your last chance for some discretionary leniency by the frontline officer – will it matter what you look like, who is with you, or whether you know the officer (for good or ill)? Of course it will. And some of the same factors may make a difference later, if you decide to contest the ticket before the traffic authority.

Even a bright-line rule is not written in stone. Yet under a bright-line rule-based regime, the traffic officer is not required to explain why she does or does not give you a speeding ticket, so long as you exceeded the posted limit. We should compare this to the transparency of the approaches described above. Flexible regulation makes people say things out loud. It recognizes explicitly the influence of other factors, like faith in the market, or confidence in private industry standards, or hope for richer citizen engagement through democratic deliberation (or the state of your car), which would go unexamined – uncontemplated, even – under a set of seemingly settled and definitive bright-line rules. These other factors will operate whether we acknowledge them or not, so we are better off acknowledging them, requiring that they be justified, and having the opportunity to scrutinize our assumptions.

In contexts such as these, characterized by fundamental dissensus around priorities and how to order them, further complicated by extensive uncertainty about how particular innovations will play out and which tools will achieve which ends, decision-making obviously is difficult. Decisions should be provisional and attuned to change. Crucially, they also must be informed by an awareness of the public interest, the importance of voice and respectful deliberation, and the civic republican ethos of non-domination, as a positive and dignity-oriented understanding of citizenship. We want to try to generate productive conversations at the political level but in the meantime, regulation also needs to keep addressing real problems, and in a way that is attuned to concerns about voice and influence. Even today, pragmatic, incremental, problem-based analyses remain the most sensible response to the kinds of challenges that innovation throws up. Even if we cannot all agree on, say, the greater wisdom of securitization, regulators need to be able to reach pragmatic and responsive responses to emergent problems, like the risks associated with a *particular* kind of securitization, while keeping the public interest and its expression through deliberative means top of mind and top of practice. Developing a regulatory regime capable of adapting to a constantly changing context is no small feat, even while it is no substitute for a broader conversation. The flexible regulation scholarship, with its well-stocked toolkit and its sensitivity to both human nature and the inevitability of change, will be essential as we chart a path forward.

4

Flexible Regulation Scholarship Blossoms and Diversifies: 1980–2012

The last two chapters have traced the historical and philosophical paths of flexible regulation, in order to understand what some of its leading proponents sought, and what they assumed, in creating a regulatory model that actively opened itself to other, non-state forces including the market, non-state standard-setters, and community deliberation. By broadening our lens from the four key perspectives described in the last chapter toward the flexible regulation scholarship more broadly, we can take the measure of flexible regulation scholarship primarily as it existed at the time of the financial crisis, with a view to understanding its theoretical assumptions and underpinnings, its reliance on market-based assumptions, its relationship to the notion of innovation, and its continued relevance.

In the context of its time, flexible regulation could be understood in part as an effort to find a way forward for the state, in the straitened circumstances of globalization, manufactured risk and uncertainty, the rise of neo-conservatism, and the shattering effects of post-structuralism. Scholars learned to focus on what could be achieved through smarter and more effective regulation and through a reorientation from regulation to the broader field of governance, meaning the study of "order and disorder, efficiency and legitimacy all in the context of the hybridization of modes of control that allow the production of fragmented and multidimensional order *within* the state, *by* the state, *without* the state, and *beyond* the state."[1] In politics but in scholarship too, the 1990s and early 2000s were marked by considerable hope that it might be possible to transcend old-style, left/right political stalemates. If, following Foucault, all human interaction bears the marks of power and regulation, then focusing on beyond-state factors in particular opens up whole new possibilities for transformative change.

Different branches of flexible regulation are more or less pragmatic, more or less explicitly committed to particular normative objectives, and more or less willing to embrace the idea of means-end reflexivity – that is, the notion that one's practical experience as a regulator should deeply influence one's own regulatory goals, as well as strategies. Within the varied scholarship on innovation and regulation, at least three distinct subject matter threads are also apparent: environmental law, financial regulation and corporate governance, and administrative law. Each takes a particular perspective on innovation and its relationship to regulation, and each contains varying and even contrary positions. As a philosophical project, flexible regulation can also be more or less theoretically driven, and more or less pragmatic. What we see, in some of these models, are the after-effects of post-structuralism and critical legal theory and a program for moving past them through democratic deliberation, even while accepting the contingency and contestability of any particular set of policy prescriptions.[2]

Yet flexible regulation scholarship is not agnostic. The scholars whose work we are considering here are overwhelmingly concerned with what, in the United States and Canada at least, would be understood as politically progressive, justice-oriented, equality-seeking priorities: they want to use the new methods in order to advance more effective environmental regulation, including mitigating climate change; better workplace safety and employment discrimination; a more accountable and responsive state; more effective and more democratic oversight of financial actors; and the like. Benefit to private parties or the search for a more efficient market are not these scholars' concerns. While the environmental, finance, and administrative law scholarship is distinct, none of these subject matter areas globally takes the un-nuanced position that innovation is beneficial by definition.

The discussion below is based on a review of the 198 US law review articles that were the most influential within the flexible regulation field between 1980 and 2012, and which also discussed the topic of innovation.[3] This literature is still consequential today, as well as being historically interesting, because flexible regulation principles and methods continue to structure large swaths of contemporary regulation across Anglo-American jurisdictions (and beyond). This literature expresses not only where we have been, but where we are.

In the immediate post-crisis years, one concern was that much of flexible regulation, at least in finance, would be deemed ineffective and jettisoned in favor of more prescriptive, bright-line regimes that sometimes nostalgically and unrealistically seemed to hearken back to earlier times. For an observer like me, this raised real concerns about effectiveness in responding to the significant challenges that innovation presents for regulation. The precise balance between top-down, bright-line rules and more flexible standards may not have been struck perfectly (it almost certainly was not struck perfectly) in the years before the crisis; yet, bright-line prescriptions have well-established limitations. More recently, as populist, anti-progressive waves have swept much of the Western world, the far greater concern, especially in the United States, is that not only post-crisis but a good portion of post-1960 social, economic, and environmental regulation could be rolled back.

Charting a path forward, especially for progressive priorities, in this era of great uncertainty requires that we take the measure of where we are, including both how technically reasonable and how normatively defensible our choices have been.

AN EMPIRICAL REVIEW OF THE FLEXIBLE REGULATION SCHOLARSHIP, 1980–2012

The flexible regulation literature grew through the period of study, with the majority of articles published after about 1997. Table 4.1 characterizes the articles by primary subject matter.

Within this sample group, environmental articles formed the largest group of articles by subject matter. Financial regulation and corporate governance articles were the second largest group. Forty-one articles were identified as having an "other" subject matter and made up the third-largest group. Most of these "others" concern "big-picture" subject matters such as governance, administrative law, government relations, legal theory, and the like; a smaller subset reference specific subject matter areas. Given the shared concerns with administrative law, public law, and governance in this group, it is shorthanded as "administrative law" for the rest of this chapter.[4]

TABLE 4.1. *Primary subject matter of articles*

Primary Subject Matter	Frequency (out of 198 articles)
Environment	80 (40%)
Finance/corporate governance	45 (23%)
Other (henceforth "Administrative law")	41 (21%)
Science/technology/medicine/intellectual property (IP)	21 (11%)
Labor or occupational health and/or safety	6 (3%)
Other social services	3 (2%)
Education	2 (1%)

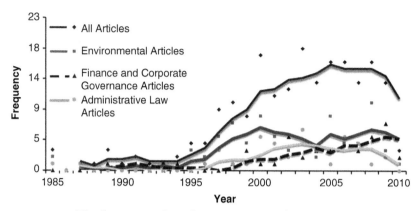

FIGURE 4.1. The frequency of articles across time. The trend lines depict the three-year moving average.

Figure 4.1 displays the number of articles in the sample that were published in each calendar year since 1985, when the earliest articles in the sample were published.[5] It shows that the vast majority of the most influential scholarship was published after around 1997. After 2002, the volume of publications remained relatively steady.[6] The graph also disaggregates the distribution of environmental, financial and corporate governance, and administrative law articles. Environmental law articles were the first to rise in number, around 1995, and output remained high and relatively stable from the late 1990s onward. Administrative Law articles began to rise around 2000, but numbers dropped off relative to the other categories around 2008. The number of financial and corporate governance articles rose slowly and steadily from the late 1990s forward, numerically surpassing the administrative law articles around 2006.

Looking at the relationship between innovation and regulation that this project has sought to unearth, the literature displays a remarkable and, in retrospect, predictable consistency: regulation scholars are interested in regulation. That is, the vast majority (91 percent) of the articles in the sample deal with *regulatory* innovations – not innovations in and by the private sector actors operating in those sectors. This result reflects the primary concerns, law and regulation, of the scholars whose work was captured.[7] It is a forceful reminder of the scholarly community operating here: these scholars are examining regulatory innovations and considering proposals for and the application of new regulatory forms. Private innovation, and the question of whether it is beneficial or not, is simply not their central concern.

Therefore, if a positive view about private sector innovation was operating in this literature, it could not have been because private sector innovation was a direct object of study. It would have had to be operating at the level of background assumptions about what kinds of regulatory innovations were beneficial, and why.

HOW IS FLEXIBLE REGULATION MEANT TO BE BETTER?

The new governance and experimentalist work helps to highlight just how far the scholarship had moved, by the 2000s, toward a regulatory model that embraced change, including human-generated innovation, and was designed to respond to the attendant contingency and uncertainty. The point is not that this scholarship directly influenced regulatory strategy most of the time, though it may have influenced it in indirect ways. The point is that flexible regulatory approaches, including most recently the new governance approaches, are of a piece with their disintermediated, heterogeneously populated, (aspirationally) deliberative, and "disruptive" times, and alive to the regulatory challenges, including the increasing contingency, variability, and dynamism that characterized many regulated spaces.

A post-crisis observer could be concerned that a flexible regulator using these methods could become so fractured in its approach, with all this variability and contingency in methods and standards, that it loses sight of its regulatory goals, and the public interest, altogether. So what exactly is the point of all this flexibility again? This scholarship claims that it is arguing for flexibility, not for its own sake or purely on efficiency grounds, but because it will also make regulation more *effective*. It claims that its arguments for flexibility are not in fact arguments for deregulation in disguise. As Table 4.2 demonstrates, the main reasons that the literature advanced flexibility was as a means for improving regulation overall, with regulatory *congruence* – achieving the regulator's goals – appearing as the primary justification twice as frequently as does making regulation less costly, or more efficient.

Table 4.2 sets out the multiple justifications that underlie flexible regulation's preference for flexibility. After congruence and efficiency, the third most common justification for more flexible regulatory structures was to make regulation more transparent and accountable; the fourth was to make it more flexible and adaptable (generally appearing in articles where the stated worry was that industry practice was moving quickly and the regulator needed to be able to respond adequately); the fifth was to enable more consultative, collaborative processes; and the sixth was to improve fairness. This suggests that, at least in terms of the overarching arguments they were making, flexible regulation scholars remained heavily concerned with familiar public law

TABLE 4.2. *Type of justification for flexible regulation in the literature by frequency*

Why regulatory innovation is "good" relative to what came before	Frequency
1. Congruence: the old way was ineffective/didn't work/didn't "fit"/ didn't achieve the innovator's (including regulator's, if regulator is innovating) goals	72 (36%)
2. Cost: the old way was costly/inefficient	34 (17%)
3. Flexibility: the old way was inflexible/couldn't move, adapt quickly enough	25 (13%)
4. Transparency & accountability: the old way was unaccountable/ not transparent/captured	29 (15%)
5. Fairness: the old way was unfair/undemocratic	15 (8%)
6. Process: (beyond traditional understandings of democratic methods) the old way was not consultative or collaborative enough, unrepresentative, dealt with wrong communities, or didn't include necessary stakeholders	21 (11%)
TOTAL (Missing = 2)	196

values: transparency and accountability, process, fairness, and achieving stated regulatory goals. Concerns about efficiency are clearly present, but this is not scholarship that emphasized efficiency, cost, or market-oriented assessments of return or value at the expense of other regulatory values.

Of course, aspirations are one thing and methods are another. What, then, are the mechanisms through which flexible regulation scholarship, in general, sought to achieve these aims of congruence, efficiency, transparency and accountability, flexibility, better process, and greater fairness?

The Regulatory Scaffolding and the Spaces Within It

One helpful way to describe flexible regulatory approaches is through the metaphor of legal "architecture."[8] Put another way, we can think of flexible regulation as constructing "regulatory scaffolding."[9] The term "scaffolding" evokes an image of public actors or regulators establishing the overarching boundaries, foundations, and institutional framing of a regulated space, while intentionally leaving pre-defined, framed-out spaces open. The key to understanding flexible regulation's approach is that it does not aim to delimit exhaustively every contour or detail of the regulatory regime. It aims to be permeable – to change coming from outside the regulatory structure and to the impact of other non-legal forces, such as markets and community norms.

At the same time, it is an intentionally designed structure. It is more than an inert casing, like a balloon, for whatever fills it out. Each of the four perspectives described in the last chapter adopts some form of scaffolding approach.

What does this mean? Recall how the classic Welfare State established a built regulatory environment characterized by bright-line requirements that set out and then comprehensively regulated the four corners of an industry. In the United States for example, whether for the regulation of common carriers (rails, trucks, telephone companies) under the Interstate Commerce Act of 1887, or for banks under the Glass-Steagall Act of 1933, the Welfare State established the scope of an industry (separating one common carrier's coverage from another, or commercial banking from securities); set top-down, universal standards for it (up to and including rate-setting and interest rate controls); and monitored industry's implementation of and compliance with those rules.[10] Sanctions for non-compliance were laid out in rule-based terms. The Welfare State and the regulatory state overlapped in time and share many common features – they are not watertight compartments – but it is nevertheless descriptively accurate to say that Welfare State regulation especially was characterized by floors, ceilings, boundaries, and (at least on paper) immovable requirements.

Understanding regulation as open, meta-level scaffolding provokes a shift in regulatory approach at every stage of that regulatory project.[11] For example, when a scaffolding approach is used around regulatory standard-setting, it manifests as a shift from a bright-line approach to one that can incorporate changing technical knowledge within industry. In environmental emissions regulation, then, the standards would change from a static limit of parts-per-million of effluent to a standard based on the "best available technology" – a more dynamic and iterative placeholder.[12] In that case, new improvements in environmental technology would set an evolving standard against which industry actors' performance could be measured. (Less successfully, the same instinct underlay other decisions, like that under the Basel II capital adequacy standards discussed earlier, to allow designated financial institutions to use their own proprietary risk analytic systems to determine how much capital they needed to keep on hand.)

Ayres's and Braithwaite's *Responsive Regulation* presents another version of the shift from two-dimensional "floors and ceilings" toward three-dimensional regulatory scaffolding (and *Smart Regulation* builds in even more dimensionality).[13] At the monitoring and implementation stages, for example, as interactions move up and down the regulatory and enforcement pyramids, responsive regulatory approaches give regulators and enforcement staffers a more structured, yet still customizable set of decision-making tools than a non-negotiable, statutorily defined, centrally enforced bright-line floors-and-ceilings approach could provide. Flexible regulation – in responsive regulation, meaning the enforcement and regulatory pyramids based on tit-for-tat interaction – frames an iterative decision-making process just as architectural scaffolding would frame a building.

For flexible regulation to function effectively on its own terms, its initial underlying design principles should be generally correct, and then it must be capable of being modified and improved based on experience. In any environment, certain actions – criminal conduct, for example – must still be prohibited outright. Not everything will be amenable to modification, and part of the challenge is to identify where flexibility will be useful and where it will not.[14] Reflexive law and experimentalism in particular erect the firmest bits of their scaffolding around ensuring that duly democratic, deliberative, procedurally fair decision-making occurs within institutions and organizations. Every regulatory structure will be a mix of bright-line, top-down, rule-based requirements and more flexible ones. Nevertheless, the leitmotiv animating flexible regulation is the conviction that one can build, within the regulatory/administrative space that lies between private action and political action, a new kind of decision-making, analytic, or jurisdictional architecture that can evolve and respond to information, even while reflecting the public interest.

The very idea of scaffolding regulation also captures the more pluralist notion of legitimate authority that characterizes (post)modern conceptions of regulation. Scholars and regulators have pinned their hopes not on regulation as a force unto itself, so much as on regulation as an effective mechanism for leveraging other forces operating in society.[15] Those other forces operate "in the shadow of" law or regulation, and the point of the regulation is to influence and channel them.[16] All the same, the very fact that regulation aims to be flexible – to erect scaffolding, not the whole building – implies that there must be something, some legitimate force possessing agency, that regulation could seek to frame and channel and not just supplant.

What fills in the spaces in the scaffolding depends on the model, and the choice tells us a great deal about how "neoliberal," "progressive," or agnostic flexible regulation actually turns out to be. Three main forces fill in the regulatory framework, according to different groups of scholars: market forces (in various versions, as described below); deliberation and community norms; and private industry standards. The three are not totally comparable: the first two are processes while the third relates to concrete standards, which can be influenced by the first two processes. But what is crucial is the role these mechanisms play: they are the prime movers in the account, with direct public regulatory intervention operating more "at a distance."[17]

How Central Were Market Forces?

In the current moment, when much of the regulation scholarship of the last thirty years is being re-evaluated, this is a pressing question. What *kind* of regulatory innovations were being advanced by the 91 percent of articles in the sample that dealt with regulatory, as opposed to private sector, innovations? Did regulation scholarship privilege market forces or market-based evaluation methods over other forces and, if so, what were the anticipated distributional effects? Why was this regulatory innovation considered by the scholar to be "good" relative to what came before? Who were the standard-setters in the account; that is, who decided whether that "good" was being achieved? And finally, what was the evaluation method for determining whether that "good" was being achieved?

What we see is a split in the strategies that different scholars advocate. More detail is provided in Appendix C and the notes to this chapter but here are some high points. Only a small minority of the articles advanced straight-forward market-based arguments: only 6% deployed pure "market forces" as the primary basis of the regulatory innovation.[18] On the other hand, 31% of the articles advanced new regulatory strategies or structures that neverthe-less, in terms of continued public authority and agency, maintained a strong and relatively top-down regulatory presence. Within this category, 21% of all the regulatory innovation articles in the set describe "other" innova-tions, which were essentially concerned with reallocating authority between branches or levels of government.[19] These are less relevant to our inquiry, in the sense that they are not really flexible regulation proposals. A further 12% of the regulatory innovation articles argued for imposing new mandatory or bright-line regulatory standards. To a certain degree, the purely market-based articles on one side, and the "other" and bright-line mandatory stan-dards articles on the other represent polar perspectives, in ideological terms, that we might have recognized before flexible regulation: deregulation and market-based programs, versus bright-line rules.

Of greater interest here, almost half the regulatory innovation articles in the set advanced arguments in favor of regulatory innovations that were sig-nificantly more porous to and cooperative with industry or private actors than traditional regulatory structures were, while not being deregulatory. This is perhaps the signal change that the regulatory state brings. In those accounts, industry or private actors were often to be motivated using engagement, dia-logue and incentives rather than traditional sanction-oriented regulatory tools. Almost half these articles envision either greater cooperation with pri-vate actors, or developing incentives-based regimes. On their own, these cat-egories do not explain the nature of the cooperation or how heavily those incentives rely on market-based, or other, structures; however, at a minimum they bring home the degree to which cooperation with regulated actors, and the economics-derived rational actor model on whom incentives-based models rely, underpin close to half the regulatory prescriptions in the set.

Arguments in favor of new information-forcing standards stand somewhat in the middle between old and new, traditional (in its bipolar forms) and regulatory state/cooperative: they are mandatory top-down standards that require private actors to disclose information (without trying to cooperate or extending a great deal of faith to private actors), on the assumption that that information will catalyze non-state forces to respond (thereby activating indirect incentives and moving costly enforcement and sanctioning obligations out of the hands of the state).[20] Dispositionally they straddle the more opposing positions.

Figure 4.2 depicts the four most popular regulatory innovations over time, not including the "other" category. The most frequently advocated or described new regulatory methods were those that spanned the so-called public/private divide or were more collaborative in some way; followed by, tied with the "other" category, regulatory innovations in mandatory standards; then incentives-based regulatory design; and then new information-forcing requirements.[21] We see that articles advocating mandatory standards, incentive-based strategies, and information-forcing regulations have remained fairly steady since the mid-1990s. While numbers are small, arguments in favor of mandatory standards rose slowly over the last decade covered here, and information-forcing regulations probably show a general upward trajectory, while incentive-based recommendations have dropped. The strategy of spanning the public/private divide or incorporating private players or standards

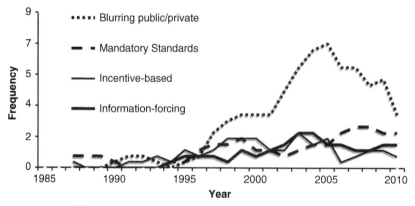

FIGURE 4.2. The frequency of articles for the four most popular regulatory innovations advocated across time. The lines depict the three-year moving average.

into regulation experienced a dramatic increase between about 1995 and 2005, and dropped off sharply thereafter.

What Was the Regulatory Innovation Trying to Achieve?

The impression of a split in the scholarship is reinforced if we look at the questions of what the primary priorities advanced by the regulatory innovation are meant to be; why the scholar considers the regulatory innovation they are advocating or examining to be "good" relative to what came before; and who, according to the description in the article, decides whether that "good" is being achieved and on what basis. The full account is too complex to depict here – more information is contained in Appendix C – but in brief, the following emerges: first (reflecting the dominance of the environmental law scholarship in the set), about one-third of the time, the primary good being advanced by the new regulatory technology is environmental protection or natural resources conservation. National or collective economic benefit is the next most popular "good," cited in one-quarter of the articles, and each of "equality, greater human flourishing, public health" and "enhanced democracy/citizen engagement/community participation/voice" are identified in a further one-eighth or so of the articles. This suggests that public values, not private gain, continue to be the overwhelming goals of regulation. This should not be surprising, but it does put to rest overbroad arguments that regulation scholarship over the last three decades has been directly or primarily concerned with private gain, not public wellbeing.

Strong claims that the regulation scholarship was neoliberal in its assessment methods – meaning that value was defined primarily in terms of economic performance – also seem overstated. As noted above, in terms of why the regulatory innovation is seen as "good" relative to what came before, 17% of the articles claimed that the old way was *inefficient* and the new way less costly. By contrast, 36% claimed that the old way was *ineffective* and the new way more likely to produce outcomes congruent with regulatory goals. Another 16% of the articles were concerned either with fairness or process, on the basis that the old way was unfair, undemocratic, unrepresentative, or insufficiently consultative or collaborative. As well, 79% of articles still identified existing state-based regulators as the standard-setters who had the authority to determine whether the good in question was being achieved by the innovation. Articles that would place that responsibility with the private sector were a distant second, with 11% of the articles.

It is in the "evaluation method" – that is, the method regulators were meant to use to determine whether the regulatory "good" they sought was being achieved – that the data become most mixed. When it comes to the evaluation method by which the standard-setter (overwhelmingly a state regulator) was to determine whether the good in question was actually being achieved, 32% of articles would require the standard-setter to check against static, bright-line or rule-based requirements. On the other hand, 26% would use the efficient market as the evaluation method, on the assumption that the best ideas will rise to the top through competition. Next in line was the use of more context-specific and/or flexible metrics like formal outcome analysis or performance-based analysis, at 23% of the articles. Dialogue, deliberation, consultation and/or consensus were the evaluation methods in 13% of the articles, and self-monitoring and inter-firm comparative analysis in another 6% of them. What this may suggest is greater collective confidence about ends – the good they were seeking – and the importance of state standard-setting; combined perhaps with less conviction about means, and a greater willingness to accept the market as a reasonable mechanism for achieving those ends.

Taken together, what emerges from this analysis is an image of a diverse scholarly community that has taken on board, to a significant extent, notions of incentives and performance assessment – this is in keeping with what we might expect from our earlier description of the rise of the regulatory state, and economics. However, this work cannot be described on a comprehensive basis as prioritizing market forces and market evaluative methods above other forces or methods. In other words, while the scholarship is divided, regulation scholarship across the last three decades has not embraced unalloyed market fundamentalism. The flexible regulation scholarship also contains rich veins of public-minded, fairness-oriented, and deliberative methods and priorities.

Does a Rising Tide Lift All Boats?

Also notable is the distributional effect that the articles in question expected to see from the innovations they were discussing. A central correlative to neoliberalism has been that it privileges a particular, economic definition of worth pursuant to which there will be clear winners and losers in a zero-sum game. This turns out not to be the imaginary that these articles inhabit, or seek to advance.

Slightly more than half the articles in the set anticipated that there would be winners and losers, and that the innovation in question would provide a competitive advantage for one group over another. Interestingly, however, 73% of articles about finance and financial regulation were of this view. This is notable because the finance articles are exceptional in sometimes sounding the alarm about the private innovation in question, rather than celebrating a regulatory innovation. Several articles presciently identified the risks associated with private sector innovation, and to some degree anticipated problems that gave rise to the financial crisis.[22] Among these articles, the idea that there would be winners and losers associated with an innovation should not be interpreted to mean that the author thought that was either good, or inevitable. In many cases, the opposite was true.

Just as interestingly, however, almost half of the articles in the total set argued that there would in fact be no losers, and that the rising tide produced by the innovation would lift all boats. Almost two thirds of these fell into the administrative law or environmental law category.[23] We may be able to interpret the "there will be no losers" analysis in a few different ways, but one thing that is clear is that many of these articles were theoretical in nature, and were more directed toward envisioning new possibilities for the regulatory state than concrete responses to particular regulatory challenges. (Certainly at least in the financial regulation context, the claim that everyone will benefit as a result of a new arrangement seems harder to sustain now.[24] We come back in the next chapter to observe how politically attractive simplified everyone-wins accounts sometimes turned out to be). Thus, both sides of the distributional analysis – those who argued that there would be winners and losers, and those who argued that everyone would benefit – need to be qualified to some extent. Neither perspective can be automatically associated with a stronger commitment to either neoliberal or egalitarian objectives.

Financial Regulation Scholarship as Outlier

The financial regulation scholarship's significant skepticism about who will benefit from new innovations is significant, and makes that literature qualitatively different from what we see in the environmental and especially the administrative law realms. The financial regulation articles were more heavily skewed towards recognizing winners and losers, and toward identifying this as problematic. The financial regulation scholarship is also qualitatively different in terms of the primary priorities the regulatory innovation is seeking to advance; why the innovation is "good" compared to what came before; and the evaluation methods used to determine whether the "good" in question was actually being achieved. Given this book's concern with financial innovation in particular, these are salient differences.

First, in terms of the nature of the innovation for which the scholarship is advocating, financial regulation articles are much more likely to advocate for "new mandatory standards or top-down strategy – e.g., ex ante licensing, bright-line rules or certification requirements." Almost half of the twenty-four articles recommending new mandatory standards or a new top-down strategy are concerned with securities, banking, or corporate law and corporate governance. This is disproportionate. Finance articles are also relatively less likely to advocate for "more context specific and/or flexible metrics." In terms of the evaluation method for determining whether the regulatory "good" in question is being achieved, as well, almost half the finance-related articles would check against static, bright-line, or rule-based requirements. Across the entire set, only about one-third would do so. At the same time, in what at first looks like a paradox and is discussed further below, the finance articles are also more likely than the articles generally to identify the efficient market as the method for determining whether the regulatory "good" in question is being achieved: more than one-third of the finance articles make this recommendation, as opposed to just over a quarter for the database as a whole.

Second, the financial regulation articles differ somewhat in terms of the primary priorities that the recommended innovation is trying to achieve, and its arguments for why that regulatory innovation is better than what came before it. In terms of the good that the proposed innovation is seeking to advance, financial regulation articles tend to be slightly more concerned than average about congruence and regulatory effectiveness, and slightly more concerned about transparency in regulation, but substantially less concerned about improving process by being more collaborative or doing a better job of including stakeholders. In terms of its primary priorities, a disproportionate number of financial regulation articles – 58%, as opposed to 24% across the database as a whole – identify "national or collective economic benefit" as their primary priority. This makes sense, though the proportion is striking. Put another way, more than half of the forty-eight articles that identified national or collective economic benefit as their primary priority come from the financial regulation topic area. (Environmental protection and/or natural resources conservation is the dominant priority in the set as a whole, but for obvious reasons is not the main priority within the financial regulation scholarship.) At the same time, ten of the sixteen total articles that identified *private* economic benefit or competitiveness as their primary priority are also from the financial regulation topic area. This priority is identified in only 8% of the articles across the set, but 22% of the articles in financial regulation. Equality and greater human flourishing, and enhanced democracy and citizen engagement, scarcely feature in the financial regulation literature.

While we might anticipate a neat overlap, there is a less-than-perfect correspondence between the ten financial regulation articles that identify private economic benefit or competitiveness as the innovation's primary priority, and the twenty financial regulation articles that identify the efficient market as the basis of determining whether the good is being achieved. Because the arguments across the articles are nuanced, it is not really possible to identify distinct and non-overlapping schools of thought within the finance articles, except to identify that a spectrum runs from articles that emphasize the value of private benefit and efficient markets; through those that link public benefit and efficient markets (though often in complex or critical ways, like some of the prescient articles described above that identified the risks associated with the private sector innovation and anticipated some of the problems that gave rise to the financial crisis); and onto articles that emphasize public benefit and the importance of static, bright-line rules. The fact that so few financial regulation articles draw on the deliberative or enforced self-regulatory instincts that animate flexible regulation more broadly is also noteworthy. It signals perhaps a lost thread in the scholarly fabric, which needs to be picked up once again.

Finally, another striking difference is the degree to which financial regulation scholarship seemed to be concerned with particular, specific innovations rather than with generalized phenomena such as climate change or globalization. Among the financial regulation articles that were coded as responding to manufactured risk, the breakdown is different relative to the dataset as a whole. Two-thirds of the environmental regulation articles, and almost all the administrative law articles in the dataset are really concerned with "background change" – that is, general knock-on effects of human innovation, like pollution or climate change or complexity. The distribution within the financial regulation articles is quite different: while fully half are also responding to background change, more than a third are responding to an identified, specific change in markets or the economy, and a further 12% are responding to a specific new product or technology. The prescient, critical articles identified above fall into the latter category. In other words, financial regulation articles seem to be more likely to be concerned with the particular underlying innovations that produce effects like globalization, with their attendant regulatory challenges, and relatively less likely to be responding to those generalized effects themselves.

WHAT RELATIONSHIP BETWEEN PRIVATE INNOVATION AND REGULATORY INNOVATION?

For present purposes, this final point may be one of the most illuminating. The clear majority of the regulatory innovations discussed in the articles were catalyzed by new human-created risks – Giddens's manufactured risk – which produced regulatory problems to which regulatory innovation in turn was seen to be the appropriate response. At first blush this suggests that this literature was a direct response to private sector innovation, presumably underpinned by a robust and well-informed understanding of how innovation and regulation intersect. Table 4.3 depicts the frequency with which the literature pointed to different varieties of risk and opportunity, as well as necessity, as catalysts for innovation.

However, the prominence of manufactured risk in the coding is actually deceiving. As Table 4.4 shows, two-thirds of the articles in the database coded as responding to manufactured or human-created risk turned out to be responding to background change or the effects of innovation, such as climate change or globalization in general terms, rather than to any specific new technology. While these background changes are themselves a product of technological innovation(s), the actual technological innovations themselves were not the main concern in these accounts. Their concern was *effects*: climate change, pollution, and the like.[25] Only about a third of the articles in the sample, a disproportionate number of which come from the

TABLE 4.3. *The frequency of catalysts for innovation in the literature*

Catalyst(s) for the innovation	Frequency
1. risk	0
1a. longstanding natural risk	2 (1%)
1b. new manufactured/human-created risk	129 (65%)
2. opportunity	2 (1%)
2a. for private benefit	13 (7%)
2b. for public benefit	31 (16%)
3. necessity	21 (11%)
TOTAL (Missing = 0)	198

TABLE 4.4. *Kinds of manufactured/human-created risks described in the literature*

Type of manufactured/human-created risk	Frequency
1. New product/technology	10 (8%)
2. Specific change in markets/economy	13 (10%)
3. Specific change in law/policy	21 (16%)
4. Background change	85 (66%)
TOTAL (Missing = 0)	129

financial regulation field, dealt with risk generated from specific new technologies or products, or specific changes in the markets or economy, or in law and policy.

Moreover, when charted across time, we can see that the one-sixth of articles in which regulatory innovation was being advocated in order to respond to specific changes in law and policy started to grow beginning around 1997, corresponding with the growth of environmental articles. Reviewing the articles shows that much of this growth could be attributed directly to new environmental policies advanced by the Clinton Administration, like Project XL, which was launched in 1995. Since these articles were really about a *regulatory* change in response to a *policy* change, they still operate at some distance from any underlying private sector innovations that might have been taking place.[26] Figure 4.3 depicts the frequency of articles responding to these different categories of human-created, or manufactured, risk.

This leaves really just one-fifth of the articles, which potentially directly address how regulation was or should be responding to manufactured risk produced by specific private sector innovations. Within these we see a second spurt of articles, responding to new products and technology, in the mid-2000s. On inspection, these articles tend to correspond to the growth of information and telecommunication technologies during this time period (e.g., WiFi, smartphones, etc.), or the greater information available to government as a result of the internet and advances in computing.[27] We then see the beginnings of the rise in number of articles responding to new changes to the market and economy, following the financial crisis in 2008.[28]

Taken together this suggests that, although human-created or what Giddens calls "manufactured" risk was the stated catalyst for regulatory innovation in almost two-thirds of these articles, more than 80% of *those* articles were

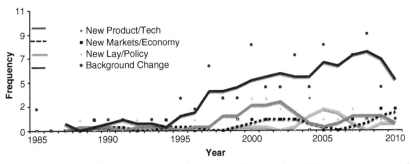

FIGURE 4.3. The frequency of articles responding to the different categories of human-created or manufactured risk. The lines depict the three-year moving average.

primarily concerned either with responding to the effects of human-created innovation, with which the article did not directly concern itself; or with responding to government policy change. In other words, notwithstanding its considerable other merits (and with the exception of some of the financial regulation articles discussed above), the regulation-and-innovation scholarship captured here was *not* focused on thinking about how one might tailor a regulatory response to a precisely defined and well-understood risk, produced by a precisely defined and well-understood private sector innovation.

Interestingly, the most-cited articles in the database were also qualitatively different from the database as a whole, in terms of what catalyzed the regulatory innovation in question. Specifically, of the fourteen most-cited articles, only five described themselves as responding to human-created manufactured risk.[29] Seven others described the regulatory innovation in optimistic terms, as responding to opportunity for either public[30] or private[31] benefit. The last two – first and third on the list of most-cited articles in this database – described the regulatory innovation in question as responding to necessity.[32] Care should be taken not to give too much emphasis to these distinctions, since the often-overlapping distinctions between risk and benefit and public and private in these articles sometimes turn on fine semantic distinctions. All the same, it may suggest that the most influential articles to consider the relationship between innovation and regulation during this time period framed the discussion in relatively urgent or optimistic terms, potentially lending forward momentum to the conversation while also obscuring the link between particular, concretely defined regulatory problems, borne of innovation-related risk, and their proposed solutions.

FLEXIBLE REGULATION AND INNOVATION

In a sense, flexible regulation scholarship considered here, and the different approaches within it, reflects our broader social relationship to the idea of innovation as a whole. We are happy to celebrate and foster it where we can. We want to believe that innovation has the capacity to address some of our most intractable problems. Pro-social innovations, like better environmental technology, get a lot of attention. Similarly, in the administrative law space, the prospect of transcending entrenched ideological divides and generating a more inclusive, engaged, responsive, and well-tailored public sphere through better regulatory technique is deeply appealing. It is primarily only when it comes to identifying and responding to specific, antisocial private innovations by powerful actors like financial institutions that we are willing to sound the alarm – as if those institutions have betrayed something essential about the innovative project, rather than just playing it out in a different context. If this literature is any guide (and I think it is), we seem unwilling to look carefully at innovation writ large as a potential challenge, perhaps because we are unwilling to contemplate the kinds of trade-offs we sense might be involved in doing so.

Considering innovation itself as a regulatory challenge, one that calls for an informed and considered regulatory response, does not require that we reject innovation wholesale. The fact that something is a challenge does not mean it must be eliminated. On the contrary, flexible regulation scholarship points the way to the kind of flexible, pragmatic, problem-solving regulatory structure that is capable of engaging with private sector innovation in a much more targeted, context-sensitive way. The next step for this scholarship, though, is to return to the Turner Review's allegation and to flip it on its head: to start from the premise that innovation is a potential regulatory *challenge*, almost by definition. The next several chapters of this book begin to investigate how innovation, including financial innovation, actually develops and evolves. Bright-line rules will have their place in responding to the challenge that innovation presents, but we will need access to all the tools at our disposal. Abandoning the tools that flexible regulation offers, on the basis of some mistaken sense of their equivalence with neoliberalism or market fundamentalism or some other pre-crisis wrong turn, would leave us bereft of some of the tools that will be most essential to our success. Abandoning the regulatory project under the banner of populism, and thereby rejecting the emancipatory, egalitarian instincts that underpin this work, would be even worse.

This scholarship emerged from a particular set of priorities, and it is not exactly fair to measure it from a different set of priorities. Nevertheless, from the perspective of someone interested in the private sector financial innovations taking place simultaneously, the scholarship demonstrates insufficient attention to what private actors were doing with the space accorded them within the regulatory scaffolding, including to its distributive effects. Some of this is a function of history: flexible regulation emerged first and primarily in environmental law, and financial regulation followed. In environmental regulation, many private sector pollution control innovations were actually generally positive. Articles on more controversial kinds of private sector environmental innovations, like fracking or deepwater oil drilling, are scarcely present in this literature. In the administrative law articles, as well, much of the literature operates primarily at the theoretical or general plane. Its prescriptions can be more exhortative than descriptive. The financial regulation articles do relatively better on this measure. Their main limitation, based on this sample, seems to be in the absence of thinking about how to build in deliberative or public-representative priorities into the regulatory architecture in the way that we see elsewhere in the flexible regulation work. In other respects, though, the financial regulation articles as a whole still bear the imprints of the regulatory and historical flexible regulation conversation of which they are a part.

5

Why Flexible Regulation Was Not Simply a Misguided, Neoliberal Project

What, in the final analysis, should we make of the flexible regulation literature as it relates to the challenge of innovation? Is there still a place for it following the financial crisis and its political sequelae, including the rise of angry populist politics? None of the claims in the last few chapters concerning the variety and possibility inherent in flexible regulation will be satisfactory if, *as an idea*, flexible regulation still seems so tainted by the somewhat anti-state, ideologically tongue-tied era in which it emerged that it cannot offer a prescription for meaningful financial regulation going forward. Even though the Turner Review does not reflect the prescriptions that regulation scholars were advancing – even though these scholars demonstrably did not think that innovation was beneficial by definition because the efficient market would winnow out unproductive ideas – was the very linkage with private sector actors that we see in the regulation and governance literature problematic? Did it reflect a milquetoast public agenda that failed to give the state its due as the legitimate voice of the polity on questions of public policy? Did it cede too much authority and agency to private actors or the market? These are consequential questions.

Flexible regulation is enmeshed with capitalism, though not with full-bore market fundamentalism. David Levi-Faur's very name for his theoretical account – "regulatory capitalism" – aims to acknowledge how fundamentally embedded contemporary flexible regulation is in capitalism.[1] Regulation constitutes the market, but regulation is also reciprocally bound up with the capitalist structure in which it is located.[2] It is a vast overstatement to say that regulators, or even more so regulation scholars, have been intellectually captured en masse over the last two decades by some form of market fundamentalism. However, as Levi-Faur observes, we should acknowledge that what has been called the "golden age of regulation"[3] is an age in which regulation is embedded in capitalism, and capitalism in turn is dependent on regulation. It has been an age of "regulatory capitalism."[4] In this respect, the flexible regulation literature is limited (though far from indefensible) in its ideological range.

Flexible regulation has been bounded, too, in that it has attended to regulatory technique without always giving adequate attention to the political context within which that technique operates. As innocuous a limitation as this may be in theory, in practice it seems to have taken on a different and more serious caste: by focusing on technique, the flexible regulation literature became susceptible to misunderstanding and misapplication. It allowed itself, sometimes, to be limited to a technocratic conversation that could be exploited in practice by political figures who neither appreciated nor valued its deep structure.

The third difficulty, already alluded to, is that flexible regulation models, porous and dynamic though they were, did not always attend sufficiently to the specific ways in which private sector innovation intersected with and affected regulation itself. This is not a small point: in failing to investigate the real-life nature of private innovation, both as a destabilizing force and a framing device, flexible regulation was missing an important source of power and influence, a generator of inequality, and a challenge to its progressive aspirations. Flexible regulation scholarship is not beyond reproach, in theory or (far more so) as imperfect facsimiles of it developed in practice. Nevertheless, the abiding merit in flexible regulation scholarship lies in its sensitivity to the complexity, dynamism, and uncertainty that inevitably characterize – will continue to characterize – the regulatory task, regardless of politics. As such it offers the indispensable jumping-off point for developing a regulatory structure that is capable of appreciating innovation for the regulatory challenge that it truly is.

FLEXIBLE REGULATION AND IDEOLOGY

Politics: Flexible Regulation and Progressive Values

Flexible regulation's provenance as a reaction to rigid Welfare State rules, and particularly concern about the gap between ostensibly authoritative state rule-pronouncing and those rules' practical force, left its mark. The fact that flexible regulation was a reaction to a regime that was thought to be inefficient and ineffective influenced and limited the scope of what flexible regulation described itself as doing. Flexible regulation argued in favor of flexibility and fit-to-context in part to reduce regulatory costs and increase efficiency. According to scholars like Sunstein and Stewart, flexible regulation promised to achieve good results more efficiently than traditional regulation, by harnessing other forces, notably incentives, that were already operating on the regulatory subject. But flexible regulation also claimed that its methods would allow regulation to achieve its own goals better – for example, by focusing on root causes rather than symptoms, and by crafting context-specific solutions that would be more congruent with regulatory intentions.

Flexibility is far from being a bad thing across the board, and rigid regulation is hardly a good thing across the board. Even if we sometimes underestimate how effective traditional bright-line regulation actually is, it makes no more sense to instinctively prefer rules-oriented, top-down regulation in all cases than it does to prefer flexible regulation in all cases. What we need to notice, though, is that there were times, especially in the early 1990s, when some (in fact many, though not all) flexible regulation scholars made a conceptual leap from the assertion that regulatory rigidity causes inefficiency and/or ineffectiveness, to the conclusion that flexibility would necessarily reduce inefficiencies and/or ineffectiveness. Moreover, they did so really without equivalent attention to the costs on the other side of the ledger, or the conditions – such as adequate regulatory capacity! – required to make it so.

We can get a sense of how over-determined the flexibility-equals-effectiveness story was at some points by considering a subtle analysis of rules and principles that Colin Diver developed more than thirty years ago.[5] Diver sees the difference between detailed rules and more high-level principles as a question of the "optimal precision" with which a regulatory requirement could be set out. He then considers the importance of precision in statutory or regulatory drafting, in terms of three underlying priorities: transparency (meaning that the words chosen have well-defined and universally accepted meanings within the relevant community); accessibility (meaning that the law can be applied to concrete situations without excessive difficulty or effort), and congruence (meaning that the substantive content of the message communicated by the words produces the desired behavior). In broad brush strokes, transparent rules ensure equality, and accessible rules promote communal values, while congruent rules foster the law's substantive aims.

Flexible regulation, with its context-specific application and its negotiable, interactive premises, has the potential to be high on congruence but relatively lower on accessibility and, if weakly developed or poorly implemented, potentially lower on transparency too. Diver points out that it is difficult to measure these qualities, and that there are often trade-offs between them. Different trade-offs will be appropriate to different contexts, and different regulatory problems. Ultimately, perhaps almost inevitably given the era, Diver adopts an economics-influenced solution to thinking about the difficult trade-offs involved: he suggests that we might balance each attribute against the others based on net social utility in a given situation. What he does not do, however, is to assume that flexibility is always optimal, or that efficiency is the only relevant measurement of optimality.

The fact that regulatory change, particularly in the 1990s, advocated forcefully for greater flexibility is significant, and was not inevitable. The background factors discussed earlier – the rise of economics, the critical challenge to the state, the increased salience of manufactured risk – meant that some form of regulatory change was likely. Popular support for deregulation and antipathy toward the state through the late 1970s and the 1980s demanded some sort of response from those disinclined to just deregulate. The progressive response was to try to protect the core of the regulatory project, while jettisoning its precise form if need be – to argue that regulation remained essential and could be salvaged through new methods that made it more efficient, or did not impose the pointless costs it was charged with imposing. Whether it was inevitable that regulatory scholarship would have settled on greater flexibility as the necessary prescription is harder to say. That it did had significant implications for the course of regulatory scholarship, including its relationship to manufactured risk and privately generated innovation.

The idea of improving regulatory efficiency and effectiveness specifically through flexibility and fit-to-context introduced not only unprecedented contingency and context-sensitivity into regulation, but also scope for negotiation and compromise. It opened the possibility that regulation could – perhaps should – be molding itself around its environment, including regulated actors' situations and expectations, rather than forcefully asserting its authority over that environment. Flexibility as a regulatory preference implies that there is some other important and legitimate consideration, around which regulation needs to mold itself, if it is to be efficient and effective. Partly as a product of globalization and increased transnational competition, flexible regulation accepts that regulation can no longer afford to be as rigid as a cardboard box, built around some inherent policy logic of its own, without regard to whether regulated actors were prepared to accept those confines or might even have better ideas of their own. Having internalized the economic analysis of law, flexible regulation accepted that efficiency was a valid measure of whether regulation was operating well (though for most scholars, it remained just one measure among several).

In terms of its authoritative position, the move toward flexibility, with its attendant defensiveness about how regulation had operated in the past, marked an important shift in the presentational authority of the state. We should also recognize the reactive, almost absolutist terms in which the flexibility-versus-rigidity dichotomy was sometimes cast, and the implications that flow from a knee-jerk preference for flexible methods. The rules-versus-principles conversation and other versions of the box-versus-suit argument can really only be understood in historical context, as a sort of overdrawn reaction against the kind of regulation that (or so it was presented at the time) existed previously. This is not to say that flexible regulation does not continue to be an important tradition; it is, and in contemporary financial regulation, with its complexities, it is perhaps more important than ever.[6] Nevertheless, to the extent that dogma ever accumulated around the perceived virtues of regulatory flexibility across the board, it is time to reject the dogma and set out some clear philosophical priors for the flexible regulation project.

Authority and the Market: Milton Friedman or Karl Polanyi?

Karl Polanyi once argued that the emergence of the self-regulating market in the eighteen, nineteenth, and early part of the twentieth centuries was then unique in human history, in that it required society to submit itself to the laws of the market rather than the other way around. Polanyi argued that the rise of the self-regulating market was partly an intentional social experiment – liberalism believed free exchanges to be the natural order – and, in this way, the "free" market was actually planned. At the same time, the self-regulating market produced an unnatural separation of economic life and political life, in which society is subservient to the market.[7] Polanyi's work has enjoyed a resurgence in recent years, particularly among those who point to the outsized influence that market-oriented values – or market fundamentalism, drawing on influential economist Milton Friedman's work – have in contemporary life.[8]

Ronen Shamir is among the contemporary scholars that would criticize the regulatory state, and its linkages between public and private actors, as part of a pernicious move toward the primacy of market-oriented values.[9] Speaking in the context of corporate social responsibility, he adopts Polanyi's view of the separation between "the market" and other social institutions. Because it was cut free of social institutions, the market was also cut free of the collective bond to ethical standards that more socially embedded institutions provided. Markets were no longer intertwined with moral sentiments.

According to Shamir, during the Welfare State era, the presence of government and its role in addressing negative social externalities produced by the "(ethically) free markets" gave business organizations a free pass to behave in purely self-interested ways. With the rise of the regulatory state, however, as government abandoned its privileged position of authority, a multiplicity of authorities emerged. The result was a "market of authority" in which mechanisms such as multi-stakeholder consultation, negotiated rulemaking, and democratic participation replaced coercive ordering activity.[10] In the process, the "logic of the market" was exported to other social domains and the public-regarding voice of the state was drowned out.

One consequence of putting government on the same level with market entities was a renewed expectation that market entities would import elements of the moral and social into their operations. For Shamir, corporate social responsibility initiatives are the product of this "responsibilization of market entities" and the "moralization of markets."[11] The barb, though, was that a "marketization of morals" meant also that morals became marketized in return: moral considerations lost their transcendent quality and became translated into the instrumental form of business opportunities.[12] In other words, for-profit private actors translated moral language into capitalist language – remember the slogan "doing good is good for business" – and in the process, stripped it of its moral resonance and its claim to freestanding legitimacy.

In a market of authority, the state also finds itself limited in how far regulation can go in pushing corporate behavior in public-regarding directions, or in getting a for-profit actor to internalize an other-regarding view. As Christine Parker warns, in trying to engage in responsive regulation, regulators cannot rely on undisputed political or cultural support for their actions.[13] (Then again, could they ever?) Corporations' strong influence and the linkage between business priorities and ethics can undermine the potency of the moral message that regulators are trying to convey. They cannot count on having legitimacy in the eyes of those they regulate. If they push too hard and are perceived as unfair or stigmatizing, regulated entities may be less inclined to comply, so regulators may be tempted to enforce "softly" or formalistically. For Parker, this is the "compliance trap," and it demonstrates the imaginative and practical limits that are baked into any effort to fold private regulated entities into the regulatory task.

There is truth in these accounts. They highlight the difficult tensions that underlie both the move toward flexible regulation in the first place, and the stubborn limits to its ideological range. The compliance trap, while not inevitable, would seem to be a logical consequence, and a significant cost, associated with shared authority. The tools that characterize flexible regulation – market mechanisms, information-forcing mechanisms, collaboration with regulated actors – very often locate the agency for change in the hands of someone or something other than the state itself. We understand why; reflexive law theory is probably the most explicit on this, though new governance has a lot to say too. Still, while the work is often characterized as being concerned with *regulatory* innovation, the effect of that regulatory innovation is often to pull dynamic forces and private innovations into the regulatory project. Often, market forces play a role as well, and in social policy terms this is not a value-neutral choice. So no matter what progressive commitments flexible regulation scholars may claim to have, for some, whenever the state collaborates on anything near equal footing with private actors, it undermines its own authority.

Vis-à-vis corporations in particular, Shamir's critique goes to the root of public/private collaborative strategies. It applies less easily to the work on cross-cutting collaborative strategies with other public institutions such as prisons, schools, hospitals, and so on, except to the extent that those institutions have also adopted a consumer-oriented, efficiency-minded frame. Where it has much less to say is vis-à-vis the strong civic republican and anti-domination instincts that underlie responsive regulation and much of experimentalism and new governance. Flexible regulation scholars are not oblivious to the risks of co-optation or capture by private forces, which is why many emphasize the need to make corporations accountable to social forces, through tripartism or "triple-loop learning" in which corporate actors must respond to a broader group of stakeholders.[14]

The piece that so often was lost in the translation from theory was the necessity for real deliberation *in action, in practice*, led and managed by a well-resourced and suitably independent-minded regulator guided by a strongly felt responsibility to the public interest, and an anti-domination ethos. A great deal of literature now holds, for instrumental reasons but also for philosophical and emancipatory ones, that rolling a broad range of participants into the process of governance, including self-governance, when properly done, can make regulation more effective. Some of this is pragmatic: enlisting actors' own incentives to guide their own self-regulation can save resources and it can at least sometimes promote "buy-in" by regulated actors. Some of it is, perhaps, resigned to the limits of the modern state: through our contemporary eyes it seems unrealistic to imagine that the state alone, without any help from private actors, should be the guardian of our collective morality and our social and environmental futures. It even seems naïve to imagine that we can achieve much through "civil society" and government combined, without at least substantial cooperation by a significant number of purely private interests. As Jody Freeman suggests, "[w]hatever version of 'good governance' one seeks to facilitate ... to the extent that one has a normative agenda, it seems necessary to enlist not only agencies, but private actors as well."[15] But under all of this, the key strands of flexible regulation scholarship underpin their arguments with a philosophical commitment to equality and human dignity.

We are overdue in restoring this priority to its central position in regulatory thinking, notably including financial regulatory thinking.

We would also do well to remember – as any American 1960s radical would tell you, and as anyone who has worked in government would probably agree (assuming the two were not in the same room) – that the state is not some pure, unalloyed transmission device for the enlightened will of the people. On the other side of the ledger from those progressive scholars who worry about how the regulatory state dissipates state authority, we have those progressive scholars who worry about how the regulatory state, by using a broader range of ordering tools, creates a totalizing and panoptic state.[16] State institutions are as imperfect and complex as any other human arrangement, including "civil society" and "the people" themselves. They are animated by their own internal logics and, it should be conceded, to some degree their self-interest too. The 1970s-era complaints about bureaucratization, interest group influence in regulation, and ineffectiveness were not completely unfounded. For these reasons, the way forward is not through a nostalgic turn back to the Welfare State: it is through a new kind of state action that locates deliberation, polycentricity, and anti-domination sentiment at its core while still appreciating the complexity of modern economic and social arrangements, and the irreducible need for flexibility in responding to them.

Decentralization: James Madison or Friedrich Hayek?

Flexible regulation overall was neither a market-oriented nor a deregulatory project. Important strains of it are heavily animated by these same civic republican ideals of greater equality and more engaged citizenship, which put the citizen – not the consumer, and not the market – at the center of the state's concerns. However, flexible regulation does advocate decentralizing state responsibilities. This can be an arresting concept for traditional Welfare Statists. One of the challenges for new governance scholarship in particular, as a program for progressive action in the world, has been its superficial similarity to less progressive and more deregulatory agendas that also favor decentralization. The subtlety of its crucial distinctions from neoconservative strategies could be all too easy to ignore, in favor of a superficial and ultimately false consensus around decentralization, self-regulation, and knocking down rigid pre-existing regulatory apparatuses.

Flexible regulation generally values context-specific, local, community-based, or industry-based knowledge. Very often, this work accepts that centralized regulators or bureaucrats are too far removed from the details of daily processes to develop wise process-based rules, though they still need to establish, oversee, and enforce high-level regulatory goals and outcome requirements. Sometimes, particularly in the environmental scholarship, substantial decision-making and operational implementation authority are moved to private actors.[17] But decentralization may also move authority to conventional state public service providers,[18] or community groups,[19] sometimes assisted by more open and deliberative court structures.[20] Along with the scaffolding approach more generally, decentralization is a mechanism for bringing in a broader range of knowledge and resources, so that regulation can work in tandem with other social actors and can respond to changing circumstances.

These are not neoconservative, anti-progressive, or Hayekian views. Flexible regulation scholars share with neoconservatives an affinity for decentralized decision-making, but they do so based on a very different set of assumptions about human and collective behavior. While some progressive scholars have been skeptical of old-style, rigid rights formulations and have argued that they should be opened up to contestation, the point was not to roll back labor rights or the hard-won successes of equality-seeking groups but rather to enrich those rights.[21] While some adopted locally driven (often private sector) innovations as an element of regulatory change, they did not imagine that self-regulation on its own was a prescription for greater social welfare; rather, they sought to link private learning with a public, and meaningfully implemented, set of goals.[22] In the United States the term "principle of subsidiarity", which is used to justify decentralization, has tended to be invoked by politically conservative scholars, but its community-empowering objectives (and its roots in Catholic social thought) span a broader set of views than that.[23] Professor Resnik's argument, in explaining her "cross-cutting trans-local organizations of government actors" (TOGAs), a new governance form of flexible regulation, is typical there:

> We could conceptualize TOGAs' work within pluralist theory as improving deliberative democracy by bringing in not only more voices but a particularly interesting set of voices ... They help bring onto the national stage points of view that are more structurally embedded in the problems of states and localities.[24]

Within flexible regulation, new governance and experimentalism in particular have been explicit about the value of decentralization and local knowledge. In an important article,[25] Amy Cohen has examined the fine but material distinctions between the kind of state-denying neoconservative perspective developed by Friedrich Hayek and his followers,[26] and the flexible regulation perspective as developed by the experimentalist Charles Sabel.

Experimentalism particularly emphasizes democratic engagement and broad citizen empowerment, but emphasizes the need to establish regulatory architecture dedicated to fostering and ensuring those features. Like flexible regulation generally, experimentalism favors decentralization, and facially that position shares a lot of ground with Hayek.

Both Sabel and Hayek advocate something similar: based on claims about the limits of individual knowledge and the impossibility of developing full-blown satisfactory responses in conditions of extreme uncertainty, Sabel and Hayek claim that government should refrain from imposing prior substantive or distributional ends. Decentralization, as a response to deep uncertainty – Knightian uncertainty, into which as we know human subjectivity factors at least as much as complexity or the state of empirical understanding – characterizes both approaches and is utterly central to the relationship between flexible regulation, manufactured risk, and ultimately private sector innovation.

Cohen's observation is that the apparent similarities between the Hayekian deregulatory project and the progressive experimentalist one are misleading. Cohen points out, correctly, that decentralization on its own is not a politically charged act. Decision making can be decentralized in the service of a range of distinct goals, and on its own it is agnostic about those goals. While both Sabel and Hayek advocate decentralization, they do so based on different sets of assumptions about the capacity of the individual, or the collective, to engage in and evolve through a process of *reasoned decision-making*.

The animating conviction underlying decentralization is what Cohen has called "unknowingness." What scholars from Hayek to Sabel share is a sense that it is simply not possible to know, as a centralized regulator, all the things one must know in order to govern effectively. For Hayek, though, this understanding is overlaid with a conviction that regulators are irremediably incapable of knowing much, or of learning practically anything. Because for Hayek knowledge is tacit, almost incommunicable, the mechanisms of collective public action cannot succeed (unless they are totalitarian, with access to totalitarian-state levels of knowledge about private concerns). Because private knowledge is tacit and therefore cannot be aggregated, regulators cannot know enough to do more than cause unintended, and generally negative, consequences. The best thing the state can do is to maximize individual freedom, enact "simple rules for a complex world,"[27] and get out of the way. For Hayek, then, decentralization is very much a deregulatory and anti-state project.

Where experimentalism fundamentally differs is in its faith in human reason and the capacity for growth. Sabel's faith in the human ability to reason, and his faith in society's potential to develop and evolve through explicit reason-giving and disciplined dialogue, leads him to a very different justification for decentralization. For him, meaningful and broadly participatory citizen deliberation can improve regulatory outcomes and also offer a fuller and more respectful model for citizenship and for democracy. Cohen's examination of Friedrich Hayek's and Charles Sabel's thinking leads her to conclude that experimentalism actually has a great deal more in common with liberal legalism than with Hayekian *neo*liberal legalism.

I would go farther, in fact, to emphasize the strong civic republican strains that animate experimentalism as well as much of flexible regulation scholarship. Unlike classic liberalism, civic republicanism is based on a richer and more engaged understanding of what it means to be a citizen. Civic republicanism is not only about negative liberties from state interference; it is about allowing individuals the resources, including the participatory and public resources, needed to allow them to realize their authentic, socially engaged selves. This strain of flexible regulation scholarship, still accepting fundamental unknowingness, sees decentralization as a means of bringing in local knowledge, engaging lay citizens in a fuller democratic project, preventing domination, and expanding the circle of participation in the public sphere. The unknowingness here stems not from the inherent incapacity of individual rationality or collective action, but rather from the multilayered and complex nature of human experience.

Unlike Hayek, flexible regulation scholarship generally rejects the view that knowledge is tacit and instead embraces the possibility that mutual understanding and collective capacity can evolve and increase through reason-giving and dialogue.[28] The goal for prescriptions like experimentalism, management-based regulation, principles-based regulation, and meta-regulation is therefore to develop mechanisms that can pull local knowledge up into the state apparatus, not to shut the state apparatus down. The same is true with respect to financial innovation. The context demands an engaged, well-resourced regulatory intervention into industry innovation, in the context of a structure that is capable of both learning and adapting, and giving voice to authentic public priorities.

TRANSLATION TO PRACTICE: PROMISING THE MOON AND THE SKY THROUGH REGULATORY INNOVATION

As we have discussed, flexible regulation scholars have made various claims about why flexible regulation was better than what had come before – it was more efficient, more likely to be effective, more participatory, and so on. As a whole, this has been a progressive body of scholarship produced by a progressive group of scholars. Yet now, with the benefit of hindsight, some may see reason to question flexible regulation's complicity with a pre-crisis worldview that was insufficiently attentive to progressive concerns about power, regulatory capacity, and inequality. While this is not accurate as a description of the scholarship, is there nevertheless something about flexible regulation scholarship that has allowed its generally progressive commitments to be misunderstood by subsequent observers, and both misunderstood and misapplied by regulators in practice?

In general, under a flexible regulation model, normative conversations take place off-stage. The flexible regulation literature has not always worn its ideological or normative commitments on its sleeve (though sometimes, as with the explicit commitments to civic republicanism we see in *Responsive Regulation* and experimentalism, it has). In some instances, normative commitments to, for example, more meaningful and effective environmental regulation are actually embedded into the project itself. In other cases, scholars that were tempted to articulate forceful ideological positions may have stayed their hands precisely because of the commitments to pragmatism and democratic deliberation contained in their prescriptions. In some versions of the respectful attention to others' views that deliberation requires, flexible regulation explicitly aimed to transcend ideological divides, to operate "post-politics," and to find the unexpected areas of accommodation and agreement that entrenched ideological positions did not permit. The point, to be sure, was to advance a strategy to reduce domination. Yet in its presentation, this relative normative reticence puts pre-crisis flexible regulation scholarship out of step with the more explicitly ideological positions that have been voiced since the financial crisis, in an era characterized by much more immediate and concrete concerns about inequality and power.[29]

In any case, the consequences are twofold: first, at least through the 1990s, flexible regulation scholars did not claim an explicit ideological position from which to critique other apparent fellow travelers who advocated for similar things but for different reasons – like the Hayekians, who were also arguing for a version of decentralization. As well, for principled and defensible reasons related to the regulatory role, which is to implement public policy and not to usurp the democratic process or make that policy, flexible regulation sometimes became a somewhat esoteric conversation about regulatory technique. Worse than esoteric, this meant that the very idea of regulatory technique was vulnerable to being "spun" by others, for instrumental and even contrary reasons, in the realm of practice and politics.

Again, flexible regulation has not been applied faithfully across the board in practice, and certainly was not applied in any meaningful sense in financial regulation in the era leading up to the crisis. Gunther Teubner did not cause the financial crisis (as he apparently was accused, jokingly, of having done).[30] Yet political actors and regulators, especially regulators competing transnationally for, say, capital markets business, seized on the language of "flexibility" or "principles-based regulation." As implemented, their interpretations of flexible regulation were uneven and wildly under-resourced. The language of flexibility and "better regulation" was perhaps most notable as a marketing or political technique, not a regulatory one.[31] Indeed, it would be difficult to establish that more "flexible" systems like the United Kingdom's more principles-based system were any more (or less!) susceptible to gaming or weaker in regulatory terms than more rigid, bright-line systems like the United States'. Across jurisdictions, underfunding, under-resourcing, lack and misdirection of information, lack of focus, and lack of regulatory independent-mindedness were the common thread, and they had far more to do with how pre-crisis financial regulation failed than theory – any theory – did.[32] No regulatory regime can succeed when it is badly under-resourced.

Flexible regulation cannot be blamed for the ways in which some facsimile of it was misapplied in practice, or for its superficial similarity to those false friends, the deregulatory and "light touch" approaches.[33] At the same time, it is now clear that where scholarship chooses to focus on technique and to downplay the emancipatory, progressive ideological substrate on which it necessarily lies, it risks having its political valence seized upon by others to be used in unintended and even contrary ways.

The fact that flexible regulation transcended entrenched normative positions and opened up unexpected areas of consensus has been identified more than once as proof of its promise.[34] While this may be true, the broad consensus about flexibility, as it developed in real-life financial regulation, also helped obscure the civic republican priorities and principles that underpinned much of flexible regulation theory. The absence of sufficiently explicit normative priors in the regulatory conversation, pre-crisis, made it difficult to sound the alarm about any particular policy step by reference to ideological or policy commitments. In theory, a focus on just process and regulatory design could be understood and maybe even celebrated as a deeply pragmatic, incremental regulatory approach. In practice, regulation (including financial regulation) is always embedded within ideological and political choices, whether or not we state them explicitly.[35]

As well, pre-crisis flexible regulation scholarship did not universally translate into an energetic and progressive practical democratic project, in part because its fixation on regulatory design and technique was disproportionately what was received in the practical arena. Rod Rhodes and Mark Bevir once charged that governance and public administration scholarship tends toward "modernist-empiricism," meaning that it sees public administration as improvable and even perfectible through measurement and empirical analysis.[36] This is an overstatement, but it is true that regulation is an instrumental thing. It attends to technical goals and processes – data and outcome analysis, benchmarking, performance assessment – and less explicitly to the choice of the broader goals that are to be advanced. The principled reasons why a civic republican regulatory philosophy would do so, and would defer making normative choices, did not make it through the grinder of translation to practice. It is also true that much of regulation scholarship, though less so in the financial regulation context, was optimistic that better regulation could "lift all boats" rather than generate sets of winners and losers.

In the context of pre-crisis financial regulation in particular, given the wealth that capital markets activity can generate, optimism about the perfectibility of regulatory technique folded into a broader hopefulness about financial innovation and the capital markets generally. The relationship between innovation and power, and the ways in which innovation can produce disproportionate benefits and framing opportunities for powerful actors, faded into the background. The promise of finance, like the promise of innovation, has throughout history sometimes tempted us collectively to ignore its dark side, at least so long as markets are on the upswing and seemingly everyone is benefiting. Because the costs of regulation are easier to quantify than the benefits, and because no one tends to think too hard about regulatory muscularity and strict enforcement during a bubble, reducing the "regulatory burden" can become a central concern at those times.[37] Thus, in practice, the structure of financial regulation before the crisis – principles-based, delegating details to regulated entities, relying on social and market forces to buttress regulatory requirements – was sometimes premised on the possibility of what Julia Black once called a "regulatory Utopia," within which the self-examining, responsible firm, which possesses the greatest contextual information, helps to elaborate the detailed content of regulation through ongoing dialogue with a flexible and outcome-oriented regulator, in the service of their shared goal of optimized regulation.[38]

Regulators were therefore happy to envision "everyone wins" scenarios. Some regulators, glossing over the details that scholars tended to worry more about, argued that more flexible regulatory structures could be simply superior all around. For example, in describing the UK FSA's move to a more principles-based regulatory approach, FSA Chief Executive John Tiner argued in 2006 that principles-based regulation produced simply "better" regulation, meaning *simultaneously* "(1) a stronger probability that statutory outcomes are secured; (2) lower cost; and (3) more stimulus to competition and innovation."[39]

What we see is the translation of a technique-oriented, modernist-empiricist tendency in the scholarship to be spun, in practice, into the notion that better regulatory technique *on its own* can somehow transcend the difficult trade-offs between effectiveness and cost, individual initiative and systemic fairness, that have always bedeviled regulation. The reality of course is that even if most regulated actors behave well most of the time, and even though incorporating privately generated information can make regulation more efficient and congruent with its goals (because it provides better access to information), we neither could nor should try to eliminate the fundamental, valuable distinction between regulators' objectives as guardians of the broader public interest, and regulated actors' objectives.[40]

WHERE THE SCHOLARSHIP DOES NOT REACH: UNDERSTANDING INNOVATION AS A REGULATORY CHALLENGE

While flexible regulation scholarship was not perfect, or perfectly communicated, where it falls short unless one rejects capitalism as a whole is not at the political or ideological plane. As an overarching perspective it is not inherently beholden to an anachronistic or misguided market fundamentalist or deregulatory political worldview. We cannot entirely blame the scholarship for the failure in translation to practice.[41]

At the same time, can we be sure that flexible regulation is worth the candle? If innovation will seep around any regulatory structure, is there any reason to bother with the more complicated and elaborate scaffolding structures that flexible regulation argues for? If we are serious about controlling the undermining effects of financial innovation on regulation, in the service of progressive public priorities, why not go even further to limit it? During his remarkable political run in 2016, former US Democratic candidate Bernie Sanders proposed much more top-down, bright-line proposals including imposing a sweeping financial transaction tax, breaking up the largest banks, and imposing a 15 percent cap on credit card interest rates.

Senator Sanders's proposals deserve attention even now. Yet we delude ourselves if we think that, when dealing with financial innovation, we can develop some kind of idealized bright-line, rules-based regulation that really controls it once and for all. The first and most obvious problem, as discussed in the Enron example in Chapter 1, is that bright-line rules are at least as easily circumvented, in explicit and implicit ways, as more flexible, principles-based, or outcome-oriented rules.[42] In fact, they are almost certainly much more easily circumvented. The more realistic but still productive regulatory changes we have seen since the financial crisis look, instead, like scaffolding-style flexible regulatory structures that are designed to change private parties' incentives and make new financial products more comprehensible and transparent – not to shut them down ab initio.[43] There are also legitimacy-oriented and practical reasons to continue with the flexible regulation project.

Think back to the examples in Chapter 1, purely in terms of how transparent the regulatory regimes were in their assumptions and operations, and how explicit they were in recognizing the mechanisms at work. The more flexible regulatory regime in Basel II was more explicit about the private sector standards it was incorporating than either the Canadian ABCP regime or the accounting regime in the Enron era. (The Volcker Rule example makes a broader point about the influence of expertise on regulatory standards and on public capacity for input, which cuts across all regulatory regimes.) All three of these regimes necessarily incorporated the private actor's technical assessments of, respectively, who owned particular assets for accounting purposes, what counted as asset-backed commercial paper, and how much capital the private actor had to keep in reserve in order to cover the risks it was running. Yet only Basel II, the one most resembling a new governance approach (albeit a desperately flawed and under-supervised one), in which the content of principles were explicitly filled in through transparently incorporating private sector decision-making methods, actually acknowledged the role that private industry standards were playing. Framing regulatory requirements in terms of bright-line or detailed rules does not actually cut private actors' judgment out.

The same can be said about contemporary bank regulation in the United States. These days some prudential regulators, like the New York Fed, embed a dozen or more dedicated examiners into large financial institutions. (Their work is shored up by another layer of staff that slices the same institutions by cross-cutting subject matter area, or "risk departments", and by policy staffers and others as well.) Yet even under this intense and engaged supervisory model, firm-focused examiners cannot actually run the institution, generate the data to assess independently the risks it is running, or develop its compliance processes.[44] This is not a new problem: the "public" and "private" spheres of action have never been watertight compartments, even when the Welfare State imagined them to be. Unless regulators actually intend to *run* regulated actors' operations, they will always be reliant on regulated actors' internal compliance systems.

From this perspective, incorporating private standards, as flexible regulatory approaches like management-based and meta-regulation do, simply acknowledges explicitly what regulators must do anyway under any regulatory regime.[45] Acknowledging the continued private role in public regulation is the precursor to thinking clearly and systematically about how formal regulatory structures can best interface with these other mechanisms, with a view to improving regulatory technique and ensuring that public priorities are advanced.

There is still another reason why we should not imagine that we could create a set of bright-line, shut-down rules that could resolve conclusively the regulatory challenge that innovation presents: modern financial markets really are complex, dynamic, transnational webs. This has not changed. We can and should criticize the way in which complexity arguments were pressed into service by self-interested financial institutions seeking to reduce regulatory oversight. We can and should take a dim view of complex chains of financial products or arrangements that are structured that way primarily in order to skim benefit off for rent-seekers at each intermediate step along the chain.[46] Even so, an irreducible core of complexity remains as the byproduct of the varied, dynamic and interconnected world we live in. As Julia Black has said, "the conditions of complexity, uncertainty, fragmentation, ungovernability and dynamism which cause [traditional 'command-and-control'] regulation to fail, and to which new governance techniques are meant to offer a superior response, all remain."[47]

Flexible regulation offers a rich set of regulatory tools, and a more nuanced understanding of those tools' relationships to other forces of social and economic ordering. Reframing regulation around the mutable and slippery nature of private sector innovation, as this book has argued that we must do, will depend on flexible regulatory strategies far more than on gameable blanket prohibitions and bright-line rules. That said, post-crisis we also have a keener appreciation for the limits on scope that characterized flexible regulation, as it was read in practice. We see the relatively non-ideological and technical band within which it has sometimes operated, and we understand that better regulation cannot, contrary to some accounts, actually improve regulatory outcomes along all axes at once. We can appreciate the consequences that flow from a decision not to foreground the anti-domination and equality concerns that also define the flexible regulation approach.

It should also be clear that flexible regulation needs to be much more attentive to the particular challenges that innovation presents, if it is to achieve its potential in responding to those challenges. In effect, many flexible regulation scholars in the 1990s and early 2000s were engaged in a conversation across time about the relative merits of different regulatory methods, with the then-discredited Welfare State as their focal point. Regulatory innovation was a response to past models' perceived failures, notably their perceived rigidity and inadaptability, but flexible regulation scholars were primarily just speaking to other regulation scholars about regulation. They were not generally engaged in a conversation about specific kinds of manufactured risk, or the private side of innovation that paralleled the regulatory innovations they argued for. The flexible regulation scholarship was not concerned enough about the potentially risky consequences of private innovation or its potentially subversive effects on regulation – not because it was excessively optimistic about innovation, as the Turner Review would have it, but because private sector innovation was not actually its central concern. Flexible regulation scholarship was a manifestation of a broader societal celebration of innovation itself during this era, but it was not prescient enough to anticipate the ways in which, for example, scaffolding-style regulation could actually accelerate innovation, the nature of which was poorly understood, or alter its distributive consequences in unjustifiable ways.

Thus armed with a better sense of the flexible regulation scholarship, and the conviction that it will continue to be a crucial approach going forward, the next step is to turn our attention to this gap in our understanding. One of this book's main points is that, without really understanding the private side of the innovative phenomenon, regulation – flexible and otherwise, financial and otherwise – cannot respond adequately to the challenge that private innovation itself presents, and the regulatory and distributive problems it generates. What does private sector innovation look like, anyway, what regulatory challenges does it create, and how should regulation – especially financial regulation – respond to it?

6

Refocusing Regulation around the Challenge of Innovation

FLEXIBLE REGULATION, INNOVATION, AND FINANCE

As we know, innovation seeps under, around, and through regulatory structures and undermines them and their boundaries in unanticipated ways. The most gameable kind of regulatory structure and the easiest to undermine is the kind of top-down, rigid, rule-based regulation that characterized, for example, the accounting rules that Enron circumvented through its derivatives and special purpose vehicles. Likewise, the old Welfare State, with its hard-to-change statutory rules, hierarchical decision-making structures, and disengaged, arm's-length relationship to regulated actors (even conceding that it was more nuanced in action than on the books) was simply not designed to respond to, or even to recognize, shape-shifting and unpredictable regulatory objects like derivatives.

The contemporary regulatory state now has a much broader and more varied range of regulatory tools at its disposal. Economic analysis introduced notions of efficiency, and identified ways in which regulation could incorporate and work with market-based forces. Regulators learned to use empirical analysis, the concept of risk, and a more pragmatic, functional approach to try to respond to uncertainty and dynamism. As the state's normative authority fell away, regulators learned to base their legitimacy on accountability, transparency, and consultation. As the state's apparent capacity to control broad swaths of economic and social action fell away, regulators reached across the old conceptual division between "public" and "private" spheres, incorporating a broader set of stakeholder views, learning to collaborate, and leveraging other forces like the market and public opinion. The flexible regulatory state that sprung up was quite different from what had come before, but it was based on a coherent set of assumptions about what accountable and effective contemporary state power looked like.

Some flexible regulation scholars take the inevitability of change and the utter postmodern contingency of the regulatory project to their logical conclusion, allowing means and ends to roll into each other in an ongoing, reflexive process. Experimentalism and meta-regulation, for example, in some ways not only recognize or leverage dynamic processes, but try to "throw a rope" around the leading edge of human-generated innovation through mechanisms like "rolling best practices rulemaking"[1] or "triple-loop learning".[2] But new governance, experimentalism, and meta-regulation are just saying explicitly something that operates in the background of contemporary regulation as a whole. Contemporary regulation is a dynamic and contingent process that seeks to operate within a dynamic and uncertain environment.[3] It tries, in various ways, to avoid building the proverbial regulatory Maginot line. The relationship between regulation and private sector action is reflexive, too, meaning that, just as non-state actors are influenced by state action, so do non-state forces influence state action in turn. In this way both the challenge, and the promise, presented by continual change are deeply embedded in contemporary regulatory technique.

And yet, for all their sophistication, the more modern regulatory approaches we discussed in Chapter 1 (speaking there of the practice, not the theory) were undermined by financial innovation too, albeit in different and less obvious ways. In particular, the Basel II capital adequacy regime, in its efforts to respond to the gamesmanship that had undone Basel I, developed a set of rules that inadvertently made space for financial institutions, by relying on their own internal risk assessment methodologies, to reduce their regulatory obligations. The technically complex nature of modern finance also squeezed the possibility for meaningful public participation out of the rulemaking process around the Volcker Rule, to a degree that may give civic republicans pause. Nor can we be confident that the Volcker Rule's ultimate objective – to insulate government-insured banking functions from a financial institution's proprietary trading on its own behalf – has necessarily survived the rulemaking process intact, or that those financial institutions have not simply found other innovative ways to achieve the same effect of trading on their own account without running afoul of that detailed rule.[4] Flexible regulation may be better at being transparent about what it is doing, and it can respond more explicitly and transparently to complexity, uncertainty, and dynamism, but it is not immune to innovation's undermining effects.

Up to this point, this book has focused on the *how* of regulation in practice and theory. This is what regulation is basically about – the instrumental work of figuring out how to achieve certain ends. Less well understood, it seems, is the *what* of innovation – the nature of this phenomenon that can so compromise its functioning. In some cases, this means that regulation and its associated scholarship have developed based on a partial or sometimes even flawed understanding of forces that are central to its project.

In the immediate wake of the financial crisis, suspicion about financial innovation in particular took off. Some regulators and policy makers, especially in Europe, floated the possibility that financial innovation should be reined in. The more forceful regulatory reform proposals contemplated trying to get "back to basics," to "de-intensify" or simplify capital markets and to promote only "socially useful" kinds of innovation while limiting the rest.[5] Paradoxically, proposals of this nature are both too radical, and not radical enough.

They are *too radical* to the extent that they aim to make advance decisions about what kinds of innovation should be promoted and what kinds tamped down, seemingly more in reaction to the crisis than as a result of careful analysis or policy formation. If we do collectively decide, as we are entirely entitled to do, to limit financial innovation, our decision should be based on a better understanding of financial innovation than we currently possess. (It should also be made based on a meaningful, deliberative, fair process, a prospect we return to in the this book's final chapter.) As Josh Lerner and Peter Tufano have compellingly demonstrated, financial innovation is neither all "good" nor all "bad."[6] Much of it has indisputably been good, and our current standard of living substantially depends on some aspects of it, even while much of it has indisputably been bad in the sense of permitting anti-social and rent-seeking behavior. Moreover, the costs and benefits of particular financial innovations change over time, based on those innovations' evolution and changes in their environments. The notion that we could validly distinguish "good" or "socially useful" innovation from "bad" innovation in advance, at some overarching level, is misguided.

This concern extends to current and future financial innovations, as well as the innovations that underpinned the financial crisis. Innovation, including financial innovation and "fintech," holds enormous potential even as it carries risks. Certainly, we need to be alive to the risks – to investor protection, to fair and efficient capital markets, to systemic stability, to sheer regulatability – that may accompany financial innovations such as high-frequency trading and dark markets. Nor do we yet know how investors will fare under new equity crowdfunding provisions. But consider also the positive influence that mobile banking and mobile money have had on the developing world's access to credit and banking services;[7] or the consumer-facing fintech products that make banking, student loan payments, investing, and financial management less costly for non-wealthy individuals.[8] Other fintech companies aim to give small companies easier access to funding and business advice,[9] to make trading cheaper or more individualized,[10] to make international money transfers (especially remittance payments) less costly,[11] or to make charitable giving and socially responsible investing easier.[12] Still others, for all their merits, have the potential to undermine regulatory assumptions about how a market operates, who operates in it, and what regulation is accomplishing.[13] No one regulatory approach, back-to-basics or otherwise, could be appropriate across such a range of innovations.

The back-to-basics proposals are also *not radical enough*, in that they still seem to assume that traditional regulatory tools, including bright-line "shut down" style rules, can be deployed to simply harness or rein in innovation at will. We know better. The four examples at the beginning of this book are only a small set of instances in which innovation has undermined regulatory structures. Innovation has undermined and denatured regulation, including financial regulation, for centuries and it has undermined many more regulatory structures than we discuss here.

Financial innovations like securitization and the creation of derivatives have now conclusively shattered the atom of property, with real consequences for attempts to regulate finance, the corporation, or innovation along traditional lines. Extensive work by scholars in the last several years has made clear that we should be very careful before we get too comfortable in thinking that we even know what a "share" is anymore, or a debt instrument, or an investor, or a public market.[14] Innovation can also produce shape-shifting: as Bill Bratton and Adam Levitin have pointed out, things that used to be comprehensible as qualities of *institutions* can now be set up through the entirely separate legal construct of *contract*.[15] The opposite is also true. Old regulatory categories lose their fit as, for example, the profitable activities of intermediaries change, or non-bank entities start doing bank-like things without being subject to the prudential regulation imposed on banks themselves. Regulators are left focusing on the wrong things.[16] New players can emerge seemingly from nowhere: in his book *Flash Boys*, popular finance writer Michael Lewis describes an occasion in which his protagonist, an experienced Wall Street trader, suddenly learns about a market player who occupies ten percent of the published securities market but of whom the trader had never even heard. That market player was a high-frequency trader.[17] Global investment in financial technology, or "fintech," has also increased dramatically in the last decade. That aspects of this sector should be regulated is surely indisputable, but its imprecise boundaries have posed questions of who the regulator should be, which players or activities even fall within this space, and what effective regulation would look like.[18] Many fintech initiatives hold real promise in social welfare terms – yet these are the kinds of basic definitional questions that, from a regulatory stand-point, should raise alarm bells.

We should be concerned about how financial innovation is continuing to evolve, even as we generate post-financial crisis responses to the last set of problems. Consider the international response to problems of systemic risk. International institutions and agencies, like the Financial Stability Board (FSB) and the International Organization of Securities Commissions (IOSCO), have made a great deal of progress in understanding how finan-cial institutions are interconnected and what makes particular institutions systemically significant.[19] Relevant assessment methodologies vary by industry but include, for example, an institution's size, complexity, and interconnect-edness.[20] This is all well and good, and it is a reasonable response to the last financial crisis. But to the extent that this kind of analysis is still based on formal designations, thresholds, and a particular image of how systemic risk will arise, those are framing devices that yet again lock us into a particular, time-bound perspective.

What if the next serious systemic risk comes from a different kind of arrange-ment? What if it arises not at the level of institutions but rather at the level of markets, or products? The framing device of the institution-as-subject, which is the dominant approach to systemic risk regulation in the US, the UK, and the European Union, could distract regulators and observers from a serious accretion of risk across the system as a whole.[21] (My own country is consider-ing a somewhat different approach.) For example, what if the next serious sys-temic risk arises not from a large, complex, or interconnected global financial institution, but from a "cloud" of countless individually insignificant, shift-ing, unreachable transactions or moments that together create enormous sys-tem effects? If this sounds too much like science fiction, we should consider again high-frequency trading, which operates very much in a cloud-like, near-instantaneous, diffuse manner and which has the potential – as the May 2010 Flash Crash demonstrates – to affect markets profoundly.[22]

As promising as some of financial innovations may (or may not) turn out to be, disintermediation and innovation are not virtues unto themselves and their merits cannot be assumed, without further consideration, to outweigh their attendant risks or to outweigh other social priorities. Public regulation's essential function is to ensure that the fundamental normative commitments we have made as a society are given effect. Innovation is a challenge for regu-lation at this fundamental level. Innovation itself should not be quashed on a sweeping basis, but careful attention needs to be devoted to ensuring that its fluid, water-like, erosive properties do not undermine regulatory structures, which embody our important social commitments.

If regulation is to be forward-looking, we need to ask some more fundamental definitional and epistemological questions about *what* financial innovation actually looks like and how it operates before we can start to consider the *how* of regulating innovation.[23] There can be no getting away from the need to make assumptions when making regulation. A regulatory regime would be incoherent if it did not rest on some set of general theories and assumptions about its context, object, and purpose. But difficulties arise when, thanks to innovation, the assumptions that undergird a regulatory regime no longer hold true. This book's question is whether it is possible to develop a regulatory approach whose fundamental underlying assumptions include – instead of assumptions about the nature of a product or a market or a firm's proprietary risk management software or the like – the default presumption that innovation will be continually changing the regulatory context and object, undermining and potentially circumventing regulation, and potentially obscuring or making irrelevant its stated purposes. In other words, can we build regulation that genuinely appreciates innovation as an almost existential challenge to its effectiveness?

The first step would be to think more systematically about the nature of innovation. What does innovation look like and how does it progress? Does innovation look different in the financial sector than it does elsewhere? We need to move entirely beyond the flexible regulation scholarship to understand this phenomenon. It turns out, though, that we also need to move beyond the conventional literature on innovation, which presents a relatively narrow picture of the drivers of innovation and only a nascent description of how financial innovation in particular may be unique. What follows is a brief, largely descriptive review of the general innovation studies scholarship, which we can use as a springboard for considering financial innovation in particular. Many aspects of the topic call for further research; but what we can do at this point is to begin to frame a new set of questions for regulation and regulatory scholarship, which more explicitly considers the ways in which innovation challenges its structures and assumptions.

STARTING POINTS FROM THE INNOVATION LITERATURE

Current kinds of innovation, and our understandings of and responses to them, are the unique product of our particular time. Yet we have been innovating ourselves into problems (such as the extinction of big game because hunting techniques became so effective) and back out of problems (such as through the potentially related development of agriculture) throughout our existence.[24] We are right to celebrate the human capacity for inventiveness and adaptability, but the overall tale of our development also sometimes smacks of some kind of collective action problem whose general outlines remain familiar today – and which remains at the core of the modern regulatory task.

Niccolò Machiavelli wrote about innovation in *The Prince* in 1513, as did Francis Bacon in *Of Innovations* in 1625.[25] But it is Joseph Schumpeter who is typically considered the father of innovation studies.[26] Schumpeter initially believed that bringing an innovation to fruition demanded a visionary individual entrepreneur, capable of overcoming societal inertia.[27] In his later work, however, he recognized that innovation was more often the product of a cooperative process, which needed to be studied beyond the individual level.[28] As familiar as the invention-to-innovation story may be, or the story of the brilliant, visionary individual, the actual development of innovations tends to be messier and less linear than that account suggests.[29]

Schumpeter insisted that in order for innovation to emerge, potential innovators must see benefits deriving from it. They do not need to capture 100 percent of the benefits – as later researchers have pointed out, innovations can and often do produce positive spillover effects for society that exceed what the innovator can capture personally.[30] The benefit to the innovator certainly does not have to be pecuniary.[31] All the same, the self-interested pursuit of profit in a capitalist economy forges a clear link between innovation and reward.[32] While the theory on the relationship between capitalism and innovation is extensive and disputed, as factual matters it seems clear, first, that capitalist economies tend to be very innovative; and second, that a self-interested profit motive has generated a large portion of innovation within capitalist societies.[33]

The First Industrial Revolution (1760–1850), as a story about innovation, remains an important anchoring narrative in our collective thinking about innovation. It kicked off a new era of firm-driven innovation, and its characteristics continue to shape our understanding of how innovation occurs. During the First Industrial Revolution, virtually all sectors of the British economy saw significant innovation and industrialization, from the well-known sectors like textiles (e.g., the spinning jenny) and power (the Watt steam engine), to the less well-known, including glass production, agricultural equipment and machinery, food (baking, brewing, and milling), chemicals, and more.[34] Industrial Revolution-style innovation, as something primarily driven by for-profit organizations producing practical goods, remains the archetype in the modern field of innovation studies.

Background social, cultural, and physical environmental factors also obviously influence innovation. In the case of Britain's rise during the Industrial Revolution, for example, important factors included geography and access to coal energy, the emerging social recognition of wealth as conferring status, legal changes such as the development of company law and patent protection for new inventions, and managerial innovations like the time clock.[35] The fact that Britain was politically stable, yet participated in technology-fostering war efforts, may have contributed. That government was decentralized, thus not draining talent from the provinces, may also have helped develop local innovation hubs.[36] Foreign trade and the sheer amount of wealth generated through imperialism indisputably played a role.

Notably, scholars do not believe that new scientific advances or research were the primary factors driving innovation during the Industrial Revolution. Britain at the time was neither a particularly scientifically advanced society, nor a particularly well-educated one. Instead, innovation was driven by individual craft workers who could engage "in collective and cumulative learning" in the new British industrial districts – that is, in local areas characterized by vertical specialization (across different steps in the manufacturing process) and horizontal competition (with other manufacturers and sometimes other districts).[37]

As Britain grew in global influence and gained access to more raw goods, new specialized manufacturing firms, often established by craft workers themselves, sprang up. Those that were geographically concentrated could enjoy economies of scale in such things as delivery of materials. This gave rise to production districts. Economist William Lazonick therefore argues that it was the district, or sometimes even the town, that was the "learning unit" in this era. Within the districts, senior workers who owned and managed their own firms, as many did, had both the economic incentive and the strategic capacity to innovate. Another factor that contributed to the new learning model was "regionally based on-the-job apprenticeship arrangements," within which senior workers passed on knowledge to junior workers. In the process, formerly tacit knowledge was codified, which helped diffuse knowledge more rapidly.[38]

Industrial Revolution-era craft-based firms did not engage in research and development or generate large-scale technological innovations themselves. Their innovations were more often to the means of production, which trained generations of flexible, skilled workers capable of doing customized work for a range of different users. The important technical inventions of the era – chlorine bleaching, food canning, gas lighting, mechanical spinning – were very often made overseas, particularly in France. However, according to economic historian Joel Mokyr, British technological success was the result of its comparative advantage in tweaking, refining and applying those processes and making them useful.[39] In Mokyr's words, "[a]s long as technological advances did not require a fundamental understanding of the laws of physics or chemistry on which they were based and as long as advances could be achieved by brilliant but intuitive tinkerers and persistent experimenters, Britain's ability to create or adapt new production technologies was supreme."[40]

As a result, innovations during the First Industrial Revolution proceeded along a particular trajectory, which continues to influence our thinking today: the key innovations were *incremental*, and emerged within industries and *districts*, as a product of collective human learning in concrete situations, motivated by *economic self-interest*. They were not linear (for example, from research, to development, directly to a predictable application) and as a general rule they were not generated in a top-down manner (for example, through R&D grants – or perhaps the era-appropriate equivalent in the UK would be Royal Charters). Innovation was the result of a process, or series of processes, of collective learning and micro-innovations, generated through various feedback loops, in a practical commercial context.[41]

Literature on more recent innovations reinforces the connection between innovativeness and practical problem-solving. Public education and training, and efforts to coordinate research and development across public research institutions, do promote innovation.[42] However, the path from invention to innovation tends not to be sequential or linear. Rather, firms see a commercial opportunity and generally try to take advantage of that opportunity via the shortest, cheapest, and quickest routes first, for example by combining knowledge they already have in new ways. If and only if this does not work will they reach out to unfamiliar new knowledge, or to the costly project of doing their own problem-solving research.[43]

Sometimes an invention will respond directly to an existing opportunity. At other times, time and context do not cooperate so readily. In particular, it is unwise to assume too early that we can identify the value of an invention, or an innovation (or the *nature* of its value – to individuals, to social welfare, to competitive advantage). Sometimes an invention's highest-impact application is not evident for some time. For example, Thomas Edison invented the phonograph in 1877, but it took him another twenty years to acknowledge that his invention's most significant real-life application was to record and play music.[44] In the meantime, other changes including urbanization, the rise of popular restaurants (and speakeasies during Prohibition in the United States), the growth of the music industry, the development of electric amplifiers, and mass production techniques had made the environment newly receptive to the phonograph.

Structural firm properties and informal cultural qualities also reportedly contribute to innovation, though the literature on this topic can be quite stylized.[45] Enormous ink has been spilled within the organizational studies literature (and in countless entrepreneurial How-Tos) on creating an innovative firm environment. Attributes thought to positively influence innovativeness include how much structural flexibility and decision-making freedom employees have; whether workers have adequate resources, and reward and recognition structures that support innovation; whether the firm values open communication and participatory decision-making; how entrepreneurial and how cohesive it is; and how much it emphasizes learning and development.[46]

Innovation involves many, continual interactions and feedback loops. It is a learning process, meaning that a firm's analytical blind spots will have an effect. Past events, self-reinforcing feedback loops and lock-in (collectively often described as path dependence – the idea that history and routines can entrench processes or conditions, even if they are not ideal) can limit a firm's real or perceived options.[47] Internal firm hierarchies make a difference too. For example, photographic industry leader Polaroid committed early to developing a business based on digital imaging. It had the technical resources to develop the new technology. In the end, however, it failed to do so because of resistance and skepticism from established power structures within Polaroid itself.[48] In competitive terms, an innovation may have a critical advantage over slower-to-react competitors if it can gather and respond to information feedback quickly.

There is also the question of "fit" between how a firm understands its products and its mandate, and whether a particular innovation will take off there. Firms tend to want to stick with what they know best, especially if they are already successful and the perceived risks associated with innovation are high.[49] Consider the now-famous example of Xerox. By the late 1970s, Xerox's Palo Alto Research Center (PARC) had developed a number of computing technologies including the personal computer, the graphical user interface (with icons and pull-down menus), email, and improvements on the mouse. It failed to capitalize on any these products, apparently because its management saw the company as a chemicals-on-paper company, and the "paperless office" concept as a risk to its core business. It did not conceive of these innovations as part of what Xerox did, nor wanted to support. The geographic distance between PARC and Xerox's other business units – its headquarters in Stamford, Connecticut, manufacturing in Rochester, and office systems in Dallas – also made technology transfer difficult.[50] It was left to Steve Jobs of Apple to launch the Macintosh computer in 1984, after visiting the Xerox research center in 1979.

There are nearby limits on how much we can generalize about slippery concepts like culture and fit. Firms are "lumpy" internally, in terms of the strength and openness of their ties and other aspects of structure, and their lumps differ. Each firm has a unique profile. As a regulatory matter, the lesson is certainly that industry sector, "fit," and structural firm properties matter to how innovative firms might be, though the precise ways in which those considerations play out will vary.

HOW DO INNOVATIONS DEVELOP? CREATION, DIFFUSION, AND SWARMING

A key distinction in the innovation scholarship is between so-called "radical" and "incremental" innovations (to which was later added the idea of the "disruptive" innovation).[51] In 1997, Christopher Freeman and Luc Soete coined the terms "radical" and "incremental" to describe how much of a step change a particular product innovation represented, relative to current technology.[52] The terms caught on quickly and remain influential. Radical innovations are about big, paradigm-shifting, transformative change. Incremental innovations are small, seemingly mundane improvements based on learning through experience. The radical innovations in history (Freeman's examples are steam power, electricity, motorization, synthetic materials, and radio communications) were thought to be the ones that became catalysts for major structural changes in the economy, because they considerably reduced the cost of key inputs.[53] Later work seriously undermined this the initial dichotomy between "important" radical innovations and "unimportant" incremental ones. Measured in terms of impact, it now seems clear that the cumulative social and economic effects of incremental innovation are just as great as, if not greater than, those of radical innovations.[54] While on its own each incremental innovation is relatively innocuous, they are many and they build on each other.

The innovation literature tells us that geography also matters a great deal to innovation, in part because tacit knowledge (meaning subtle, context-specific, difficult-to-communicate knowledge) does not travel easily. It travels best through face-to-face interaction between people who share basic commonalities, like language, local knowledge, and shared assumptions. (Neither Charles Sabel nor, presumably, Friedrich Hayek would disagree with that.) Beyond just tacit knowledge, geography matters because innovation emerges through social interaction.[55] Even industries that rely on analytical knowledge tend to cluster geographically. Knowledge spillovers occur locally, meaning that new ideas tend to be communicated first through word of mouth before they are published. As well, once a region has attracted a critical mass of workers in the same industry, the concentrated career opportunities and the area's reputation as an industry center will be more likely to generate "buzz" and attract even more talent.[56]

How a firm is situated relative to other firms or actors in its space also matters. For example, sectors that are stable and dominated by a few large, established firms will present significant barriers to entry for innovators.[57] As well, recent scholarship has focused on how certain "network properties" may promote innovation, and the diffusion of innovations.[58] Networks can be held together by formal, contractual relationships or by informal ties. Either kind can be strong ("embedded") or it can be weak ("arms-length").[59] The scholarship suggests that weak ties are useful for searching for, finding and transferring novel information, while strong ties are better for transferring fine-grained or complex knowledge.[60] Optimally, in terms of capacity to innovate, firms will have both kinds of ties.[61] Individual or organizational relationships, as well, can be highly fluid, or relatively closed.[62]

How tight-knit a network is, and how embedded a particular firm is within it, also affect how innovative that network is likely to be. Of course, networks will be lumpy just as firms will be, and may be tightly knit in some places and not in others. In general, though, if a network's density is too low, the innovation scholars tell us that knowledge is not absorbed as efficiently into it. On the other hand, if a network's density is too high, novel information can be both harder to come by and harder to process.[63] Actors near the center of large, informal networks, with cross-organizational access to information and ideas, may be more innovative.[64] Actors with a relatively large number of links to others in the network are sometimes called "hubs." On the other hand, an entrepreneur who can bridge a "structural hole," connecting two networks or firms that have complementary information but are not otherwise connected, may be able to reap the significant benefits that flow from being a crucial connection point.[65]

Networks are enormously complex and varied, and this discussion only scratches the surface of the research that has been done by scholars in that field. Even once we have mapped a network's structure, the process by which information *diffuses* across a network adds another layer of variety and complexity. Innovation does not diffuse in a sequential, linear fashion, and the speed and degree of diffusion is not directly correlated to how useful the innovative idea seems to be. Factors that may affect the rate of diffusion include the perceived attributes of the innovation itself (its relative advantages, how compatible it is with existing technology, how complex it is, and whether it is testable or its results easily observable); but also the type of innovation decision needed (for example, it is easier to adopt an innovation if only one person has to make that decision, rather than a collective or organization); the communication channels available (for example, mass media or interpersonal exchange); the nature of the system (meaning the norm system into which the innovation would insert itself, the degree of interconnectedness, etc.); and simply how hard the innovator works to promote the innovation.[66]

Sometimes, as well, diffusion patterns have more to do with the status of the innovation initiator than with the innovation's inherent value. For example, "hubs" in networks can gather information from a large number of contacts, consolidate that knowledge, and propagate new ideas more easily. Innovations championed by hubs will diffuse more readily. On the flip side, this also means that the hub's ideas can outcompete other, even potentially superior, ideas.[67] Diffusion may also occur along cultural lines and can be affected by branding, as it were: that is, by how the innovation connects to useful or salient categories or relationships. For example, once psychologists defined dyslexia, technological reading innovations like speech recognition software and new type fonts, which were thought to respond to the needs of this new category of people, diffused more quickly.[68] As valuable as any particular innovation may be, these kinds of boosts also have an element of luck and timing to them, making the diffusion process unpredictable and uneven.

Isomorphism – meaning conformity or structural similarity – can also influence how innovations diffuse. As sociologists Paul DiMaggio and Walter Powell famously described, organizations sometimes come to resemble each other over time. Sometimes, especially under conditions of uncertainty, they engage in mimetic isomorphism – basically, imitation.[69] Sometimes, imitation is pure duplication that diffuses an innovation, potentially even into quite different contexts, without altering it at all.[70] Often, though, as an innovation diffuses, imitators will further innovate on the original innovation, in large and small ways, to adapt it to new circumstances and to gain an edge over their competitors.[71] This in turn can provoke significant growth and change.

For practical purposes, the extent of an innovation's diffusion may be at least as significant as its initial development. As Christopher Freeman and his coauthors have said,

> What matters in terms of major economic effects is not the date of the basic innovation... what matters is the diffusion of this innovation – what Schumpeter vividly described as the "swarming" process when imitators begin to realize the profitable potential of the new product or process and start to invest heavily.... Once swarming does start it has powerful multiplier effects in generating additional demands on the economy ... [which], in turn, induces a further wave of process and applications innovations. It is this combination of related and induced innovations which gives rise to expansionary effects.[72]

CAN WE APPLY THESE INSIGHTS TO FINANCIAL INNOVATION?

What emerges from this brief sketch of the general innovation literature is a sense of the unpredictable, complicated, almost organic way in which innovation develops, and the reason why it – and its undermining effect on regulation – is such a considerable challenge. Yet in many respects, the general literature is not entirely fit for purpose in trying to assess financial innovation. Narrowing the lens now to consider the structural attributes of the financial industry in particular, and how those attributes relate to its innovativeness, generates richer and more fruitful lines of inquiry. From there, we are in a better position to think about how financial regulation should be thinking about the phenomenon.

The innovation literature tells us that "big picture" contextual factors matter at a number of levels, and surely this is true in finance too. The overarching fabric of the legal system, and of economic and social systems, clearly matter very much in structuring background rules and innovation-philic conditions, including access to resources, stable rules of contract and property (including intellectual property), and the like. New technology, or inventions, may be catalysts for innovation; then again, they may lie fallow until and unless the necessary conditions for translation into practice arise. As a subject of regulation, it is the innovation – the practical implementation – and not the invention that should attract our attention.

Whether and how a particular opportunity will generate significant industry response in the form of new innovations clearly depends on multiple and nuanced contextual factors. Innovation arises within industries, sectors, geographic locations, firms, and networks as a shared practice, and the nature of those environments will influence how innovations are generated and transmitted. The relationship between a particular innovation and those environments matters too – some innovations are more "legible" than others to those that might seize on them. Framing, timing, receptivity, and reputation also influence how quickly and completely innovations are taken up. Phenomena like path dependence, isomorphism, and network effects demonstrate that the market does not operate as some pure force that lifts great new innovations into use, unadulterated, and ensures their strong adoption. Yet in the context of financial regulation, we still know relatively little about financial institutions' firm and network qualities, as they bear on how innovation develops within them.

For example, is it reasonable to assume that innovation across the global financial sector in the twenty-first century will necessarily evolve in the way that craft-based innovation did during the First Industrial Revolution?

(Probably not.) Will strong or weak, formal or informal ties operate in the same way? Some familiar attributes – the incrementalism, the importance of learning feedback loops, the fact that economic self-interest acts as a driver, and the creative energy produced by having to solve concrete problems – will likely continue to be important. In other ways, problems of complexity and scale make contemporary financial regulation much more complicated. It may be that financial instruments' intangible nature, and the shape-shifting possibilities inherent in innovation around them, make financial innovation more of a challenge for financial regulation than innovation is to regulation in other fields.

There is still a great deal that we do not know about precisely how financial innovation has evolved, and of course we cannot know for certain how it will evolve in the future. Nevertheless, with the innovation literature as a foundation we could begin to think about how to locate the challenge of innovation more centrally into the project of financial regulation. Any such effort would have to be tailored to the specific regulatory priorities that engaged, say, securities regulators or banking regulators at different scales. It would also have to be revisable based on experience and the meaningful examination of public priorities, and as industry conduct and contexts evolved. The focus on innovation as a regulatory challenge is not meant to replace existing provisions directed toward antifraud, protecting investors, fostering fair and efficient capital markets, or requiring microprudential standards and mitigating macroprudential risks. It is intended to ensure that the regulatory regime can continue to address those substantive purposes, even as financial innovation, dynamism, and uncertainty continue to alter the terrain on which it operates.

With this in mind, and extrapolating from the innovation literature described above, below are four high-level, epistemological questions to help structure decision-making around how exactly innovation is likely to present a challenge to regulation, in finance in particular. These questions also form one part of a broader decision-making roadmap for regulating around financial innovation, further developed in this book's Conclusion.

Who Is Innovating?

What do we need to know about the subjects of financial regulation, in terms of who is innovating? How do considerations like the nature of the innovative actors and their industry environment affect their innovative inclinations?

Finance being the somewhat chest-beating industry it is, Wall Street innovation stories often incline toward a sort of Great (or Infamous) Men of History-style, prominently featuring individuals like Michael Milken at

Drexel Burnham Lambert, Blythe Masters at JP Morgan, or John Meriwether at Salomon Brothers. Surely individuals have played key roles in the development of financial innovation, but experience shows that similar innovations were often being undertaken across the industry, suggesting not just firm-level but economy- or industry-level innovative drivers. The innovation literature also tells us that innovation is a social process and that we should look at firms, their institutional characteristics, and the networks in which they are embedded if we want to understand it.

Just trying to understand the firm and network characteristics of the New York-based, wholesale market financial innovators before the crisis – those geographically concentrated financial institutions that were creating and selling securitized and derivative assets on the OTC market, with other "sophisticated parties" – still leaves us with a rather large conceptual piece to chew on. Retail-oriented innovators, hedge funds, buy-side firms, London-based and international financial institutions, disruptive fintech firms, and others all operate in distinct ecosystems, and several may be relevant at once. Within the Wall Street subset, the industry was highly competitive, money-oriented (in the sense that one's status in the firm had a good deal to do with how much money one made), risk-taking, and generally aggressive. The Wall Street firms tended not to be loose, non-hierarchical adhocracies, in the way that tech companies typically aim to be; but nor were they orderly, routine-oriented work organizations in the mold of a mid-twentieth-century General Electric.

Years ago William Silber suggested, following Kenneth Arrow, that oligopolistic market structures in the American futures market incentivized innovation.[73] Whether American finance operates in an oligopolistic fashion is of course a question of great social, political, and economic consequence. For present purposes, though, whether Wall Street is oligopolistic and how this affects its influence in broader capital markets matters primarily in terms of how that would affect the development and diffusion of innovative ideas. Certainly we know that certain markets are concentrated,[74] and otherwise-small players may occupy large positions in particular niche markets, for example for particular commodities.[75] As well, in the years leading up to the financial crisis, large Wall Street firms increasingly found themselves on both sides of transactions, through what the innovation literature would describe as weak formal ties.[76] The link between concentrated markets and innovativeness appears to hold in the US financial sector, where large investment banks before the crisis reportedly were consistently the leading innovators,[77] and in the Canadian financial sector, where both market share and geographic centrality within hubs have been found to be positively associated with innovativeness.[78]

There also seems little doubt that New York and London were *hubs* for innovation in the wholesale market in the lead-up to the crisis.[79] Hubs propagate ideas more easily, and innovations championed by hubs diffuse more readily. Among the questions for which we do not currently have answers are: does innovation travel along the same contagion that risk does? Are network hubs necessarily also systemically important financial institutions? Presumably there would be overlap, but we do not know how much. As we discuss further in the next chapter, hubs do not exist only in economic space. They also, by virtue of their privileged position in social space, possess a degree of prestige that lends their innovations additional credibility and gravitas. As a function of cognitive or reputational geography, innovations that have been transmitted outward from recognized hubs may be more likely to be accepted on faith.

As a regulator trying to understand who the key innovators in one's industry are likely to be, conscious attention to hubs, culture, and market characteristics can help indicate where one should be concentrating one's energy. As well, as the innovation literature would propose, a regulator should be on the lookout for boundary-spanners, with a view to understanding what boundaries they are spanning and what new opportunities present themselves as a result of their involvement. A regulator must also be on the lookout for new players and outsider innovators seeking entry into lucrative markets or seeking to establish new ones.

As formal as all of this may sound, financial industry players and their regulators likely already have a good deal of contextual knowledge about these questions. More, and more granular, less anecdotal knowledge would be better. Yet even as a map is developed of a network and its properties, it will remain dynamic. Not only will firms' orientations toward innovation and their positions in particular markets change, but other firms – remember the high-frequency traders, and remember fintech – may be actively disrupting established networks or hubs, along with the products and markets with which they are preoccupied. To develop a fine-grained sense of one's industry network with a view to better understanding who the innovators are, only to miss another set of profoundly disruptive innovators because they do not fit into the schematic, would be ironic in the extreme.

What Are Their Innovations and Why Are They Pursuing Them?

Cross-country data on financial innovation are scarce, in part because financial firms historically have not sought to patent their innovations.[80] R&D expenditures and research staff data for financial institutions tend not to be collected either.[81] Tracking technical innovations is challenging, though not impossible through the kinds of efforts we see at the US Treasury's Office of Financial Research.[82]

It makes sense to begin by considering what kinds of purposes the innovator is seeking to advance through the innovation. Assuming the substantial presence of self-interest of the capitalist variety (as is probably safe in this industry, even if firms are not always perfect judges of what is in their self-interest), what advantages do the innovators hope to gain from the innovation, and how do these perceived benefits affect the nature of the innovations? In light of its characteristics, is this an innovation that is likely to diffuse across the industry and, if so, for what purposes?

Sometimes, financial innovations are developed for the purpose of putting assets to their most productive use, addressing inefficiencies and completing markets. Hedging risks as a form of insurance, or engaging in mutually beneficial arrangements like the currency swap that Salomon Brothers brokered for IBM and the World Bank in 1981, fall into this category. Where financial institutions can come up with ways to address inefficiencies on behalf of a paying client, we can expect to see innovations geared to those objectives. Innovations geared toward arbitrage opportunities across time and space – such as when high-frequency traders take advantage of tiny information gaps across exchanges, or when corporations engage in transfer pricing arrangements with overseas subsidiaries in order to avoid paying domestic tax – may be generally more problematic in public policy terms, even if strictly speaking they are still efforts to address inefficiencies. Even among these efficiency-oriented drivers of innovation, there are clearly differences between different kinds of innovations in terms of the purposes for which innovation is being undertaken, who is benefiting, and their potential social value. However, innovation may also be directed toward ends that have nothing at all to do with market efficiency, such as gaining a first-mover advantage,[83] edging out competitors,[84] extracting rents, or circumventing the burdens of regulation.[85] While some such goals are more pro-social (or, rather, somewhat less anti-social) than others, each puts a particular torque on the nature of the innovation, carries potentially unanticipated consequences, and leaves a potential gap between the innovator's private interest and goals, and the public's interest and regulatory goals.

In trying to understand what innovations firms are pursuing and why, one should consider where in the firm the innovation is happening, and what drives those units' operations. Most often, a financial institution's market-oriented or client-oriented profit centers will have the strongest incentives to develop profitable innovations in marketable products. This seems obvious, now, but it might not always have been so. As the Basel II Capital Accord structure arguably makes clear, before the crisis there was a certain degree of willingness to believe that the highest-performing financial institutions were as innovative around, for example, their risk modeling and compliance processes as they were around their wholesale business lines.[86]

Specific regulatory structures can also create specific new opportunities for innovation. It was the low regulatory burden imposed on asset-backed commercial paper in Canada, for example, that made ABCP such an attractive capital-raising vehicle and caused it to grow in volume, shape-shifting in the process. Regulation itself can also transform a sector profoundly enough to undermine established business functions or roles.[87] As the law changes, opportunities can change.[88] The deregulation of nearby spaces can also play a role, not only in how private actors choose to structure their innovative products and processes, but also in how regulators understand and implement their mandate.[89] On the other hand, as Lawrence Baxter puts it, "prohibiting an activity can just as surely generate innovation, either desirable or destructive, as permitting it."[90] On that front, regulators should pay particular attention to innovations that, for example, create products that can achieve the same ends as a regulated product without triggering regulation (as money market funds did). They should also pay particular attention to innovations that, like swaps at one point, are legible to the market – everyone understands the purpose they are serving – even while they are illegible to the regulatory structure.[91]

Again, none of this work can proceed on the assumption that market opportunities or the market itself will remain static. The most disruptive opportunities may well arise outside conventional financial structures, particularly in a context, like today's, in which advances in data analysis and communication technology have made peer-to-peer lending and other forms of (partially) disintermediated interactions efficient and effective.

How Do Innovations Develop?

An innovation in one discipline can also have unexpectedly broad knock-on effects. For example, a key invention that made the innovation of securities derivatives really accelerate was a mathematical one: the Black-Scholes option pricing model.[92]

Options have been around for a long time, and traders long bought and sold them based on a sort of instinctive assessment of their value. Many considered options markets to be little better than gambling.[93] Then, in 1973, economists Fischer Black and Myron Scholes published a new formula, which came to be called the Black-Scholes model. It established a better mathematical basis for calculating the premium of an option and thereby its present value.[94] Establishing the present value of an option with greater clarity made option contract pricing easier, more transparent, more replicable, and more consistent.[95] As applied in the markets, it was an innovation that moved options pricing from the realm of instinct and experience to the realm of calculability.

Black-Scholes revolutionized options markets. The model was so important that a leading electronics manufacturer created a handheld calculator specifically designed to use the Black-Scholes model.[96] However, its effects were even more wide-ranging than that. As Donald MacKenzie has argued in his insightful sociological account of how financial models affected financial markets, the model also transformed how people *saw* options markets. It conferred an aura of legitimacy on derivatives, reframing their pricing from some form of gambling to a model for "efficient pricing" and perfecting markets (meaning allocating risk precisely to the parties most willing to bear it).[97] The model slotted smoothly into an existing commercial opportunity, an essential precondition to a successful and widely diffused innovation, but to some extent it was the model's legitimacy-conferring powers that transformed the market as a whole.

The innovation literature also tells us that innovators often "make do," repurposing existing tools and knowledge rather than investing in costly and time-consuming new discovery efforts. This suggests that splashy new inventions are not necessarily the thing to look for. Even the notorious quantitative analysts working on some lower floor of a pre-crisis Wall Street investment bank are more likely to work from existing knowledge and products than to start completely fresh. Thinking of ways to tweak existing tools to try to solve a discrete, slightly different problem generates new iterations of a product and new uses for it. Invention can lead to innovation, and an invention can have a strong impact on an existing market, as the Black-Scholes model did on options markets, but one would want to look equally at what products or innovations seem to have been repurposed or translated to new contexts, or seem for some reason to have emerged from dormancy.

One difficulty particular to tracking private sector financial innovations is that financial institutions are more likely to protect their innovations by bringing products to market as quickly as possible, rather than for example by seeking patent protection for them before marketing them. Speed is secrecy. The amount of advanced or even real-time information available about private financial innovations will be limited. Instead, regulators may need to try to track other telltales.

For example, all of these things may be markers of innovation: sharp changes in supply and demand, the emergence of new asset uses and transaction patterns, changes in the use of assets, the sudden rise of a new market (like asset-backed commercial paper), industry actors suddenly taking on large positions (as AIG did in credit default swaps before the crisis) or showing sudden enthusiasm for a new market structure (like the multiple exchanges that now exist outside New York City), or rapid growth in substitution and combinations of financial instruments or contracts.[98] Other unexpected or seemingly inexplicable phenomena – a decision to build a fiber-optic cable from Chicago to New Jersey,[99] or a sudden decision to reallocate legal work to different law firms – would also, to the extent that they became known to regulators and are appreciated as relevant, provide clues to significant new business innovations on the part of financial institutions.[100]

Tracking changes in perception and norms, not just products, may be useful as well. This requires a separate level of familiarity with the industry, and of familiarity across time. One could watch language and look out for assertions that "this time is different" (sometimes accompanied by the observation, when talking to regulators, that there is nothing different going on over here at all); one could assess the continued or diminished in-house prestige of those who might once have been recognized as "wise old bankers."[101] If wisdom and experience seem to be marginalized within a firm, this may suggest something about the speed of cultural and business change, and it may signal that there are new limits to one's visibility into the firm as well. In times of change one should not assume that senior financial institution leaders necessarily understand all of what is going on, and one should not assume that things are necessarily the same as they were even a short while ago. At the same time, one should not necessarily accept assertions, like those that were pervasive before the crisis, that regulation is behind the times and needs to work harder to keep up with industry. Comments of that nature may be a sign that the regulatory regime is at risk of being undermined and needs to respond, but in skeptical and independent-minded, not catch-up, ways.

Where and When Does "Swarming" Happen?

The innovation literature is helpful in that it helps us to recognize the difference between radical, or seismic and incremental, or sedimentary innovation patterns. All the same, and even if we concede for now the existence of these pure types (which we return to in the next two chapters), even an incremental development in finance still seems to proceed remarkably quickly. Entirely new markets emerge with startling speed. Why is this?

Part of the answer may be that, unlike craft-based innovation around physical objects during the First Industrial Revolution in Britain, modern financial innovation innovates around intangibles, and employs (or did, quite recently) large numbers of exceptionally talented quantitative analysts to participate in that innovation. Certainly, the financial instruments that have been developed over the last few decades rely on complicated mathematical formulas and multi-layered payout structures, risk analytics and the like. This is not the whole story, however.

Weak or ineffective intellectual property rights regimes combined with the relative ease with which new financial products can be reverse engineered means that, historically, successful financial innovations are quickly imitated.[102] Financial firms innovate in order to gain first-mover advantage and hopefully to acquire a larger market share than those who adopt the innovation later.[103] Imitator firms also want to reproduce innovations and enter the market as soon as possible after the original innovator, because in at least some contexts, the benefits dissipate quickly: every new market entrant ends up receiving a smaller share of the market over the long term.[104] A herding effect can easily develop as each additional firm chooses to adopt an innovation, and the pressure to follow suit increases among those firms that have not yet adopted it.[105] Because the benefits dissipate so quickly, firms have an incentive to create ever more innovations more frequently in pursuit of the first-mover advantage.[106] For all of these reasons, it is not unusual in the financial sector for initially successful innovations to experience rapid and widespread diffusion, even before the long-term effects of the innovation are understood. Schumpeter's "swarming" process is turbocharged. In markets, like the emerging peer-to-peer lending market or other aspects of the sharing economy, where developing a critical mass of market presence is key to success, the rush to move products to market will be even stronger.

Moreover, financial innovation is not always subject to the same market-based or regulatory limits that would slow the growth of innovation in other sectors. Transparency and price discovery are hindered in the OTC derivatives markets for several reasons: the complex nature of the products being sold makes them hard to understand; what Ben Bernanke called a "global savings glut"[107] meant that new products that promised higher returns were scooped up rather indiscriminately; and there is the uncertainty associated with multifactorial events in the capital markets. Often there will be winners and losers associated with a product, but unlike a "lemon" of a car or a defective consumer product, with intangible financial products it can be difficult to determine after the fact whether the product was flawed, or whether money was lost for other reasons.[108] All of this undermines market-based penalties for poor quality products.

To make matters worse, at least with respect to mortgage-backed securities, the originate-to-distribute model that was adopted in the United States meant that those creating the original securitized products for sale had no remaining economic interest in the underlying mortgages, thereby stripping out internal accountability. What was perceived as an implicit government guarantee for the large banks – the conviction that the US government would not allow large financial institutions to fail – swept away whatever additional internal discipline might have otherwise remained. Finally, by comparison to some other industries, financial innovators also have considerable autonomy.[109] While innovators in some other industries are generally subject to independent quality control checks – in the way that the US Food and Drug Administration licenses foods and new pharmaceuticals – financial innovators are not.

Meanwhile, imitation and diffusion continued unabated. In fact, it turns out that imitation may be more likely to have dangerous consequences in highly uncertain environments, like the derivatives market, because herding behavior continues even while outcomes lag.[110] In other words, imitators in particular may choose simply to keep replicating an innovation until there is some signal not to. This may be the case in a sector like finance, where long-term outcomes for innovative products may be difficult to anticipate in real time and, as the financial crisis demonstrates, may not be apparent until a sudden and widespread negative shock occurs.

All of these factors may contribute to swarming, with the result that a financial innovation develops a substantial market presence before its risks are recognized. Yet as instructive as the postmortem above may be on the limits of market discipline before the financial crisis, it may not say a great deal about how the next crisis, borne of financial innovation, may develop. Even as we build potential new regulatory responses to financial innovation, we should recognize that the next challenging innovation may come from outside these parameters. For example, the Uber ride-sharing company argues that it is simply not a taxi company, and therefore is not subject to regulations that govern taxi companies. Are some kinds of fintech, then, just not banking (or securities, or money)?

TAKEAWAY POINTS: REFRAMING REGULATION AROUND INNOVATION

Recall the three misperceptions described at the end of Chapter 1, as a way of thinking about the problems that financial innovation has presented for regulation. The first misconception relates to the impact and significance of complexity in finance. Financial innovation produces real complexity, which needs to be taken seriously, even while we should be also mindful of how complexity arguments can be pressed into service by private financial institutions in order to try to reduce regulatory oversight. We should not underestimate the importance of articulating an agenda for regulation that does not get caught up in the frisson and fascination associated with financial complexity. Second, we should not assume that the regulatory moment is the crucial one, since innovation alters products and contexts before and behind that moment, and alters conversations after it. Addressing this problem requires greater mindfulness about *when* problems associated with innovation arise – when does financial innovation arise and, just as importantly, can regulation reach out beyond formal regulatory moments and capture significant before-and-after considerations? Third, we should not imagine that regulation sits outside innovation and is unaffected by it. This misconception, as well, requires that we look more closely at the ways in which regulation and innovation intersect, and the effects that innovation has on regulatory conversations, regulatory boundaries, and regulatory bearings. I offer a more general model for developing innovation-ready regulation in this book's Conclusion. Even at this point, though, the innovation literature has given us a new vocabulary to try to talk about these vexing problems, and it offers some conceptual handholds for trying to grapple with them.

For example, in finance anyway, the absence of internal or market-based safeguards to validate a financial innovation's viability may demand a stronger regulatory presence at the "front end," before such products make it to market at all.[111] It may also be useful to look at other critical control points or junctures, bearing in mind however that innovation will not constrain itself to those moments. Adopting either strategy will require that regulators have a clear technical understanding of the products in question. But every bit as important as that technical knowledge will be that the regulator maintain a sense of its bearings and a general appreciation for why, details aside, the regulator's function is to safeguard the public interest at a broader level. Structurally building in new mechanisms for fostering greater representativeness is part of the puzzle, as discussed in this book's Conclusion.

Regulators should also bear in mind the possibility that by the time they are having a detailed discussion with an industry actor about the technical merits of a particular innovation, as US credit rating agencies did with mortgage backed securities (not that they did not have other problems that undermined their credibility), or as the SEC did with respect to rulemaking around Dodd-Frank, at a certain fundamental level they have already ceded substantial ground. The point is not that detailed regulation-making can be avoided, or that consultation and expertise are irrelevant; only that the regulator must come to such engagements with a clear understanding of its perils, and of the regulatory mandate vis-à-vis the public interest.

As well, as above, it will always be essential to watch the boundaries and assumptions that delimit the regulatory sphere, not least if licensing or other potentially substantial regulatory requirements will be implemented, and there are nearby unregulated spaces to be colonized.[112] One should even assume that regulation will provoke further innovation – particularly in a field like finance, where regulatory requirements shape so much of the framework for these intangible products – sometimes in unanticipated ways and quite potentially in ways that undermine the regulatory structure itself.

Diffusion complicates the regulatory task too, because we cannot assume that a particular financial innovation will look the same as it diffuses. (We discuss diffusion further in Chapter 8.) Imitators and diffusers can be expected to incrementally modify some innovations that enter their spheres of conduct. As well, there can be translation from one field to another (such as new mathematical concepts affecting finance, as the Black-Scholes option pricing model did) and also contagion across scales or jurisdiction. An innovation that operates a particular way in one field can have very different effects in another. Remember that Black-Scholes had an effect on individual transactions' pricing, but by legitimizing derivatives pricing it also provoked a massive growth in the industry as a whole. Consider also that in the run-up to the financial crisis, changes in microeconomic policy (around, for example, how financial institutions track the amount of capital they need to keep in reserve) directly, if unexpectedly, affected macroeconomic policy (for example, the amount of credit available in the economy as a whole).

Jurisdictional boundaries could affect a financial regulator's ability to see a phenomenon's full effects. Whether a regulator decides to track the effects of the innovation at the individual level as a consumer protection regulator might, or at the systemic level as a prudential regulator might, can influence what it sees as the "main effect." Regulators would want to communicate about innovations with crosscutting significance and across geographical or jurisdictional boundaries as innovations diffused. The fact that the regulator is tracking dynamic innovations, rather than specific, theoretically static products, should not change the importance of regulatory communication (and it will not resolve its failings or tensions).[113] As always, it is crucial that the necessary regulators are involved in decision-making and are coordinating effectively with each other. And always and perpetually, the best-laid plans above will need to be revisited, time and again, as (or hopefully before) new waves of innovation break. One cannot commit too much to a static vision of an industry without losing sight of innovations happening at the margins, or beyond the realm of that vision.

Erik Gerding has argued that financial innovation has been a manifest feature of every major financial bubble over the last several hundred years.[114] So, he says, has "regulatory instability" – the fact that regulation cannot sustain itself across time, as memory of the bust fades and new innovations crop up. The problem is that regulation gets swept up in the zeitgeist and erodes. It cannot keep its bearings in a bubble. There is something markedly time-bound about our conception of innovation – a sort of psychological procyclicality in our thinking. When the "stock" of financial innovation is soaring, contrarians and others – including the formerly "wise old heads" of banking[115] – who would suggest that we be cautious, are marginalized, if not ridiculed. When the "stock" of financial innovation is down, it has few defenders in the public arena (even while we can hardly imagine actually doing without it).

The regulatory response across time has either been to address the *specific* loophole or regulatory opportunity through which the new bubble expanded, with financial innovation as its mechanism, or to try to mitigate against the negative *effects* of innovation – limiting its potential downsides – in both cases without paying a lot of attention to the underlying phenomenon itself. This is a mistake. The urge toward innovation and creative boundary-pushing in the service of pecuniary gain has not been drummed out of the financial sector, or out of the economy as a whole. It is not evident that, post-financial crisis, we are better informed or more thoughtful in our regulatory approach to innovation than we were pre-crisis. Closing loopholes and addressing obvious incentive problems, as we have tried to do in the wake of the financial crisis, is surely part of a good regulatory response, but it does not confront the fact that financial innovation will – over time but recurrently – erode or undermine or circumvent whatever regulatory structures we erect.

Our experience with the financial crisis has undermined the idea that "simply better" technical regulation could "harness" innovation in the service of better outcomes for everyone. The alternative claim, more popular after the financial crisis, that we might be able to distinguish "good" innovation from "bad" *ex ante*, and foster the first while stifling the second, is equally misguided. As different as these assertions may be, both assume that regulation can somehow impose its will on this force, innovation, which in these accounts is still not more than partially described or understood. There is no need to either condemn or blindly celebrate innovation at some ideological level, but there is a need to recognize its persistently corrosive effect on regulatory fit and effectiveness over time.

Perhaps the main thing that comes out of this chapter's inquiry is a realization of how much contextual information we must actually have, not only about how financial innovation in particular develops but also about how to track innovation's effects across scales, if we hope to build regulation that is capable of operating within such a fluid environment without simply ceding its authority to those it aims to regulate. The above proposes a series of questions geared toward developing a regulatory regime that is more problem-oriented, data-heavy, and flexible than even the most flexible regulation schemes, even while it adopts those strategies *not* in the pursuit of more innovation, but in the stubborn pursuit of beyond-innovation regulatory goals aligned with our broader social values.

Time, and timing, are persistent challenges for regulation and the next two chapters consider innovation in that vein. We talk more about so-called seismic (radical) and sedimentary (incremental) innovations and the kinds of specific technical regulatory responses we might find useful in responding to each one. Of course, real-life innovations do not fall into these two neat conceptual categories. All the same, in trying to grapple with the problem of time, the labels are useful as framing devices. Relatively more seismic or more sedimentary innovations can raise different regulatory challenges and should attract different kinds of regulatory attention, even while we strive to remember that the world is not so tidy as that.

7

Seismic Innovation: The Radical Step Change as Regulatory Opportunity

Technology does not inflate like a balloon, expanding human power over nature evenly in all directions and at all scales. It grows like a sea urchin: long spines of ability radiate out towards specific needs and desires.[1]

This chapter's purpose is to describe the idea of a seismic innovation as a phenomenon and, just as importantly, as a framing device for regulation. It is important to be up-front about one thing: at any universal level, the very existence of a seismic pattern of innovation is highly disputable. A seemingly seismic pattern will always depend heavily on embedded questions of scale. Yet this is not to say that it may not be useful to talk about it, in particular contexts and for particular purposes.

The innovation scholarship talks a lot about seismic, or what it calls "radical," innovations. It draws a distinction between radical and "incremental," or what I call sedimentary, innovation. Radical innovations are described as typically involving "a *discontinuity* in products and processes," often produced through research and development departments.[2] Mensch describes a radical innovation as one that requires a new factory and/or market for its use.[3] Perhaps more accessibly, we can think of this kind of innovation as creating a need, and the opportunity to fill it, where we had not previously identified one. I did not imagine, let alone "need," a smartphone as a central personal accouterment until it existed. This is the paradigm shift, the disruption, the transformative break with the past. It is this image of innovation that captures the romantic imagination. Radical, or what I prefer to call "seismic," innovation produces the dramatic step changes that we humans are naturally adept at recognizing,[4] that we tell stories about, and that most centrally capture the hopes and dreams that we hold out for innovation.

Business scholars often define radical/seismic innovations in terms of how disruptive they are to the status quo. That is, they focus on the infrastructural investments and market share that are overturned when a seismic innovation transforms its business environment.[5] We can think of many examples – of how, seemingly overnight (though not really) Netflix undermined Blockbuster; Google maps undermined dashboard GPS gadgets; smartphones with cameras undermined the digital camera industry (after it in turn had undermined film, darkroom developing, and so on); Uber and Airbnb are undermining the taxi and hotel industries; and container shipping undermined break bulk shipping and the economies built around it, vastly accelerating globalization in the process. Because we are concerned with the regulatory implications of seismic innovation, however, its disruptiveness to other market players is less central here than its relationship to regulation, including its potentially disruptive effect on regulatory capacity.

While the two concepts are similar, the metaphor of radical innovation as "seismic" underlines its dislocating, ground-shaking, unpredictable character. It helps us to focus on the magnitude and location of the transformative innovative event, meaning that our conceptual lens can incorporate multi-firm or even industry-wide innovations, in ways that are relevant if what we care about is the innovative phenomenon itself and the challenge it presents for regulation. Seismic changes are transformative and sudden, but not necessarily characterized by the kind of intentionality that has come to be associated with the word "radical." As well, like human responses to earthquakes, the response to seismic innovation is heavily human-dependent, and heavily dependent on prior structures (like building integrity in the physical context, or regulatory capacity and prior industry features in the financial innovation context). The word "radical" has an acontextual quality and suggests a total break with the past but, in reality, background conditions will always influence how an innovation is received and responded to.[6]

For our purposes, then, a seismic innovation is one in which:

(1) an innovation, or a suite of closely related innovations, is newly or unexpectedly being applied at a level – in terms of volume, or breadth, or magnitude – that outstrips prior experience, such that a regulator does not have useful comparables from which to extrapolate in making sense of the new seismic innovation,

(2) with a rate of adoption or diffusion that is too rapid to allow the regulator to gather sufficient data in real time to know how to react, and,

(3) with the potential to significantly alter the landscape on which regulation operates.

Faced with such a phenomenon, how should a regulator react?

The first difficulty arises in identifying something as authentically seismic. Consider Figure 7.1. Is the increasing use of asset-backed commercial paper in the United States from 2000 to 2009, as compared to the use of "normal," non-securitized commercial paper, evidence of a seismic innovation there?

The answer may be yes; that is, that we could defensibly describe the trajectory above, across the timeframe above, as such. As Figure 7.1 shows, over a short period of time, US ABCP came to be issued at a volume that at its peak was more than sixty times the level of old-style commercial paper issued by non-financial firms at the same time. The rate of adoption may have been too rapid to allow the regulator to gather sufficient data and to know how to react, though this may be more debatable. Arguably, a regulator might have twigged to the significance of the new kind of commercial paper somewhere in the two years prior to the peak, during which commercial paper volumes were increasing steadily. Certainly, ABCP had the potential to alter the landscape on which regulation operated, and it did. As we know from Chapter 1, commercial paper (in Canada, and the US as well, and elsewhere) has been around a long time and has historically been considered to be low-risk, because it was thought that only large, well-capitalized corporations would find a market for their unsecured debt, and the chances that a such a corporation would suffer an adverse credit event within such a short time window was very low. Asset-backed commercial paper is the newer product of securitization plus commercial paper, which changed the very nature of the asset. Unlike old-style commercial paper, asset-backed commercial paper was not

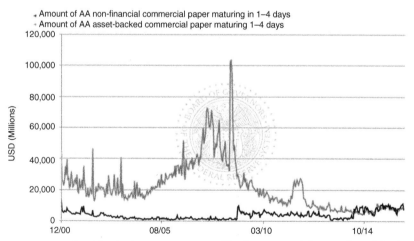

FIGURE 7.1. Asset-backed versus non-securitized commercial paper issued in the United States, 2000–2009 (data source: US Federal Reserve Flow of Funds).

safe, and was not backstopped either by the assets of a sound institution, nor by the market discipline that the regulatory structure assumed would come to bear on unsecured loans.

What about deepwater oil drilling in the Gulf of Mexico? Figure 7.2 is taken from the US National Commission struck in the wake of the 2010 BP Deepwater Horizon Oil Spill and Offshore Drilling, which depicts wells drilled in the Gulf of Mexico by water depth.

Looking at the definitional criteria above, is the increase in the number and depth of wells across this timeframe sufficiently steep to qualify deepwater oil drilling as a seismic innovation? Was adoption too fast to allow the regulator to develop sufficient data on the risks associated with deepwater drilling and to react appropriately? Did deepwater oil drilling have the potential to significantly alter the landscape on which regulation operated?

Three observations flow from these questions. First, what counts as a "seismic" innovation will be a matter of interpretation, and it is far easier to identify something as putatively seismic after the fact than it is in real time. Typically, the difference between a seismic and sedimentary innovation will be a matter of degree, not kind, and will depend heavily on scale.[7] Whether an innovation looks seismic will depend on one's frame of reference, not only across time but also across geography, industry, regulatory jurisdiction, and any number of other factors. The diagram above only examines one geographical region

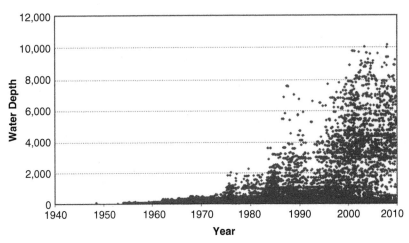

FIGURE 7.2. Wells drilled in the Gulf of Mexico by water depth, 1940–2010. (source: National Commission on the BP Deepwater Horizon Oil Spill and Offshore Drilling (ed.), *Deep-water: The Gulf Oil Disaster and the Future of Offshore Drilling* (United States Government Printing: Washington, DC, 2011), p. 41)

within one jurisdiction, and of course deepwater drilling operated in a broader and more varied way than that. Moreover, something that looks like a significant spike in new activity at a particular scale and in retrospect may be exceedingly difficult to identify as significant while it is taking place, particularly in more complex environments, which are more likely to be characterized by a lot of what economists call "noise."[8] These make for frustrating conditions for regulation.

Second, regulatory structures and public action can produce conditions that lead to seismic innovations in different ways. In the context of deepwater oil drilling in the Gulf of Mexico, for example, given the US regulator's now well-documented shortcomings, the question of whether an innovation is being adopted too quickly for a regulator to be able to respond cannot be divorced from the question of how robust, effective, and responsive the regulatory infrastructure is in the first place. In each of the three examples we discuss below, public action in the form of regulation or judicial intervention co-created seismic innovations by establishing conditions that incentivize growth, either actively or through inaction, deregulation, and delay.

Finally, given that public legal architecture can play a role in co-creating seismic innovations, public actors like regulators should not be apologetic about intervening in forceful ways in what they may have the power to *deem* as seismic innovations, particularly where (as may often be the case) a seismic innovation proceeds along an unanticipated trajectory, at unexpected speed, or while throwing off unexpected consequences. The argument here is not that some innovations will be irrefutably recognized as seismic; that may not be the case, but as a framing device the label of seismicity is still important. Our popular romance with innovation notwithstanding, seismic innovations as defined here raise particular challenges for regulators and risks for society, and responding to them may sometimes require proactive and muscular regulatory responses. Surely it need not always take a disaster to gin up the necessary political will and regulatory resources to act.

Note that responding will require a regulator to make a subjective determination that in fact a seismic innovative phenomenon is at work. The fact that a determination is subjective, however, does not make it invalid. Identifiably "seismic" innovations will be less common than sedimentary ones. However, so long as it is done judiciously and plausibly, labeling an innovation as such may in fact help to highlight the urgency of the situation for others (like elected representatives) whom the regulator may need to enlist for support. Among its benefits, describing an innovation as seismic or radical can be a crucial rhetorical tool.

THE CHARACTERISTICS OF SEISMIC INNOVATION

The innovation literature tells us that, most of the time, innovation develops in a sedimentary fashion, with layers of relatively modest modifications, translations, and imitations building incrementally on underlying innovations as they diffuse, collectively producing significant change over time. We discuss these in the next chapter. Sometimes, though, a particular innovation develops in a seismic pattern. Even if it is difficult to draw a bright line, for practical purposes the distinction between seismic and sedimentary innovation is not meaningless: as a matter of degree, we can agree that certain innovations are faster-moving than others, and bring with them quickly developing and transformative consequences. As well, if we have a particular reason to be concerned about developments at a particular scale, it can be useful, even necessary, to recognize a seismic pattern for those purposes, regardless of whether the same pattern is evident at some different scale.

For example, using *The Economist*'s simile, an initial seismic innovation (such as a financial instrument with strikingly new characteristics) may create a new sea urchin "spine" that heads in a new direction (for example, creating a new market or business model). Thereafter, even though other firms rush to imitate and incrementally innovate around that first innovation, the suite of closely related innovations remain collectively identifiable as a "spine" for the rapid adoption of the innovation and its close variants, and the concentration of the innovators' efforts around something with which no one has more than limited experience.

In finance, as a function of financial innovators' desire to seize the first-mover advantage in a competitive market characterized by weak property rights, combined with minimal "backstop" market or regulatory mechanisms to slow innovation down, innovation may proceed more quickly and new technology may diffuse more rapidly. Potentially this makes some financial innovations candidates for framing as seismic. The industry's own imagery may support this: more than one observer has described trading in futures or derivatives markets as equivalent to another kind of voyage into the unknown – space exploration.[9]

According to the innovation scholarship, there is also a size component to innovation, in that (at least in pharmaceuticals, and perhaps in other industries) a large majority of the most transformative innovations come from a minority of well-resourced firms. Seismic innovation can require high amounts of managerial, technological, and entrepreneurial skill and financial support.[10] Thus, active efforts at innovation are risky ventures in which only the most dominant firms usually partake.[11] Although the drivers in finance are different from those in the pharmaceutical industry, large firms are the leading innovators in finance as well, presumably as a function of resources.[12] Whether they are leaders in producing seismic innovations is less clear, although the large US investment banks' enormous exposure to risky derivatives markets, as demonstrated by the crisis itself, suggests that they were heavily implicated in generating those pre-crisis innovations.[13] Understanding how seismic innovations develop, and the characteristics of the private firms involved in their development, can provide crucial information to a regulator concerned with the phenomenon.

The literature also tells us that dominant firms may benefit more from seismic innovations, and that market players near the center of their networks are better able to diffuse their innovations. Large firms' advantages in terms of superior product support and expertise also enhance the value, to them, of their seismic innovations as compared to innovations by less dominant players.[14] For example, all else being equal, a dominant bank that launches a peer-to-peer lending platform will have a better chance of becoming dominant in that sector as well, than would an external challenger. Seismic innovations also may be more valuable to their innovators than sedimentary ones, in terms of the ability to capture market share and seize greater profit margins. Truly new products have a greater financial value than updates of existing products, and highly innovative products seem to surpass moderately innovative products in terms of their success rate and return on investment.[15] In the aggregate, this means that the benefits of seismic innovations may be both greater, and more likely to be concentrated among already-dominant players.

Below are three narrative examples that might help us to think further about the relationship between seismic innovation and regulatory action, including responses to it: railway industry financial innovation during the American Gilded Age, deepwater oil drilling in the Gulf of Mexico, and the growth of securitization and the derivatives market in recent decades. The point is not that these three stories are necessarily typical; the research needed to make that claim has not been done. The point of these anecdotes is just to get us wondering about the relationship between regulation and seismic innovation, in particular around the claim above: that regulatory structures may generate opportunities for seismic innovation to take off. As a result, without downplaying how challenging it is to label something as "seismic" in real time, regulation may also have both the opportunity and the obligation to intervene as it is emerging. In particular, if an ostensibly seismic innovation fits the three criteria above – growth that outstrips prior experience and existing data, a rate of adoption that is too rapid to allow for gathering data, and significant potential to alter the landscape – a regulator should seriously consider whether it should be taking steps to intervene, before a disaster forces its hand.

American Railroads and Financial Innovation in the Gilded Age

Railroads were transformative, nation-building, revolutionary forces in American history across much of the nineteenth century. In the years prior to the Civil War, railroads' funding needs created the modern investment banking house, centralized and institutionalized the American capital market in New York, and established modern trading and speculation activity, including on margin, on the New York Stock Exchange. Trading volumes soared, from a low of only thirty-one shares traded on one day in March 1830, to hundreds of thousands of shares being traded weekly by the 1850s.[16] The changes the railroads wrought – and not only in finance but in immigration, urban construction, and trans-Atlantic connections – can plausibly be described as seismic across the time scale of those antebellum decades.[17] Yet even though the state was involved in funding railroad construction in these years, the lack of public or regulatory oversight makes the example less germane for our purposes than the Gilded Age period of railway development, in which public institutions (in the form of courts) played a more structural role.

Railroad building in the United States boomed after the Civil War as the population surged, important technological inventions were made (in steel manufacturing, electricity, investment capital and communications), and the industrial economy grew. Within this context, the development of transcontinental railroad lines, with the help of generous federal land grants, was transformative. Their growth generated demand for multiple other industries, including glass, lumber, and steel, and opened much of the western United States to settlement.[18] Through the second half of the nineteenth century, railroads continued to be the largest and most strategically important industry in the United States.

This is not to say that all railroads were necessarily well run or economically viable, however, and the industry was rife with corruption. In many parts of the country, competition was fierce. Fixed costs associated with railroad building were always exceptionally high. The economic Panic of 1873 bankrupted many companies and temporarily ended growth; in the Panic of 1893, which was substantially caused by concerns about railway overbuilding and inefficiencies, fully one-quarter of American railroads failed.[19] Then followed a period of consolidation such that, by 1906, nearly two-thirds of railroad miles were controlled by seven entities, many of them under the effective control of bankers, notably J.P. Morgan and Company as well as Kuhn, Loeb and Company, who had invested heavily in defaulting railroads and then helped to reorganize and then monitor them.[20] How did that happen?

Among other factors, the challenges associated with railroad financing spurred an extraordinary surge in financial innovation in the late 1800s. As Peter Tufano describes it, the reason that railroads fell into distress so often was twofold: first, due to high fixed costs and fierce competition, they needed a lot of cash. Distressed railways needed large influxes of cash over the short term simply to keep running. Second, over the longer term, corporate governance had to be improved if they were to be kept from failing again.[21]

Railroad regulation was minimal in this common law era. Courts were the primary public players, and it was courts that solved the railways' short-term cash flow problem. In view of the perceived public interest in keeping the railroads running, judges modified existing security contracts and the law of liens, often to the bewilderment of the business community. For example, they established new super-senior priority rights for new investors, so that new investors would not be inferior to existing creditors in being paid out (and therefore had an incentive to invest). They limited junior creditors' ability to hold up receiverships by establishing "upset values," which were court-ordered prices for dissenting creditors' interests in the event that a consensual reorganization agreement could not be reached. Courts tended to set the upset values low, so they operated like a penalty default that ratcheted up creditors' incentives to reach agreement.[22]

Since there was no stable national bankruptcy statute in the United States until 1898, courts also developed common law bankruptcy and reorganization rules. In particular, they developed the equity receivership, under which courts appointed an interim manager (the receiver) to run the company and help direct its reorganization into a new business entity. With support from those receivers, courts held that secured creditors of the bankrupt organization could not seize and sell off railroad assets on bankruptcy. In exchange for losing this well-established creditor's right, they received new post-reorganization control rights over management in the form of covenants (binding positive and negative obligations on the part of the firm to bond holders), and sometimes exceptionally strong new voting rights, for example, for preferred shareholders. In addition, it became common practice to establish "voting trusts" – committees of three to five experts, again generally the bankers, to oversee a reorganized railway's management and, standing in the shoes of ostensibly dispersed shareholders, to decide voting matters for five years after reorganization.

Notably, courts seem to have established super-senior priority rights on reorganization, low upset prices, and new legal arrangements on the advice of reorganization committees – that is, those same bankers, especially J.P. Morgan and his associates, who tended to be appointed to manage, oversee, and reorganize the railways. The courts would only have done so if they accepted the argument that the rights of creditors appearing before them had to be sacrificed to the broader need to put the railroads on sounder footing. In direct response to judicial interventions in the financial markets,[23] private parties – again, principally the same professional trustees – then engaged in their own round of innovations. Some of the key innovations they developed, which were aimed at making cash payment obligations more manageable over the long term, included deferred coupon debt (which provided for temporary reductions in interest with the coupon rate stepping up over time, or which paid interest on existing bonds with additional bonds, or which provided for extremely long maturity rates – even over 100 years – with low interest rates); contingent charge securities (which allowed companies to skip annual cash payments to bond holders without being considered to be in default, either if the company failed to collect enough earnings or simply at management's discretion); and the creation of voting trusts as described above. Taken together, these innovations created stronger *ex ante* control measures over corporate management, even while reducing *ex post* creditors' rights in the event of bankruptcy – and sidelining courts. Interestingly, weakening creditors' rights was what it took to make bankruptcies less likely, but also had the advantage, from the creditors' perspective, of "reduc[ing] one element of risk faced by investors; namely, judicial redefinition [of their rights]."[24]

Together, these inter-dependent public and private innovations amounted to a wholesale change to securities and receivership strategies over slightly more than two decades. They also probably made possible the enormous consolidation that took place in the railroad industry after 1893, and made J.P. Morgan and his associates dominant players in the railroad industry and in finance generally. The concentration of power within the railroad industry produced its own problems, of course, and ultimately attracted antitrust attention.[25] From 1887 through 1980, the railroads then became subject to the Interstate Commerce Commission's regulation of common carriers, with the obligations and benefits accruing from that Welfare State-era structure.[26]

Whether or not this suite of financial and legal innovations qualifies as a seismic innovation in today's terms, certainly by the standards of its time it was extraordinary in its rapid development, the breadth of its diffusion across the industry and beyond, and the depth of its impact. We should also notice the coordinated public/private effort through which these innovations were adopted and absorbed, and the non-trivial state involvement (in the form of courts, in that common law era, with the guidance and encouragement of the private parties) in addressing the challenges posed by railroad financing. According to Tufano, courts were committed participants in restructuring the railway industry and its financing because they viewed their efforts as advancing the public interest in the railway industry itself – in this way, perhaps not unlike those more contemporary regulators who have celebrated fast-moving private innovation in the service of national competitive advantage and economic growth. Public/private coordination and the shared focus on solving specific, pressing concerns produced rapid innovation, and wide diffusion. More unexpectedly, it also paved the way for industry consolidation and increased the private innovators', that is, the particular bankers', economic power and industry influence. And, ultimately, one of the more profound effects of this cooperation (this mostly through the private parties' innovations) was to structure corporate finance and corporate governance so as to make railways more resistant to court intervention in the future.

In the context of widespread, messy, structurally based bankruptcies in a key industry, courts could be pleased to have helped innovate themselves out of a job, even at the expense, it seems, of creditors, established legal rights and, to a degree, rule of law values including certainty and predictability. An important question that we cannot yet answer is whether this is an instance of a more general rule: whether public/private collaborations around financial or legal innovation tend, over the course of their development, to squeeze the public role out. Our experience with how financial industry actors framed the problems of complexity, described in Chapter 1, suggest that we should at least remain alert to the possibility of this occurring in other public/private cooperative contexts as well.

Deepwater Oil Drilling

The year 1936 saw the first freestanding oceanic oil-drilling platform, located in the Gulf of Mexico.[27] Ocean drilling developed rather slowly until the 1970s, when digital 3D imaging and then the rise of computers in the 1980s enabled companies to identify deepwater oil fields. 3D seismic imaging effectively tripled or quadrupled estimated oil and gas reserves in the Gulf of Mexico. Through the first half of the 1980s, however, the American economy was weak and oil and gas prices were flat, so drilling was limited. The industry did acquire tracts in deepwater to develop later. As economic conditions picked up for oil companies, so did drilling. In 1988, Shell installed a 162 story-high, $500 million fixed platform – a structure that was taller than the tallest building in the world at the time, the Sears Tower in Chicago.

Technology improved rapidly in the early 1990s. During the same period, US government policy shifted offshore drilling away from all other areas along the United States coast, and to the Gulf and some parts of Alaska. Offshore drilling outside the Gulf had always been unpopular (even while it had produced substantial government revenues). In 1990, US President George H.W. Bush issued a memorandum that canceled all scheduled deepwater lease sales off the California, southern Florida, Washington, Oregon, and North Atlantic coasts and withdrew those areas from leasing until after 2000. Then, in 1995, the Deepwater Royalty Relief Act[28] provided royalty relief for oil companies drilling in the Gulf of Mexico's outer continental shelf, accelerating a race that by that point was already underway. The US Congress, through its House Appropriations Committee, also singled out the Gulf of Mexico for offshore drilling by imposing a series of recurring one-year moratoriums on the Interior Department's annual budgets, which effectively prohibited exploration, development, and new leasing activities across the outer continental shelf of North America, except for the Gulf and a few areas off Alaska.

The combination of improved technology and drilling-friendly regulation intensified deepwater work in the Gulf of Mexico. Figure 7.2 above depicts the increasing number of deepwater wells in the Gulf, and the increasing water depth of those wells. In 1996, in a moment of poetic parallelism, Shell produced oil from its *Mars* platform six months before NASA launched its Pathfinder probe to the planet Mars. Shell's *Mars* was three times more expensive than the Pathfinder, costing $1 billion, and arguably boasted more sophisticated technology. By 2006, tests by Chevron at the Jack 2 field established that "ultra-deep" drilling – down through more than 7000 feet of water to the sea floor, and then a further 20,000 or more feet below that – was viable.

The relevant US regulator, established during the Reagan era, was the Minerals Management Service (MMS). It was imperfectly designed from its creation (and before it: it was the product of longstanding tensions between environmental concerns and a desire for US energy independence). Its mandate contained a built-in conflict of interest: it was required to ensure federal revenues from drilling leases, even while regulating the industry. In the 1990s, its resources decreased sharply. Its budget reached its lowest point in November 1996, even while major development activities in deepwater were rapidly expanding. (It did not see the royalties that were being collected.) As the National Commission on the BP Deepwater Horizon Oil Spill later observed,

> As MMS's resources lagged behind the industry's expansion into deepwater drilling – with its larger-scale and more demanding technology, greater pressures, and increasing distance from shore-based infrastructure and environmental and safety resources – the agency's ability to do its job was seriously compromised. Of particular concern, MMS was unable to maintain up-to-date technical drilling-safety requirements to keep up with industry's rapidly evolving deepwater technology. As drilling technology evolved, many aspects

of drilling lacked corresponding safety regulations. The regulations increasingly lagged behind industry and what was happening in the field.[29]

Industry efforts were regularly directed toward resisting more effective oversight. In the late 1990s, the oil industry globalized, restructured, and underwent a massive consolidation phase. In September 2009, the Deepwater Horizon rig drilled the deepest oil well in history, down to a total vertical depth of 35,050 feet. Then in April 2010, at a separate location within the Gulf of Mexico, the same rig experienced a blowout that caused an explosion, killing eleven crewmen and producing the largest ever oil spill in US waters. It became shockingly clear that neither industry nor regulators were prepared for the risks they were running at these "frontiers of experience."[30]

The factors that led to the intensification of deepwater, and then ultradeepwater, drilling in the Gulf of Mexico included an improved economic environment, a pro-drilling regulatory regime that included government incentives for drilling, increasing industry competition as a result of those more attractive economic conditions, and the improvements in technology needed to capitalize on them. The fact that MMS was ineffective and underfunded is a separate phenomenon, which did not directly contribute to the growth in deepwater drilling. However, in the absence of meaningful and meaningfully enforced regulatory requirements, regulation provided no meaningful brake on the competition-driven rush to drill ever deeper and ever more aggressively. In this sense, both the pro-drilling policy environment and the weak regulatory presence in the space helped to co-create the seismic innovation that occurred.

Twenty-First-Century Financial Innovation in Securitization and Derivatives

As we have discussed, financial innovation – the engineering of new financial products and processes – proceeded at an extraordinary pace in the two decades leading up to the financial crisis. The number, volume, and complexity of structured products, especially those trading in the virtually unregulated over-the-counter derivatives markets, surged upward.[31] As Lynn Stout has demonstrated, changes to legal architecture helped spur that growth. The dismantling of regulations prohibiting derivatives speculation in the 1980s and 1990s, and the formal legalization of speculative over-the-counter derivatives trading in 2000, gave rise to a vast speculative wave.[32] The fact that some aspects of derivatives became standardized also made it possible for other aspects to become far more varied. Specifically, the fact that the International Swaps and Derivatives Association (ISDA), a global private trade association, had developed a "master agreement" that established background rules around collateral and other aspects of derivatives contracts created a substructure on which a range of innovative, purpose-built derivatives could then be erected.[33] The pace of change accelerated dramatically, and markets and institutions became tightly interconnected.[34]

Andrew Haldane of the Bank of England has noted that the extraordinary growth of derivatives contracts from the early 2000s to 2009 outpaced the growth in world gross domestic product by a factor of three. The market for the derivatives known as credit default swaps outpaced Moore's Law – in other words, while the density of transistors on computers' integrated circuits doubled every two years, the number of CDSs more than doubled.[35] In the United States, the securities sector far outpaced the growth in other sectors of the economy, including the household sector, the non-financial corporate sector, and the commercial banking sector. In fact, while the other three sectors grew roughly 80-fold between 1954 and 2009, the securities sector grew roughly 800-fold.[36] We should be able to safely call this a seismic innovation, with predictable consequences for regulatory reach and capacity.

The causes of the financial crisis are complex, and there is no need to rehearse them for current purposes. The relevant point is that, once again, we can identify that the regulatory structure played a role in co-creating seismic growth in the OTC markets, through a series of structural choices we have touched on (including the faith that the market could be counted on to regulate OTC derivatives, and the way mortgage-backed assets were treated for capital adequacy purposes). As with deepwater oil drilling, product development exploded in part because of the competitive environment in which it operated, and the absence of regulatory or market-based brakes on its growth and diffusion. As with both the railway innovations and the deepwater drilling examples, the private innovations with which public regulation was ostensibly partnered eventually managed to consume the standard-setting space formerly accorded to regulation, and to squeeze the public voice out of the public/private collaborative arrangement.

Hindsight analyses make things seem simpler than they seemed at the time, and they flatten complex real life events into deceptively linear causative relationships. No doubt, this narrative risks doing so. The point is simply this: that regulation may regularly help co-create innovation phenomena that we could plausibly call "seismic," and those phenomena go on to present real, if hard-to-track, challenges to regulation itself in terms of its autonomy and its scope. Seismic innovation has implications. It may concentrate power among already-dominant firms, and it may shift important decision-making power from public regulators to private actors. It may grow and diffuse at a rate that swamps regulatory capacity, particularly in competitive environments and in the absence of regulatory or other (for example, market-based or social) retardants.

Regulatory structures and public action can help produce conditions that lead to seismic innovations in different ways, but the fact that they help to co-create seismic innovations suggests a corresponding regulatory responsibility to address them. The fact that seismic innovations generate risks for society generally is one thing, but seismic innovation also generates particular risks for regulation itself. To the extent that seismic innovation makes regulation extraordinarily difficult, or even outright impossible, our romantic association with innovation should not prevent us from taking steps to make the environment more capable of being regulated, in the interest of other priorities we also hold dear.

WHAT KINDS OF PROBLEMS DO SEISMIC INNOVATIONS PRESENT FOR REGULATION?

Uncertainty and Illegibility

Both seismic and sedimentary innovations can be hard to track and to grapple with, though for different reasons. Seismic innovations are challenging because we lack data about them and their likely trajectory, we may lack the regulatory infrastructure to recognize the change, and we tend to be best able to identify genuinely seismic changes only in retrospect. Included in this, we may even lack contemporaneous understanding of how the regulatory environment helped co-create the seismic innovation in the first place.

How well we can respond to seismic innovation will depend on and be bounded by the structures and assumptions that have been put in place. Yet in its purest incarnation, a seismic innovation is capable of entirely outstripping expected rates of growth, and completely outstripping existing risk management strategies. As is true of sedimentary innovation too, our prior regulatory structures and assumptions may be ill-suited to responding to it. Yet what further characterizes the seismic innovation is the lack of data, or even a frame for noticing the new phenomenon, combined with rapid growth in adoption or diffusion and the potential for transformative consequences over a short time frame.

Seismic innovation (using the term here in its pure, theoretical form) is risky for societies and challenging for regulators because it entails real uncertainty, as Frank Knight used the term.[37] One of Knight's key contributions was the insight that uncertainty is the product not only of the lack of data

that accompanies genuine novelty, which certainly applies to seismic innovation, but also of the fact that inevitably, our understanding will be infused
with our own subjective beliefs about the future.[38] In other words, when it
comes to uncertainty, we lack evidence and experience because the situation
is so unprecedented, but we are also at a disadvantage in making sense of the
phenomenon – of identifying the relevant comparators or useful analogies
and extrapolating from them. Arguably, the greater the sense of unpredictability and regulatory resource inadequacy, the more tempting it may be to
reach for a sense of recognition and security by identifying analogous cases or
comparator responses. The sense of security will be not only false, but actively
detrimental, if the comparator is inappropriate as a way of understanding the
new event.[39]

From a regulatory perspective, the fact that seismic innovators may be dominant industry firms makes the initial challenge of tracking such innovations
easier – so long as that situation persists. The regulator will face separate concerns in terms of the industry's transparency and the enormous resources it has
at its disposal to resist regulation, along with potential antitrust or concentration concerns, but at least it can identify an initial set of players. On the other
hand, the risk is that focusing on the existing dominant players and their methods could blind a regulator to a surge in seismic innovation from outside that
core. In spite of their initial resource advantages, it is always unclear whether
incumbent firms will continue to be dominant, and is specifically unclear
today, in finance, in view of the ongoing innovation by technology companies in fintech, much of it aimed at disrupting costly intermediary functions
like financial advising and investment banking functions.[40] While regulators
may want to begin with a focus on dominant industry players, the risk is that
they become anchored to the existing universe of players in a way that, like an
inappropriate comparator, is actively detrimental to their ability to see a new
phenomenon forming.

Similarly, as we have already discussed, innovation can undermine existing
regulatory categories, and make plausible comparators actually quite inapposite. Robert Merton, writing in 1995 about the growth of financial derivatives,
notes some of the challenges innovation poses for regulators. For example,
these innovations destroy traditional boundaries relied upon by regulation,
and they also outpace regulation and infrastructure in development. Speaking
of the Basel I Capital Accord, he says:

> [The rules] were organized along categories of products or asset types …
> in the US for example, if a bank were managing and holding mortgages on
> houses, it would have to maintain a capital requirement of 4%. If, instead,
> it [engaged in functionally identical mortgage based swaps agreements], the

[Basel I] capital calculation, instead of it being 4%, appears to produce a capital requirement using the swap route of about 0.5%.

... many of those institutional categories (not only for institutions but for the very products themselves) will have to be redefined to be operationally effective.[41]

Recall also the Asset-Backed Commercial Paper regime in Canada, which assumed that a particular market would reliably function as a regulatory back-stop when in fact the market had been utterly transformed. The innovation that Merton describes above – which reduces the amount of capital a finan-cial firm has to keep on hand through financial innovation, even though the asset being held is functionally equivalent – is another example of the way that innovation can denature a particular financial product and cause it to slip from one category to another without the regulatory scheme properly reg-istering and responding to the change. Much the same can be said not just of new products, but across the shadow banking institutions and services that arose in the early years of the twenty-first century: among other new prod-ucts and techniques, non-bank financial institutions used financial innovation to develop bank-like products, including products that could be marketed to retail investors. Since they were not recognized as banks under the traditional regulatory structure, however, those institutions were exempt from traditional banking capital requirements and so could operate more cheaply – even while ultimately availing themselves of the implicit government subsidy that their size and systemic significance afforded them.

While regulatory mismatch is a problem whenever innovation alters the envi-ronment, we can also think of these problems as particularly associated with seismic innovation patterns, whose pace far outmatches what statutory draft-ers, democratic institutions, or even the nimblest regulators could consistently match. Seismic innovation means that new things fall between the cracks of structures built to respond to a different environment. It also means that cog-nitive embeddedness within existing structures makes it difficult to recognize seismic innovations as significant, as they occur. We lack what James Scott (and, following him, Michael Moran) described as "legibility" with respect to struc-tures and innovations that do not fit with our existing institutional and cognitive understandings of the environment.[42] Our existing structures impose blinkers on us that make it hard to recognize new, different, ill-fitting phenomena.

Uncertainty means that regulators' ability to anticipate new threats or risks will be sorely limited; and, significantly, that involving private actors – the innovators themselves – in their own regulation may seem especially attractive, given that they possess closer and more direct experience with their own inno-vations, and therefore may seem better able to anticipate and respond to an

emergency arising through that innovation. (Consider that it was BP, not its regulators, which devised the infamous "junk shot," "top kill," and other strategies
to respond to the Deepwater Horizon disaster.) As we discussed in Chapter 1,
fields like financial innovation that are characterized by substantial complexity
are even more susceptible to potentially self-serving industry arguments that the
regulator should cede some of its decision-making authority to the private innovators themselves. Of course, the fact that private parties have more direct access
to information does not mean they can be trusted, without regulatory oversight,
to implement effective self-regulatory controls. As Diane Vaughn noted in her
celebrated analysis of the 1986 Challenger space shuttle disaster,

> A logical assumption is that organizations producing high-risk technological
> products will play an active role in their own regulation, if for no other reason
> than because they have the technical knowledge to do so. Self-regulating sys-
> tems, however, are "fundamentally suspect". Any organizational system that,
> like NASA, regulates resources and their exchanges, in effect, concentrates
> influence over those resources. As a consequence, self-regulation of risky
> technical enterprise may, by definition, be accompanied by dependencies
> that interfere with regulatory effectiveness.[43]

Hindsight Bias, Ex Post Overreactions

High-salience disasters like the Deepwater Horizon disaster or the financial
crisis may generate a shift in image and attention that provokes regulatory
change. Sometimes, this shift in perception gives us the small consolation of
presenting an opportunity to catch up on regulation that had lagged before the
crisis.[44] Seismic innovations can produce highly visible disasters of this nature,
and can open a window within which more forceful regulatory responses are
possible.

However, we should not assume that our immediate post-crisis regulatory
instincts are necessarily the best guides to designing optimal regulation. To
begin with, the hindsight bias and the proximity of the event may make it
difficult to identify what reasonably ought to have been expected by industry
actors before the crisis. A certain amount of interpretation will accompany
any after-the-fact assessment. Weak signals that seem unremarkable or ambig-
uous before a disaster may take on great narrative significance afterward. As
Starbuck and Milliken have pointed out, writing about hindsight bias in the
wake of the Challenger disaster,

> Retrospective analyses always oversimplify the connections between behaviors
> and outcomes, and make the actual outcomes appear highly inevitable and
> highly predictable ... Retrospection often creates an erroneous impression

that errors should have been anticipated and prevented. For instance, the Presidential Commission found that 'The O-ring erosion history presented to Level I at NASA Headquarters in August 1985 was sufficiently detailed to require corrective action prior to the next flight', but would the Commission members have drawn this same conclusion in August 1985 on the basis of the information then at hand?[45]

Thinking back to the first two diagrams in this chapter, we may ask the same question about the growth of ABCP or deepwater oil drilling. If it is difficult to confidently label an innovation as seismic after the fact, surely it is even more daunting to try to do so in the absence of a focusing disaster.[46]

As many scholars have observed, we also seem inclined to over-regulate in the wake of a high-visibility disaster of the seismic type.[47] In a society in which increased or changed regulation is seen as a solution to a wide range of problems,[48] major events that leave regulators looking flat-footed present risks to the regulator, and seem to demand a forceful, credibility-restoring *ex post* response. Sometimes optics dictate that the response be more forceful than a regulator might have designed in the absence of that focusing event and the attendant pressure. Regulators, needing to bolster their reputation after the fact, may engage in regulation as a rearguard action. More cynically, regulators may engage in politically motivated posturing. This was Roberta Romano's charge in the wake of the dot-com collapse in the early 2000s, when she colorfully labeled the Sarbanes-Oxley Act an example of "quack corporate governance."[49]

The lack of data affects *ex post* regulation too: sometimes the natural response is to build a regulatory version of the "Maginot line" that responds to the last crisis, not the next one. In environments marked by rapid change and innovation, quantification models that try to aggregate risks based on the assumption that future behavior will mirror past behavior can prove to be very flawed.[50] Moreover, even better performance post-disaster is not necessarily proof that the post-disaster regulatory responses were needed. We may overstate the effectiveness of regulation because we imply causation when we see a pattern of disaster, followed by regulation, followed by fewer disasters. Yet improvements may actually have come about due to learning, not regulation. All of these challenges exist whenever we try to regulate, but they may be more likely to materialize in the wake of a high-salience disaster flowing from unaddressed seismic innovation.

We also need to take care to ensure that the high salience of a spike, if we see it, does not distract us from other phenomena that might be equally consequential. Recall the growth of the ABCP market, depicted in Figure 7.1.

Over the last year depicted, from August 2015 to August 2016, ABCP and regular, non-financial commercial paper has been issued in relatively similar volumes. This may suggest that the market has reached some kind of equilibrium, and that we need no longer be concerned with the growth of ABCP as a seismic innovation. At the same time, Figure 7.3 is a close-up depiction of volumes of the two kinds of commercial paper over these seemingly stable twelve months:

What is causing the historically unusual volatility in non-financial commercial paper? Perhaps, looking for seismic events is only part of the challenge of understanding what potentially new use commercial paper is being put to now.

To the extent that post-crisis regulatory reforms are rearguard actions characterized by confusion about how to deal with the risks posed by industry innovation, we should also be concerned that they will be ill-suited to the next challenge that financial innovation will throw up. Regulatory reforms initiated immediately after a crisis may focus too much on short-term fixes to address the perceived causes of the crisis, while ignoring other less salient risks, producing ill-conceived regulation that may hinder innovation or reform in the future while also not preventing problems.[51] We do not need to share Romano's fundamental distaste for regulation to agree that some approaches to regulation are more promising than others, and that the immediate post-crisis moment may not be a time when we are thinking especially clearly.

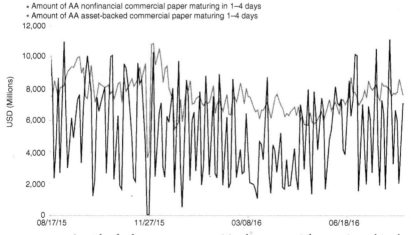

FIGURE 7.3. Asset-backed versus non-securitized commercial paper issued in the United States, August 2015–August 2016 (data source: US Flow of Funds).

WHAT REGULATORY RESPONSES TO SEISMIC INNOVATION
MAKE SENSE?

Here are the problems, then: an imperfect understanding of how regulatory structures co-create seismic innovation in different circumstances; the lack of data or experience on the part of regulators with the seismic innovation, potentially to the point of producing outright Knightian uncertainty; the fact that most of what data there is rests in the hands of innovators themselves, not regulators; a potential mismatch between problem, once it arises, and regulatory infrastructure (which affects cognition and recognition); the problem of recognizing a seismic innovation in "real time;" and concerns about hindsight bias and politically motivated *ex post* reactions. While more work needs to be done, three paths forward suggest themselves. All draw on the tradition of flexible regulation that we have discussed.

Developing a more sophisticated understanding of the nature of innovation, as this book advocates, will help regulators develop better strategies for responding to seismic innovation. Even though the labels of "seismic" and "sedimentary" cannot be true at all scales and for all purposes, they may be reasonable and meaningful across a particular industry, geographical jurisdiction, or time frame. Then, instead of engaging in potentially haphazard or *ex post* rearguard action, regulators could identify and implement strategies as a seismic innovation is developing, tailored to dealing proactively in particular with uncertainty and data scarcity. Below are three options, focused on addressing the uncertainty and risk associated with seismic innovations.

Meta-Regulation or Experimentalist Regulation

First, we can potentially do better in gathering and making sense of information, if we approach regulation as a continually learning-oriented exercise, in the way that meta-regulation or experimentalism aims to do. As we have discussed, new governance approaches such as meta-regulation and experimentalism focus on developing regulatory systems that can learn from experience, which may be an effective stance from which to make sense of seismic innovation both as a phenomenon in its own right and as a regulatory challenge. Meta-regulatory approaches are based on continual data gathering and process improvement based on feedback, and may impose rigorous information-forcing requirements on industry. For example, Bradley Karkkainen has proposed a "regulatory penalty default" similar to the penalty defaults that the upset rules represented in the nineteenth-century railway story. A regulatory penalty default would impose harsh terms that incentivized regulated actors to produce and/or generate information and devise solutions to identified risks.[52]

The main challenge is that meta-regulation requires substantial regulatory capacity, if the regulator is not to cede the field to the private actor. It must still be in a position to independently identify and assess risks; evaluate industry conduct and evaluate its own information-gathering, analytic and decision-making capacity; and use its own experience with monitoring to improve its own practice, in a conscious and systematic way. While not impossible, we should not underestimate the resources and political commitment that meta-regulation requires, for the distance between ineffectual self-regulation and meaningful meta-regulation lies in that gap. Effective meta-regulation may actually require *more* resources than other strategies (though it has the theoretical potential to be more effective too), and it almost certainly requires substantially more resources than was generally realized before the financial crisis.[53]

Safety-Case Regulation

According to the World Economic Forum (WEF), the financial crisis produced precious little that could not be handled through better self-regulation within the financial industry. Rather, the WEF recommended that industry participants improve their enterprise risk management, their own internal new product development and approval processes, their incentive design (e.g., around compensation related to innovation), and that they recommit to "consumer-friendly principles of product and business process design to steer innovation in a direction that will regain customer trust and create a better alignment of interests between the bank or insurer and its customers." The Forum had some recommendations for regulators too: to build a pro-competitive marketplace on the principles of "do no harm," "use the lightest touch" and "prefer market solutions;" to strengthen systemic risk oversight, as the only environment where the regulator was in a position to monitor over-arching risks stemming from innovation; and to monitor and oversee industry by supporting and extending the industry's own efforts. The Forum's view was that "concerns over innovation outcomes do not require an entirely new innovation governance framework, but enhancements to existing ones."[54]

In fact, the better view is that the financial crisis very seriously undermined the financial industry's arguments in favor of self-regulation. Financial industry-specific conditions aside, that recognition should also provoke some general concern about any industry's ability to manage the broader effects of its innovative processes. Yet, the informational problem persists. It continues to be the case that innovators will have more granular, immediate, and contextually informed information about their innovations than any regulator is likely to.

Not all public/private collaborative exercises are created equal. While collaborative exercises may present the real risk that the public partner will be squeezed out, this may not be inevitable so long as a regulator remains adequately resourced and maintains a sufficiently skeptical mindset. Unlike drilling in the Gulf of Mexico, for example, collaborative safety-case regulation of deepwater oil drilling in the North Sea seems more successful.

Safety-case regulation – something the MMS in the United States never managed to implement except on a voluntary basis – is an outcome-oriented rather than prescriptive approach that requires operators to identify all potential hazards and show risks are below a certain tolerable level.[55] It was developed for offshore drilling platforms in the late 1980s and early 1990s, in Norway and then in the UK, in response to drilling tragedies in the North Sea. It tries to take advantage of industry's own information while still insisting on information-forcing and effective regulatory oversight, and in this sense shares features with the new governance varieties of flexible regulation in particular. Under safety-case regulation, a regulated private actor is required to submit a safety plan to the regulator for approval, which includes among other things a risk analysis and corresponding management system. The regulator audits the plan. If it is satisfactory, as would also be the case under Ayres's and Braithwaite's enforced self-regulation model, that safety-case forms the basis for accreditation. The regulator's role is not to prescribe what action the private actor should take but rather to accredit the safety-case and oversee its implementation.

Among its advantages, safety-case regulation may increase the knowledge base and credibility of the safety-case itself, particularly if actual front-line workers are involved. The fact that industry actors must continually update their safety-cases may be useful in seismic innovation contexts, in the sense of providing regulators as well with more up-to-date information than they otherwise might have.[56] In contrast to pure self-regulation, safety-case regulation continues to engage public regulation because regulators are expected to actively challenge the private actor to demonstrate that its systems work in practice. Safety-case regulation also recognizes the challenge of dealing with complex, heterogeneous organizations and safety problems. If the relative absence of drilling disasters in the North Sea is any indication, when properly implemented it can be more effective for addressing the particular safety and environmental challenges confronting a particular facility, because it requires that the private actor engage with site-specific information rather than with standardized regulatory requirements. In contexts like nuclear and chemical power plant operation, air traffic control, North Sea oil drilling, and space shuttle operation – where the context is inherently risky and consequences of failure very serious – safety-case regulation has been a central and substantially successful strategy allowing so-called "high reliability organizations" to avoid failure.[57]

On the other hand, like other new governance strategies, safety-case regulation is vulnerable to under-resourcing, and there is nothing inherent to the safety-case that would make it immune to the risk of erosion as seismic innovations, and the attendant data asymmetry and orientation toward industry expertise, potentially take over. Once again, the need for the regulator to have adequate resources cannot be overemphasized.[58] Safety-case regulation is also probably not well suited to environments where regulator/industry relationships are not fairly stable and long-lasting, or to any situation where the regulator does not, for whatever reason, have the capacity to convincingly "kick the tyres" on the innovator's safety-case.[59] It may be also insufficient in environments where innovators do not themselves bear the whole burden of a seismic innovation gone wrong. Finance, where systemic risk means that the innovator may not be the only victim of its own failure, may be such an environment in the absence of genuine political and regulatory commitment to address the industry's negative externalities.[60]

The Precautionary Principle and/or Ex Ante *Licensing*

The two proposals above are variations on existing flexible regulation approaches, which could be modified to be more aware of the particular risks that seismic innovation presents for regulation, and for society and the environment at large. Meta-regulation and safety-case regulation can be compatible approaches. Together they can help address the uncertainty problem, at least to some degree, by recognizing its existence and taking steps to mitigate it. They can improve the quantity and quality of the data in regulators' hands, including by imposing information-forcing requirements on industry actors. Through better regulation before the fact, they may be able to prevent both disasters and politically motivated *ex post* regulatory responses, motivated by hindsight.

On the other hand, neither approach is fully capable of tackling the deepest, most epistemological challenges associated with seismic innovation. It is one thing to take the potential for Knightian uncertainty seriously, but it is quite another to know how to react within its bottomless well, where even the nature and origins of the seismic innovation phenomenon itself can be hard to make out until it is too late. The problem of the potential mismatch between regulatory structure and seismic innovation exacerbates sense-making difficulties, not only in terms of being able to recognize new phenomena, but also in the sense of being able to understand how complex regulatory choices helped to co-create the conditions within which seismic innovation gestated in the first place. Finally there is the persistent tendency for public resourcing, regulatory skepticism, and even the public role to slide "downhill" toward more acquiescence or reactiveness in the face of complexity and dynamism. If these are the problems we are concerned with, the two regulatory strategies above, on their own, will not be enough.

Another option is the precautionary principle, which would shift the burden of proof to the innovator to demonstrate, for example, how its innovation would produce a benefit, or would not exacerbate systemic risk, or would otherwise advance the public interest or at least not undermine regulatory priorities. In its strongest form, the precautionary principle would prohibit new innovations until and unless its advocates could demonstrate that the innovation did not throw up prohibited kinds of risks. When accompanied by a licensing requirement, the precautionary principle could incorporate product development or testing requirements. Like safety-case regulation, the precautionary principle and licensing requirements have the potential to impose a high regulatory threshold that the innovator must clear before it can implement or market its innovation. This is far more than what we are accustomed to seeing in a field like finance, where licensing or public interest tests have so far been anathema. Yet it can also be broader than what we are accustomed to seeing in safety-case regulation of deepwater oil drilling. Depending on how it is designed, licensing requirements based on the precautionary principle could involve priorities well beyond just site safety.

To be clear, we should expect that adopting the precautionary principle would slow (visible, permission-required) innovation down.[61] The question, which is a normative one, is under what conditions this is justified. There may be some contexts where we would not want to adopt such a demanding standard, or where we may want to apply it in a modulated or staged way. In some areas, however, the benefits associated with responding forcefully to identifiable risks may outweigh the costs. For example, Geoffrey Underhill has argued that new financial products should be subject to "precautionary capital charges," meaning that they would be subject to high capital adequacy requirements, like the riskiest assets under the Basel Capital Accords, for at least one business cycle. The onus would be on financial institutions to demonstrate, through the course of that business cycle, that financial products are safe before they can attract regular, risk-weighted capital charges. Underhill argues that reversing the onus in this manner also helps to reduce herding, and helps assure that the new product is comprehensible, adequately disclosed, and can be explained transparently.[62] In a different vein, Lawrence Baxter has suggested that a proposed merger that would make a huge bank even larger would be a situation in which the precautionary principle in its fullness may be justified.[63]

Other legal academics have developed the related idea of creating a pre-market licensing requirement for financial innovations. As Omarova has argued, the "most radical and direct method of reducing systemic risk is to insert regulatory controls at the point of product development, before the risk is introduced into the financial system."[64] Both she and, independently, Eric Posner and Glen Weyl advocate for a product approval/licensing system similar to the one the US Federal Drug Administration (FDA) imposes on pharmaceuticals.[65] The burden would be on the financial institution to pass the "economic purpose" test – which addresses the social and commercial utility of the instrument; the "institutional capacity" test – which addresses the firm's ability to monitor and manage the risk posed by the instrument; and the "systemic effects" test – which addresses whether and how the instrument increases systemic risk.[66]

Unlike new governance or safety-case strategies, licensing and precautionary principle-based strategies are not designed to be flexible or context-sensitive. They are not regulatory scaffolding so much as they are floors. In this sense they suffer from all the shortcomings of bright-line rule-based regulatory techniques, including over- and under-inclusiveness, non-transparency, and gameability. There will be gaps, potentially significant ones, between how they appear on paper and how they operate in practice. Bright-line threshold requirements have their place in any regulatory regime, but their limits should be borne in mind. As well, we should remember that product approval processes like this are expensive, and may inherently favor larger firms.[67] By imposing high barriers to entry, we may be exchanging an innovation-related risk for a competition-related one. In this way, even as we consider forceful mechanisms for slowing the pace at which seismic innovations are launched and diffuse, the problem of power persists.

REFLECTIONS ON RESPONDING TO SEISMIC INNOVATION

Some regulatory responses to seismic innovation, especially the precautionary principle, share some ground with regulatory responses that are skeptical of innovation generally: in its strongest form the precautionary principle is a blanket, *ex ante* prescription that emphasizes imposing regulatory prohibitions sooner rather than later, that does not see the regulatory exercise as provisional or iterative or incremental, and that is not flexible but rather operates, out of an abundance of caution, with "shut down" as a default position. As controversial as this may be, *not* being willing to consider shut-down options under any circumstances amounts to endorsing a questionable status quo in which regulators, faced with fast-moving innovations, may be powerless to even make sense of events. More than that, if the narratives above are any guide, it may amount to that questionable status quo, *plus* an implicit decision to allocate even greater power or influence to dominant private parties, *plus* another implicit decision to squeeze out public regulation's capacity and its room to maneuver as the seismic innovation gathers steam.

In the high-reliability industries like nuclear power, where the consequences of a disaster to society or the environment are too enormous to risk, we understand our priorities. Outside those industries, our choices thus far seem to indicate that we are willing to wager on positive outcomes from seismic innovation, even in the absence of a genuine conversation about whether in fact we are comfortable with the degrees of complexity, uncertainty, and even illegibility that characterize finance, deepwater oil drilling, nanotechnology, genetic mapping and research, and other highly innovative technical endeavors. In fact, our choices even suggest that we are fairly comfortable about the prospect of seismic innovation fundamentally undermining regulation (as opposed to presenting direct risks to society), even though undermining regulation ultimately gets us to the same, risky, place.

In trying to evaluate regulatory options for dealing with seismic innovation, our own incoherence about what we want from regulation writ large becomes plain. That incoherence affects regulatory responses to sedimentary innovation too, but our troubles are more baldly on display here. What do we want from regulation? Do we want to try to identify seismic innovations and head off risks before disasters occur, even if this comes at a cost to innovation generally? Do we care about regulation, and the public voice it represents, enough to genuinely worry about how innovation can undermine it? Do we actually want to try to identify and decelerate seismic innovation (bearing in mind the challenges of doing so, and intense transnational economic competition, and the likelihood that others may not do the same), even if we accept that that is required to give regulators the time to generate data and chip away at the uncertainty? Our post-disaster teeth-gnashing notwithstanding, is the truth actually that we are prepared to pay the (unequally distributed) price of Deepwater Horizon disasters and financial crises in exchange for the hope and romance that seismic innovation still carries with it? Some of these questions engage difficult normative choices. Any technical regulatory prescription we develop for dealing with seismic innovation will not eliminate the need for us to make them.

High-salience disasters and what seem like clear examples of seismic innovative shifts can also be opportunities for learning, and for reframing the conversation around a particular industry's practices. Moments when seismic innovations seem to be occurring have the potential to focus resources and stiffen the resolve to address important problems that might otherwise remain unaddressed for too long. Granted, what constitutes a genuinely seismic innovation is difficult to define, especially in real time. Yet whether a particular innovation comes to be described as seismic also has a good deal to do with framing, context, scale, and even hype. Given that public legal structures, like regulation or judicial decisions, often structure the spaces within which seismic innovation occurs, regulators should not shy away from trying to confront innovation directly across its life cycle, or from dealing with what they deem to be seismic innovation as forcefully as necessary when it threatens regulatory capacity.

8

Sedimentary Innovation: Responding
to Incremental Change

For all their splashiness, seismic innovations as described in the last chapter are not actually that commonplace. Incremental improvements on new inventions, arising through collaboration or knowledge networks and based on imitation, tweaking, translating, and diffusion, are the main means through which innovation happens. Innovation scholar Christopher Freeman describes the shift in emphasis in regulatory and policy work from radical innovations to "incremental" or sedimentary innovations:

> [R]adical innovations ... tended to overshadow incremental innovations, both in policy making and in descriptive analysis for a long time ... an important change in emphasis in policy making [has been] the recognition that the vast majority of firms do not make radical innovations, but all can and should make incremental innovations and adopt new products processes first made by others.[1]

A simple, one-move example of an incremental innovation would be Apple Corporation's iPad. Unlike the obvious, seismic potential that smartphone technology was immediately recognized to have, the iPad's launch was accompanied by debate about whether it was an innovation at all, or just a scaled-up version of an iPhone.[2] With the smartphone as a cognitive anchoring device, it was difficult to imagine that an iPad might be something different, yet what seemed like just a difference in physical size altered the user experience in considerable ways, and gave rise to follow-on innovations and functions.[3] (Both phone and tablet also of course generated imitators.)

Or, more subtly perhaps, consider rail safety: in July 2013, an unattended freight train carrying 72 cars of crude oil derailed and exploded in Lac Mégantic, Québec, causing forty-seven deaths.[4] It produced one of the largest oil spills in Canadian history. Freight trains are not new, of course, and nor are oil spills. Yet the Lac Mégantic derailment serves as an example of the risks and unpredictability of sedimentary innovation. The sedimentary innovation here was a process one, of major rail shipment of crude oil products, stemming from increased oil prices and political pressures not to build pipelines, combined with railway deregulation,[5] and inadequate enforcement[6] to create serious gaps in rail safety. Leading up to the disaster, shale oil and bitumen transported by rail in Canada had increased from 500 carloads in 2009 to an estimated 140,000 carloads in 2013, in an effort by oil companies to reap profits from the increase in oil prices then occurring.[7] As Tim Shufelt writes, "For the Canadian oil patch, railways were an inelegant – if necessary – substitute for highly controversial pipelines."[8]

Another recent train derailment, in Oregon, introduces another element: the sheer weight of heavy crude oil versus its lighter variety. In June 2016, a train carrying heavy crude derailed in Oregon's Columbia River Gorge, when a number of the bolts that fastened the tracks together were sheared off.[9] Since 2001, US freight railways have only seen a 12 percent increase in the number of cars they transport, but after taking into account the weight and mileage that the system is subjected to, railroads have actually experienced a 24 percent increase in "ton-miles."[10] Like the Lac Mégantic disaster, the derailment in Oregon was a multi-causal phenomenon. It was not caused solely by technological advances in oil extraction, or process innovations in transporting oil by rail, or because the properties of heavy crude undermine the safety of tank cars, or because of a lack of sufficient regulation. It was caused by each of these phenomena converging to intensify the strain on the system, making the track as a whole more prone to failure.

In these examples are the hallmarks of the phenomenon I want to consider: "sedimentary" layers of innovation, each perhaps unremarkable on its own and not flashy in technological terms and yet, collectively, highly consequential. In contrast to seismic innovations, "sedimentary" (or incremental) innovations are built up through multiple small modifications to equipment or organization or use, made by engineers (including financial engineers), technicians, managers, salespeople, product users, and others.[11] In high-risk, technologically complex environments like nuclear power plants, the accretion of small operator errors can produce catastrophic accidents, which are nevertheless "normal" in the sense that their causes are so common, unremarkable, and ultimately inevitable.[12] As we know from Chapter 6, important sedimentary innovations may not always be underpinned by a significant technological change, or a clearly visible trajectory from specific technology to innovative outcome. Changes in business processes or in how and where a tool is deployed count too. The move to rely on rail to transport crude oil in these quantities is a process innovation, and produces manufactured risk, but its incremental development and multifactorial causes make it hard to detect until a focusing event, like a large oil spill, arises. By then much damage has been done.

Our language and our literature are full of allegories for the problems posed by the small drip-drip of incremental change: one can suffer death by a thousand cuts, Gulliver was tied down by Lilliputians, there is a last straw that can break a camel's back, and (apocryphally) frogs can be boiled alive if the water in a pot is heated gradually enough.[13] While the concept of sedimentary innovation is in some ways analogous to the more familiar idea of incremental innovation, the metaphor of *sedimentary* innovation also helps emphasize the dangers of gradually increasing, piling-up innovation in a way that the word incremental does not. Sedimentary innovation can bury the structures designed to contain it, and can fundamentally shift the landscape even while not appearing to be doing much at all.

Alongside these darker images, we also have a romantic account of sedimentary innovation, just as we have a romantic account of seismic innovation. The image of vision-plus-perseverance as the basis of innovation, or the eccentric who, in the fullness of time (and perhaps posthumously) was proved right, is a familiar cultural stock figure whose existence affirms the idea that imagination and hard work should ultimately pay off. Sedimentary innovations may be less magical in the popular imagination than the seismic form, but they too occupy a space in our normative, and narrative, universes. Sedimentary innovation also occupies a space in the flexible regulation literature, which we need to understand before we can delve more deeply into the ways in which sedimentary innovation not only intersects with but also represents a challenge for that literature.

In this chapter, we go a bit deeper into the influence of networks, the first-mover advantage, and the problem of innovative bricolage ("making do") as each one affects our understanding of sedimentary innovation as a regulatory challenge. Thereafter, we can consider the particular cognitive barriers that human beings encounter when trying to recognize sedimentary innovation accreting in real time. Finally, we turn to some possible regulatory responses to the challenges associated with dealing with sedimentary innovation in particular.

SEDIMENTARY INNOVATION AS REGULATORY OPPORTUNITY AND REGULATORY CHALLENGE

The image of sedimentary innovation, and progress, underpins a range of pragmatist, experimentalist, and evidence-based regulatory prescriptions. In fact, the idea of incremental, step-by-step progress underlies important regulatory touchstones such as the "race to the top," and the use of decentralization and competition to foster productive innovation. Because flexible regulation so often emphasizes the value of bottom-up learning, former US Supreme Court Justice Louis Brandeis's notion of multiple "laboratories" for democracy is a recurrent theme in flexible regulation scholarship. As Brandeis famously said,

> The discoveries in physical science, the triumphs in invention, attest the value of the process of trial and error. In large measure, these advances have been due to experimentation ...
>
> It is one of the happy incidents of the federal system that a single courageous State may, if its citizens choose, serve as a laboratory; and try novel social and economic experiments without risk to the rest of the country.[14]

Brandeis's famous claim that federalism permits multiple laboratories for democracy in fact *assumes sedimentary innovation*: it establishes a legal architecture for running parallel experiments, with a view to increasing the rate of beneficial discoveries and innovations. Focusing on the upside potential of sedimentary innovation, Charles Sabel and his colleagues in particular have described developments in hospitals, prisons, schools, and other public institutions in terms of the benefits that can arise from multiple laboratories.[15] The experimentalists adopt the term "bootstrapping" to describe the process in which incremental innovations in different jurisdictions create a structure conducive to experimentalism, arguing that it is a positive self-reinforcing process. Outside the federalism context, the same faith in permitting regulatory improvement by fostering private sector experimentation underpins the "regulatory sandbox" initiatives around fintech, which were launched in multiple jurisdictions in 2016.[16]

Laboratory and sandbox initiatives can have many virtues in improving regulation, including by helping to develop best practices and giving regulators access to more detailed and up-to-date information about the ways in which industry actors are innovating. At the same time, we should remember that innovators may innovate not only to make markets more efficient, but also to avoid regulation; that there may not be external market backstops that can quickly assess and reflect back the social welfare benefits (or detriments) associated with financial innovations; that innovations will both develop and diffuse in hard-to-predict ways; and that even the bounds of a regulatory sandbox are not likely to be immune from the undermining effects of innovation. A regulatory sandbox focused on fintech innovations could find itself expanding its definition of what fintech is, or what kind of play is permitted in the sandbox. Especially in the context of growing inter-jurisdictional regulatory competition for fintech business – a factor that is influencing all this interest in sandboxes in the first place – we should be mindful of the possibility that private sector innovation could become the driver of the experiment to such a degree that public regulatory priorities are undermined.

Regulatory competition for innovative financial work between London and New York has often been blamed for a general lowering of regulatory standards in the lead-up to the financial crisis. Regulatory competition within the United States also provoked increased innovativeness by American banks, but not without a price. As Art Wilmarth has noted, prior to the financial crisis, competition among US state banking regulators and between state and federal regulators promoted further instances of cooperative innovation between the private and public sectors. Competition helped generate a reflexive loop of regulatory innovation, ultimately producing very significant change. On the upside, Wilmarth points to private sector innovations that go on to achieve success once they are embraced and championed by regulatory actors, operating in competition with each other:

> [T]he dual banking system has permitted states to act as "laboratories" in experimenting with new banking products, structures, and supervisory approaches, and Congress has subsequently incorporated many of the states' successful innovations into federal legislation. In addition to the examples … of checking accounts, bank branches, real estate loans, trust services, and NOW accounts, the state banking system originated reserve requirements, deposit insurance, adjustable-rate mortgages, automated teller machines ("ATMs"), bank sales of insurance products, interstate electronic funds transfer systems, interstate bank holding companies, and supervisory agreements that promote cooperative oversight of multistate banking organizations by state bank regulators, the FRB, and the FDIC.[17]

Ultimately, however, the downside revealed itself. Increasing competition between state and federal bank regulators then spurred further innovation, eventually in ways that threatened regulatory standards. The result of competition and innovation was pressure on regulators to adopt a more innovation-friendly and flexible stance:

> During the 1980s and early 1990s, the [US Office of the Comptroller of the Currency]'s success in obtaining court decisions expanding intrastate branching opportunities for national banks forced many states to adopt laws granting statewide branching privileges to state banks. During the same period, state initiatives allowing state banks to offer securities and insurance products encouraged federal regulators to take similar steps. These state and federal regulatory innovations helped persuade Congress to enact [the

Gramm-Leach-Bliley Act] in 1999, which removed legal barriers separating the banking industry from the securities and insurance businesses. Thus, the regulatory competition for bank charters has placed continuing pressure on state officials and the OCC to demonstrate that they can provide innovative, responsive, and cost-effective supervision to their regulated constituents.[18]

Saule Omarova has also tracked how the business of banking changed over time. She looked at the way in which, from the mid-1980s onward, the OCC gradually broadened its statutory interpretation of what a bank does, using first the "look-through," then the "functional equivalency," and finally the "elastic definition" approach. Omarova emphasizes how, at each stage, decisions by regulators precipitated the growth of financial innovation, allowing financial institutions to take greater and more complex risks. The relationship is a reciprocal and reflexive one. Moreover, like the innovations to which they contributed, the regulatory innovations were subtle, incremental, and operated "under the radar" in a way whose consequence could only be recognized in retrospect. As Omarova says,

> Contrary to an implicit assumption underlying most conventional explanations, the financial innovation of recent decades did not happen "naturally"; it was not some generalized evolutionary force but, to great extent, a product of policy choices and decisions by regulatory agencies. Moreover, some of the most influential of those decisions escaped public scrutiny because they were made in the subterranean world of administrative action invisible to the public, through agency interpretation and policy guidance.
> ... It was not the highly visible acts of Congress but the seemingly mundane and often nontransparent actions of regulatory agencies that empowered the great transformation of the U.S. commercial banks from traditionally conservative deposit-taking and lending businesses into providers of wholesale financial risk management and intermediation services.[19]

The banking story illustrates the nature of sedimentary innovation, as well as the relationship between regulatory innovation and private sector innovation: these are series of incremental changes, which collectively lay down a markedly different landscape than existed prior – even while a clean, coherent account may readily present itself only after the fact. In similar fashion, the broad-scale securitization of residential mortgages did not happen overnight. It took place, as did other moves toward maturity transformation, the speculative use of derivatives, and the growth of leverage, in incremental steps.[20]

The point is not that sedimentary innovation, laboratories for democracy, or regulatory sandboxes are bad; far from it, they can in fact be very positive, especially if their promise is measured relative to easily-gamed bright-line regulatory rules. The point is simply that sedimentary innovation, like innovation generally, can exert powerful undermining forces on regulation itself across time. The fact that it is incremental change, which proceeds by degrees, can make it seem more benign in terms of its effects on regulation than it ultimately turns out to be.

The Impact of Network Effects: Brandeis and the "Swarm"

Examples like the railway oil spills, the evolution of banking, or the ABCP Crisis in Canada show how inputs from multiple different arenas – (a) increased oil prices plus political pressure not to build pipelines plus the sheer weight of heavy crude oil, for example; or (b) regulatory competition plus an evolving banking business model; or (c) the development of structured financial products and a new banking model, plus a global "savings glut" and low interest rates, plus a looming mortgage crisis next door – can together accrete into a new set of practices or conditions on the ground, which profoundly alter, in unexpected ways, the conditions with which regulation must grapple. Sedimentary innovation is a multifactorial phenomenon. What is more, the process by which sedimentary innovation accretes is an organic, contingent, somewhat unpredictable one that bears little resemblance to the clear, linear, mission-oriented innovative process we sometimes imagine.

The experimentalist account of regulatory bootstrapping, and the deep potential of incremental change, is important. At the same time, managing sedimentary innovation – having the presence of mind to bootstrap the "right" things and curtail the "wrong" things – is a challenging prospect. Sedimentary innovation holds out the possibility of meaningful benefits, certainly; as an object of regulation, however, it can also be hard to see, and hard to handle. The first problem is our own human fallibility as identifiers of relevant information and as rational decision-makers. Beyond that lie further problems that relate to the nature of innovation itself.

Claude Lévi-Strauss coined the term bricolage in its current usage. The bricoleur, in Lévi-Strauss's elegant twentieth-century formulation, is someone who works with his or her hands. However, what distinguishes bricoleurs from other craftspeople is that while they are skilled in many diverse tasks, their projects do not depend on having particular materials or tools on hand. They make do. In Lévi-Strauss's words, the bricoleur's

> Universe of instruments is closed and the rules of his game are always to make do with "whatever is at hand," that is to say with a set of tools and materials which is always finite and is also heterogeneous because what it contains

bears no relation to the current project, or indeed to any particular project, but is the contingent result of all the occasions there have been to renew or enrich the stock or to maintain it with the remains of previous constructions or destructions. The set of the "bricoleur's" means... is to be defined only by its potential use or ... because the elements are collected or retained on the principle that "they may always come in handy."[21]

Sedimentary innovation can be marked by bricolage, whether one works with one's hands or in more intangible realms like finance. In the financial context, Engelen et al. suggest that the idea of bricolage "has a double relevance to the process of financial innovation because it both describes the result of innovation, which ... has become a series of fragile long chains and it also characterizes the activity of innovation by the bricoleur at one nodal point in a chain."[22] That is, the fragile long chains of innovation they describe are the product of financial intermediaries fashioning retail-ready financial products out of the wholesale material available, rent-seeking at each juncture along the way. Bricolage is also occurring at each discrete nodal point, since "financial innovation does not correspond one-on-one with specific knowledge or technology."[23] Engelen et al. challenge the dominant accounts of financial innovation "in mainstream finance, social studies of finance and Marxist political economy which, all in different ways, argue or imply that science (represented by finance theory) or some other form of rationality (like class interest calculation) either is financial innovation or drives financial innovation." Instead, they argue, bricolage undertaken under changing, unstable circumstances will produce, inherently, unstable long chain innovations like the complex structured products we saw in the run-up to the financial crisis.[24]

The idea of bricolage is consistent with what we know about how innovation, including financial innovation, develops. Robert Merton once famously described what he called the "financial innovation spiral effect" – the idea that particularly useful or versatile financial innovations can spawn multiple knock-on financial innovations and collateral agreements. Once developed, a custom-made financial innovation can serve as a baseline for other commoditized agreements that ostensibly further fine-tune risk allocation between other parties. In Merton's words, the "synthesizing of custom financial contracts and securities is for financial services what the assembly-line production process is for the manufacturing sector. Options, futures, and other exchange-traded securities are the raw 'inputs' applied in prescribed combinations."[25]

The spiral effect makes the path of financial innovation more complex and more unpredictable, and that complexity is then multiplied by its deployment within the complex, varied, and interconnected financial system. The financial system is a complex network of institutions such as domestic banks, overseas banks, central banks, insurance companies, and investment firms, and they are linked together in multiple ways: through transactions, through products and services, through markets, and through the financial infrastructure of clearing, settlement, and trade depository functions. This is not a sea urchin-like "spike" of activity; it is a progressive spread.

From a regulatory perspective, the complex network characterizing the financial sector also means that certain hubs, like Wall Street or the City of London, should attract particular scrutiny. So should financial institutions that by virtue of their size, relationships, or influence are key vectors for transmitting risk, and therefore are important to systemic stability.[26] However, understanding the importance of networks to innovation is one thing, and defining relevant networks in a useful way is quite another. Financial system networks are multiple, variable, dynamic, and overlapping, and they can gain purchase at several different levels, as described below. They transmit innovations, as well as their effects (including risk), but the innovations are also altered, tweaked and repurposed as they diffuse. Financial network analysis is still in its early stages, though the US Treasury's Office of Financial Research (OFR) considers it a "promising new tool."[27] In furtherance of this project, however, we cannot forget that institutional network connections are only one, and the most formal, of the kinds of networks that bind the financial system together. As the innovation literature points out, network ties can be formal or informal, and strong or weak. While formal contractual relationships may be the most important elements for purposes of transmitting risk, understanding how innovation is transmitted will be more complicated. Along with institutional network analysis, we will also want to consider social and financial geography. As well, we will want to understand the precise nature of the products in question: it turns out that as a function of weak property rights and strong competition, financial innovations may diffuse through networks in particular ways.

Networks as Institutional and Social Phenomena
In the years since the financial crisis, network analysis based on computer simulations has begun to provide new insight into global financial interconnectedness and how such networks can or cannot absorb stress. Network analysis can help us develop a better image of the relationships through which goods, information, and risk all travel (even if any analysis will only provide a snapshot of a discrete moment in time). For example, when Sheri Markose and her colleagues modeled the US CDS market as of late 2007 and early 2008, they found J.P. Morgan to be the dominant bank in the network,

followed by European banks, and then other US banks like Goldman Sachs and Citibank.[28] Figure 8.1 reproduces their model of this network.

Recent work by Richard Bookstaber and Dror Y. Kenett for the OFR breaks interbank relationships down in a more granular, if less visually networked, way. Focusing on former US investment bank Bear Stearns's and two of its hedge funds during the financial crisis, their map, reproduced as Figure 8.2,

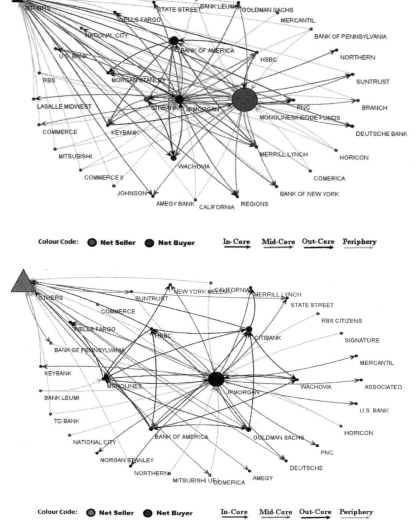

FIGURE 8.1. CDS network (Markose, "Too interconnected to fail," 640, note 28 above).

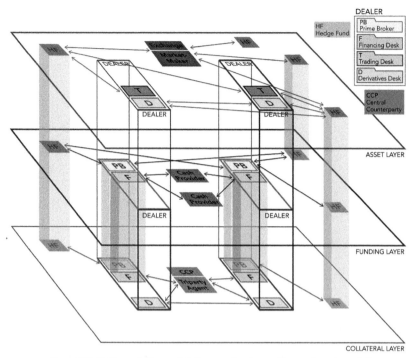

FIGURE 8.2. US Office of Financial Research, three-dimensional multilayer network map of the financial system (Source: Richard Bookstaber & Dror Y. Kenett, "Looking deeper, seeing more: a multilayer map of the financial system," OFR Brief Series (July 14, 2016) at p. 7).

identifies three layers of connections (across short-term funding, assets, and collateral flows) through which risk was transmitted across the financial system:

Schemas like these are helpful in understanding vectors along which risk may be transmitted. While there may be some overlap, financial *innovation* networks probably look somewhat different. If mapped, they could be equally useful in understanding how particular innovations are being transmitted. Yet, as valuable as these institutional network maps may prove to be, mapping institutional connections for purposes of tracking innovation must incorporate insights from social geography as well.

Within networks, geography – including social geography and cognitive geography – influences how innovative ideas diffuse, and how they evolve through diffusion. In some cases, physical geography may affect economic activity. Geographical proximity is a component that contributes to how and where network hubs develop, and isolation can have effects as well: for example, Hampton and Christensen have argued that small island economies can become locked into dependence on offshore finance, and therefore into tax haven activities.[29] The rate of diffusion of consumer-facing financial innovations like ATMs, debit cards, and direct deposits can also depend heavily on the demographics of the market, including education, race/ethnicity, and age.[30] Even despite heavy supply-side pressure to adopt innovations, the demand-side can be resistant to adopting innovations in certain contexts as a result of geography.

But perhaps the most interesting aspect of the social geography of financial innovation, when considering innovation as a regulatory challenge, is the way in which "supply-side" social networks seemingly influence the incremental development, diffusion and evolution of new technology, products, and practices. Sociologist Donald MacKenzie has described the famous 1998 downfall of the hedge fund Long-Term Capital Management (LTCM) in social network terms.[31] Salomon Brothers, headed by John Meriwether, reputedly "the most talented bond trader of his generation," developed LCTMs, with Nobel laureate partners Robert Merton and Myron Scholes (both instrumental to developing and perfecting the Black-Scholes option pricing model discussed earlier).[32] The fund was so successful that other investors started imitating it, and the result was something of a "super-portfolio" of overlapping arbitrage positions. Network effects thus created unanticipated homogeneity, which in turn decreased the entire system's stability and increased contagion effects.[33]

What may have been especially important in the globalization of securitization is what we might call "cognitive geography," or even the geography of professional social hierarchy: this is the sense that innovations diffuse out from knowledge or practice hubs, much in the way that Boaventura de Sousa Santos describes "focal objects" in his analogy of law to cartography.[34] De Sousa Santos refers to the distortions that are unavoidable aspects of map-making as *projection*. Projection and distortion happen outward from a focal object determined by the context surrounding the creation of that particular map. De Sousa Santos applies the concept of "focal objects" to law, and argues that the legal accounts that are created with a particular focal object at their center will be distorted in various ways when moving out from that point. Financial innovation, too, seemingly rippled outward from financial network hubs in a way that demonstrated the intellectual and reputational sway of centers like London and New York.

Reflecting on how local or regional crises beginning in the US subprime mortgage market could have turned into a global one, Roger Lee expresses surprise at:

[T]he geographical spread of the CDO market from New York to London, and then on to continental Europe ('contra' home bias and the historical significance of local markets). At that distance, decisions appear to have been made on the 'reputations' of offering banks, the claimed superior innovativeness of Anglo-American markets and the rumour-mill of actions taken by competing banks in other jurisdictions. Whereas institutions involved in currency trading have had to develop rigorous checks on cross-market positions on a 24/7/365 basis, this type of discipline was apparently not applied to participation in exotic products.[35]

Lee notes that by taking on the known and unknown risks associated with the CDO market, institutions were effectively gambling on the stability of the Anglo-American markets. These institutions "joined (perhaps unwittingly) the leverage applied to those markets by agents who stood most to gain, at least in the short-term from the leverage game."[36] In other words, network hubs were not only better able to transmit their innovations, but the reputational sway they wielded – their status as focal objects, in prestige terms using de Sousa Santos's cartographical metaphor – meant that other, more peripheral network players may also have been *less likely to scrutinize* those innovations. Diffusion took a particular form, which was the product not only of law and regulation, particular innovations, and network centrality, but of subjective reputational factors as well.

Of course, social geography also meant that the crisis, like economic shocks generally, imposed a differential effect on the poor. Where unemployment rose in the US and UK, levels of malnutrition and even death were expected to rise in the poorest parts of the global economy. As Minouche Shafik, then the permanent Secretary of the UK's Department for International Development, noted:

> [T]hose consequences are far more severe, frankly than anything we will experience as a result of this crisis ... And if this crisis is unfolding in poor countries more slowly more quietly and perhaps a bit less dramatically – it's because the families who are having to cut back on the quality of food they eat are poor and isolated and in rural areas and so we don't see them on the front page of the Financial Times or the Wall Street Journal, but that doesn't make the effect any less real.[37]

Herding and the First-Mover Advantage
Along with institutional relationships and the impact of cognitive and social geography, a third consideration that can help us to understand sedimentary financial innovation is the nature of financial products themselves. As we discussed in Chapter 6, financial innovation is particularly susceptible to herding because financial innovations are characterized by weak property rights, meaning first-movers have a considerable advantage.[38] In addition, common

incentive systems across financial institutions – a short-term profit orientation and the bonus structure, for example – gave each bank an incentive to evade capital requirements and take risks so long as its competitors were doing the same, generating a collective action problem.[39]

This was not the case back in 1931, when John Maynard Keynes famously observed that "[a] 'sound' banker, alas! is not one who foresees danger and avoids it, but one who, when he is ruined, is ruined in a conventional and orthodox way along with his fellows, so that no one can really blame him."[40] Banking has changed utterly, and is now an innovative industry where once it was a sleepy one. And yet based on a different set of economic drivers, Chuck Prince, Citigroup CEO, uttered a strikingly similar conformist sentiment in 2007. Dismissing concerns about liquidity in the credit-fueled economy, he just as famously said, "[w]hen the music stops, in terms of liquidity, things will be complicated. But as long as the music is playing, you've got to get up and dance."[41]

Consider that the following factors operate simultaneously and can reinforce each other: the pre-crisis environment was innovative in part because of the first-mover advantage. It was susceptible to collective action problems because of the additional incentive structures that operated within its institutions. Regulators who were seeking to be nimble and flexible in a competitive regulatory environment endorsed innovative activity. Innovations diffused in complicated and hard-to-track ways through institutional interconnections, but also as a result of the social and reputational sway that particular hubs enjoyed. And, the innovations in question were often the product of a process of bricolage that gave the impression that each incremental evolution was relatively unremarkable. Even while regulators were working to be receptive to financial innovation, they were not in a position to really understand how far from safety those innovations had taken them.

MAKING SENSE OF SEDIMENTARY INNOVATION

Humans Struggle to See Sedimentary Change

We probably all know, by now, that humans are not terribly good decision-makers under all conditions. For example, we tend overall to read too much into things that make a forceful impression on us, particularly where we have personal experience with them, and we read too little into things that do not make such an impression. Thanks to the availability heuristic, we also tend to confuse how easy it is to bring an example of something to mind with the probability it will occur (e.g., my friend lost money to a pump-and-dump scheme, so losing money in pump-and-dump schemes must be more common than I thought).[42] Perhaps for this reason, when making inter-temporal choices, we tend to value the present more than the future.[43] When calibrating the costs of low-probability, high-impact events – something else we struggle with, and which affects our thinking about seismic innovations too – we tend to discount future events even more. Thanks to anchoring and adjustment, we are also liable to judge future probabilities by reference to pre-existing starting points, which may or may not be reasonable or even relevant to the question at hand. Then, we tend to see what we want (or expect) to see. Confirmation bias, meaning the tendency to interpret evidence in a way that confirms existing beliefs and expectations,[44] distorts our perception of risk and inhibits our ability to see the unexpected, including the kinds of unexpected developments that may arise from sedimentary innovation.[45] Nor are we especially numerate. Anything above basic numeracy, like the complex probabilities that characterize risk, is challenging for most of us.[46]

Humans' familiar and predictable cognitive limitations take a particular form when it comes to sedimentary innovation. Put bluntly, we do a poor job of registering more incremental phenomena. We are simply not wired to detect gradual change very well.[47] In psychology, Weber's Law says that humans' ability to detect differences in the magnitude of a stimulus will depend on how large it is relative to the background situation. For example, while most people can hear a whispered voice in a quiet room, they may not notice someone shouting in their ear at a rock concert if the shouting is not louder, by a certain minimum proportion, than the background concert noise.[48] We acclimatize; we habituate; we become "change blind." How we respond to risk will be a function of how much risk we are already taking (as anyone who has ever traded a large debt in for a larger one knows). How much we register change, meaning innovation, will also be a function of how much change and innovation we are used to. Thus, sedimentary innovation can escape notice and, absent a focusing event, we seem able to become accustomed to very high levels of risk so long as it accretes slowly.

There is more. We may over-extrapolate from our own experience, and assume too much about what we do not know. We may anchor our perception of risk to something that has proven not to be risky for us individually (statistics notwithstanding), or not risky at our particular *scale*. For example, we may imagine that a financial innovation that seemingly presents low risk to the firm that developed it also poses a low level of risk to an entire sector, to systemic stability, or to society generally. Or, because a past financial innovation was considered to be low-risk, a newer and similar but in fact much riskier financial innovation may be judged to be lower risk than it is because we mentally characterize it as only an adjustment to, and recognizable in the terms of, the earlier low-risk innovation.

On the other hand, we tend to jump to conclusions about significance when confronted with striking events. They cause us to see patterns and discern pressing, widespread problems. As Rajeev Gowda says,

> [P]eople can be readily persuaded that a few examples of unfortunate results are an adequate representation of a policy's overall performance. Presenting a sequence of inferences which seem believable may persuade people towards such conclusions. This could lead to support for an unwarranted overhaul of the policy. The representativeness heuristic could also affect people's willingness to support risk management policies, e.g., flood risk-reduction measures, if the adduced sequence of future events leading to such disasters does not seem believable.[49]

This suggests, as already discussed, that the decision to frame an identified innovation as seismic can open windows of opportunity for regulatory action. By contrast, sedimentary innovations do not register with the same significance. In the regulatory context, this means that (to the extent we think about regulation at all when things seem to be going fine), even if we understand that sedimentary innovation is more common and often more influential, we may still respond rather too listlessly to it, because of the absence of a striking event.

The biases and heuristics above are only some of the reasons why our rationality is bounded.[50] Humans do not always even *try* to operate on a rational plane. We are also emotional beings, and our decision-making process can be influenced, or even dominated, by emotion.[51] Fear and anxiety can be strong emotional drivers of regulation and risk-related decision-making. Consider the heavy regulatory burden imposed on nuclear power compared to conventional fossil fuels. As journalist William Saletan noted when writing on the Fukushima crisis, there have only been 31 direct fatalities from nuclear power in the last 40 years, but over 20,000 in the oil supply chain and 15,000 in the coal supply chain. The ratio of fatalities per unit of energy produced is 18 times greater for oil than for nuclear energy.[52] Yet the fear of nuclear disaster provokes dread in a way that a steady stream of conventional fatalities does not, and to a substantial degree we regulate in response to our dread.[53]

We also experience anxiety where we perceive something as unknown, and where we cannot (rightly or mistakenly) slot it into a pre-existing narrative. Therefore, phenomena that seem new or different inspire more regulation than phenomena that seem like an extension of the familiar.[54] How vivid the imagery associated with a bad event, and how far into the future it may occur, also influence its emotional valence.[55] Sedimentary innovation is less unfamiliar and less emotionally evocative. In contrast to seismic innovation events, where particularly after a disaster risk is salient and people may over-estimate risk and over-regulate, when it comes to sedimentary innovation people may persistently under-estimate risk and under-regulate. This may be even more the case for financial risk, because it tends to be counterbalanced by the glittering promise of financial return. As well, financial risk tends not to generate the same imagery as, for example, environmental risk. The media-ready images of physical destruction, tar-covered shore birds or children being tested for toxin-related illnesses are absent.

Finally, the status quo bias also contributes to our passivity in the fact of sedimentary innovation. Given the choice, humans generally tend to prefer to maintain the status quo or to refrain from acting.[56] The status quo and confirmation biases may make us unwilling to recognize, in the absence of a striking event, that facts on the ground have changed and demand a response. Coupled with the prospect theory – that we tend to value avoiding potential losses over having potential gains – these biases may help explain why regulators may be more inclined to act aggressively *ex post* than comprehensively *ex ante*. Why change anything if there is no salient risk? Why "take the punch bowl away" when everyone is enjoying the party and nothing bad has happened?[57]

This presents a form of slippery slope problem as well, for both regulators and firms, in terms of accountability. Let us imagine that early on in the trajectory of some financial innovation, matters seem stable. There is risk associated with the innovation, but it seems to be operating within a tolerable range. With every day that sedimentary innovation accretes, the regulator (and the firm's compliance personnel) will have to consider afresh not one, but two questions: the first is whether the risk has now exceeded tolerable levels. The second, equally difficult one, is: why intervene today when we did not intervene yesterday? The regulator must not only justify its present intervention, but somehow establish the difficult claim that some *de minimis* change suddenly justifies acting, even though yesterday the regulator had judged in all its wisdom that things were fine. In settings such as this, the human mind opts for consistency, rejecting a potentially awkward change in posture, until disaster ensues.[58]

Epistemological Problems and Awareness Problems

One other cognitive bias hints at the larger epistemological problem that underlies sedimentary innovation as a regulatory challenge: the hindsight bias. The hindsight bias causes us to imagine, after viewing an outcome, that

that outcome was always clear.[59] The hindsight bias influences policy evaluation. As Gowda says,

> When faced with negative outcomes, the hindsight bias may lead people to criticize the decisions leading to failure as if the negative outcome should have been foreseen as inevitable rather than merely probable. Closely related to the hindsight bias, the outcome bias leads people to judge the goodness of risk-related decisions on the basis of their outcomes ... The hindsight and outcome biases could generate charges of incompetence or corruption to explain the failures of policies which may have failed by chance.[60]

These biases also make it simpler for us to conclude after the fact that we were mistaken to ever have run the risks we did. For example, while in view of the retrofitting costs we may honestly have imagined in 2010 that we were willing to run the tiny risk of an enormous tsunami flooding a major nuclear power plant in central Japan, it feels quite impossible to sustain that view in mid-2011, after a disaster has occurred. But the fact that the terrible thing happened does not mean that we had not measured the risk, and (even if not in this case, then in others) been willing to run it earlier. Our societies could not function without running some risks. Our after-the-fact assessment of which risks have been worth running is heavily skewed by which risks actually came, perhaps just by chance, to pass.

The hindsight and outcome biases are a problem for policy analysis regardless of the subject matter or innovation in question. However, the particular way in which they manifest in regard to sedimentary innovation is that they imposes *ex post* a level of certainty that simply was not present *ex ante*. They suggest not only that damage could and should have been avoided, but also that we can do better in avoiding it next time. In other words, when it comes to sedimentary innovation, the hindsight bias blinds us to the persistence of uncertainty itself. Every effort to improve regulation and avoid future harms – including the one we are engaged in here – is based on the idea that we can avoid regret later, if only we improve our risk management processes enough.

In fact, we are hampered by our inability to see, in the moment, precisely what is going on. Anticipating problems or identifying key turning points, in a complex world full of noisy signals, is extraordinarily difficult.[61] Moreover, it is impossible to predict which of multiple possible or probable outcomes will actually come to pass. This is not necessarily (or not only) a function of our limited ability to think clearly, to separate the causal wheat from the epiphenomenal chaff. It is also a function of the complex nature of causation. So, while there is a behavioral component to the challenge of regulating, including regulating sedimentary innovation, there is also a more fundamental epistemological one.

What may be less immediately obvious is how fragile any such coherent explanation is bound to be. Though it is no less true of the seismic innovation story, it is especially with respect to sedimentary innovation that we can *see* the contingency and subjectivity in the causal account. The causal account of the relationship between regulation and sedimentary innovation is a complex one. Like determining proximate cause of injury in a complex tort situation, determining (or predicting) how technological change and sedimentary innovation will co-evolve is an indeterminate process. Understanding financial innovation as most often a form of sedimentary, rather than seismic, innovation may be a useful analytical lens, because it yields a different interpretation of the problem at hand and generates different prescriptions for its resolution. At the same time, we need to be alive to the ways in which this account, like any other, cannot be more than partial and imperfect in its *ex post* explanations.

Regulatory Boundaries and Coordination Problems

Another aspect of the phenomenon of sedimentary innovation is that in complex, multipart systems, sometimes very consequential events happen in the interstices between existing regulatory regimes, or regulatory moments, or regulatory objects. Each component of regulation may focus on the "main effect," from its vantage point, and miss developments in the cracks in between. The anchoring effect of existing regulatory structures makes it harder to see interstitial phenomena with the color and depth that more central objects have. The legibility of a new innovation is a challenge for sedimentary innovations just as it is for seismic ones.

Entities operate within a complex factual and regulatory matrix, with layers of rules. Regulators may not see the connections between how public and private regulations interact, or how transnational and domestic regulations interact.[62] Transnational governance does not overpower domestic legal regimes, but rather intersects with domestic and customary systems to generate elaborate combinations of regulations.[63] Even leaving aside the impact of complexities such as private ordering and transnational regimes, it seems difficult to coordinate formal regulatory regimes.[64]

Moreover, interactions may not be obvious because different regulators may interact in unanticipated ways. Consider the relationship between bankruptcy law, the capital requirements imposed on financial institutions, and housing policy in the United States pre-crisis. Presumably the size and robustness of the subprime mortgage market was not the main concern of the Recourse Rule in the United States, which allowed financial institutions to keep only one-fifth as much capital on hand to cover triple-A rated mortgage-backed securities as for business and consumer loans.[65] Capital adequacy, not housing policy or access to credit, was the Rule's concern. Similarly, 2005 amendments to American bankruptcy provisions in 2005[66] expanded the definitions of a "repurchase agreement" (a "repo" agreement) to include mortgage loans, and interest on mortgage loans.[67] These amendments had the effect of facilitating the expansion of short-term repo financing. However, they also distorted creditor behavior and increased systemic risk.[68] The amendments essentially subsidized derivative financial activity with bankruptcy benefits, thus increasing the use of derivatives and reducing market discipline.[69] Of course, neither the derivative markets nor housing and mortgage policy was the Bankruptcy Code's main concern. The same is true of the relationship between capital adequacy rules and macroeconomics – they interacted in unexpected ways, effectively increasing the money supply and fueling an asset price bubble in housing.[70]

It is difficult in the abstract to do enough systematic comparison of the interactions between different regulatory regimes or strategies, and this is a problem that exacerbates and is exacerbated by sedimentary innovation. Coordination failure between regulators is a familiar problem, not limited to the innovation context, but it is a problem that is particularly relevant to the regulatory challenge that sedimentary innovation presents. These, too, are incorporated into the technical roadmap in this book's concluding chapter.

Sedimentary Innovation and Flexible Regulation

As we know by now, bright-line rules' rigidity in the face of incremental innovation makes it likely that the rules will be out of step almost by the time they are promulgated. Flexible regulation, which lays out a more nuanced and variable set of regulatory options, has been in part a response to that problem. Among the regulatory options it lays out is the idea of having a regulator set high-level principles or outcomes that regulated entities must meet, while leaving the details of implementation to the regulated actors themselves. In principle, this is the kind of system that should be able to adapt to sedimentary innovations while keeping sight of "big picture" regulatory objectives.

However, as the Volcker Rule account in Chapter 1 pointed out, moving the discussion of details to the technocratic plane can neutralize public participation, and it allocates substantial influence to those still in the room after the public moment has passed. Worse yet, if an agreement on principles or high-level outcomes is in fact masking the regulatory incapacity to understand or work with the actual firm-driven innovations being developed – as was the case in the UK around principles-based prudential regulation,[71] or in the US around the CSE Program[72] – then the regulator will simply have ceded the regulatory field to private actors. The crucial difference between what Ayres and Braithwaite call "enforced self-regulation"[73] on the one hand, and outright deregulation on the other, is precisely there. It matters very much what back-end processes are in place, exactly, through which indeterminacy will be resolved and the spaces in regulatory scaffolding filled in. Sedimentary innovation can undermine flexible regulatory structures, like other regulatory structures, if the regulator is not possessed of considerable capacity to register change across time, including effects outside the discrete regulatory moment at issue, and to appreciate its potential impact and the necessary responses to it.

We should flag two other potential problems that might be particularly associated with flexible regulation and sedimentary innovation. The first is that, as the Basel II capital adequacy account, or Omarova's description of the changing nature of the "business of banking" makes clear, flexible regulatory structures can actually *increase* the speed and prevalence of sedimentary innovation. Jeffrey Gordon has engagingly demonstrated that in a "constructed system" like financial regulation, any new, non-trivial change to the regulatory regime alters the context in which it operates.[74] Regulation changes behavior. In Gordon's words, "regulatory benchmarks inevitably become a management target; the exogenous becomes endogenous."[75] In such a reflexive system, a regime that puts private sector innovation-embracing strategies at the core of its own standards, as Basel II or banking regulation did, can expect one of its outputs to be more private sector innovation.

Second, we should be aware of the ways in which the particular structure of regulation may not be well situated to deal with sedimentary innovation. Risk-based regulation, one of the touchstone concepts within flexible regulation, may be such a structure. Specifically, Julia Black and Robert Baldwin have pointed out that, in risk-based regulation, "the tendency is for regulators' gaze to be drawn to their highest risks and for regulators to be encouraged to pull back resources from lower risks."[76] Risks that individually look low may never trip the alarm in such a system, notwithstanding that collectively they may be very significant. Nor do we understand the interactions between them in a complex system. Sedimentary innovation, too, can appear innocuous to a risk-based regulator until it has progressed well down the road, and – because it develops incrementally, through the actions of multiple parties and in response to multiple stimuli – by that time it can be very difficult to unwind.

As difficult a task as it may be, developing viable regulatory responses to extensive and continuous private sector innovation requires careful attention to these interactions, and an appreciation for just how much regulatory structure interacts with and is affected by private sector innovation taking place within its bounds.

POTENTIAL REGULATORY RESPONSES TO SEDIMENTARY INNOVATION

In terms of potential regulatory responses, first should be the recognition that loopholes and disconnects will be exploited. Innovation presents a clear and persistent risk – perhaps the single most significant and under-analyzed risk – to regulation itself. We can and should improve on the quality of information we have about just how sedimentary innovation works its way through, and in the process expands, the spaces and arbitrage opportunities within the regulatory fabric. Better harmonization and collaboration between financial regulatory regimes domestically and transnationally (including around accounting rules, prudential regulation, bankruptcy, and living wills) would also help reduce opportunities for regulatory arbitrage.[77] In the run-up to the financial crisis, private parties engaged in regulatory arbitrage between overlapping US regulators.[78] Transnational arbitrage, prominently between New York and London, also played a role. Gaps such as these can be addressed, and we can design incentives that reward better decision-making by banks and seek to limit herding behavior.[79]

But all of that is familiar ground. While useful, these suggestions do not respond to the question of how better to understand sedimentary innovation and its effects; nor do they address the epistemological and awareness problems that dog our efforts. There is no regulatory silver bullet. Yet promising options exist that can help to augment regulatory capacity to track and respond to sedimentary innovation.

As we have noted, developing a better understanding for how financial innovation develops – considering market structure, incentives, transmission vectors, and the presence or absence of "off" switches – is key to being able to understand innovative phenomena as they grow and to appreciate some of the ways in which they may be undermining, circumventing, or swamping regulatory structures. It may be useful to draw on experience about the parts of the financial system that seemed to remain stable or enforceable while others did not.[80] It may be useful to consider, as well, taking steps to identify those areas where financial institutions already have some incentive to self-regulate, for self-interested reasons, and those where they do not.[81] Without relying too heavily, or at all, on assumptions about the reliability of self-regulation, this may provide the opposite piece of information: a preliminary indication of what priorities most urgently need to have regulatory resources allocated to them.

Second, there is value in more explicitly considering the ways in which regulators, along with the rest of us, struggle to make sense of sedimentary innovation as it is developing. Are there ways that we might improve this capacity? The first way would be to take intentional steps to build better analytical capacity of the kind needed not just to understand the industry (though that is obviously essential), but also to identify behavioral cascades earlier, and to track "creep" in industry assumptions or standard practices over time. In the United States, the OFR has a mandate that can encompass these kinds of efforts.[82] A compatible suggestion would be Chuck Whitehead's, that regulators adopt a "Goldilocks Approach," meaning an approach whereby regulators are authorized to roll out, suspend or forgo regulatory steps over time, as information and experience improve understanding.[83]

It may also make sense to build an "institutional contrarian" role into the regulatory environment, particularly where regulators may be participating in sandbox exercises or other semi-collaborative engagements with private innovators. Regulatory contrarians as Brett McDonnell and Daniel Schwarcz describe them are "devil's advocates," with three key characteristics: 1) they are in a position of persuasive authority with access to media and officials (or, here, decision makers within the regulator), 2) they are affiliated with a regulatory entity but independent, and 3) they study the regulatory process to suggest improvements and point out flaws (or, as modified here, to point out assumptions or misperceptions about innovation that could undermine regulation).[84] Including a diversity of voices within a regulatory structure, combined with a formal structural role for presenting alternative views, may help increase the chances that a regulator will be able to identify, make sense of, and respond to sedimentary innovation in a timely and well-calibrated manner.

Third, regulators will want to understand sedimentary financial innovation as the network-based phenomenon that indeed it seems to be. This approach counsels treating the industry ecosystem as a network and focusing on its hubs rather than on specific instruments or institutions.[85] It would mean recognizing that, in regulatory terms, diffusion and herd behavior based on overall social and geographical networks can be just as problematic, in the aggregate, as any one institution that is considered "too big to fail" or "too interconnected to fail" on its own. Risk-based regulation that relies on bright-line matrices, like threshold asset size, risks missing important aggregate effects.

In addition, regulation could focus on breaking the connections through which sedimentary innovation diffuses, in the way that systemic risk management tries to do with respect to systemic risk. Using an engineering-based approach as Steven Schwarz has suggested to manage systemic risk, regulators could also choose to implement modularity within innovation networks – for example, by closing off some components and only allowing them to interact with others in certain ways, to make it possible to repair the component before the entire system fails.[86] No doubt, this idea will be less popular with respect to the prospect of cabining innovation than it is for cabining risk. Whether it is a tool worth deploying would depend on the regulator's (and perhaps the broader policy-maker's) assessment of how many other safeguards were in place to manage the disadvantages associated with a particular sedimentary innovation, and whether it made sense to try to close off the innovation, rather than *ex ante* to try to close off the risks associated with it. Yet for innovations that, in policy-makers' estimation, seem over time to have lost their social value – such as financial innovations that a policy maker has determined have no function other than rent-seeking – it is an approach that should not be dismissed out of hand.

Each of these options, and combinations of them, may make sense as responses to sedimentary innovation. The challenge will be to develop regulatory capacity and to implement these measures in a much more thorough and effective way than has been attempted so far, in keeping with the magnitude of the challenge that innovation presents for regulation's ability to meet its other, substantive, goals.

9

Innovation-Ready Regulation: Learning to See Financial Innovation

This book began by linking the current apparent ascendancy of political populism and its potential roots in frustration around inequality, with financial regulation and its associated scholarship. The relationship between equality, regulation, and innovation, particularly financial innovation, is in fact enormously complex and contingent.

If we think of innovation as a great flowing river, we should remember that not everyone will be swept up in it. For better and for worse, sometimes by choice but mostly due to circumstance, some will remain on its banks. Of those that are swept up, some quickly will be swept under while others will be carried along its surface, at least for a time. Indeed, at some point in our lives, *none* of us, not even the most capable and well resourced, will be at the vanguard of innovation and in a position to benefit directly from it. Some very thorny political and normative questions about fairness, equality, and justice arise around innovation – the very questions that sometimes lay buried under flexible regulation's preoccupation with technique.

The question of whether innovation is "good" or "bad" is almost impossible to answer in that crude form. Good for whom, and how? Leaving aside the easy cases where innovation is undertaken apparently just for rent-seeking or to circumvent regulation, what if an innovation benefits the most disadvantaged while simultaneously increasing inequality? Is that good? Most theories of justice agree that extreme deprivation is presumptively unjust. If we think about justice as being primarily concerned with the problem of extreme deprivation, then an innovation that addresses it is likely to be seen as improving justice. If we expand the concept of justice to include considerations of inequality, power disparities, or domination, however, the answer is not so simple.[1] The Green Revolution may even be such a case. We are right to celebrate its tangible successes: technological advances in high-yield seed varieties contributed directly to improving food security and reducing rural poverty in places such as India, with real and significant benefits to peoples' lives. At the same time, its benefits have gone disproportionately to richer farmers, and Green Revolution innovations have had environmental effects, including lowering the water table, that are likely to have consequences for future generations.[2]

As well, do we care about inequality at the local, or national, or global level? Benefits at one level will not necessarily yield benefits at others, and may yield costs. Advances in shipping technology contributed to creating many thousands of jobs and markedly improving standards of living in developing countries, at least over the short term, even while stripping manufacturing jobs from developed economies. Nor does the equation always flow in that direction. For every innovation, like mobile money systems, that benefits local economies in developing countries, there may be a corresponding innovation developed by and for the benefit of the Global North, which threatens the livelihoods of poor people in the Global South.[3] Nor, in fact, is there any unequivocal answer to the question of the relationship between innovation and equality. Innovation can reflect and reinforce inequalities, or undermine them. Moreover, innovation has a reflexive relationship with inequality just as it does with regulation: they influence each other in complex ways.[4]

The same is true of financial innovation. We cannot make credible *ex ante* determinations about whether a particular financial innovation will bring social benefits and, if so, how diffused those benefits will be. Soete has asserted that even though innovation often produces Schumpeterian "creative destruction," there are times, including in finance, when it produces only "destructive creation."[5] Yet, there does not seem to be any rule that allows us determine, unequivocally, the social benefits or costs associated with any particular financial innovation. As Elul has suggested, introducing a new financial product can have "almost arbitrary effects on agents' utilities." A new product can "generically make all agents strictly worse off, or all agents strictly better off, or favor any group of agents over another."[6] Indeed, even the recent financial crisis was underpinned by financial innovations, such as home equity lines of credit and mortgage securitization, that could have been and in some cases were actually significantly welfare-enhancing for ordinary people across a non-minimal time period. Until they spun out of control and produced systemic effects (in part because, through innovation, regulatory safeguards had been circumvented and undermined), in some cases these new financial technologies allowed households to smooth consumption patterns, and allowed more people to obtain mortgages and acquire real property.[7] The underlying innovations were not inherently malign. (Other things were – predatory lending and mortgage fraud were. But securitization itself was not.)

Assessing innovation's benefits against different standards of justice or fairness is part of a debate that has been raging, and continues to rage, and (as with many such debates) it will probably never admit of an easy answer. This book does not advance a comprehensive theory of justice as it concerns innovation, except to insist that innovation – the capacity to be innovative, the ability to frame new initiatives in the simultaneously aspirational and silencing language of innovation – is a form of power, and is unequally distributed. Any progressive instincts notwithstanding, a regulatory analysis that cannot see and grapple with innovation, as a significant source of power and influence and as a framing device for legitimizing conduct, will be missing an essential consideration. It will fail to recognize the magnitude of the challenge that innovation presents. We can do better at solving the immediate, pragmatic problem – the fact that regulation consistently struggles to identify and respond to innovation effectively. As well, we can take steps, energized by flexible regulation's ability to manage postmodern uncertainty and disagreement through participatory and deliberative mechanisms, to develop a more legitimate and defensible approach to generating the very goals that our financial regulatory regimes seek to accomplish. In this way, the project ahead is one that involves both procedural, and substantive, justice.

RESPONDING TO INNOVATION AS A TECHNICAL REGULATORY CHALLENGE

We know now that financial innovation can have significant and underappreciated effects on the human-built legal fictions and cognitive architecture that house it. Across this book we have discussed multiple examples of the ways in which innovation can denature products, like commercial paper, which was transformed across a short time frame from a sleepy, safe corner of financial practice to a complex, short-term, and risky borrowing mechanism. Innovation has denatured practices too, like the "business of banking" as its regulatory definition in the United States evolved, with the help of industry lobbying and inter-regulatory competition, across a few short decades. Indeed, financial innovation in the form of equity derivatives in particular has shattered the atom of property, blurred the lines between products and practices, and made structures that were previously comprehensible in one form (for example, as institutions) now reappear in entirely different guises (for example, as contractual relations), avoiding regulatory requirements even while performing operations that, from the market's or the consumer's point of view, were functionally identical.

We should not forget that many of the financial innovations described here are as much legal innovations as they are strictly financial ones. Financial innovation includes changes to formal legal fictions and the legal treatments of assets, not just new financial technology. Innovation for the sake of avoiding regulation is as much lawyers' doing as it is bankers' or accountants'. Lawyers are intimately implicated here, and their inimitable ingenuity is part of the challenge that regulation needs to acknowledge and confront.

Financial regulation is one, particularly consequential, example of how our cognitive architecture can be undermined by innovation. Financial innovation made a mockery of bright-line accounting rules in the Enron scenario. Swaps went essentially unregulated for years because it was difficult to put them into any of the pre-existing regulatory categories of futures, securities, or loans. Presentations of innovative finance also, due to their framing as technical matters of esoteric expertise and high complexity, undermined longstanding mechanisms for public input into regulatory rulemaking in the United States, as the Volcker Rule example in Chapter 1 describes. The story of financial innovation in nineteenth-century American railroad development also suggests that, at least some of the time, seemingly public/private cooperative arrangements can over time lose their public aspect, as persistently involved and interested private actors slowly occupy the decision-making field. Nor did innovation limit its effects to established regulatory silos. The role of "shadow banks" – financial institutions performing bank-like functions without being subject to banking's prudential regulatory requirements – is quite familiar now, but consider also the bleed-overs from one realm of finance to another, such as those from bankruptcy rules to the size of the subprime mortgage market. There are many such examples.

Regulation was not just a passive bystander to, object of, or victim of these processes. The relationship between innovation and regulation is intricate and reflexive. Consider, for example, the ways in which regulation can accelerate innovation – potentially, by deregulating (as with deepwater oil drilling, or the ABCP prospectus exemption under Canadian securities regulation), but also by regulating in particular ways (as we saw with the gameable Enron-era accounting rules). We should recall, as well, the tendency of innovation-framing, scaffolding-style flexible regulation to unintentionally spur more innovation, simply by creating opportunities within its porous structures for more private sector creativity. This was the case with the Basel II capital adequacy rules. Regulation – like financial modeling itself, and like legal fictions and framing devices generally that shape their environments through their descriptions of it – truly can be, in Donald McKenzie's words, an engine and not just a camera.[8]

Innovation has had broader cognitive implications as well, which are related to but which extend well beyond the general pro-innovation caste of contemporary society. For example, as we have seen, complexity-borne-of-innovation arguments were pressed into service by industry actors and, in a form of creeping cognitive capture, helped to undermine regulators' independent-mindedness and to chasten their ambitions. On the other side of the equation, adopting mathematical modeling, in the form of the Black-Scholes option-pricing model, into finance produced more than just an apparent improvement in pricing certainty. It also transformed the whole tenor of derivatives markets from something akin to gambling, to a far more legitimate-seeming, even noble, method for allocating risk and perfecting markets. Innovation can also be difficult to track or to make sense of, for cognitive reasons. As it develops at different speeds and along different trajectories, innovation can throw up distinct regulatory challenges. Our cognitive shortcomings figure prominently in our efforts to respond to them: we may struggle to recognize sedimentary innovations in real time, or struggle to "pull the plug" on an evolving innovation after not having done so the day before; even while we are prone to over-reacting to high-salience disasters after the fact.

Consider, also, the organic, very human, and socially derived paths along which innovation seems to develop and diffuse. Formal network effects are part of the account, but so are "fuzzy" reputational effects, and softer forms of influence. Similarly, while technical advancement has been part of this narrative, innovation is the product not only (or even not mainly) of invention but also of messy, idiosyncratic, multi-nodal bricolage and improvisation. Getting a better handle on innovation for regulatory purposes will be as much an epistemic, and perhaps microsociological, undertaking as it is a quantitative one. This book hardly scratches the surface of that project.

In focusing on innovation, the risk of reductivism is significant. The claim here is not that innovation is at the root of every single challenge that financial regulation faces. Clearly there are other contributing challenges, prominently including regulatory coordination problems across jurisdictions, and what we might call (at best) a sometimes-ambivalent political stance toward regulating finance and curbing financialization. The reason we would want to focus on innovation is not that it is demonstrably at the root of all our difficulties, but rather that learning to *see* it, and to see it as a central challenge to regulation, is perhaps the single most direct and effective thing that financial regulation can do to establish some bearings in a most fluid, contingent space. It is Occam's Razor.

We can discern an image – still grainy and anecdotal, with more work to be done – of how financial innovation evolves. Alongside it, hopefully, we will develop a sense of the importance and urgency of the task we face from here. Chapter 1 closed with three observations: first, that narratives about complexity and dynamism, while grounded in reality, can be "spun" and co-opted by industry actors arguing for regulatory restraint. Financial industry actors' success in helping to convince regulators that their main concern was that they not fall behind fast-moving private sector developments contributed to regulators' difficulty in articulating a forceful, skeptical, independent regulatory stance from which to critique that private sector innovation. The second observation is that we should not simply assume that the formal regulatory moment – the implementation or triggering of a rule, for example – is the most important one. Technical innovations made in the spaces before and behind the rule's operation can alter its effect or even neuter it. Discursive and lobbying efforts after its implementation, concerning its technical details, can pose similar risks. The third observation was that we should not assume that regulation sits outside innovation and is not directly implicated by it. On the contrary, regulation and its environment, including the innovations being developed there, are in an ongoing, reflexive relationship in which each continually influences the other.

Taken together, along with the other narratives woven through this book, what emerges is the sense that regulation has been insufficiently aware, at a very fundamental level, of the nature of the challenges – the cognitive, interpretive, structural, and temporal challenges – that it faces as a function of innovation. The necessary epistemological reckoning has not yet taken place. Part of this book's purpose is to improve our capacity to understand innovation, particularly financial innovation, as a phenomenon – a swamping, swarming, sedimentary, and potentially seismic one – that, we should assume, will continue to threaten and to undermine our best-laid regulatory plans. Recognizing financial innovation for the regulatory challenge that it genuinely is requires both a technical/procedural, and a substantive, set of responses.

Regulatory design will never be a sufficient or perfectible instrument for achieving social goals. We would be wise to maintain a degree of humility about what any *ex ante* effort to channel collective behavior may achieve, particularly if it becomes divorced from lived experience and historical context. Moreover, a preoccupation with technique on its own may have been one of the reasons why flexible regulation found its scope and its practical influence limited, and sometimes co-opted, in the years leading up to the financial crisis. At this stage, the aim must be to move beyond technical conversations about how to improve regulatory efficiency and effectiveness, and to reclaim regulation – especially financial regulation – as the fundamentally progressive project it has been since the 1930s. Regulating effectively means embodying public priorities, and it calls for expressing and hewing to explicit normative choices about regulatory priorities.

At the same time, if we want regulation to succeed, we will also want to make the best instrumental choices we can about which regulatory tools to use. The last three decades of regulatory experience and (perhaps especially) scholarship have yielded important new insights into how regulation works; how it relates to other forces, like the market or community norms, that also channel and influence behavior; and the range of mechanisms that can be deployed to achieve regulatory outcomes more reliably and at lower cost. Flexible regulation was generated not only out of the claims to legitimacy that transparency, accountability, and deliberation afforded in the postmodern environment, but also on knowledge gleaned from economics, norms scholarship, behavioral psychology, and more. The question, though, here and persistently, is whether the regulatory schemes we seek to rely on have yet inquired into their priors and premises sufficiently to understand from where the risks and challenges from innovation will be coming.

With this object in mind, financial regulators should be addressing three discrete but interrelated sets of considerations in seeking to meet the challenge that innovation presents for regulation: the basis of the regulator's knowledge and the nature of its assumptions; how the regulatory regime is structured, and what implications flow from that structure; and finally, what mechanisms exist to allow the regulatory regime to learn and adapt, and whether they are adequate. Each of Chapters 6 through 8 closed with specific recommendations and avenues of inquiry for thinking about and confronting financial innovation. The questions below aggregate the claims made in those chapters, and build on the foundation that flexible regulation scholarship itself has established.

Figure 9.1 illustrates the three main sets of considerations, after which follows Table 9.1, which breaks each component down further into a set of provisional questions, which are meant to be revisable based on experience. The relationship between the three sets of considerations is more porous than this diagram can depict, and regulators' learning loops should weave across all three. The volume and granularity of information needed here is considerable, but we should remember a few things: first, regulators in specific sectors likely already possess a fair bit of it. Second, others in the vicinity of the regulation (industry actors, relevant third parties and regulatory surrogates, and broader stakeholders including members of the public) are likely to possess more. Flexible regulation scholarship has taught us a good deal about how to gain access to and incorporate that information, and about when it

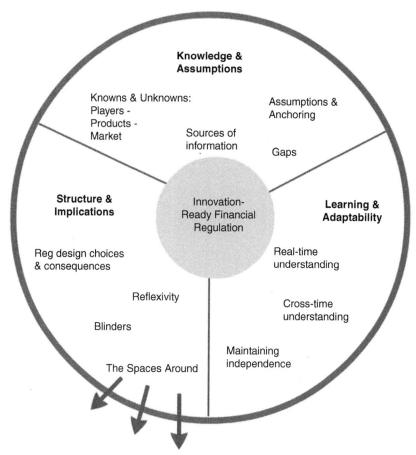

FIGURE 9.1. Aspects of innovation-ready financial regulation.

might make sense to do so. Third, if actual informational scarcity is a problem, then it will be a problem whether we acknowledge it or not. Identifying gaps in knowledge can be essential to augmenting a regulator's capacity to see and fully understand its field, including the innovative challenges arising within it.

Trying to understand innovation, for purposes of regulating it, is not the same thing as trying to develop some *ex ante* assessment of whether a particular innovation is "good" or "bad." That is a fool's errand. Far better to think of our assessment methods as relying on continual checking and re-checking, asking the right questions and re-checking the questions too, to confirm that we are both *seeing* financial innovation as it occurs – an epistemological project – and *assessing its effects* by reference to pre-established normative

TABLE 9.1. *Framework for innovation-ready regulation*

	Knowledge and assumptions: What does the regulator know, and how does it know it? What does it not know?
	Who are the main (incumbent) players in the regulated industry? This will affect the kinds of innovations they pursue.
	• What are their key relationships? How are they positioned within knowledge transmission networks? What influence do they have within those networks and more broadly? This includes their formal and informal institutional connections but also, crucially, their location within the industry's cognitive and social geography.
	• What are these players' core business areas, and what kinds of innovations likely fit most easily with their business models, structure and approach? Is their business model based on providing services that, evidence suggests, are
Knowledge about potential *innovators*	currently particularly vulnerable to disruption? Who is rent-seeking?
	• What incentives do they have (pecuniary or otherwise, short-term and longer-term), and not have? E.g., there are far fewer internal quality control incentives with respect to underlying mortgages under an originate-to-distribute model. Are industry actors particularly more or less likely to be able to self-regulate (e.g., where they share a "community of fate") with respect to any aspects of their business?
	Who are the disruptive outside innovators who may be changing the landscape? What is known? What is knowable but not known (in the realm of evidence deficit)? Why is evidence missing and what can be done to acquire it? Are there even genuinely uncertain aspects of their natures, businesses, relationships, strategies, and incentives?
	• This includes innovative uses for existing products. Consider both product and process innovations; and both highly technical and seemingly unremarkable ones where their use seems to be evolving, increasing, or shifting.
Knowledge about potentially innovative *products*	• Consider purposes: to what degree is innovation being undertaken to ostensibly serve clients and perfect markets, to rent-seek, to protect market share or raise barriers to entry, or to avoid regulation (or for some other reason)? How are these purposes being advanced? The purpose being pursued will affect the nature of the innovation.
	• What do we know about what is happening before and behind the regulatory moment? E.g., can we detect innovation around the nature or use of a product, like commercial paper, which is not being reflected in its regulatory treatment? What regulatory structures are in place for investigating this? Are they adequate?

- What characteristics of the innovative product will affect how it diffuses? E.g., financial innovations are characterized by weak property rights, which generate a strong first-mover advantage and can produce herding.

- How competitive is the particular market segment in question, among incumbents as well as between established players and disruptive newcomers? How is this competition likely to affect how innovative ideas are developed and deployed, and how they diffuse? Consider how interfirm competition produced a collective rush toward excessive leverage in the years leading up to the financial crisis.

Knowledge about industry *context* and market

- Are market forces likely to operate to slow, or accelerate, innovation and its diffusion? E.g., the lack of transparency and price discovery in the OTC derivatives market, combined with a potential "global savings glut" and the uncertainty associated with multifactorial events in the capital markets, meant that market discipline did not operate in the pre-crisis OTC markets. Securitization produced an appetite for assets (including debt and already-securitized debt) that created an artificial, outsized, and unsustainable financial economy. Is innovation altering its market environment and weakening market discipline and, if so, how? Are there other reasons (e.g., implicit government subsidies for too big to fail financial institutions, in the run-up to the financial crisis) to think that market discipline will not operate?

- Where is the regulator getting its information? E.g., from proprietary systems developed by regulated actors (as with Basel II), or from intermediaries who may have conflicts of interest (as with credit rating agencies in the United States)? Why and how is the regulator's data limited or imperfect in terms of quantity or quality? Is innovation producing or exacerbating these knowledge gaps (or, as with the complexity account described in Chapter 1, is industry innovativeness being used to make a case for regulatory passivity)? How significant are these limits, and how can they be addressed?

Knowledge gaps and sources of information

- What is the reason for knowledge gaps? Are they because the right information is not being sought, or because of genuine uncertainty (e.g., with respect to apparently "seismic" innovations)? What developments seem to be too complex or too fast-moving to comprehend and respond to? Does this lack of knowledge suggest the need for new precautionary principle or pre-licensing requirements?

(continued)

TABLE 9.1 (continued)

| | • Is information and feedback being gathered from a suitably broad range of perspectives? This is important to ensure that good information is being developed, and it helps ensure a level of congruence between regulatory practice and social priorities. It also contributes to a level of perceived legitimacy. Where and how does public voice enter – whether through deliberative mechanisms (assess how meaningful) or representative ones? If voices articulating public priorities are muted or absent, why is this the case and how can it be addressed? |
| Regulatory assumptions | What assumptions are baked into the regulatory structure? Assumptions are inevitable, but they can be more or less appropriate. How do they limit perception or understanding, and anchor thinking? E.g., what assumptions are being made about the influence of market forces (as with the ABCP regime in Canada), the reliability of privately generated information, or private actors' incentives not to run excessive risks (e.g., the Basel Capital Accords' use of banks' proprietary risk analytic software)? What assumptions are being made, and why, about what is in the public interest? Does the regulatory approach focus on institutions (e.g., SIFI designations), in which case it risks missing market-focused or crowd-based phenomena; or vise versa? How are key terms defined (and potentially defined differently by adjacent regulators, producing opportunities for regulation-avoiding innovation)? How could innovation, notably under-the-radar sedimentary innovation, potentially be undermining key regulatory assumptions? |

How is regulation structured, and what flows from these choices?

| | • What roles are formal thresholds, designations, and bright-line or detailed rules playing in the regulatory structure? What are their effects (e.g., in imposing an important minimum floor or meaningful boundaries on conduct; or binding regulation to concepts that, due to innovation, no longer reflect practice)? How effective are they in practice? How can they be gamed, and what resources does the regulator need to determine whether they are being gamed through innovation? |
| Regulatory design choices and their implications | • Does regulation adopt a cooperative stance with regulated actors? If so, at what stage and for what purposes? E.g., in terms of standard setting, monitoring, implementation, enforcement? What are the implications, positive and/or negative, for the regulator's access to information, and its capacity to act to respond to innovation? Is the public role being squeezed out of the public/private cooperative endeavor, as with late nineteenth-century American railroad |

restructuring? Does the cooperative structure look more like North Sea safety case regulation, or more like Gulf of Mexico deepwater regulation under MMS? Is the regulator adequately enough resourced, given that cooperative schemes demand significant resources if they are to be implemented responsibly?

- Does the regulatory structure anticipate input from the public in some form? How? Does the regulatory structure anticipate input from other third parties or regulatory surrogates (e.g., insurers, trade associations) and, if so, can it track how those parties' incentives may evolve as innovation alters the terrain? (US credit rating agencies' conflicts of interest were exacerbated, as complex securitized assets became a larger proportion of their business.) Does the regulatory structure anticipate that industry behavior will be channeled in pro-regulatory ways by other forces, such as social pressure or market forces? What do we know about how effective these mechanisms are in practice, and how they will be affected by innovation? What resources does the regulator need to determine whether they are effective across time?

Reflexivity

What is the reflexive relationship between the regulatory structure and innovation? How is regulation creating new opportunities for innovation (e.g., by creating easily gameable structures, imposing different regulatory burdens on functionally similar asset types, or similar regulatory burdens on functionally different asset types)? Is this intentional (e.g., on the assumption that innovation, or certain kinds of innovation, will be beneficial or are easily controlled), or is it unintentional? Is regulation accelerating innovation or producing more of it, as a function of an innovation-friendly but under-designed structure? Is it co-creating innovations, including what we might think of as "seismic" ones? Is the content of detailed, technocratic discussions about regulatory content ramifying back to, and potentially undermining, broader understandings of regulatory goals and the public interest (as may have been the case around the Volcker Rule)? How should these consequences be assessed, and responded to?

Blinders

How does regulatory jurisdiction (horizontally between, e.g., banking and securities regulators, vertically across state/federal/regulation lines, through different scales of individual/industry/professional/market) potentially impose limits on understanding? Innovations that take place at the margins of jurisdiction, or even beyond them, will be harder to see even while they may have strong and adverse effects on regulatory capacity or overall regulatory goals. This was the case with the growth of shadow

(continued)

TABLE 9.1 (continued)

	banking. Products (e.g., interest rate and foreign exchange swaps) can be legible to the market while being illegible to regulatory structures, in the sense of being hard to categorize. How can the regulator remain aware across time of the effects of these blinders, and what can be done to address their effects vis-à-vis boundary-spanning innovations?
The spaces around	What factors outside the regulator's immediate bailiwick may affect innovation within it? E.g., if there are adjacent unregulated or less-regulated spaces, innovation may gravitate toward them, with consequences that will be felt within regulated spaces too. What about regulatory competition – is it operating? Are regulators competing for innovative business in particular (as with fintech sandboxes)? How might this influence innovative activity and regulatory standards? Does the regulatory regime anticipate any other backstops (such as marketability or market discipline) operating to limit or channel innovative activity? How might regulation within one area affect other nearby spaces (as with the bleed over from bankruptcy provisions to the subprime mortgage market, or from microprudential to macroprudential spaces)? Conversely, how might innovation within one regulatory space affect other nearby spaces, and with what effects on broader socioeconomic conditions? What resources does a regulator require to be able to answer these questions?

Learning and adaptability: making regulation more resilient in the face of innovation

Strategies for identifying and responding to innovation in *real-time*	• What structures does the regulator require to obtain and work with good information in real-time? How will it identify innovations, their substitutive potential, and their structural impact? This may include developing a regulatory approach that prioritizes learning, in the way that experimentalist and meta-regulatory systems do; and continuous awareness of what the regulator actually knows, and does not know. It also calls for additional methods (including perhaps information disclosure requirements as terms of entry to regulatory sandboxes) for gathering and then validating information from industry and others. This includes structures for checking the information inputs it is receiving, including after-the-fact (e.g., at the notice-and-comment rulemaking stage, when important details are determined and having a diversity of informed opinion in the room is essential). It also includes acquiring and analyzing information across boundaries, space, and scale as described above (e.g., noticing the way that new mathematical innovations, like the Black-Scholes option pricing model, or new inputs, like changes to bankruptcy or other rules, are driving innovation).

- What mechanisms are in place to ensure the regulator is able to continually re-check its assumptions to confirm they are still operating as assumed, in spite of innovation's effects; to notice when the fit between regulatory structure and actual industry conduct seems to be loosening, opening new spaces for regulatory arbitrage; and to notice how assumptions – like the significance of complexity – may be serving industry purposes at the expense of regulatory goals, or undermining transparency or legibility? Are these mechanisms embedded or institutionalized into regulatory practice and regulatory incentive structures in a way that makes them meaningful and robust?

- How can regulation be specifically structured to continually re-examine how its blinders and the limits of its own jurisdiction may be causing it to miss important effects? How collaborative and congenial are relationships with adjacent regulators? How strong, structured, and regular are communication paths with adjacent regulators? (E.g., supra-regulatory consultation and oversight bodies, like the Financial Services Oversight Council in the US, the European Systemic Risk Board in the EU, and the Bank of England's Financial Policy Committee in the UK were designed in part, post-crisis, for this purpose; at the international level, the Group of Twenty and the Financial Stability Board serve somewhat similar functions.) Are processes adequate to ensure that crosscutting innovations that are not the "main effect" in anyone's jurisdiction are nevertheless not ignored?

Noticing sedimentary innovations in particular requires that regulators develop strategies for overcoming human cognitive shortcomings. In the case of seismic innovations, the challenge is to respond before disaster strikes. In all cases, regulatory thinking tends to soften in the midst of a bubble and to harden, with the benefit of hindsight, after the fact. Preoccupied as it inevitably is with the formal regulatory moments – the licensing decision, the exemption decision, the moment of disclosure – regulation also can fail to see crucial changes, wrought by innovation, in the spaces before and behind and after those formal ones. Lifting regulation out of its time-bound moment is not simple, though recognizing the problem is an important part of the solution. Consider, for example: has the regulator developed the institutional capacity to track "creep" over time, including swarming, or the kinds of changes in industry practice that suggest that new products are being substituted for old, or that bricolage has transformed a market? Are there ways to gather and use quantitative and qualitative data to help alert humans to relevant changes that might otherwise go unnoticed? Does the regulator have the ability and access needed to identify normative changes within the industry, demonstrated perhaps by the rising and falling fortunes of different professionals, or firms, or of the "wise old heads of banking?"

Strategies for identifying and responding to innovation *across time*

(continued)

TABLE 9.1 *(continued)*

	Responding to the effects of innovation requires courage on the part of regulators and a willingness on the part of policy makers to accept that there will be tradeoffs – that there is no magical formula that can simultaneously increase competitiveness, spur productive innovation, stifle unproductive innovation, achieve regulatory objectives efficiently and effectively, and reduce the regulatory burden.
Strategies for maintaining regulatory independent-mindedness	What strategies can be developed to help regulators to maintain independent-mindedness, in the face of industry persuasion and across time? Consider, e.g., embedding institutional contrarians, and paying conscious attention to diversity, so that the regulator is continually exposed to a plurality of perspectives. What mechanisms for public voice, in some form, are in place to help shore up a regulator's independent vantage point and its sense of public purpose? Are regulators adequately resourced? Do they have access to meaningful and valid data, and the means to validate data? Is there a risk of cognitive capture (or outright capture) associated with a revolving door between regulation and lucrative private industry practice? Could inter-jurisdictional regulatory competition be posing risks to independent-mindedness, as regulators compete with each other for business? How are industry actors framing their innovations when engaging with their regulators – asserting, for example, that there is "nothing to see here (e.g., ABCP is like normal commercial paper)," or that regulators should "leave the details / the complexities to us", or that "this time is different?" In retrospect, assertions like these may have been useful tell-tails of important innovative shifts in industry practice in the lead-up to the last financial crisis, which pointed to a heightened need for critical assessment and scrutiny on the part of regulators.
	Regulators should understand that they can frame things too, including framing an innovation as "seismic" innovations where required.

priorities.[9] Technical regulatory strategies such as these are essential to allow financial regulation to grapple with the considerable challenge that innovation presents to its functioning. The other essential piece is normative, and requires that we consider what legitimate and workable options exist for allowing our treatment of innovation, particularly financial innovation, to conform more closely to our collective priorities and concerns.

THE NORMATIVE PIECE: ON DELIBERATION AND CONTINGENCY

What gets lost in overbroad accounts of the last few decades of regulatory theory is also the key to both good information and justifiable process today: it is the centrality of deliberation, contestation, and dialogue to flexible regulation theory. James Scott once described the ways in which the state, along with other agents of "homogenization, uniformity, grids, and heroic simplification," including capitalism, tend to flatten out lived reality into forms that are legible for its own purposes.[10] This book's purpose is not to try to impose some top-down, simplified or homogenized vision of elegant regulatory design in response to financial innovation. Flexible regulation, as embodied in the scholarship we have considered here, has never been a purely technocratic project. Granted, institutions like *Responsive Regulation*'s tripartism and experimentalist broadly participatory deliberation can be effective for instrumental reasons: they can enrich and improve the information in the system, and reduce herding and groupthink. But bringing local knowledge up into a state-level regulatory project is more important for social and political reasons than for instrumental ones. In helping to ensure that a multiplicity of voices and perspectives are present for the regulatory conversation, we avoid not only Scott's dystopic expertise-driven calamities, but also the domination that is civic republicanism's main concern.

The idea of domination includes concerns about economic inequality, and also concerns about voice and representation. For civic republicans, the ethic of non-domination means not just negative freedom, as with liberalism – not just freedom from explicit state interference; it means freedom from domination in all its forms, including representative and economic ones. Genuinely instantiating a civic republican non-domination ethos into financial regulation, as it relates to financial innovation, must include substantive goals – taking steps to notice whether a playing field is level in multiple senses, notably including voice and access, and to try to level it where needed – as well as structural regulatory choices geared toward ensuring that the public interest in its many forms and guises is genuinely represented. Financial regulation should therefore be buttressed not only by a clear sense of its public purpose, but also by regulatory structures that facilitate and perhaps even sometimes mandate voice and participation.[11]

This book aims to recover the particular civic republican thread within flexible regulation literature, and to position it as a normative lodestar for structuring and clarifying decision-making around financial innovation in particular. But this is only part of a broader legal project, now overdue, which would link law's justice-oriented and socially embedded commitments to thinking more carefully about financial regulation. Legal thinking is uniquely suited to programmatically and normatively confronting the kinds of intractable, real-life social questions that occupy us here. For all the radical transactionalism that sometimes characterizes legal practice, improving financial regulation – making it structurally better able to see innovation, and making it substantively more alive to concerns about voice and domination – is a project that demands the attention of legal scholars and practitioners.

Law is a form of applied ethics based on rule of law values such as justice, legality, human dignity, non-arbitrariness, and accountability. The content of these jurisprudential values will continue to be contested, appropriately, and we will inevitably fall short of the mark in giving them real effect in the world. Nevertheless, these philosophical priors and animating motivations are invaluable in guiding the legal project as it focuses, as it must do, on practical problem-solving and application.

Law's magpie nature is helpful too. Law will always be less theoretically pure than mathematics, or economics, or even finance, because it is the product and the reflection, so profoundly, of lived human experience. Law, like regulation generally, implicitly and explicitly draws on other disciplines including economics, sociology, political science, and much more. Its methods, too, span versions of social science methods but also humanities methods, philosophical analysis, and increasingly other strategies developed by systems engineers and big data analysts and others. These methods are not just a motley assortment of cast-offs and knock-offs. They are practical tools, made coherent when interpreted through the lens of legal values and objectives. There are disputes in law, obviously, about what priorities should govern, what methods are most valid, how much certainty or predictability or accountability is required in general or in specific contexts. But through its disputatious tradition, law is uniquely positioned to generate a dynamic, socially attuned form of practically-embedded morality. Law's comfort with ambiguity makes it adept with the awkward balancing exercises and temporary accommodations between competing priorities – economic growth and economic security; innovation and stability; human dignity and personal autonomy – that inevitably must be struck.

Accepting that we need to inject a louder, clearer and more independent-minded public voice into financial regulation is not, of course, the end of the matter. Working out how to make that voice workable is challenging in any venue, but especially when dealing with technical, arcane, and often unsexy topics. Most of the time, most people do not occupy themselves terribly with the minutiae of financial regulation. As the Volcker Rule story made clear, it is even harder to obtain relevant, useful, detailed public input where, along with the technical esoterica, an aura of complexity and expertise helps to marginalize popular concerns. Expertise is not irrelevant, even while it is not the only basis for valid opinion on matters of broad public import.

While there will be no easy solution, we have starting points: we have the responsive regulatory argument for tripartism; we have experimentalism's emphasis on local learning underpinned by faith in collective learning; we have the idea that decentralization supported by the resources needed to aggregate learning need not be a deregulatory project; and we have an appreciation for the ways in which conversations about technical matters or details can allow fundamental normative or allocative questions to go unexamined. Among the representative (as opposed to direct) options for ensuring that the public interest is explicitly part of regulatory decision-making, we also have new, real-life examples such as the US SEC's Office of the Investor Advocate, and an investor advisory panel in Canada.[12] Taken together these suggest a few things: above all, they demand that we pay more conscious attention to how exactly the public voice will be represented. It may be time to consider whether, for example, notice-and-comment rulemaking can support the legitimacy-conferring weight it now must bear. Notice-and-comment is, in the United States, an artifact of the Welfare State; in a country like mine, there is not even that much mandatory consultation built into most administrative law regimes. In the regulatory state, however, where consultation plays a more substantive legitimacy-conferring role, even mandatory consultation in its current form may be entirely insufficient.

Along with helping regulators to think more explicitly about how innovation can undermine its structures and authority, along the lines described in Table 9.1, it is also time that we ask ourselves how it is, exactly, that we will ensure that the public interest is articulated within financial regulatory structures to a degree commensurate with that industry's significance to normal peoples' lives. Finance, and financial regulation, have a profound influence on everyone's fortunes (pecuniary and otherwise). The regulatory structures that we have in place for incorporating the public's voice are out of sync with the scale of the impact that financial regulatory decisions can have. Some decisions will be made at the level of formal electoral politics, but hugely consequential decisions are also taken at the regulatory level. Why, then, can its processes sometimes be so inscrutable, inaccessible, and democratically insufficient? Developing more appropriate mechanisms for public input will not be simple, but the necessity of the task is clear.[13]

ON FINANCIAL REGULATION, FAIRNESS, AND EQUALITY

The goal of innovation-ready regulation as described above would not be to supplant existing substantive regulatory objectives; it would be to ensure that those other substantive commitments can be advanced effectively. The goals of, for example, securities regulation are to foster fair and efficient markets and to protect investors. These will continue to be the objectives toward which that regulatory regime orients itself, whether or not dealing with financial innovation in particular. Similarly, systemic risk regulation (and banking regulation, and insurance regulation) will continue to be their own coherent regulatory approaches. In all cases, some regulatory responses that have already been developed will be responsive to financial innovation, and that is laudable. None of this is to the exclusion of what is advocated here.

Financial regulation – securities, banking, insurance, and systemic risk regulation – unlike tax law and policy, is not explicitly redistributive. Fundamentally, financial regulation is about allocative efficiency, and does not itself have (re)distributive ends. Yet financial regulation has never been blind to concerns about power or inequality, and dealing with financial innovation is one of the topics around which egalitarian concerns and financial regulation's historical concerns converge. Financial regulation is designed to prevent concentrated interests from pushing costs onto dispersed interests (including preventing present people from externalizing costs onto future people, as with pension funding). Securities regulation tries to force insiders to disclose information to the general public, to address information asymmetries, and to prevent adverse selection and other kinds of market failures. We can see the prudential regulation and consumer protection priorities that animate banking and insurance regulation, respectively, in terms that bear on market failures and inequitable distributions of risk.

Based on what we know about innovation, we can be concerned that the operating structures of finance, and financial regulation, are not only *not* reliably producing allocative efficiency, but can also be reflecting, perpetuating, or exacerbating inequalities in access, influence, and voice, which in turn have the potential to exacerbate broader distributive inequalities. It is not that financial regulation has a direct, proactive role to play in addressing distributive ends, but rather that it ought to be alive to the ways in which financial innovation and its regulation actually contribute, in unanticipated, dysfunctional, and indefensible ways, to inequality and unfairness in both voice and distributive outcomes.

Our social values are deeply embedded in the techniques we use to regulate. By not paying attention to innovation, we are (intentionally or not) endorsing its distributive effects and, in this case by omission, failing to take stock of its implications for capital allocation, for productivity, for stability, and for the kind of genuine inclusivity and attentiveness that is indicative of real recognition, personhood, and respect. We should be concerned about such structures not only because lack of inclusivity can produce poor outcomes, but also because inclusivity is an important democratic value unto itself. Trying to draw the unified normative thread through financial regulation as a whole may point the way to rethinking of what its priorities collectively entail. Specifically, the non-domination ethos that underpins some of the central flexible regulation scholarship may help us imagine an expanded, richer and more substantive account of the aims that financial regulation holds out for itself. Given how important finance, and the regulation of financial innovation, are to individual peoples' fortunes as well as to economies as a whole, it is time that we think about how to develop regulatory and participatory mechanisms adequate to the moral and democratic imperatives at play.

Andreas Scherer and Emilio Marti, drawing on Habermas, recently described a concept of "justifiable" financial markets, based on a thicker understanding of the financial markets' roles and obligations. They propose that, "financial markets should enhance *productivity* and thereby help people step out of poverty. Financial markets have to be *stable*, as financially induced economic crises hinder millions of people to lead a decent human life. Furthermore, financial markets should be *inclusive* as access to financial services is a prerequisite for self-development in a modern society."[4] These priorities are internal to financial regulation's own historic priorities, but they are also active. They require a public presence in financial regulation that is more than negative, and that comes to its task with its own mandate and agenda. The link to the civic republican ethos that key flexible regulation scholarship espouses, and this book endorses, is clear. This is the starting point for developing a substantive, as well as a procedural, approach to regulating financial innovation in the service of equality and non-domination.

This book ends where it began: with the subtle but profound relationship between seemingly desiccated, wonkish regulatory design questions, and the social values that we as a society hold dear. Our social values are deeply embedded in regulation. Flexible regulation scholarship was a considered and nuanced response to the ideological and economic challenges of its times. It is a valuable springboard for thinking about how to respond to financial innovation. It is also due for a fresh look, paying attention in particular to the distributional consequences of financial industry and regulatory arrangements, including ones that have been collateral to innovation. What is called for now is a regulatory structure that worries about technique but not only technique, and that remains attuned to the equality-seeking and justice-oriented priorities that the current political moment demands. The opportunity exists to build a more robust, ambitious regulatory response to financial innovation, which appreciates financial regulation for what it is: a crucial site for addressing domination in some of its most embedded and pernicious forms.

Appendix A

Methodology

For this book, I aimed to create a database of academic articles, from LexisNexis,[1] which captured a range of views on how innovation should intersect with regulation. I wanted to be sure to include articles that directly addressed flexible regulation scholarship. However, I also wanted to capture articles other than those that explicitly referred to these scholarly approaches. Although the financial crisis catalyzed this study, I did not limit the review to financial regulation scholarship. Regulatory studies span subject matter areas as well as disciplines. Moreover, financial regulation scholarship came late to the game relative to, for example, environmental regulation scholarship. Scholarly approaches developed in other areas ultimately became fundamental to financial regulation as well.

The search terms used to create this database were broad, intentionally, to try to generate a clearer sense of what regulatory scholarship around innovation has looked like since 1980. Lexis Nexis had 5382 articles in its American and Canadian archives that satisfied my search criteria, from a period of 1981 to 2012.[2]

The result is that the database generated from this search should be "theory neutral," within the literature that examined the concepts of regulation and innovation together. Several factors could have biased the representativeness of the body of literature obtained. One considerable limitation in the representativeness of the body of literature obtained is that the search was limited to articles available on LexisNexis only, meaning that only articles published in North American law reviews are represented. This is a considerable limitation when dealing with a trans-disciplinary and transnational body of scholarship, like regulation and governance, and one in which several books have made important contributions. Limiting the field to articles available through

LexisNexis was necessary because only this database permitted plain-text searching and downloading, which was needed to conduct the initial text-based query to obtain the articles and to generate the clusters discussed below. I believe the limitation to LexisNexis is justified given the number of articles returned, and given that conducting the search through computer query generated a body of articles without having to rely on subjective assessments of their relevance or impact.

The search did not capture the number of articles I initially had expected around private innovation – particularly financial innovations. This is likely in part because the specific names of these innovations (e.g., CDOs, asset-backed securities (ABSs), etc.) were not included as search terms. It also probably reflects the primary concerns – law and regulation – of the community of legal and regulation scholars whose work I captured. My search therefore captured articles about what were described as *regulatory innovations*, with relatively few references to private sector innovations. Since these were in fact the scholars whose work I was interested in, the result raised a separate question of how these regulatory innovations were linked to private sector innovations in the same regulated spaces.

SELECTION OF A SUB-GROUP OF ARTICLES TO REVIEW QUALITATIVELY

I subjected a subset of articles to a close qualitative review for three purposes: (1) to develop a more detailed description of the main "regulatory innovations" being discussed in the database, (2) to identify any cross-cutting themes and/or clusters of articles, based on shared assumptions or cross-citation, and (3) to test whether a relationship existed between the regulatory innovations being described in the database, and the promotion (explicit or implicit) of private sector innovation. With help from research assistant coders, I subjected 198 of the 5382 articles obtained in the original search to this review, using the coding protocol described in Section 3, below. The method used to obtain a practicable number of the most influential articles to subject to this qualitative review is described below.

First, after combining duplicate entries by hand, the articles were ranked according to the frequency with which they were cited within the database. I used citation counts to weight the articles, based on each article's citation count *within* the database I developed. This allowed me to identify the most influential articles within the literature I was concerned with. It established a weighting of importance/relevance to my field of interest, rather than a generic impact factor assessment. (Some of the articles in the database have been cited more than others in the broader literature, so my citation counts really are specific to this project.) The most cited articles correlate well with my independent understanding of the field's most influential US legal articles, helping to confirm the set's overlap with flexible regulation literature.

To "even the playing field" between newer and older articles, the citation count method only counted citations within five years of when the article was published. Since the database only considered articles published prior to 2012, for articles published after 2007, five-year citations were estimated based upon the citations collected until 2012. Counting citations only over five years made it possible to compare the importance of articles that appeared in different years, such that older articles were not more influential merely by virtue of having had a longer period of time in which to collect citations. This created a relatively unbiased weighting of the importance of a given article, available on LexisNexis, to the question of how innovation should intersect with regulation.

To ensure that the main schools of thought within the database had been captured within the qualitative sub-sample, with research assistance help I also conducted a cluster analysis of the articles according to the sources they cited, and set out to read and analyze the top half of each cluster. Both a six-cluster and an eight-cluster solution were identified using the *k*-means clustering approach.[3]

Cluster analysis is, generally speaking, a quantitative method of categorizing related data points into groups objectively, such that similar data points end up in the same groups. In this analysis, the articles in the database were the data points, and similarity of the articles was determined again through citations within the database.

In order to conduct a cluster analysis on the article dataset, we developed a weighting of the articles that indicated how similar they were to each other in a manner that was relevant to my analysis. This was done by counting the number of articles in the database that cited a given *pair* of articles, called the "pairwise citation count" for that pair. The idea was that the more times any given pair of articles was cited together in other articles in my database, the more similar their subject matter should be. Since we only counted citations of pairs of articles within the database, this resulted in articles being considered similar only if they contemplated a subject matter relevant to the literature I was interested in. We recorded the pairwise citation count for all possible pairs of articles in the database. For this analysis the timeframe was not limited to a five-year window as above, since the purpose was to measure the strength of similarity between articles rather than to compare the importance of the articles generally. This may have created some error in that older pairs of articles may have more pairwise citations than newer pairs of articles, but the results did not bear this out as a practical concern. In the pairwise citation count, if an article in the database cited another, the pairwise citation count for that pair of articles was incremented by one. Therefore, an article was at least considered somewhat similar to articles that it cited.

Once the number of pairwise citations of all pairs of articles in my database had been counted, that information was converted into a form that could be used to carry out the cluster analysis. A cluster analysis upon a dataset requires any pair of data points to have a "distance measure" or "weighting" between them. The distance between two very similar data points should be very small while the distance between two very dissimilar data points should be relatively large. Therefore, the higher the pairwise citation count within the database, the smaller the distance or weighting between the articles should theoretically be.

There is no generally accepted method to convert the pairwise citation count into a distance measure. The goal in conducting the conversion was to ensure that a cluster analysis could be carried out and that no new errors or biases be introduced due to the method of conversion. For that reason, numerous potential relationships between the pairwise citation count and the distance measure were considered. Two relationships seemed particularly reasonable: in the first, the pairwise citation count of a pair of articles and their distance measure was inversely proportional. In the second one, the weighting was proportional to the inverse square of the pairwise citation count. In practice, this meant that in the second method the weights decreased at a much greater rate as the citation count increased than in the first method. In the end, a distance measure determined by the first method was used to conduct the cluster analysis since, under the second method, any pair of articles with a common citation count of five or more would appear to have a negligible distance between them, which would cause them to always be grouped together by the cluster analysis.

The *k*-means cluster analysis of all of the articles in the database was conducted using the statistical software package R. The "Elbow Method" was used to determine the number of clusters in the analysis: under this approach, the percentage of the variance of the data points in the dataset explained by the clusters is graphed against the number of clusters, and a choice is made for the optimal number of clusters based on the shape of the graph. The percentage of variance explained is, loosely speaking, a measure of how much of the variation in the data points is due solely to the data points belonging to different clusters. This type of graph usually has an "elbow" that occurs for only one number of clusters, after which adding more clusters does not significantly increase the percentage of variance explained. For this dataset, this occurred when there were 8 clusters. In other words, this graphical method suggested that having more than 8 clusters would not produce a more coherent model of the schools of thought that existed in the dataset.

By carrying out the cluster analysis with R, all of the 198 most cited articles were grouped into individual clusters. These clusters seemed to be cohesive in the sense that most represented an identifiable school of thought within the database, despite being algorithmically chosen. With the help of research assistants, I then conducted a close qualitative review of these 198 articles, thereby covering the top half of every cluster, all of which had at least seven citations. Each article contained a "primary innovation," which was the main dominant innovation discussed in the article. Twenty-six articles also contained a "secondary innovation," though only primary innovations are discussed in this book.

Some clusters were "tighter" than others, meaning that they were characterized by more mutual citations. These clusters – notably clusters 1 and 8 – may more clearly reflect a "school of thought," or a collective conversation, in those clusters around new governance and experimentalism. Others seemed to be linked by a common subject matter area (like Cluster 2, concerned with market mechanisms in environmental law). Other clusters – notably Cluster 6, the one in which financial regulation in its various guises appeared most prominently – were clearly looser and "flatter," meaning that the articles in them had fewer mutual citations and a long "tail" of articles with lower overall citation counts within the database. (Cluster 5, as well, which generally contained articles in administrative law and federalism, also had a long tail.) Based on the titles of the articles, my background familiarity with the authors' work, and my review articles that were qualitatively reviewed, it was difficult to discern much substantive commonality within Cluster 7.

Some clusters were also more active than others. For example, in Cluster 8 (the most active), all twenty articles we reviewed had been cited at least thirteen times, and articles were cited thirty-one times on average. These twenty articles comprised the top half of that cluster. In the least active cluster (Cluster 2), the twelve articles we reviewed had been cited between eight and sixteen times and averaged just over nine cites each. While my decision to review the top half of each cluster means that less active clusters are overrepresented, in my view this makes sense because my goal was to identify the range of scholarly perspectives on flexible regulation rather than simply to focus on the dominant streams.

Although I found the clustering methodology to be very informative in identifying relationships between articles and, based on prior knowledge, verifying the different schools of thought that existed within the database, there were some limitations to the method as used with respect to my dataset. In general, the common citation counts for pairs of articles was not very high, and therefore it was difficult to distinguish how similar two articles were based on the database. This primarily caused categorization issues for articles on the cusp of different clusters, and had the effect of leaving the "edges" of the clusters hard to discern. As noted above, some of the less active clusters, notably Cluster 7, while recognizably part of flexible regulation scholarship and generally environmental law-oriented, overall looked relatively less like a cohesive school of thought. The third issue was with respect to articles belonging to Cluster 6, which I describe as the financial regulation cluster. Though financial regulation articles were very well represented within the database, the cluster itself was clustered much more loosely than some of the other clusters. This may be a symptom of there being many more sub-schools of thought in that particular field of study than the others. More likely, it may demonstrate that within the larger overall body of scholarship concerned with financial regulation, only some articles made it into this database because they were concerned with financial *innovation* in particular. These issues may have generated some errors in the clustering process, which I believe could be addressed by having a much larger initial dataset in which to comb through for pairwise citations. Specifically with regard to the relationship between regulation and innovation in particular, however, the clusters are still useful.

Table A.1 lists the fourteen articles that received more than thirty cites within the database.

DESIGN OF THE QUALITATIVE CODING PROTOCOL

To avoid making the qualitative review theory-driven or anecdotal, I generated coding questions based on a "five Ws and one H" approach (who, what, when, where, why, and how) to the regulatory context, considering both subject and object of the question where relevant. I developed a choice of answers based on my knowledge of the options put forward in the literature. For many questions I also included an "other" category among the response options, along with a requirement to explain through textual response, to ensure that responses other than the listed options listed could be included. Based on feedback from the coders I expanded the coding possibilities to include primary, secondary, and tertiary effects. I also sought to get "behind" the surface of the articles by asking questions such as, "who determines whether a standard has been met?" Where the coders had to imply

TABLE A.1. *The most-cited flexible regulation articles in the database*

Article	Cluster	Cites within five years
Orly Lobel, "The renew deal: the fall of regulation and the rise of governance in contemporary legal thought" (2004) 89 *Minn L Rev* 342–470.	8	73
Michael C. Dorf & Charles F. Sabel, "A constitution of democratic experimentalism" (1998) 98 *Colum L Rev* 267–473.	8	56
Charles F. Sabel & William H. Simon, "Destabilization rights: how public law litigation succeeds" (2004) 117 *Harv L Rev* 1015–1101.	1	50
Richard B. Stewart, "A new generation of environmental regulation" (2001–2002) 29 *Cap U L Rev* 21–182.	8	46
Steven L. Schwarcz, "Systemic risk" (2008) 97 *Geo LJ* 197–250.	6	41
Jody Freeman, "Collaborative governance in the administrative state" (1997) 45 *UCLA L Rev* 1–98.	8	40
Jody Freeman, "The private role of public governance" (2000) 75 *NYU L Rev* 543–675.	8	37
Bradley C. Karkkainen, "Information as environmental regulation: TRI and performance benchmarking, precursor to a new paradigm?" (2001) 89 *Geo LJ* 257–370.	8	36
Susan Sturm, "Second generation employment discrimination: a structural approach" (2001) 101 *Colum L Rev* 458–568.	1	35
Rena I. Steinzor, "Reinventing environmental regulation: the dangerous journey from command to self control" (1998) 22 *Harv Envtl L Rev* 103–202.	8	35
Kristen Engel, "Harnessing the benefits of dynamic federalism in environmental law" (2006) 56 *Emory LJ* 159–190.	3	35
Cary Coglianese, "Assessing consensus: the promise and performance of negotiated rulemaking" (1997) 46 *Duke LJ* 1255–1349.	8	33
Cary Coglianese & David Lazer, "Management-based regulation: prescribing private management to achieve public goals" (2003) 37 *Law & Soc'y Rev* 691–730.	1	33
William W. Buzbee, "Asymmetrical regulation: risk, preemption, and the floor/ceiling distinction" (2007) 82 *NYU L Rev* 1547–1619.	3	32

something not on the face of the article itself they marked the response with an "x."

The coding questions are included in Appendix B.

RELIABILITY OF THE CODING

The data were coded by five coders, all academically strong JD students at the University of British Columbia. Three of the coders worked over a relatively concentrated period of three months in summer 2012, when they were working on this project full-time. I established a dedicated workroom in the law school for the coders, to allow them to confer with one another, although the coders were also free to work from elsewhere. To ensure coding reliability, I orally went through the coding protocol in detail at a group meeting with those three, before the coding began. I subjected three articles to consensus coding, one in great depth. One coder reviewed fully 73 of the 104 articles in the subset, with the others coding 22 and 23 apiece. Fourteen articles were reviewed by more than one coder during this initial phase. While this was unintentional outside the three articles subjected to consensus coding, it confirmed that coding was largely consistent among the coders. Thereafter, I reviewed the coding on eight additional, randomly selected articles that the coders had reviewed. While the coders differed in terms of the length of their textual responses and some of their language, I found no clear differences in the coding itself among the three. The only exception was question 6 (catalysts for the innovation), in which two coders used responses 3 and 3a (respectively "necessity" and "necessity, action taken in response to a crisis") somewhat differently. For this reason it makes sense to combine those responses, which are a minority of the responses to that question in any event.

A fourth coder was retained in August 2014 to review an additional 84 articles, which were required to ensure that I had coded the top 50 percent most-cited articles in each of the eight clusters. To ensure reliability, this coder first re-reviewed five randomly selected articles that had already been coded by the others, and he and I compared his results and discussed variations. Results were quite similar and the coder's analysis was further refined through our conversation. I reviewed the coding on five additional, randomly selected articles the fourth coder coded.

A fifth coder was retained in spring 2015 to ensure final consistency and to code the "manufactured risk" category at a greater level of granularity. That coder re-reviewed many of the earlier-coded articles for consistency, which was high. I also re-reviewed most of the coded articles, at different levels of depth, while constructing Chapter 4 itself.

ANALYSIS OF THE QUALITATIVE DATABASE

For questions on the coding protocol that contained a closed number of categorical response options, the frequency with which each response option was chosen was calculated. Analyses were primarily univariate in nature. Occasionally, descriptive bivariate analyses were conducted to investigate the relationships between two variables. These bivariate analyses consisted of visual inspections of the data, including histograms and cross-tabulation tables. Because the variables on the coding sheet each contained a large number of response categories, the contingency tables upon which inferential statistics (e.g., chi-square analyses) would be based contained cell sizes too small for inferential analysis. Qualitative (i.e., textual) data was analyzed using thematic analysis, that is, the information was reviewed and categorized inductively into discrete themes.

Appendix B

Coding Questions

TABLE B.1. *Coding questions*

Q: Why innovation is good

"Innovation"

1. **What is the innovation? (in a word/phrase)**
2. **Sector/subject matter**
   1. environment
   2. labour or occupational health and safety
   3. science/technology/medicine/intellectual property
   5. education
   6. other social services
   7. finance
   8. other (describe)
3. **Who is innovating?**
   1. private sector (including individuals, corporations)
   2. ancillary private for-profit groups or their representatives (insurers, industry associations, trade councils, etc.)
   3. not-for-profit groups/civil society
   4. public sector: existing state-based regulators
      4a. federal level
      4b. state/provincial
      4c. municipal
      4d. other local unit
      4e. other global/transnational unit
   5. international/transnational regulators or networks
4. **Nature of innovation**
   1. private innovation
      1a. technical/scientific innovation
      1b. business process innovation
      1c. grassroots/community-based/social
      1d. sea urchin/radical innovation
      1e. sedimentary/incremental innovation

2. regulatory innovation

    2a. spanning public/private divide in new way, incorporating private standards or capacity, collaborating

    2b. new mandatory standards or top-down strategy – e.g., *ex ante* licensing, bright-line rules or certification requirements

    2c. incentive-based regulatory design to align private actors' interests with public interests

    2d. new information-forcing requirements

    2e. bringing in third parties as quasi-official regulatory surrogates, e.g., monitors, auditors, certifiers

    2f. bringing in civil society or community, e.g., name-and-shame or awards for industry leaders

    2g. market forces

    2h. other

5. **For regulatory innovation: labels (according to author)**

    1. co-regulation

    2. enforced self-regulation

    3. experimentalist

    4. incentive-based

    5. market-based

    6. management-based regulation

    7. meta regulation

    8. negotiated rulemaking

    9. new governance

    10. outcome-oriented/outcome-based/performance-based

    11. principles-based

    12. problem-solving regulation

    13. reflexive law/regulation

    14. responsive regulation

    15. risk-based regulation

    16. command-and-control (C&C)

    17. collaborative governance

    18. flexible regulation

    19. deregulation

    20. other (explain)

6. **What is the innovation responding to? Catalysts (please choose either 1 or 2 for overall cognitive framing of problem, then 3 where appropriate based on how author frames it)**

    1. risk

        1a. longstanding natural risk

        1b. new manufactured/human-created risk

    2. opportunity

        2a. for private benefit

        2b. for public benefit

    3. necessity: old way cannot be maintained

        3a. action taken in context of a crisis

6a. **Specific regulatory initiative being discussed, if any**

"Good"

7. What is the "good" this innovation offers? (in a word/phrase)
8. Primary priorities advanced (no more than 3)
   1. private economic benefit/competitiveness
   2. national or collective economic benefit (competitiveness, efficiency, resource allocation, etc.)
   3. environmental protection/natural resources conservation
   4. scientific/medical progress
   5. corporate social responsibility/corporate compliance
   6. occupational health and safety/labor standards
   7. liberty/freedom/choice (individual)
   8. equality, greater human flourishing (for individuals or marginalized groups), public health
   9. enhanced democracy/citizen engagement/community participation/voice
   10. newness/experimentation for its own sake
9. Who benefits from the innovation, per author?
   1. $1°$ private benefit
   2. $1°$ private benefit with public ancillary benefit
   3. $1°$ public benefit with private ancillary benefit
   4. $1°$ public benefit
10. Geopolitical level where primary benefit applies, per author
    1. "community" or local or civil society
    2. national
    3. global
11. Relative impact story, per author (choose one)
    1. there are winners: innovation provides competitive advantage for us versus them (identify: who are winners and losers)
    2. there are no losers: a rising tide lifts all boats
12. Why is this innovation "good" relative to what came before?
    1. congruence: the old way was ineffective/didn't work/didn't "fit"/didn't achieve the innovator's (including regulator's, if regulator is innovating) goals
    2. cost: the old way was costly/inefficient
    3. flexibility: the old way was inflexible/couldn't move, adapt quickly enough
    4. transparency and accountability: the old way was unaccountable/not transparent/captured
    5. fairness: the old way was unfair/undemocratic
    6. process: (beyond traditional understandings of democratic methods) the old way was not consultative or collaborative enough, unrepresentative, dealt with wrong communities or didn't include necessary stakeholders
13. Who are the standard-setters? Who decides whether the "good" is being achieved?
    1. private sector (including individuals, corporations)
    2. ancillary private for-profit groups or their representatives (insurers, industry associations, trade councils, etc.)
    3. not-for-profit groups/civil society
    4. existing state-based (federal or other) regulators
    5. international/transnational regulators or networks

14. **What is evaluation method for determining whether "good" is being achieved?**
    1. efficient market – best ideas rise to top through competition
    2. checking against static, bright-line, or rule-based requirements
    3. more context-specific and/or flexible metrics: formal outcome analysis or other performance-based analysis (based on performance indicators, best practices)
    4. dialogue, deliberation, consultation, consensus
    5. self-monitoring and inter-firm comparative analysis
15. **What new risks or challenges does the innovation produce? How are these responded to?**
    1. describe

Author's overall stance (if you can)

16.
    1. neo-conservative
    2. Third-Way
    3. experimentalist/new governance

Appendix C

Additional Coding

TABLE C.1. *Additional coding questions*

Q: Why innovation is good

About the "Innovation"[i]

	Enviro. Law	Admin. Law	Finance/ Corp. Gov.	Science/ Tech.	Other	Total (%)
2. **Sector/subject matter**	80 (40%)	41 (21%)	45 (22%)	21 (11%)	11 (6%)	198 (100%)
4. **Nature of innovation**						
1. private innovation	6 (8%)	2 (5%)	7 (16%)	2 (10%)	1 (9%)	18 (9%)
1a. technical/ scientific innovation	3 (4%)	0 (0%)	1 (2%)	2 (10%)	0 (0%)	6 (3%)
1b. business process innovation	1 (1%)	1 (2%)	4 (9%)	0 (0%)	1 (9%)	7 (4%)
1c. grassroots/ community-based/social	2 (3%)	1 (2%)	2 (4%)	0 (0%)	0 (0%)	5 (3%)
2. regulatory innovation	74 (92%)	39 (95%)	38 (84%)	19 (90%)	10 (90%)	180 (91%)
2a. spanning public/private divide in new way	20 (25%)	14 (34%)	13 (23%)	8 (38%)	6 (54%)	61 (31%)
2b. new mandatory standards or top-down strategy	6 (6%)	4 (10%)	11 (24%)	2 (10%)	1 (9%)	24 (12%)

TABLE C.1 *(continued)*

	Enviro. Law	Admin. Law	Finance/ Corp. Gov.	Science/ Tech.	Other	Total (%)
2c. incentive-based regulatory design	17 (21%)	0 (0%)	3 (7%)	1 (5%)	0 (0%)	21 (11%)
2d. new information-forcing requirements	8 (10%)	5 (12%)	3 (7%)	2 (10%)	0 (0%)	18 (9%)
2e. bringing in third parties as quasi-official regulatory surrogates	0 (0%)	1 (2%)	0 (0%)	0 (0%)	2 (18%)	3 (2%)
2f. bringing in civil society or community	0 (0%)	0 (0%)	0 (0%)	0 (0%)	0 (0%)	0 (0%)
2g. market forces	5 (6%)	1 (2%)	2 (4%)	3 (14%)	0 (0%)	11 (6%)
2h. other	18 (23%)	14 (34%)	6 (13%)	3 (14%)	1 (9%)	42 (21%)
6. **What is the innovation responding to? Catalysts**						
1. risk	63 (79%)	23 (56%)	27 (60%)	15 (71%)	3 (27%)	131 (66%)
1a. longstanding natural risk	0 (0%)	1 (2%)	1 (2%)	0 (0%)	0 (0%)	2 (1%)
1b. new manufactured/ human-created risk	63 (29%)	22 (54%)	26 (58%)	15 (71%)	3 (27%)	129 (65%)
2. opportunity	9 (11%)	11 (27%)	13 (29%)	6 (29%)	7 (64%)	46 (23%)
2a. for private benefit	3 (4%)	3 (7%)	6 (13%)	2 (10%)	0 (0%)	14 (7%)
2b. for public benefit	5 (6%)	8 (20%)	7 (16%)	4 (19%)	6 (55%)	30 (15%)
Unspecified	1 (1%)	0 (0%)	0 (0%)	0 (0%)	1 (9%	2 (1%)
3. necessity: old way cannot be maintained/ action taken in context of a crisis	8 (10%)	7 (17%)	5 (11%)	0 (0%)	1 (9%)	21 (11%)

(continued)

TABLE C.1 *(continued)*

	Enviro. Law	Admin. Law	Finance/ Corp. Gov.	Science/ Tech.	Other	Total (%)
Manufactured risk from Q6 (=1b) N= 63 enviro. articles, 22 admin. articles, 26 finance/corp. governance articles, 15 science/tech. articles, 3 other articles						
1. New product/ tech.	1 (2%)	0 (0%)	3 (12%)	6 (40%)	0 (0%)	10 (8%)
2. Specific change in markets/ economy	4 (6%)	0 (0%)	9 (35%)	0 (0%)	0 (0%)	13 (10%)
3. Specific change in law/policy	17 (27%)	1 (5%)	1 (4%)	0 (0%)	2 (67%)	21 (16%)
4. other/ background change	41 (65%)	21 (95%)	13 (50%)	9 (60%)	1 (33%)	85 (66%)
About the "Good"						
8. Primary priorities advanced						
1. private economic benefit	3 (4%)	2 (5%)	10 (22%)	1 (5%)	0 (0%)	16 (8%)
2. national or collective economic benefit	7 (9%)	7 (17%)	26 (58%)	6 (29%)	2 (18%)	48 (24%)
3. environmental protection/ natural resources conservation	64 (80%)	3 (7%)	0 (0%)	1 (5%)	0 (0%)	68 (34%)
4. scientific/ medical progress	0 (0%)	0 (0%)	0 (0%)	5 (24%)	0 (0%)	5 (3%)
5. CSR/corporate compliance	1 (1%)	1 (2%)	7 (16%)	0 (0%)	0 (0%)	9 (5%)
6. occupational health & safety/ labor standards	0 (0%)	0 (0%)	0 (0%)	0 (0%)	0 (0%)	0 (0%)
7. liberty/ freedom/choice (individual)	0 (0%)	1 (2%)	0 (0%)	1 (5%)	0 (0%)	2 (1%)
8. equality, greater human flourishing, public health	3 (4%)	8 (20%)	2 (4%)	6 (29%)	5 (45%)	24 (12%)

TABLE C.1 *(continued)*

	Enviro. Law	Admin. Law	Finance/ Corp. Gov.	Science/ Tech.	Other	Total (%)
9. enhanced democracy/ citizen engagement/ community participation/ voice	2 (3%)	19 (46%)	0 (0%)	1 (5%)	3 (27%)	25 (13%)
10. experimentation for its own sake	0 (0%)	0 (0%)	0 (0%)	0 (0%)	1 (9%)	1 (1%)
						198

11. Relative impact story, per author

	Enviro. Law	Admin. Law	Finance/ Corp. Gov.	Science/ Tech.	Other	Total (%)
1. there are winners: innovation provides competitive advantage for us-versus-them	44 (55%)	16 (39%)	33 (73%)	8 (38%)	3 (27%)	104 (53%)
2. there are no losers: a rising tide lifts all boats	36 (45%)	25 (61%)	12 (27%)	13 (62%)	8 (73%)	94 (47%)

12. Why is this innovation "good" relative to what came before?

	Enviro. Law	Admin. Law	Finance/ Corp. Gov.	Science/ Tech.	Other	Total (%)
1. congruence: the old way was ineffective	31 (39%)	12 (29%)	19 (24%)	8 (38%)	2 (9%)	72 (36%)
2. cost: the old way was costly/ inefficient	18 (23%)	6 (15%)	8 (18%)	3 (14%)	0 (0%)	35 (17%)
3. flexibility: the old way was inflexible	12 (15%)	3 (7%)	6 (13%)	3 (14%)	2 (18%)	26 (13%)
4. transparency & accountability: the old way was unaccountable	7 (9%)	7 (17%)	8 (18%)	6 (29%)	1 (9%)	29 (15%)
5. fairness: the old way was unfair/ undemocratic	3 (4%)	7 (17%)	3 (7%)	0 (0%)	2 (18%)	15 (8%)

(continued)

TABLE C.1 (*continued*)

	Enviro. Law	Admin. Law	Finance/ Corp. Gov.	Science/ Tech.	Other	Total (%)
6. process: the old way was not consultative or collaborative enough, unrepresentative, dealt with wrong communities or didn't include necessary stakeholders	9 (11%)	6 (15%)	1 (2%)	1 (5%)	4 36%)	21 (8%)

13. Who are the standard-setters? Who decides whether the "good" is being achieved?

	Enviro. Law	Admin. Law	Finance/ Corp. Gov.	Science/ Tech.	Other	Total (%)
1. private sector	4 (5%)	2 (5%)	10 (22%)	5 (24%)	1 (9%)	**22 (11%)**
2. ancillary private for-profit groups or their representatives	0 (0%)	2 (5%)	1 (2%)	0 (0%)	2 (18%)	5 (3%)
3. not-for-profit groups / civil society	3 (4%)	3 (7%)	1 (2%)	0 (0%)	1 (10%)	8 (4%)
4. existing state-based (federal or other) regulators	70 (88%)	33 (80%)	31 (69%)	16 (76%)	7 (64%)	157 (79%)
5. international / transnational regulators or networks	3 (4%)	1 (2%)	2 (4%)	0 (0%)	0 (0%)	6 (3%)

198

14. What is evaluation method for determining whether "good" is being achieved? N = 80 enviro. articles, 40 admin. law (one blank), 45 finance/corp. Gov. articles, 21 science/tech. articles, 11 other articles

	Enviro. Law	Admin. Law	Finance/ Corp. Gov.	Science/ Tech.	Other	Total (%)
1. efficient market – best ideas rise to top through competition	22 (28%)	4 (10%)	16 (36%)	8 (38%)	2 (18%)	52 (26%)
2. checking against static, bright-line, or rule-based requirements	18 (23%)	13 (33%)	21 (47%)	9 (43%)	2 (18%)	63 (32%)

3. more context-specific and/or flexible metrics: formal outcome analysis, performance-based analysis	28 (35%)	7 (18%)	5 (11%)	2 (10%)	4 (36%)	46 (23%)
4. dialogue, deliberation, consultation, consensus	12 (15%)	8 (20%)	1 (2%)	2 (10%)	2 (18%)	25 (13%)
5. self-monitoring and inter-firm comparative analysis	0 (0%)	8 (20%)	2 (4%)	0 (0%)	1 (10%)	11 (6%)
						197

i The numbering in this table corresponds to the questions in Appendix B.

Notes

INTRODUCTION: WHY INNOVATION IS NOT (JUST) ROMANTIC, AND REGULATION IS NOT DULL

1   Naomi Klein, "It was the Democrats' embrace of neoliberalism that won it for Trump," *Guardian*, November 9, 2016. The word "neoliberal" is problematic when poorly defined, and its pejorative connotations can be so strong as to make thoughtful examination difficult. This is not to say there is nothing to it. Here I adopt Michèle Lamont's definition of neoliberalism as problematic for the way that it flattens assessments of worth: "neoliberalism, a context in which definitions of worth that are not based on market performance tend to lose their relevance and in which market fundamentalism is exercising strong homogenizing pressures on collective identities and on shared definitions of what defines a worthy life." Michèle Lamont, "Toward a comparative sociology of valuation and evaluation" (2012) 38 *Ann Rev Sociol* 201–221, at 210. *See also* Chapter 5 for more discussion on this point.

2   The term "financial regulation" encompasses securities, banking, and insurance regulation as well as macroprudential (systemic risk) concerns as they derive from those areas. Before the financial crisis, the idea of talking about "financial regulation" as a whole would have seemed too imprecise. Now, we have a far greater appreciation for the linkages between these sectors. Several law schools now offer Financial Regulation courses, and two new text- or casebooks were published in the area in 2016: John Armour et al., *Principles of Financial Regulation* (Oxford: Oxford University Press, 2016); and Michael S. Barr, Howell E. Jackson & Margaret E. Tahyar, *Financial Regulation: Law and Policy* (New York: Foundation Press, 2016). Certainly, each institutional sector remains distinct and has its own priorities, even while financial regulation as a whole shares important features. Even the two new books above differ in how they balance the specific and the general. My aim in this book is not to dislodge the substantive regulatory priorities distinct to securities, or banking, or insurance, or systemic risk regulation; but rather to talk about what is required in order for regulators across all of these areas to be better able to discharge those substantive regulatory priorities. Because my goal is to begin to develop a better epistemological

approach to thinking about financial innovation and regulation generally, albeit in different ways depending on context, I am able to speak more globally.

3 UK Financial Services Authority [FSA], *The Turner Review: A Regulatory Response to the Global Banking Crisis* (2009), p. 49.

4 E.g., Mary Ann Glendon, *Rights Talk: The Impoverishment of Political Discourse* (New York: Free Press, 1991); Michael C. Dorf & Charles F. Sabel, "A constitution of democratic experimentalism" (1998) 98 *Colum L Rev* 298–473.

5 Frank R. Baumgartner & Bryan D. Jones, *Agendas and Instability in American Politics*, 2nd edn. (Chicago: University of Chicago Press, 2009).

6 See, e.g., Nell Abernathy, Mike Konczal & Kathryn Milani (eds), *Untamed: How to Check Corporate, Financial, and Monopoly Power* (Roosevelt Institute, 2016), pp. 40–55, 62–75, available at rooseveltinstitute.org/untamed-how-check-corporate-financial-and-monopoly-power/.

7 See, e.g., Martin Wolf, "Seven ways technology has changed us," *Financial Times*, January 20, 2016, available at www.ft.com/cms/s/2/7d9874c0-a25d-11e5-8d70-42b68cfae6e4.html#axzz4GPWaHGUr; Vivek Wadhwa, "The amazing artificial intelligence we were promised is coming, finally," *The Washington Post*, June 17, 2016, available at www.washingtonpost.com/news/innovations/wp/2016/06/17/the-amazing-artificial-intelligence-we-were-promised-is-coming-finally/; Manny Puentes, "How to invest in a big data platform," *Forbes*, July 8, 2016, available at www.forbes.com/sites/forbestechcouncil/2016/07/08/how-to-invest-in-a-big-data-platform/#59df025d4209; Freddie Dawson, "Sorry Google and Tesla, FiveAI will have the best driverless car," *Forbes*, July 30, 2016, available at www.forbes.com/sites/forbestechcouncil/2016/07/08/how-to-invest-in-a-big-data-platform/#59df025d4209; Kevin Murnane, "A new map of the brain that is unlike anything you have seen before," *Forbes*, August 2, 2016, available at www.forbes.com/sites/kevinmurnane/2016/08/02/a-new-map-of-the-brain-that-is-unlike-anything-you-have-seen-before/#5040f32a7a9f; Catherine Offord, "Mapping traits to genes with CRISPR," *The Scientist*, May 5, 2016, available at www.the-scientist.com/?articles.view/articleNo/46029/title/Mapping-Traits-to-Genes-with-CRISPR/; Jared Meyer, "The sharing economy won't kill the middlemen," *Forbes*, July 29, 2016, available at www.forbes.com/sites/jaredmeyer/2016/07/29/the-sharing-economy-wont-kill-the-middleman/#73b675d97565; Andrew Ross Sorkin, "Fintech firms are taking on the big banks, but can they win?," *The NY Times*, April 6, 2016, available at www.nytimes.com/2016/04/07/business/dealbook/fintech-firms-are-taking-on-the-big-banks-but-can-they-win.html; Dan Holden, "Is cyber-terrorism the new normal?," *Wired*, available at www.wired.com/insights/2015/01/is-cyber-terrorism-the-new-normal.

8 Luddites were skilled machine textile workers who protested between 1811–1816, starting in Nottinghamshire. The increasing use of labor-saving machines, combined with wage cuts, poor harvests, skyrocketing food prices, and deregulation of the industry, led to various protests that involved violent rallies and machine-breaking. Modern neo-Luddism has romanticized the original Luddite movement to reflect a general philosophical view that is anti-progress, anti-technology, and sometimes radically environmentalist. This is, at least arguably, contrary to the original Luddite movement. More recently, scholars have characterized what the Luddites were doing as "collective bargaining by riot," not social protest against

technology. Lord Byron, who defended the Luddites in the House of Lords during the riots, stated that their message was that "the maintenance and well-doing of the industrious poor, were objects of greater consequences than the enrichment of a few by any improvement, in the implements of trade." John E. Archer, *Social Unrest and Popular Protest in England 1780–1840* (Cambridge: Cambridge University Press, 2000); Steven E. Jones, *Against Technology: From the Luddites to Neo-Luddism* (New York: Routledge, 2006), pp. 54–56; David Edgerton, "In praise of Luddism," (2011) 471 *Nature* 27–29, at 29 (citing Lord Byron); E.J. Hobsbawm, "The machine breakers," (1952) 1 *Past & Present* 57–70 (coining "collective bargaining by riot").

9   See also Donald C. Langevoort, *Selling hope, Selling Risk: Corporations, Wall Street, and the Dilemmas of Investor Protection* (New York: Oxford University Press, 2016), pp. 154–157, 160.

10 See generally Evgeny Morozov, *To Save Everything Click Here: The Folly of Technological Solutionism* (PublicAffairs, 2013); Jaron Lanier, *Who Owns the Future?* (New York: Simon & Schuster, 2013); Ronald Wright, *A Short History of Progress* (Toronto: Anansi Press, 2004); Kirkpatrick Sale, *Rebels Against the Future: The Luddites and Their War on the Industrial Revolution: Lessons for the Computer Age* (Reading: Addison Wesley Publishing Company, 1995); Chellis Glendinning, *When Technology Wounds: The Human Consequences of Progress* (New York: Morrow, 1990).

11 Axel Dreher, Noel Gaston & Pim Martens, *Measuring Globalisation: Gauging its Consequences* (New York: Springer, 2008); Ming-Chang Tsai, "Does globalization affect human well-being?" (2007) 81 *Social Indicators Research* 103–126; Paul Krugman & Anthony J. Venables, "Globalization and the inequality of nations" (1995) 110 *QJ Econ* 857–880.

12 "Word Frequency Data," accessed November 16, 2012, available at www .wordfrequency.info/intro.asp. As of publication, comparable data are not available from 2012 onward (Google ngram data extends only to 2000). This linguistics analysis is based on word frequency data from the Corpus of Contemporary American English (COCAE), a 450-million word corpus. 100,000 word lists supplement this COCAE data with detailed frequency data from the 400 million-word Corpus of Historical American English, the British National Corpus, and the Corpus of American Soap Operas (for very informal language). The word list obtained from this corpus contains the top 60,000 words used in the English language. It analyzes sources from spoken word, fiction, popular magazines, newspapers, and academic sources. Within academia, discussion of innovation spans disciplines. "Innovation"'s highest frequency was in the law/political science category (25%), followed by the science/technology category (18%). The remaining 57% is spread over the remaining categories (Geog./SocSci., History, Education, Humanities, Medicine, and Misc., in descending order of frequency).

13 The ID ranks were as follows: risk = 650; growth = 787; freedom = 1149; democracy = 1507; innovation = 3684; liberty = 3865; equality = 4634; globalization = 6540.

14 Total frequency score = 8630, frequency in academic sources = 3938, frequency in popular magazines = 2663.

15 Each word in the 60,000-word list is associated with approximately 220 collocates. Collocate word list, Corpus of Contemporary American English. A word

qualifies as a collocate according to the formula below, which takes into account the frequency of the collocate in the corpus, the frequency of the collocate near the root word, and the number of words in between the collocate and the root word (to a maximum of four). In order for a word to be included as a collocate of a lemma, the collocate must occur at least 3 times, and there must be a Mutual Information Score (MIS) of 1.0 or higher. The MIS is calculated by $MIS = \log((AB^*sizeCorpus)/A^*B^*span))/\log(2)$, where:

AB^* = frequency of collocate near node word
SizeCorpus = number of words in the corpus
A^* = frequency of node word
B^* = frequency of collocate
Span = span of words (4 left and 4 right, 8-word span total)

In the COCAE's collocate list, containing 13,200,000 words, "innovation" appeared 444 times, either as a collocate or as the root word.

16   "important" MIS = 112, "key" MIS = 31, "successful" MIS = 38, "encourage" MIS = 84, "introduce" MIS = 62, "leadership" MIS = 32, "promote" MIS = 49, "progress" MIS = 49, "educational" MIS = 49, "adopt" MIS = 23, "improvement" MIS = 29, "invest" MIS = 19, "creative" MIS = 25, "initiative" MIS = 20, "discovery" MIS = 27, "inspire" MIS = 11, "embrace" MIS = 17, "remarkable" MIS = 8, "tremendous" MIS = 12, "exciting" MIS = 10, "reward" MIS = 13.

17   "Freedom" collocates usually referred to the type of freedom, such as "political freedom." "Freedom" = 1066 collocates; "political" MIS with "freedom" = 717.

18   "Liberty" = 452 collocates; "equality" = 776 collocates; "democracy" = 1231 collocates.

19   "Regulation," *Oxford English Dictionary* (online ed., August 2016).

20   E.g., Colin Scott, "Regulating everything: from mega- to meta-regulation" (2012) 60 *Administration* 61–89 at 67–68. Available at IPA: ipa.ie/pdf/Scott.pdf; also Colin Scott, "Regulation in the age of governance: the rise of the post-regulatory state," in Jacint Jordana & David Levi-Faur (eds), *The Politics of Regulation: Institutions and Regulatory Reforms for the Age of Governance* (Cheltenham: Edward Elgar Publishing, 2004), pp. 145–174 (defining "governance" as relevant to the "exercise of power among a wide range of state, non-state and supranational actors"). Michel Foucault's concept of "governmentality," as the practice of the exercise of political power, is distinct and most governance scholars are probably not committed Foucaultians; but see, e.g., Ole Jacob Sending & Iver B. Neumann, "Governance to governmentality: analyzing NGOs, states, and power" (2006) 50 *International Studies Quarterly* 651–672.

21   Philip Selznick, "Focusing organizational research on regulation," in Roger Noll (ed.), *Regulatory Policy and the Social Sciences* (Berkeley: University of California Press, 1985), pp. 363–367 at 363.

22   Julia Black, *Critical Reflections on Regulation* (London: Centre for Analysis of Risk and Regulation, London School of Economics and Political Science, 2002), p. 19. Available at LSE: eprints.lse.ac.uk/35985/1/Disspaper4-1.pdf.

23   Christopher Hood, Henry Rothstein & Robert Baldwin, *The Government of Risk: Understanding Risk Regulation Regimes* (New York: Oxford University Press, 2001), p. 23.

24 This variability is implicit in Coglianese's discussion of regulatory tools: "Although the array of instruments available to any decision maker may seem large, regulatory tools all share common attributes. All regulatory instruments consist of some rule or rule-like statement having normative force and backed up with some type of consequences. Given these core similarities, the differences between the myriad regulatory instruments can be explained in terms of four variables: the regulator, the target, the type of command, and the type of consequence." Cary Coglianese, "Engaging business in the regulation of nanotechnology," in Christopher J. Bosso (ed.), *Governing Uncertainty: Environmental Regulation in the Age of Nanotechnology* (Washington, DC: Resources for the Future Press 2010), pp. 49–50; U of Penn, Inst for Law & Econ Research Paper No. 12-07; U of Penn Law School, Public Law Research Paper No. 12, at 5. Available at SSRN: ssrn.com/abstract=2002983.

25 E.g., the telecommunications regulations in Canada have been promoting more competition by relaxing foreign ownership rules both judicially in *Globalive Wireless Management Corp* v. *Public Mobile Inc.*, 2011 FCA 194 (leave to SCC declined), and legislatively by amending the *Telecommunications Act* to allow companies into the industry as long as they own less than a 10% share in the market, see *Telecommunications Act*, S.C. 1993, c. 48, s. 16(2)(c). Prior to this, like the US airline industry in the pre-Alfred Kahn days, it tended to protect cartels, see Thomas K. McCraw, *Prophets of Regulation: Charles Francis Adams, Louis D. Brandeis, James M. Landis, Alfred E. Kahn* (Cambridge: Belknap Press, 1984), pp. 259–296.

26 McCraw, "Prophets of regulation," 224–226, 239–243, note 25 above (discussing marginal cost pricing in the power sector). Feedback is also a good example of a means to encourage energy conservation. For a literature review, see Sarah Darby, *The Effectiveness of Feedback on Energy Consumption* (2006). For an example of how innovators are implementing this research, see www.carbonculture.net.

27 E.g., the Global Analyst Research Settlement was due to conflicts of interest created between independent sell-side research analysts and their connection to investment bankers due to the deregulation of brokerage commissions. See Press Release, US Securities and Exchange Commission, *Ten of Nation's Top Investment Firms Settle Enforcement Actions Involving Conflicts of Interest Between Research and Investment Banking* (April 28, 2003), www.sec.gov/news/press/2003-54.htm. For how the post-settlement regulatory environment has since affected sell-side research, see Ohad Kadan et al., "Conflicts of interest and stock recommendations: the effects of the global settlement and related regulations" (2009) 22 *Rev Financ Stud* 4189–4217.

28 Orly Lobel, "The renew deal: the fall of regulation and the rise of governance in contemporary legal thought" (2004) 89 *Minn L Rev* 342–470, at 354.

29 *Dunsmuir* v. *New Brunswick*, 2008 SCC 9, [2008] 1 SCR 190, para. 136 (per Binnie J.)

30 "Innovation," *Oxford English Dictionary* (online ed., August 2016).

31 Tufano, Peter, "Financial innovation," in G.M. Constantinides, M. Harris & R. Stulz (eds), *Handbook of the Economics of Finance* (Amsterdam: Elsevier, 2003), pp. 307–335, at 311. (For Tufano, financial innovation includes invention and diffusion as well.)

32 Certain background conditions would also be crucial. It would be essential to have in place an overarching social value system that generally rewarded and valued innovation over tradition, change over stability. We would also want to recognize property rights in innovations so that innovators could own their innovations, be protected from free riders, and reap the benefits of their work. It would be helpful to establish programs, perhaps funded by governments (like National Science Foundation in the United States), which use targeted research grants to try to foster innovation. Tax-free geographic zones for particular industries could serve a similar purpose. But these kinds of initiatives operate in the background here. Our main concern is how we should build *regulation* – the quotidian oversight of industries or practices, generally by formal regulatory agencies in some degree of partnership with their regulated actors and potentially other parties – in order to foster innovation.

33 Tom R. Tyler, *Why People Obey the Law* (New Haven: Yale University Press, 1990).

34 See, e.g., Ian Ayres & John Braithwaite, *Responsive Regulation: Transcending the Deregulatory Debate* (New York: Oxford University Press, 1992) (describing the enforcement and regulatory pyramids).

35 Erik F. Gerding, *Law, Bubbles, and Financial Regulation* New York: Routledge, 2014).

36 See Chapter 5 for a comparison of Friedrich Hayek's and Charles Sabel's views on uncertainty. I, and most of flexible regulation scholarship, adopt Sabel's stance.

37 See, e.g., Peter F. Drucker, *Innovation and Entrepreneurship: Practice and Principles* (New York: Harper & Row, 1985).

1 INNOVATION AS A REGULATORY CHALLENGE: FOUR STORIES

1 See Merton H. Miller, "Financial innovation: the last twenty years and the next" (1986) 21 *J Financ Quant Anal* 459–471; Erik F. Gerding, *Law, Bubbles, and Financial Regulation* (New York: Routledge, 2014).

2 Lon Fuller, *The Morality of Law* (New Haven: Yale University Press, 1964); Joseph Raz, "The rule of law and its virtue," in Joseph Raz, *The Authority of Law: Essays on Law and Morality* (New York: Oxford University Press, 2009), pp. 210–232.

3 Ronald Dworkin, "Law as interpretation" (1982) 9 *Crit Inquiry* 179–200.

4 We know this – law and economics scholars, discussing gap-filling in incomplete contracts, have long argued that there can never be such a thing as a totally complete contract – but the point applies to regulation too. See Kimberly Krawiec, "Cosmetic compliance and the failure of negotiated governance" (2003) 81 *Wash U LQ* 487–544; E. Allan Farnsworth, "Disputes over omission in contracts" (1968) 68 *Colum L R* 860–891; Ian Ayres & Robert Gertner, "Filling gaps in incomplete contracts: an economic theory of default rules" (1989) 99 *Yale LJ* 87–130; Charles Goetz & Robert Scott, "Principles of relational contracts" (1981) 67 *Virginia L Rev* 1089–1150.

5 Edwards v. Canada (Attorney General), [1930] AC 124, 1929 UKPC 86 (describing the "living tree doctrine"); Guido Calabresi, *A Common Law for the Age of Statutes* (Cambridge: Harvard University Press, 1982).

6 For example, Under the American Procedure Act, 5 USC §533 (b)-(d) (1946).

7   Julia Black and her co-authors distinguish, accurately, between "bright-line" rules, which are structured around a single, non-negotiable threshold criterion; detailed rules, which set out detailed or complex criteria for their application; and principles, which establish a regulatory requirement at a higher level of generality. The distinction is useful in conversations about the relative merits and demerits of each approach. For present purposes, I treat detailed and bright-line rules together since both are based on static regulatory prescriptions, around which innovative processes or products can move. Julia Black et al., "Making a success of principles-based regulation" (2007) 1 *L & Fin Markets Rev* 191–206 at 194–195.

8   But see William H. Simon, "Optimization and its discontents in regulatory design: bank regulation as an example" (2009) 4 *Reg & Gov* 3–21 (describing the ways in which the "vulgar optimization" approach in the Basel II regime fell short of what experimentalist regulatory design would have prescribed). To be clear, the financial crisis is in no way a story about the failure of innovation-framing regulation as a theoretical approach, let alone about flexible regulation as a broader category. Financial regulation in the run-up to the crisis was not responsive regulation, new governance regulation, meta-regulation, or any of the other versions of flexible regulation that this book discusses. This crucial point should not be obscured: many of the so-called regulatory failures of our era are properly traced back further to private sector behavior. We can say that regulation and regulators ought to have done better, without letting private actors off the hook for errors and bad behavior that ultimately lay with them. But bracketing for now the extraordinarily poor conduct of industry actors, the main regulatory failures implicated in the crisis were functions of gaps in regulation, inadequate resources, the widespread underestimation of industry interconnectedness and systemic risk, and an ill-informed and insufficiently skeptical regulatory mindset. What I hope emerges from the observations here is an appreciation of the enormous challenge that the pace of private sector innovation presents to regulatory structures of all stripes.

9   See Tim Bartley, "Transnational governance as the layering of rules: intersections of public and private standards" (2011) 12 *Theo Inq L* 517–542.

10 On the origins of securitization, see Sarah Lehman Quinn, "Government policy, housing, and the origins of securitization", unpublished PhD dissertation, University of California, Berkeley (2003) (on file with author); *Protecting Homeowners: Preventing Abusive Lending while Preserving Access to Credit*: Joint hearing before the Subcomm. on Housing and Community Opportunities and the Subcomm on Fin Institutions and Consumer Credit, 108th Cong 117 (2003) (Statement of Cameron L. Cowan, Chair of Legislative and Judicial Committee, American Securitization Forum), available at www.gpo.gov/fdsys/pkg/CHRG-108hhrg92983/html/CHRG-108hhrg92983.htm. On derivatives and their early treatment see, e.g., Lynn A. Stout, "Why the law hates speculators: regulation and private ordering in the market for OTC derivatives" (1999) 48 *Duke LJ* 701–786 at 704–705, 712–734; Frank Partnoy, "The shifting contours of global derivatives regulation" (2001) 22 *U Pa J Int'l Econ* 421–495, at 435–442. For a straightforward explanation of what securitization and derivatives are, see generally Steven L.

Schwarcz & Adam D. Ford, *Structured Finance: A Guide to the Principles of Asset Securitization*, 3rd edn. (Practising Law Institute, 2002).

11   Adolf A. Berle & Gardiner C. Means, *The Modern Corporation and Private Property*, 2nd rev. edn. (New York: Harcourt, Brace & World 1968), pp. 8–9 (describing the corporation as producing "dissolution of the old atom of ownership into its component parts, control and beneficial ownership").

12   The literature here is extensive but see, e.g., Henry T.C. Hu & Bernard S. Black, "The new vote buying: empty voting and hidden (morphable) ownership" (2006) 79 *S Cal L Rev* 811–908; Frank Partnoy, "Financial innovation in corporate law" (2006) 31 *J Corp L* 799–827; Ronald J. Gilson & Charles K. Whitehead, "Deconstructing equity: public ownership, agency costs, and complete capital markets" (2008) 108 *Colum L Rev* 231–264; Tamar Frankel, "The new financial assets: separating ownership from control" (2010) 33 *Sea U L Rev* 931–964; Steven L Schwarcz, "Regulating complexity in financial markets" (2009) 87 *Wash UL Rev* 211–269.

13   Erik F. Gerding, "Code, crash, and open source: the outsourcing of financial regulation to risk models and the global financial crisis" (2009) 84 *Wash L Rev* 127–291.

14   Ibid. at 153–159; Kenneth A. Bamberger, "Technologies of compliance: risk and regulation in a digital age" (2010) 88 *Tex L Rev* 669–739.

15   Ben S. Bernanke, "The global saving glut and the U.S. current account deficit", Remarks at the Sandridge Lecture, Virginia Association of Economics, March 10, 2005, available at www.federalreserve.gov/boarddocs/speeches/2005/200503102/.

16   Adam Davidson, "What does Wall Street do for you?" *NY Times Magazine*, January 15, 2012, available at www.nytimes.com/2012/01/15/magazine/what-does-wall-street-do-for-you.html.

17   Gilson & Whitehead, "Deconstructing equity," note 12 above.

18   Josh Lerner & Peter Tufano, "The consequences of financial innovation: a counterfactual research agenda" (2011) Nat'l Bureau of Econ Research, Working Paper No. 16780 2, at 71–82, available at www.nber.org/papers/w16780.

19   Another example is the relationship between technology and regulation around high-frequency trading itself. As Chris Brummer describes it, the US SEC passed Regulation NMS (National Market System) in response to the market fragmentation problem that electronic trading networks had created. Regulation NMS attempted to improve fairness and price transparency across exchanges. The SEC also promulgated Rule 144A, which provided exemptions from the normal securities regulation registration requirements, to help investors gain access to innovative new capital-intensive firms. The unanticipated combined effect, however, was to move trading off public markets (for Rule 144A companies) and to spur high-frequency trading based on Regulation NMS price standards, to the detriment of both price discovery and fair treatment for retail investors. Chris Brummer, "Disruptive technology and securities regulation" (2015) *Fordham L Rev* 977–1052.

20   Among the many helpful sources on the Enron debacle, one particularly useful one on the relationship between Enron and derivatives is Frank Partnoy's testimony in *The Fall of Enron: How Could it have Happened? Hearing before the Comm. on Governmental Affairs U.S. Senate*, 107th Congress, 103 (January 24,

2002) (statement of Frank Partnoy), available at www.banking.senate.gov/public/
_files/partnoy.pdf. The discussion in this section draws on this testimony.

21   For a description of the criticism and response to the FASB, and a comparison of
     the US GAAP to British GAAP, see Frederick Gill, "Principles-based account-
     ing standards" (2003) 28 *NC J Int'l L & Com Reg* 967–982; *But see* William
     W. Bratton, "Enron, Sarbanes-Oxley and accounting: rules versus principles
     versus rents" (2003) 48 *Vill L Rev* 1023–1056 (arguing that auditor failure, rather
     than the existence of a rules-based GAAP regime, was to blame for the Enron
     crisis).

22   Financial Accounting Standards Board, *Proposal: Principles-based Approach to
     U.S. Standard Setting* (2005), available at www.fasb.org/project/principles-based_
     approach_project.shtml; Securities and Exchange Commission; US Securities
     and Exchange Commission, *Study Pursuant to Section 108(d) of the Sarbanes-
     Oxley Act of 2002 on the Adoption by the United States Financial Reporting
     System of a Principles-Based Accounting System* (2003), available at www.sec.gov/
     news/studies/principlesbasedstand.htm.

23   See, e.g., Peter Jeffrey, "International harmonization of accounting standards,
     and the question of off-balance sheet treatment" (2002) 12 *Duke J Comp & Int'l
     L* 341–351; David Kershaw, "Evading Enron: taking principles too seriously in
     accounting regulation" (2005) 68 *Mod L Rev* 594–625.

24   A recent example would be Goldman Sachs' use of its merchant banking arm to
     engage in the kind of proprietary investments that many had believed the Volcker
     Rule would prohibit. See Nathaniel Popper, "Goldman Sachs investments test
     the Volcker Rule," *NY Times*, January 13, 2015, available at dealbook.nytimes.
     com/2015/01/21/goldman-investments-are-testing-volcker-rule/?emc=edit_
     dlbkam_20150122&nl=business&nlid=12532775&_r=0.

25   Even outside the innovative context, disclosure-based regimes are imperfect and
     sometimes deployed without enough attention to context and fit. See, e.g., Omri
     Ben-Shahar & Carl E. Schneider, "The failure of mandated disclosure" (2011) 159
     U Pa L Rev 647–749.

26   Canadian Securities Administrators, National instrument, 45–106, Prospectus
     and Registration Exemptions, s. 2.35 (short-term debt) (2011), available at www
     .bcsc.bc.ca/Securities_Law/HistPolicies/HistPolicy4/PDF/NI_45-106/.

27   John Chant, "The ABCP Crisis in Canada: the implications for the regulation
     of financial markets (research report prepared for the Expert Panel on Securities
     Regulation)" (2009), available at www.expertpanel.ca/documents/research-
     studies/The%20ABCP%20Crisis%20in%20Canada%20-%20Chant.English.pdf.

28   "Credit crisis 'made in Canada,'" *National Post*, September 27, 2007, available at
     www.nationalpost.com/news/story.html?k=63868&id=3f92dc01-2dce-41a1-8035-
     358 121a6725a.

29   John Greenwood, "ABCP maker misled investors: OSC," *Financial Post*,
     September 28, 2011, available at business.financialpost.com/2011/09/28/regulator-
     finds-coventree-failed-to-disclose-problems-with-abcp-market/.

30   The SEC established the CSE program in June 2004 and terminated the program
     in 2008. It may have been meant to be somewhat equivalent in purpose to Basel
     II, but the CSE Program was not at all equivalent in scope or effect: it covered
     only the US-based broker-dealer arms of global financial institutions, since those

broker-dealers were subject to SEC regulation, and compliance by those broker-dealers' parent institutions was entirely voluntary. US Securities and Exchange Commission, "Chairman Cox Announces End of Consolidated Supervised Entities Program" (2008), available at www.sec.gov/news/press/2008/2008–230.htm.

31 Basel Committee on Banking Supervision, "A brief history of the Basel Committee" (2015) *Bank for International Settlements*, available at www.bis.org/bcbs/history.pdf.

32 Jean Dupuis, *The Basel Capital Accords* (Ottawa: Parliamentary Information and Research Service, 2006).

33 Globally, Basel II implementation was uneven. By 2008, forty-five jurisdictions had comprehensively implemented Basel II including Canada, Australia, Hong Kong, and the EU, and partially adopted by an additional eight countries by 2008. Eleven countries chose to implement the basic approaches of Basel II as well as Pillar II and III by 2008, but the advanced approaches more gradually. Nineteen countries, including the United States, partially implemented Basel after 2008, while eighty-four countries chose not to implement Basel II at all. The original intention was for Basel II to be implemented in the US in 2008 but the financial crisis delayed its implementation. Therefore, by 2008, only international banks with more than $250 billion in total assets or with foreign exposures greater than $10 billion were required to implement the advanced approaches for calculating capital charges for credit risk and operational risk under Basel II. The Federal Reserve Board, "Basel II Capital Accord: notice of proposed rulemaking (NPR) and supporting board documents" (2006), available at www.federalreserve.gov/generalinfo/basel2/draftnpr/npr/section_2.htm. Further, in 2001, the US implemented the Recourse Rule, which applied the (then developing) Basel II ratings-based approach to privately issued securitized assets to commercial banks and savings and loans in the US. It essentially extended the Accord's risk differentiations to securities. This had the effect of incentivizing certain assets by reducing the capital required under Basel I by 80 percent for the top-rated tranches. Jeffrey Friedman & Wladimir Kraus, *Engineering the Financial Crisis* (Philadelphia: University of Pennsylvania press, 2001).

34 First, with respect to the capital that a bank had to keep on hand, the Accord divided regulatory capital into two tiers. It required supposedly safe, high-quality "Tier 1 capital" to make up at least 50 percent of a bank's total capital base. Tier 2 capital was designated "supplementary capital" and was comprised of lower-quality capital, such as undisclosed reserves. Second, Basel I required international banks to hold capital equal to at least 8 percent of its risk-weighted assets (of which, as noted above, 50 percent had to be Tier 1 capital). To calculate how much capital it had to keep on hand, a bank was required to weigh the risks associated with the assets it held. For this purpose, under the Accord, a bank's assets were divided into just four categories of credit risk, assigned (in order from least risky to most risky) risk weights of 0 percent, 20 percent, 50 percent, or 100 percent. Where an asset was assigned 0 percent risk weight, the bank did not have to hold any capital in reserve for it. However, when an asset was assigned to the riskiest category (100 percent risk weight), the bank was required to hold the full 8 percent of its value as capital, 50 percent of which had to be Tier 1 capital. Basel Committee on Banking Supervision, "International convergence of capital

measurement and capital standards" (1988) *Bank for International Settlements*, available at www.bis.org/publ/bcbsc111.pdf.

35 Peter King & Heath Tarbert, "Basel III: an overview" (2011) 30 *Banking & Financial Services Policy Report* 1–19 at 2; Jeffrey Friedman & Wladimir Kraus, *Engineering the Financial Crisis* (Philadelphia: University of Pennsylvania press, 2001), p. 63.

36 Basel Committee on Banking Supervision, "International convergence of capital measurement and capital standards" (1988), at 12, available at www.bis.org/publ/bcbsc111.pdf.

37 King & Tarbert, "Basel II,", 2, note 35 above.

38 Basel Committee on Banking Supervision, "Working paper on the regulatory treatment of operational risk" (2001), available at www.bis.org/publ/bcbs_wp8.pdf.

39 Anna S. Chernobai, Svetlozar T. Rachev & Frank J. Fabozzi. *Operational Risk: A Guide to Basel II Capital Requirements, Models, and Analysis* (Hoboken, NJ: John Wiley & Sons, Inc., 2007), p. 26.

40 Ibid.

41 Regulatory arbitrage can be defined as legally taking advantage of the gap between the economic substance of a transaction or arrangement, and its legal or regulatory treatment. For a comprehensive treatment see Victor Fleischer, "Regulatory arbitrage" (2010) 89 *Tex L Rev* 227.

42 Basel Committee on Banking Supervision, *Basel II: International Convergence of Capital Measurement and Capital Standards: A Revised Framework* (June 2004), available at www.bis.org/publ/bcbs107.htm.

43 Marianne Ojo, "Basel III – Responses to consultative documents, vital aspects of the consultative processes and the journey culminating in the present framework (part I)" (2011) 30 *Banking & Services Policy Report*, 26–46; Alexey Lobanov, "Current trends in prudential regulation of market risk: from Basel I to Basel III," in Didier Sornette et al. (eds), *Market Risk and Financial Markets Modeling* (Springer, 2012), pp. 129–139 at 129.

44 UK Financial Services Authority, Internal Audit Division, *The Supervision of Northern Rock: A Lessons Learned Review* (March 2008), available at www.frank-cs.org/cms/pdfs/FSA/FSA_NR_Report_25.4.08.pdf.

45 Marc Levinson, "Faulty Basel" (2010) 89 *Foreign Aff* 76, at 83.

46 Dupuis, "Basel Capital Accords," note 32 above; Harald Benink & Clas Wihlborg, "The New Basel Capital Accord: making it effective with stronger market discipline" (2002) 8 *European Financial Management* 103–115.

47 Adrian Blundell-Wignall & Paul Atkinson, "Thinking beyond Basel III: necessary solutions for capital and liquidity" (2010) 1 *OECD Journal: Financial Market Trends* 1–23, at 15, available at www.oecd.org/finance/financial-markets/45314422.pdf, at 9–33.

48 King & Tambert, "Basel III," 3, note 35 above.

49 Ibid.

50 Ibid., at 7.

51 Jeffrey Friedman & Wladimir Kraus, *Engineering the Financial Crisis: Systemic Risk and the Failure of Regulation* (Philadelphia: University of Pennsylvania Press, 2011). The Basel capital accords operated somewhat differently in the United

States where, among other things, the US Securities and Exchange Commission adopted Basel II's Pillar I advanced approach for broker dealers operating under its regulatory jurisdiction. US Securities and Exchange Commission, *Alternative Net Capital Requirements for Broker-Dealers that are Part of Consolidated Supervised Entities, Exchange Act Release* No. 34-49830, 69 Fed Reg 34, 428 (2004), available at www.sec.gov/rules/final/34-49830.pdf. In the process, it transported the Basel II structure, including its incentives toward holding mortgage-backed securitized products, into this "shadow banking" context. The SEC's CSE Program has long been criticized for catalyzing a mad rush toward greater leverage among the broker dealers, but the better account now seems to be that the CSE Program simply replicated Basel II's own flaws in a different and highly competitive environment, where the capital adequacy rules were deployed with particular gusto. See Bethany McLean, "The meltdown explanation that melts away," Reuters, March 19, 19 2012, available at blogs.reuters.com/bethany-mclean/2012/03/19/the-meltdown-explanation-that-melts-away/; John Carney, "The SEC rule that broke Wall Street," CNBC, March 21, 2012, available at www.cnbc.com/id/46808453.

52   Basel III's requirements and phase-in schedules were approved in 2010. Basel III compliance compels banks to fulfil the requirements by 2019. Basel Committee on Banking Supervision, "Basel III phase-in arrangements," available at www.bis .org/bcbs/basel3/basel3_phase_in_arrangements.pdf; see also Basel Committee on Banking Supervision, "Revised Pillar 3 disclosure requirements" (2015), 1; King & Tambert, "Basel III," 3, note 35 above.

53   Connel Fullenkamp & Céline Rochon, "Reconsidering bank capital regulation: a new combination of rules, regulators, and market discipline" (2014) International Monetary Fund, Working Paper 14/169, at 5–6, available at www .imf.org/external/pubs/ft/wp/2014/wp14169.pdf.

54   Ibid.

55   Dodd-Frank Wall Street Reform and Consumer Protection Act, Pub. L. No. 111–203, 124 Stat. 1376, codified at 15 USC 8301 (2010).

56   Davis Polk LLP, "Dodd-Frank progress report," July 19, 2016, available at www .davispolk.com/Dodd-Frank-Rulemaking-Progress-Report/.

57   Ibid., at 6.

58   Administrative Procedure Act, 5 U.S.C § 500 et seq. has been in place since 1946, and requires all US federal administrative agencies to follow notice-and-comment rulemaking procedures: that is, to publish any proposed new administrative rule in advance, and to solicit and respond to public comment on it before it can be enacted.

59   Beyond administrative rulemaking, efforts to impose additional regulation on financial institutions encounter multiple other levels of resistance, including as a result of industry lobbying and politicization. For example, Dodd-Frank section 716 (known as the Lincoln Amendment), which would have limited the kinds of swaps that federally insured banks could hold, was significantly narrowed in December 2014 as part of a must-pass spending bill to prevent a government shutdown. Davis Polk LLP, "Swaps pushout provision amended: pushout requirement in section 716 now limited to certain ABS swaps," available at www.davispolk .com/.../2014-12-17_Swaps_Pushout_Provision_Amended.pdf. There is no dispute that large US financial institutions had been lobbying for years to roll back

or repeal that provision: see, e.g., Victoria McGrane, "Swap talk: why are people fighting over Dodd-Frank and derivatives?" *The Wall Street Journal*, December 10, 2014, available at blogs.wsj.com/washwire/2014/12/10/swap-talk-why-are-people-fighting-over-dodd-frank-and-derivatives/. The Dodd-Frank provisions that would impose additional regulatory requirements on "too big to fail" financial institutions (known as systemically important financial institutions, or SIFIs) was also dealt a blow in spring 2016 when MetLife Inc. successfully argued before the United States District Court for the District of Columbia that its designation as a SIFI should be struck down: *Metlife, Inc.* v. *Financial Stability Oversight Council*, C.A. No. 15–0045 (D.D.C. March 30, 2016). At the time of publication, that decision was under appeal to the DC Circuit.

60   Prohibitions and Restrictions on Proprietary Trading and Certain Interests In, and Relationships With, Hedge Funds and Private Equity Funds 17 CFR Part 75, codified at 12 USC § 1851.

61   Davis Polk LLP has produced a flowchart that graphically, across more than twenty pages of small-font diagrams, sets out the dozens of nested questions that a financial institution must answer to identify whether the Volcker Rule applies to its activities: "Proprietary trading flowcharts," December 13, 2013, available at volckerrule.com.

62   Kimberly D. Krawiec, "Don't 'screw Joe the plummer': the sausage-making of financial reform" (2013) 55 *Ariz L R* 53–103, at 71–74.

63   Ibid., at 73.

64   Ibid., at 74.

65   Ibid., at 101.

66   See, e.g., Wulf A. Kaal, "Dynamic regulation for innovation" in Mark Fenwick, Wulf A. Kaal, Toshiyuki Kono & Erik P.M. Vermeulen (eds), *Perspectives in Law, Business & Innovation* (New York: Springer, 2016), available at ssrn.com/abstract=2831040.

67   We return to this discussion in the books' final chapter, which sets out three sets of technical/epistemological questions that regulators should be asking themselves, on a continual basis, in order to maintain a bead on the phenomenon of financial innovation as it proceeds: (1) Knowledge and assumptions: what does the regulator know, and what does it not know?; (2) How is regulation structured, and what flows from these choices?; and, (3) learning and adaptability: how can we make regulation more resilient in the face of innovation?

68   Peter Bachrach & Morton S. Baratz, "Two faces of power" (1962) 56 *Am Pol Sci Rev* 947–952 Another highly relevant kind of power, which we discuss in the last part of this book, is "normative power". Financial institutions wielded normative power because they had the capacity to present compelling and well-crafted arguments and had access to policy makers at multiple levels. In a different historical, political, national, and industry environment, flexible regulation would certainly have played out differently than it did in the context of early twenty-first-century Anglo-American financial regulation. In that context, though, agenda-setting and power had a broader and mutually reinforcing knock-on effect on overarching theories of regulation and social ordering. Existing pillars in the normative framework, such as faith in market forces and optimism about innovation generally, could be leveraged as justifications for increasingly sweeping arguments in favor of

self-regulation. The apparent normative force of these claims in turn contributed to understaffing and under-resourcing of key regulators, and to regulatory timidity.

69   Pierre Bourdieu's idea of "habitus" – the idea that we collectively take in complex ideas of what is "appropriate" or "done" or "in good taste," based heavily and implicitly on social hierarchy – could be seen to underpin agenda-setting power, even though these scholars do not reference each others' work; See also Pierre Bourdieu & Loïs J.D. Wacquant, *An Invitation to Reflexive Sociology* 119 (1992); see generally Pierre Bourdieu, Richard Nice (tran.), *A Social Critique of the Judgment of Taste* (Cambridge: Harvard University Press, 1984).

70   Frank R. Baumgartner & Bryan D. Jones, *Agendas and Instability in American Politics*, 2nd edn. (Chicago, University of Chicago Press, 2009).

71   The Sarbanes–Oxley Act of 2002 Pub. L. No. 107–204, 116 Stat. 745, codified at 15 USC §§ 7201 was the statute that resulted. According to one scholar, this moment of "high politics" produced very little real value, see Roberta Romano, "The Sarbanes-Oxley Act and the making of quack corporate governance" (2005) 114 *Yale LJ* 1521–1611; Others disagree of course, see, e.g., Lawrence A. Cunningham, "The Sarbanes-Oxley yawn: heavy rhetoric, light reform (and it just might work)" (2003) 35 Conn L Rev 915–988.

72   See, e.g., Manuel Roig-Franzia, "Brooksley Born, the Cassandra of the derivatives crisis" (2009) *The Washington Post*, May 26, 2009, available at www .washingtonpost.com/wp-dyn/content/article/2009/05/25/AR2009052502108.html; see also, Katrina vanden Heuvel, "The woman Greenspan, Rubin & Summers silenced," *The Nation*, October 10, 2009, available at www.thenation.com/blog/ woman-greenspan-rubin-summers-silenced.

73   See, e.g., John Braithwaite, "The essence of responsive regulation" (2011) 44 UBC Law Rev 475–520; see also Joe Nocera, "Risk mismanagement," *New York Times Magazine*, January 2, 2009, available at www.nytimes.com/2009/01/04/magazine/ 04risk-t.html?pagewanted=all&_r=1&.

74   Michael Lewis, *Flash Boys: A Wall Street Revolt* (New York: W.W. Norton & Company, 2014).

75   Steve Schwarcz, "Regulating complexity in financial markets" (2009) 87 *Wash UL Rev* 211–269, at 213.

76   Malcolm Sparrow, *The Regulatory Craft: Controlling Risks, Solving Problems and Managing Compliance* (Washington, D.C.: Brookings Institution Press, 2000), p. 132.

77   UK Financial Services Authority Internal Audit Division, *The Supervision of Northern Rock: A Lessons Learned Review* (March 2008), available at www.frank-cs.org/cms/pdfs/FSA/FSA_NR_Report_25.4.08.pdf.

78   Frank R. Baumgartner & Bryan D. Jones, *Agendas and Instability in American Politics*, 2nd edn. (Chicago, University of Chicago Press, 2009).

79   Louis Kaplow, "Rules versus standards: an economic analysis" (1992) 42 *Duke LJ* 557–629.

80   Indeed, the Volcker Rule continues to be the subject of intense and often successful lobbying by banks. See, e.g., Jesse Hamilton & Cheyenne Hopkins, "Fed grants Volcker reprieve in banks second big win this month," *Bloomberg News*, December 18, 2014, available at www.bloomberg.com/news/articles/2014-12-18/ fed-grants-banks-two-year-delay-of-volcker-ban-on-private-funds.

81   Filling the gaps between legal construct and reality must account for how all of those layers interact in a specific political context. Bartley, "Transnational

governance," 518–519, note 9 above. Since regulatory design is our main interest here, however, it is the focus of the discussion above.

82   Frank Partnoy, "The shifting contours of global derivatives regulation" (2001) 22 *U Pa J Int'l Econ* 421–495, at 423–428; also Russell J. Funk & Daniel Hirschman, "Derivatives and deregulation: financial innovation and the demise of Glass-Steagall" (2014) 59 *Admin Sci Q* 669–704.

83   Beyond this chapter's scope, the corporate share itself also has been disassembled through the use of options and swaps, in ways that separate share ownership from economic stake. The result has been the new phenomenon of "empty voting" and "vote buying" that has fundamentally undermined corporate accountability and the market for corporate control. See Henry T.C. Hu & Bernard S. Black, "The new vote buying: empty voting and hidden (morphable) ownership" (2006) 79 *S Cal L Rev* 811–908; Even the traditional legal model of the corporation has been undone to some degree by SPVs whose relationship to the parent corporation is determined by contractual terms instead, as Raptor's with Enron was. This makes it difficult for regulators to recognize and respond to structural problems. See William W. Bratton & Adam J. Levitin, "A transactional genealogy of scandal: from Michael Milken to Enron to Goldman Sachs" (2013) 86 *S Cal L Rev* 783–868.

84   Donald MacKenzie, *An Engine, Not a Camera: How Financial Models Shape Markets* (Cambridge: MIT Press, 2006).

85   In 2015, initiated by its outgoing editor-in-chief, Alan Rusbridger, the Guardian newspaper launched a campaign called Keep It in the Ground. The campaign aims to persuade large investors, including the Bill and Melinda Gates Foundation and the Wellcome Trust, to divest from fossil-fuel companies.

86   Matthew Desmond, "Is democratic regulation of high finance possible?" (2013) 649 *Annals Am Acad Polit & Soc Sci* 180–184, at 182–183.

87   Neil Gunningham, Robert A. Kagan & Dorothy Thornton, *Shades of Green: Business, Regulation, and Environment* (Stanford: Stanford University Press, 2003).

88   See, e.g., Greg Myre, "The 1973 Arab Oil Embargo: the old rules no longer apply," *NPR*, October 16, 2013, available at www.npr.org/sections/parallels/2013/10/15/234771573/the-1973-arab-oil-embargo-the-old-rules-no-longer-apply; see generally, The White House, "Driving efficiency: cutting costs for families at the pump and slashing dependence on oil," available at www.whitehouse.gov/sites/default/files/fuel_economy_report.pdf.

89   See, e.g., Jacob Goldstein, "What is Bitcoin?," *NPR: Planet Money*, August 24, 2011, available at www.npr.org/sections/money/2011/08/24/138673630/what-is-bitcoin;

90   As of January 31, 2014, it appears that no country had successfully banned Bitcoin, although in many countries its legal status was unclear, see Kashmir Hill, "Bitcoin's legality around the world," Forbes, January 31, 2014, available at www.forbes.com/sites/kashmirhill/2014/01/31/bitcoins-legality-around-the-world.

91   See, e.g., "Silk Road successors," *The Economist*, May 29, 2015, available at www.economist.com/blogs/graphicdetail/2015/05/daily-chart-13; see also Christopher Ingraham, "How the FBI just made the world a more dangerous place by shutting down Silkroad 2.0 and a bunch of online drug markets," *Washington Post*, November 6, 2014, available at www.washingtonpost.com/blogs/wonkblog/wp/2014/11/06/how-the-fbi-just-made-the-world-a-more-dangerous-place-by-shutting-down-silkroad-2-0-and-a-bunch-of-online-drug-markets/.

92 David Bonilla, "Fuel taxes, fuel economy of vehicles and costs of conserved energy: the case of the European Union," in Oliver Inderwildi & Sir David King (eds), *Energy, Transport, & The Environment* (Springer, 2012), pp. 285–301; see also John Mikler, *Greening the Car Industry: Varieties of Capitalism and Climate Change* (Cheltenham: Edward Elgar, 2009) (comparing the UK, EU, and Japanese emissions control regimes).

93 See, e.g., "The lure of shadow banking," *The Economist*, May 10, 2014, available at www .economist.com/news/leaders/21601826-shadow-banks-helped-cause-financial-crisis-better-regulated-they-could-help-avert-next; see also "Shadow and substance," *The Economist*, May 8, 2014, available at www.economist.com/news/special-report/ 21601621-banks-retreat-wake-financial-crisis-shadow-banks-are-taking-growing.

94 David Johnston, Kathleen Rockwell & Cristie Ford, *Canadian Securities Regulation*, 5th edn. (Markham: LexisNexis, 2014).

95 John Tiner, Chief Executive, Financial Services Authority, "Better regulation: objective or oxymoron," Remarks at the SII Annual Conference (May 9, 2006), available at www.fsa.gov.uk/pages/Library/Communication/Speeches/ 2006/0509_jt.shtml.

2 HOW WE GOT HERE: THE HISTORY AND ROOTS OF FLEXIBLE REGULATION

1 Lord Peter Mandelson, Speech to Labour Party Congress, September 28, 2009, available at www.theguardian.com/politics/2009/sep/28/lord-mandelson-speech-in-full.

2 For a series of thoughtful treatments of contemporary capture theories and their limits, see Daniel Carpenter & David A. Moss (eds), *Preventing Regulatory Capture: Special Interest Influence and How to Limit It* (New York: Cambridge University Press, 2014).

3 See, respectively, The Financial Crisis Inquiry Commission, *Final Report of the National Commission on the Causes of the Financial and Economic Crisis in the United States* (2011), available at www.gpo.gov/fdsys/pkg/GPO-FCIC/pdf/ GPO-FCIC.pdf, at xvi; and House of Commons Treasury Committee, *The Run on the Rock* (London: The Stationary Office Limited, 2008), available at www .publications.parliament.uk/pa/cm200708/cmselect/cmtreasy/56/56i.pdf (respectively on the financial crisis in the US and the failure of Northern Rock in the UK); National Commission on the BP Deepwater Horizon Oil Spill and Offshore Drilling (ed.), *Deep Water: The Gulf Oil Disaster and the Future of Offshore Drilling* (Washington, D.C.: United States Government Printing, 2011) p. 122, available at www.gpo.gov/fdsys/pkg/GPO-OILCOMMISSION/pdf/ GPO-OILCOMMISSION (on the Deepwater Horizon oil spill and associated regulatory failures); and James M. Acton & Mark Hibbs, "Why Fukushima was preventable," (2008) *Nuclear Policy*, available at www.carnegieendowment.org/ 2012/03/05/why-fukushima-was-preventable-pub-47361 (on why the Fukushima nuclear disaster was preventable, including by regulators).

4 The New Deal refers to the sweeping changes put into place during Franklin D. Roosevelt's first term as US President (1933–1937), which established the

US-style Welfare State and the precedent for much contemporary federal government regulation in that country. The original Glass-Steagall Act in the United States was the Banking Act of 1933, which prohibited commercial banks from offering investment banking and insurance services. It was repealed by the Gramm-Leach-Bliley Act in 1999, though by that point it had already been substantially hollowed out in practice. In July 2015, Senator Elizabeth Warren and others introduced a new bill to the United States Senate with the short title the "21st Century Glass-Steagall Act of 2015," available at www.congress.gov/bill/114th-congress/senate-bill/1709/text. The bill would not actually reinstate the divisions that the original Glass-Steagall Act imposed, but the rhetorical link to the New Deal reform is instructive. (Regardless of the new bill's policy merits, it may be worth noting that my home country, Canada, has never had an equivalent separation of investment and consumer depository banking and yet has a resilient and safe banking sector.)

5   Jason Horowitz, "Bernie Sanders consistent over decades in his call for 'revolution'," *New York Times*, March 25, 2016, available at www.nytimes.com/2016/03/26/us/politics/bernie-sanders-consistent-over-decades-in-his-call-for-revolution.html?_r=0.

6   Consumer Financial Protection Bureau, "Strategy, budget and performance," available at www.consumerfinance.gov/about-us/budget-strategy.

7   K. Sabeel Rahman, "Envisioning the regulatory state: technocracy, democracy and institutional experimentation in the 2010 financial reform and oil spill statutes" (2011) 48 *Harv J on Legislation* 555–590, esp. at 84–87.

8   See eHealth, "Obamacare 101: how Obamacare health insurance works," available at resources.ehealthinsurance.com/affordable-care-act/obamacare-101-obamacare-health-insurance-works.

9   See, e.g., Christopher Hood, *The Art of the State: Culture, Rhetoric, and Public Management* (New York: Oxford University Press, 1998).

10 Giandomenico Majone, "From the positive to the regulatory state: causes and consequences of changes in the mode of governance" (1997) 17 *J Pub Pol'y* 139–167.

11 See, e.g., Julia Black, "Regulatory conversations" (2002) 29 *JL & Soc'y* 163–196, at 170.

12 As Lawrence Lessig has observed, law (here equivalent to state regulation) can directly influence a subject and can also influence that subject vicariously by leveraging other forces, which he describes with the terms "norms," "architecture," and the "market:" Lawrence Lessig, "The new Chicago school" (1998) 27 *J Legal Stud* 661–691. The term "regulation" is sometimes paired with the term "governance," which tends to be used to refer to a broader range of more informal networks of forces, including institutional forms and interpersonal pressures, which operate on social actors to constrain and channel behavior. Whether the term "regulation" is understood to include other "governance" mechanisms, or vice versa, varies from scholar to scholar. This book's concern is primarily public ordering that includes some role for the state, including where it takes the form of, for example, setting up a market for something like carbon credits.

13 We discuss Polanyi further in Chapter 5. But for now, see David Levi-Faur, "The global diffusion of regulatory capitalism" (2005) 598 *Annals Am Acad Pol & Soc*

Sci 12–32, at 14. See also Clifford D. Shearing, "A constitutive conception of regulation," in Peter Grabosky & John Braithwaite (eds), *Business Regulation and Australia's Future* (Canberra: Australian Institute of Criminology, 1993). As Cynthia Williams and John Conley have examined, in certain contexts private parties will fill in these background rules by agreement where a public regulatory presence has not done so. See John M. Conley & Cynthia A. Williams, "Global banks as global sustainability regulators?: the equator principles" (2011) 33 *L & Pol'y* 542–575.

14   See, e.g., Bronwen Morgan & Karen Yeung, *An Introduction to Law and Regulation: Text and Materials* (Cambridge University Press, 2007) at 79–113.

15   Levi-Faur, "Global diffusion," 14, note 13 above.

16   Other surveys of the scholarship and the flexible regulation approach include Orly Lobel, "The renew deal: the fall of regulation and the rise of governance in contemporary legal thought" (2004) 89 *Minn L Rev* 342–470; and Lester M. Salamon, *The Tools of Government: A Guide to the New Governance* (New York: Oxford University Press, 2002).

17   Ian Ayres & John Braithwaite, *Responsive Regulation: Transcending the Deregulatory Debate* (New York: Oxford University Press, 1992).

18   Gunther Teubner, "Substantive and reflexive elements of modern law" (1983) 17 *Law & Soc'y Rev* 239–285; Eric W. Orts, "Reflexive environmental law" (1994) 89 *Nw U L Rev* 1227–1340; Jean L. Cohen, *Regulating Intimacy: A New Legal Paradigm* (Princeton: Princeton University Press, 2002).

19   Malcolm K. Sparrow, *The Regulatory Craft: Controlling Risks, Solving Problems and Managing Compliance*(Washington, DC: Brookings Institution Press, 2000).

20   Julia Black & Robert Baldwin, "Really responsive risk-based regulation"(2010) 32 *Law & Pol'y* 181–213; Mary Condon, "Canadian securities regulation and the global financial crisis" (2009) 42 *UBC L Rev* 473–491; Bridget M. Hutter, *Anticipating Risks and Organising Risk Regulation* (New York: Cambridge University Press, 2010).

21   Cary Coglianese & David Lazer, "Management-based regulation: prescribing private management to achieve public goals" (2003) 37 *Law & Soc'y Rev* 691–730.

22   Julia Black, Martyn Hopper & Christa Band, "Making a success of principles-based regulation" (2007) 1 *L & Fin Markets Rev* 191–206; Cristie L. Ford, "New governance, compliance, and principles-based securities regulation" (2008) 45 *Am Bus LJ* 1–60; Cristie L. Ford, "Principles-based securities regulation in the wake of the global financial crisis" (2010) 45 *McGill L Rev* 257–307.

23   Gráinne de Búrca & Joanne Scott (eds), *Law and New Governance in the EU and the US* (Oxford: Hart Publishing, 2006), Orly Lobel, "New governance as regulatory governance," in David Lavi-Faur (ed.), *The Oxford handbook on Governance* (New York: Oxford University Press, 2012); Joanne Scott & Susan Sturm, "Courts as catalysts: re-thinking the judicial role in new governance" (2007) 13 *Colum J Eur L* 565–594.

24   Christine Parker, "Meta-regulation: the regulation of self-regulation," in *The Open Corporation: Effective Self-Regulation and Democracy* (New York: Cambridge University Press, 2002) at 245–291.

25   Condon, "Canadian securities regulation," note 20 above; Sharon Gilad, "It runs in the family: meta-regulation and its siblings" (2010) 4 *Reg & Gov* 485–506; Lori S. Bennear and Cary Coglianese, "Flexible approaches to environmental

regulation," in Michael E. Kraft & Sheldon Kamieniecki (eds), *The Oxford Handbook of U.S. Environmental Policy* (Oxford: Oxford University Press, 2013) 582–604.

26 Lucio Baccaro & Valentina Mele, "Pathology of path-dependency? the ILO and the challenge of 'new governance" (2012) 65 *Indus & Lab Rel Rev* 195–224; Cynthia L. Estlund, "The ossification of American labor law" (2002) 102 *Colum L Rev* 1527–1612.

27 The literature here is extensive but see, e.g., Joanne Scott & David M. Trubek, "Mind the gap: law and new approaches to governance in the European Union"(2002) 8 *Eur LJ* 1–18; Gráinne de Búrca & Neil Walker, "Law and transnational civil society: upsetting the agenda?" (2003)9 *Eur LJ* 387–400; Charles F. Sabel & Jonathan Zeitlin, "Learning from difference: the new architecture of experimentalist governance in the EU" (2008) 14 *Eur LJ* 271–327; Colin Scott, "The governance of the European Union: the potential for multi-level control" (2008) 8 *Eur LJ* 59–79; Kenneth A. Armstrong & Simon Bulmer, *The Governance of the Single European Market* (New York: Manchester University Press, 1998); Giandomenico Majone, *Regulating Europe* (London: Routledge, 2002); Adrienne Héritier & Dirk Lehmkuhl, "The shadow of hierarchy and new modes of governance" (2008) 28 *J Pub Pol'y* 1–17.

28 Orts, "Reflexive environmental law," note 18 above; Bradley C. Karkkainen, "Information as environmental regulation: TRI and performance benchmarking, precursor to a new paradigm?" (2001) 89 *Geo LJ* 257–370; Oren Perez, Yair Amichai-Hamburger & Tammy Shterental, "The dynamic of corporate self-regulation: ISO 14001, environmental commitment, and organizational citizenship behavior" (2009) 12 *L & Soc'y Rev* 593–630.

29 Julia Black, *Rules and Regulators* (New York: Oxford University Press, 1997); Cristie L. Ford, "Toward a new model for securities law enforcement" (2005) 57 *Admin L Rev* 757–828; Ford, "New governance," note 22 above; Robert F. Weber, "New governance, financial regulation, and challenges to legitimacy: the example of the internal models approach to capital adequacy regulation" (2010) 62 *Admin L Rev* 783–869.

30 Another evolutionary account is Nonet & Selznick's legal typology of repressive, autonomous, and responsive law. Repressive law serves the ruling elite, and actively makes and changes law to guide public policy. Autonomous law, on the other hand, is politically independent but cedes law-making and public policy to the legislators. The change from one legal system to the next depends on a variety of factors, including economic and political forces, legal histories, and cultures. However, Nonet & Selznick also argue that inherent weaknesses of autonomous law will naturally lead to responsive law. See Philippe Nonet & Philip Selznick, *Law & Society in Transition: Toward Responsive Law* (New York: Harper & Row, 1978). For a brief critique of the evolutionary aspect of this account, see Ayres & Braithwaite, "Responsive Regulation," 5, note 17 above.

31 Gøsta Esping-Anderson, *Three Worlds of Welfare Capitalism* (Princeton: Princeton University Press, 1990), pp. 18–19 (clustering welfare states into liberal, conservative, and social democratic regimes).

32 Majone, "From the positive," 141, note 10 above.

33 Ibid., at 141–142.

34 John Maynard Keynes, *The General Theory of Employment, Interest and Money* (New York: Harcourt, Brace & World, 1936).

35 Giandomenico Majone, "The rise of statutory regulation in Europe," in Jeremy Richardson (ed.), *Regulating Europe* (London: Routledge, 2002), pp. 54–56. This is not to say that all Welfare State structures were necessarily redistributive, or concerned with public service provision. Some initiatives, such as price controls, wage controls, interest rate controls and the like, were concerned more with stability and demand management.

36 Ibid., at 158; see also Thomas K. McCraw, *Prophets of Regulation: Charles Francis Adams, Louis D. Brandeis, James M. Landis, Alfred E. Kahn* (Cambridge: Belknap Press, 1984), at 210–221; Gary M. Anderson & Robert D. Tollison, "Congressional influence and patterns of New Deal spending, 1933–1939" (1991) 34 *JL & Econ* 161–175, at 164 (noting that nonmilitary federal spending rose from slightly over 30 percent in 1932 to over 50 percent in 1937, and that over $27 billion was spent on New Deal Programs from 1933–1939, accounting for about 55 percent of total spending during that period); Christopher Pierson, *Beyond the Welfare State: The New Political Economy of Welfare* 2nd ed. (University Park: Pennsylvania State University Press, 1998), p. 116 ("There is near universal agreement that the 'social' side of the New Deal, embodied in the 1935 Social Security Act 'declared the birth of the [American] welfare state and established a basis for its growth and development'," citing June Axinn & Herman Levin, *Social Welfare: A History of the American Response to Need* (New York: Dodd, Mead, 1975), p. 195). Expenditures from 1937–1941 averaged $9.2 billion, post-Second World War expenditures from 1947–1950 averaged $37.8 billion, and meanwhile total tax collected rose from $7.1 billion in 1941 to $44.5 billion in 1945: Jonathan R.T. Hughes, *The Governmental Habit Redux: Economic Controls From Colonial Times to the Present*, 2nd ed. (Princeton: Princeton University Press, 1991), pp. 186, 189.

37 Charles A. Reich, "The new property" (1964) 73 *Yale LJ* 733–787.

38 The absolute number of federal civilian employees in the years 1968 and 1969 totaled just over three million for each year. Over the last three decades, federal civilian employee numbers have moved between the highs of those years and lows of between 2.6 and 2.7 million, from 1999 through 2014. US Office of Personnel Management, *Historical Federal Workforce Tables*, available at www.opm.gov/policy-data-oversight/data-analysis-documentation/federal-employment-reports/historical-tables/total-government-employment-since-1962/. The late 1960s numbers have been roughly equaled or surpassed only six times since, in the years 1987 through 1992. Meanwhile, the population of the United States surpassed 200 million in 1967, was 249 million in 1990, and was just under 309 million as of the 2010 US national census. United States Census Bureau, *Historical National Population Estimates*, available at www.census.gov/popest/data/national/totals/pre-1980/tables/popclockest.txt. As discussed below, these numbers do not actually reflect state involvement in the economy since many roles were outsourced to private contractors, even while still being provided by the state.

39 Robert W. Hahn & John A. Hird, "The costs and benefits of regulation: review and synthesis" (1991) 8 *Yale J Reg* 233, at the appendix, summarize and assess multiple studies that estimate the costs of these forms of economic regulation, along with both costs and benefits of 1970s-era social and environmental

legislation including highway safety, occupational safety and health, consumer product safety, clean air and water legislation, and equal opportunity legislation. The article helpfully reviews several specific regulatory shifts that took place in the US as the regulatory state replaced the Welfare State, even if we may not reach the same conclusions today with regard to the costs and benefits of these regulatory schemes. For example, efforts to stimulate competition under the US Telecommunications Act of 1996 had the unintended effect, in radio in particular, of further concentrating the industry.

40 An engaging depiction of the trucking and shipping industries in this era, which also serves as a corrective to too much romanticization of at least the stevedores' unions and worker productivity, is Marc Levinson, *The Box: How the Shipping Container Made the World Smaller and the World Economy Bigger* (Princeton: Princeton University Press, 2006).

41 See, e.g., Wolfgang Streeck, "The crises of democratic capitalism" (2011) 71 *New Left Rev* 5–30; Pierson, "Beyond Welfare State," 99–166, note 36 above.

42 Thomas Piketty & Arthur Goldhammer, *Capital in the Twenty-First Century* (Cambridge: Harvard University Press, 2014), pp. 146–155.

43 Gøsta Esping-Andersen, "After the golden age: welfare state dilemmas in a global economy," in Gøsta Esping-Anderson (ed.), *Welfare States in Transition: National Adaptations in Global Economies* (London: Sage, 1996) pp. 1–31, at p. 1. 3.

44 Marvin B. Lieberman, Lawrence J. Lau & Mark D. Williams, "Firm-level productivity and management influence: a comparison of U.S. and Japanese automobile producers" (1990) 36 *Mgmt Sci* 1193–1215.

45 The left argued the that the Welfare State was ineffective at addressing poverty, while the right argued the Welfare State was intensifying inflation and undermining self-reliance. See, e.g., Thomas Wilson & Dorothy J. Wilson, *The Political Economy of the Welfare State* (Boston: G. Allen & Unwin, 1982).

46 See, e.g., Henry J. Aaron, *Politics and the Professors: The Great Society in Perspective* (Washington: Brookings Institution, 1978).

47 Robert E. Lucas Jr & Thomas Sargent, "After Keynesian macroeconomics," in *After the Phillips Curve; Persistence of High Inflation and High Unemployment*, Conference Series 19 (Federal Reserve Bank of Boston, 1978), available at www.bostonfed.org/economic/conf/conf19/conf19d.pdf; Alan S. Blinder, "The fall and rise of Keynesian economics" (1988) 64 *Econ Rec* 278–294; Greta R. Krippner, *Capitalizing on Crisis: The Political Origins of the Rise of Finance* (Harvard University Press, 2011). According to Krippner's compelling account, financial market deregulation and ultimately financialization itself in the US was produced, not by a grand anti-middle class conspiracy, but by incremental decisions based on political expediency, with unexpected effects.

48 R.H. Coase, "The problem of social costs" (1960) 3 *JL & Econ* 1–44 (this famous article had become a pillar of neoclassical law and economics scholarship by the 1970s). See, e.g., Richard A. Posner, "The economic approach to law" (1975) 53 *Tex L Rev* 757–782; Richard A. Posner, *Economic Analysis of Law* (Boston: Little, Brown, 1973).

49 See, e.g., Gary S. Becker, "A theory of competition among pressure groups for political influence" (1983) 98 *QJ Econ* 371–400.

50 See, e.g., McCraw, "Prophets of regulation," 270–273, 282–286, note 36 above.

51 See, e.g., Eric Helleiner, _States and the Reemergence of Global Finance: From Bretton Woods to the 1990s_ (Ithaca, Cornell University Press, 1994). Many factors have been cited to explain the (re)emergence of the modern globalized financial system, including 1) the growth of global communications technology, 2) restoration of market confidence in international financial transactions since the Great Depression, 3) growth in demand as international trade and multinational corporations grew, 4) the 1973 oil crisis, 5) dismantling of domestic financial cartels and using international activity as regulatory arbitrage, 6) market innovations like interest rate futures, options and swaps that decreased effective risks and costs of international financial operations, 7) incentives from "hegemonic" states like the US, UK, and Japan to support the globalization of the financial industry, 8) the success of the Euromarket and the resulting competitive deregulation in finance to attract more business and capital, and 9) a shift towards "neoliberalism" and the rise to prominence of thinkers like Milton Friedman and Friedrich Hayek. See McCraw, "Prophets of regulation," 6–22, note 36 above. Friedman and Hayek, and their (non)relationship to flexible regulation, are discussed further in Chapter 5.

52 Money market mutual funds allow investors to purchase a pool of securities that often offer higher rates of return than interest-bearing bank accounts and similar liquidity, but without being subject to banking regulation. From the investor's perspective, they seem to operate very much like a normal savings account at a bank. The oldest and largest of the American money funds, the Reserve Primary Fund, "broke the buck" in 2008 and was forced to dissolve when it was forced to return to investors only a portion of their investments. That fund's broken promise led to a massive exit of investors from the entire money market industry and was a catalyst of the financial crisis. See William A. Birdthistle, "Breaking bucks in money market mutual funds" (2010) _Wis L Rev_ 1155, at 1157.

53 Helleiner, "Reemergence global finance," 560–562, note 51 above. Carter did later enact a windfall profit tax on oil producers: see generally Dennis B. Drapkin & Philip K. Verleger Jr, "The windfall profit tax: origins, development, implications" (1981) 22 _BC L Rev_ 631–704.

54 Steven Morrison & Clifford Winston, _The Economic Effects of Airline Deregulation_ (Washington: Brookings Institute, 1986).

55 On the unintended predatory lending consequences of relaxing the usury laws, which had imposed interest rate ceilings, see Kathleen C. Engel & Patricia A. McCoy, "A tale of three markets: the law and economics of predatory lending" (2002) 80 _Texas L Rev_ 1255–1381.

56 The eight techniques were: marketable rights; economic incentives; performance-based standards; market-oriented compliance measures; reducing barriers to competition; information disclosure; voluntary standard setting; and adjusting standards to distinguish among categories of regulated entities ("tiering"). Memorandum From the President on Alternative Approaches to Regulation to the Heads of Executive Departments and Agencies (June 13, 1980) (published in _Public Papers of the Presidents of the United States, Jimmy Carter, 1980–1981, Book 2: May 24 to September 26, 1980_). Jimmy Carter also signed into law the Regulatory Flexibility Act, 5 USC §§ 601–612 (1980). See also Steven Rattner, "Carter asks agencies for flexible regulations," _NY Times_, June 13, 1980, at 29.

57 The Democratic Party in the United States was struggling internally with its commitment to existing programs, vis-à-vis new models. Younger Democrats in particular were advocating for a new and more "pro-business" liberal state. See, e.g., Paul E. Tsongas, "Update Liberalism, or it's a 6o's relic," *NY Times*, June 30, 1980, A19. See also Michael Barone, *Our Country: The Shaping of America from Roosevelt to Reagan* (New York: Free Press, 1990), p. 562. President Carter also encountered opposition to his more "centrist" policies from more left-leaning Democrats including Edward Kennedy, who contested the President's nomination as Democratic Party nominee in 1980.

58 John G. Geer (ed.), *Public Opinion and Polling Around the World: A Historical Encyclopedia* (Santa Barbara: ABC Clio, 2004), p. 222.

59 Eugene Bardach & Robert A. Kagan, *Going by the Book: The Problem of Regulatory Unreasonableness* (Philadelphia: Temple University Press, 1982), pp. 14–15.

60 See, e.g., ibid.

61 The term "command-and-control" seems to have been coined by economist Charles L. Schultze, *The Public Use of Private Interest* (Washington: Brookings Institute, 1977). This book avoids the term. As Jodi Short demonstrates, the term became increasingly common, and pejorative, from 1980 onward. It came to signify the dysfunctional regime against which more modern, flexible regulation contrasted itself: Jodi L. Short, "The paranoid style in regulatory reform" (2012) 63 *Hastings LJ* 633–694; see also Robert Baldwin, "Regulation: after command and control" in Keith Hawkins (ed.), *The Human Face of Law* (New York: Oxford University Press, 1997). In the process, some careful sociological work on how traditional regulatory prescriptions were translated into action – showing that traditional regulation as practiced could actually be quite sensitive to context – was disregarded. See, e.g., Kenneth Culp Davis, *Discretionary Justice* (Baton Rouge: Louisiana State University Press, 1969); Jeffrey L. Jowell, *Law and Bureaucracy* (New York: Dunellen Pub. Co, 1975); Susan S. Silbey & Austin Sarat, "Reconstituting the sociology of law: beyond science and the state," in Jaber F. Gubrium & David Silverman (eds), *The Politics of Field Research: Sociology Beyond Enlightenment* (London: Newbury Park, 1989), 150–173. Other scholars have criticized "command-and-control" because the term misleadingly exaggerates certain implicit myths and weaknesses about traditional regulatory regimes. See, e.g., David M. Driesen, "Is emissions trading an economic incentive program?: replacing the command and control/economic incentive dichotomy" (1998) 55 *Wash & Lee L Rev* 289–350; Timothy F. Malloy, "The social construction of regulation: lessons from the war against command and control" (2010) 58 *Buff L Rev* 267–355. Although terms like "traditional" or "bright-line" regulation, used in this book, are also reductionist and fail to depict the nuance that characterized regulation as an operational matter, they do not carry the same negative valence.

62 Everett Carll Ladd, Jr. & Seymour Martin Lipset, "Public opinion and public policy," in Peter Duignan & Alvin Rabushka (eds), *The United States in the 1980s* (Stanford: Hoover Institution, 1980), pp. 67–69.

63 Max Kaase & Kenneth Newton, *Beliefs in Government* (New York: Oxford University Press, 1995), pp. 67–71.

64 Giandomenico Majone, "Regulation and its modes," in Jeremy Richardson (ed.), *Regulating Europe* (London: Routledge, 1996), pp. 11–23.

65 Majone, "From the positive to the regulatory," 142, note 10 above; Majone, "Rise of statutory regulation," 55–57, note 35 above.

66 Merton H. Miller, "Financial Innovation: The Last Twenty Years and the Next" (1986) 21 *J Fin & Quant Anal* 459–471.

67 For a contemporaneous American discussion, see Harold Seidman & Robert S. Gilmour, *Politics, Position and Power: From the Positive to the Regulatory State* (New York: Oxford University Press, 1986).

68 Donald J. Savoie, *Thatcher, Reagan, Mulroney: In Search of a New Bureaucracy* (Pittsburgh: University of Pittsburgh Press, 1994), pp. 248–257. The story in Australia is somewhat different, though it still traces the same path from more directly interventionist state action to one guided more by competition and NPM-style reforms. Malcolm Fraser, the country's Liberal Prime Minister, maintained a relatively Keynesian outlook and governed until 1983, even while much of his party, including his eventual successor John Howard, was moving toward a regulatory state model. Howard did not become Prime Minister until 1996. Paul Kelly, *The End of Certainty: The Story of the 1980s* (St. Leonards: Allen & Unwin, 1992).

69 Savoie, ibid., at 12–13, 281–318.

70 On its history and development, see Joe Nocera, "Risk mismanagement," *New York Times Magazine*, January 2, 2009.

71 Though the drivers were different, the shift in governance strategies at the World Bank and the International Monetary Fund followed a similar trajectory from the 1980s through the 1990s. See Jacqueline Best, *Governing Failure: Provisional Expertise and the Transformation of Global Development Finance* (New York: Cambridge University Press, 2014). During this time these organizations shifted from a Washington Consensus era of structural adjustment policies in which "only economics mattered, and everything that mattered could be understood as economics" (ibid., at 62) to a more multifaceted and provisional form of governance focused on fostering political buy-in for development programs, developing global "good governance" standards, managing risk, uncertainty and vulnerability, and measuring outcomes.

72 Peter Aucoin, *The New Public Management: Canada in Comparative Perspective* (Montreal: Institute for Research on Public Policy, 1995), pp. 1–48; Jonathan Boston et al., *Public Management: The New Zealand Model* (New York: Oxford University Press, 1996). For an overview of New Public Management, see Ewan Ferlie et al., *The New Public Management in Action* (New York: Oxford University Press, 1996); see also Michael Barzelay, *The New Public Management: Improving Research and Policy Dialogue* (Berkeley: University of California Press, 2001).

73 See generally Karen Yeung, "The regulatory state," in Robert Baldwin et al. (eds), *The Oxford Handbook of Regulation* (New York: Oxford University Press, 2010), pp. 64–86.

74 Beryl A. Radin, *Federal Management Reform: In a World of Contradictions* (Washington: Georgetown University Press, 2012), pp. 30, 60.

75 Seidman & Gilmour, "Politics, position & power," 128, note 67 above.

76 David Osborne & Ted Gaebler, *Reinventing Government: How the Entrepreneurial Spirit is Transforming the Public Sector* (Reading: Addison-Wesley Publishing Company, 1992), p. 25.

77 The National Program Review was subsequently renamed the National Partnership for Reinventing Government. Its documents can be found at govinfo.library.unt.edu/npr/library/index.html#systemreports (last visited August 7, 2015).

78 Sparrow, "The regulatory craft," note 19 above (developing a powerful critique of this mindset in the enforcement context, where the notion of the "customer" is inapposite).

79 Michael Power, *The Audit Society: Rituals of Verification* (New York: Oxford University Press, 1997), p. 11.

80 Ibid., at 14.

81 Sometimes the fact of checking became more important than the results. Power has described the rise of the "audit society," meaning "a collection of systematic tendencies [that] dramatizes the extreme case of checking gone wild, of ritualized practices of verification whose technical efficacy is less significant than their role in the production of organizational legitimacy:" ibid., at 14.

82 We should not ignore the impact of what David Skeel has identified as the "corporatism" of the era. David Skeel, *The New Financial Deal: Understanding the Dodd-Frank Act and its (Unintended) Consequences* (Hoboken: Wiley, 2010).

83 Paul C. Light, *The New Public Service* (Washington: Brookings Institution Publishing, 1999), p. 8.

84 Tony Blair, *The Third Way: New Politics for the New Century* (Fabian Society, 1998).

85 William J. Clinton, "Address Before a Joint Session of Congress on the State of the Union," January 27, 1998, available at www.presidency.ucsb.edu/ws/?pid=56280. Whether this was actually the case – whether the government was smaller, or more progressive – is not obvious in retrospect. The point here is to describe the regulatory narrative at the time, not to assess its accuracy.

86 Ayres and Braithwaite, "Responsive regulation," note 17 above.

87 The Better Regulation Task Force was established in the UK in 1997, changed into a permanent body called the Better Regulation Commission in 2006, but closed in 2008. Better Regulation is still the term used by the European Commission, ec.europa.eu/smart-regulation/index_en.htm (last accessed August 6, 2015). See also, Claudio M. Radaelli & Anne C.M. Meuwese, "Better regulation in Europe: between public management and regulatory reform" (2009) 87 *Pub Admin* 639–654. I discuss the concept of simply "better" regulation further below, at the end of Chapter 5.

88 Neil Gunningham & Peter M. Grabosky, *Smart Regulation: Designing Environmental Policy* (New York: Oxford University Press, 1998), pp. 11–19.

89 Nocera, "Risk mismanagement," note 70 above.

90 Black, "Making a success," note 22, at 37–44; see also generally Black, "Rules and Regulators," note 29 above.

91 Parker, "Meta-regulation," 245–301, note 24 above.

92 At the international and transnational levels see, e.g., Kenneth W. Abbott & Duncan Snidal, "Hard and soft law in international governance" (2000) 54 *Int'l Org* 421–456; Errol Meidinger, "The administrative law of global private-public regulation: the case of forestry" (2006) 17 *Euro J Int'l L* 47–87; Gregory C. Shaffer & Mark A. Pollack, "Hard vs. soft law: alternatives, complements,

and antagonists in international governance" (2010) 94 *Minn L Rev* 706–799. In Europe see, e.g., Sabel & Zeitlin, "Learning from difference," note 27 above. See also, Héritier & Lehmkuhl, "Shadow of hierarchy," note 27 above (finding that voluntary agreements and self-regulation in the European environmental sector is more likely to emerge in the "shadow of hierarchy," i.e., with the threat of legislation). Some have argued that the EU is still hampered by traditional notions of the state, and governance would in fact be more effective if it was delegated to more non-state actors. See, e.g., Scott, "Governance of the European Union," note 27 above; Colin Scott, "Governing without law or governing without government? new-ish governance and the legitimacy of the EU" (2009) 15 *Euro LJ* 160–173.

93   For example, John Braithwaite noted that traditional constitutional protections against abuse of state power were ill-suited to a regulatory state that delegated so much public power into private hands. John Braithwaite, "Accountability and governance under the new regulatory state" (1999) 58 *Aus J Pub Admin* 90–94 at 90–91. Similarly, Ellen Dannin called privatization "an escape hatch that has allowed government agencies to contract out of the law." Ellen Dannin, "Red tape or accountability: privatization, public-ization, and public values" (2005) 15 *Cornell JL & Pub Pol'y* 111–164 at 143. See also, Gillian E. Metzger, "Privatization as delegation" (2003) 103 *Colum L Rev* 1367–1502; Laura A. Dickinson, "Public law values in a privatized world" (2006) 31 *Yale J Int'l L* 383–426.

94   See, e.g., Francis G. Castles, *The Future of the Welfare State: Crisis Myths and Crisis Realities* (Oxford: Oxford University Press, 2004); David Levi-Faur, "The odyssey of the regulatory state: from a 'thin' monomorphic concept to a 'thick' and polymorphic concept" (2013) 35 *Law & Pol'y* 29–50.

95   The rate of growth has not been consistently as high as in previous decades. With the 2008 financial crisis, however, welfare spending jumped on average across the OECD from 19% of GDP to historically high levels of 22% of GDP between 2007 and 2009, see *Social Spending During the Crisis: Social Expenditure (SOCX) Data Update 2012*, OECD (2012), www.oecd.org/els/soc/OECD2012SocialSpendingDuringTheCrisis8pages.pdf. Welfare spending has remained high in most OECD countries since. But see *Social Expenditure Update (SOCX) Data Update 2014*, OECD (2014), www.oecd.org/els/soc/OECD2014-Social-Expenditure-Update-Nov2014-8pages.pdf. (Indicating that social spending has decreased in some OECD countries – notably Germany, the UK and Canada – following the spending peak in 2009.)

96   Majone, "From the positive to the regulatory," 143, note 10 above.

97   Aucoin, "New public management," note 72 above; but see Michael Power, "The audit society," note 79 above (questioning the actual efficacy of the "rituals of verification").

98   Majone, "From the positive to the regulatory," 140, note 10 above; Steven K. Vogel, *Freer Markets, More Rules: Regulatory Reform in Advanced Industrial Countries* (New York: Cornell University Press, 1996).

99   Levi-Faur, "global diffusion of regulatory capitalism," 13, note 13 above.

100 American scholars had to contend directly with the rise of public choice theory, and the complex constitutional underpinnings of the American administrative state. Peter Aucoin has argued that the stronger executive control of government in Westminster systems allowed those systems to avoid interbranch power

struggles; Aucoin, "The new public management," note 72 above. Meanwhile, the European Union was being constructed as a novel entity. Compare, e.g., the work of Westminster-based scholars like Peter Aucoin, ibid.; Gunningham & Grabosky, "Smart regulation," note 88 above; Black & Baldwin, "Really responsive," note 20 above; with the work of Bardach & Kagan, "Going by the book," note 59 above; or Cass R. Sunstein, *After The Rights Revolution: Reconceiving the Regulatory State* (Cambridge: Harvard University Press, 1993). Of course there was also considerable cross-pollination and collaboration, see e.g., Neil Gunningham, Robert A. Kagan & Dorothy Thornton, *Shades of Green: Business, Regulation, and Environment* (Stanford: Stanford University Press, 2003); Ayres & Braithwaite, "Responsive regulation," note 17 above. The important work of continental European scholars, which influenced British scholars in particular, is beyond the scope of this book. See also David Levi-Faur, "Odyssey of the Regulatory State," note 94 above.

101 Vogel, "Freer markets," note 98 above.

102 Michael Moran, *The British Regulatory State: High Modernism and Hyper-Innovation* (New York: Oxford University Press, 2003).

103 For a contemporaneous account of the effect of new public management theory on responsible government and the professional public service, see Boston, "Public management," 316–347, note 72 above; Aucoin, "The new public management," 25–34, 49–82, note 72 above.

104 Clayton M. Christensen, *The Innovator's Dilemma: When New Technologies Cause Great Firms to Fail* (Boston: Harvard Business School Press, 1997).

105 7 U.S.C. § 27a. Other statutes and regulatory instruments played a role as well, including rules under the US Bankruptcy Code.

106 See Aucoin, "The new public management," 1–4, 31–38, note 72 above; see also David Heald, "The United Kingdom: privatisation and its political context" (1988) 11 *W Euro Pol* 31–48.

107 Welfare economics is now a field of study in its own right. See, e.g., N.A. Barr, *The Economics of the Welfare State*, 4th edn. (New York: Oxford University Press, 2004).

108 Johan Van Overtveldt, *The Chicago School: How the University of Chicago Assembled the Thinkers Who Revolutionized Economics and Business* (Agate Publishing, 2008).

109 See, e.g., Alfred E. Kahn, *The Economics of Regulation: Principles and Institutions* (New York: Wiley, 1970); George J. Stigler, *The Citizen and the State: Essays on Regulation* (Chicago: Chicago University Press, 1975); M. Derthick & P.J. Quirk, *The Politics of Deregulation* (Washington, DC: Brookings Institution, 1985). For an overview, see Cento Veljanovski, "Economic approaches to regulation," in Robert Baldwin et al. (eds), *The Oxford Handbook of Regulation* (New York: Oxford University Press, 2010), pp. 17–38.

110 Robert L. Rabin, "Federal regulation in historical perspective" (1986) 38 *Stan L Rev* 1189–1326, at 1318.

111 See, e.g., Anthony I. Ogus, *Regulation: Legal Form and Economic Theory* (New York: Oxford University Press, 2004).

112 See, e.g., Owen Fiss, "The Supreme Court 1978 term, foreword: the forms of justice" (1979) 93 *Harv L Rev* 1, at 6–9 ("Discrete and insular minorities" as legislative failures); John Hart Ely, *Democracy and Distrust: A Theory of Judicial*

Review (Cambridge: Harvard University Press, 1980), p. 103 (constitutional adjudication as correcting political market malfunctioning); Lani Guinier, *The Tyranny of the Majority: Fundamental Fairness in Representative Democracy* (New York: Free Press, 1995) (political market failure).

113 See, e.g., Ayres & Braithwaite, "Responsive regulation," note 17 above; Stephen Breyer, *Regulation and its Reform* (Cambridge: Harvard University Press, 1982).

114 Elinor Ostrom, *Governing the Commons: The Evolution of Institutions for Collective Action* (New York: Cambridge University Press, 1990). For non-economic regulatory scholars using traditional economic notions of efficiency to advance their work, see Lobel, "The re-new deal," 264, note 16 above ("A key strength of the new governance model is its explicit suggestion that economic efficiency and democratic legitimacy can be mutually reinforcing"); Gunningham et al., "Smart regulation," 26–27, note 88 above; Orts, "Reflexive environmental law," 1327–1330, note 18 above.

115 Karl Polanyi, *The Great Transformation: the Political and Economic Origins of our Time* (Boston: Beacon Press, 1944)

116 Ronald Reagan, First Inaugural Address, January 20, 1981, available at www .presidency.ucsb.edu/ws/?pid=43130.

117 Peter L. Bernstein, *Against the Gods: The Remarkable Story of Risk* (New York: John Wiley & Sons, 1998).

118 Anthony Giddens, *Runaway World: How Globalisation is Shaping our Lives* (London: Profile, 1999), p. 42 ("The welfare state … is essentially a risk management system. Designed to protect against hazards that were once treated as at the disposition of the gods"). Giddens attributes this concept initially to Ulrich Beck.

119 Anthony Giddens, "Risk and responsibility" (1999) 62 *Mod L Rev* 1–10, at 4.

120 Edmond Halley, better known for his work in predicting the orbit of the comet named after him, is widely held to be the father of actuarial science: see E. Halley, "An estimate of the degrees of the mortality of mankind, drawn from curious tables of the births and funerals at the City of Breslaw; with an attempt to ascertain the price of annuities upon lives" (1693) 17 *Phil Trans R Soc Lond* 596–610. For a general history of actuarial science, see Chris Lewin, "An Overview of Actuarial History," Institute and Faculty of Actuaries (lecture on June 14, 2007), available at www.actuaries.org.uk/research-and-resources/ documents/overview-actuarial-history-slides-notes.

121 Martin Lengwiler, "Technologies of trust: actuarial theory, insurance sciences, and the establishment of the welfare state in Germany and Switzerland around 1900" (2003) 13 *Info & Org* 131–150; Daniel Béland, "Ideas and institutional change in social security: conversion, layering, and policy drift" (2007) 88 *Soc Sci Q* 20–38.

122 Giddens, "Risk and responsibility," 4, note 119 above.

123 Ibid., at 3.

124 Ibid., at 2, 6.

125 Frank Knight, *Risk, Uncertainty and Profit* (New York: Houghton Mifflin Company, 1921), p. 20.

126 Ibid., at 230–232. Knight's definition of risk and uncertainty has been examined extensively. For a summary of different interpretations of Knight's classification

see Richard N. Langlois & Metin M. Cosgel, "Frank Knight on risk, uncertainty and the firm: a new interpretation" (1993) 31 *Econ Inquiry* 456–465; Geoffrey T.F. Brooke, "Uncertainty, profit, and entrepreneurial action: Frank Knight's contribution reconsidered" (2010) 32 *J Hist Econ Thought* 221–235.

127 Donald H. Rumsfeld, US Department of Defense News Briefing, February 12, 2002, transcript available at www.defense.gov/transcripts/transcript.aspx?transcriptid=2636.

128 Knight, "Risk, uncertainty and profit," 230–236, note 125 above. See also Stephen F. LeRoy & Larry D. Singell Jr, "Knight on risk and uncertainty" (1987) 95 *J Pol Econ* 394–407, at 400–401; See also Langlois & Cosgel, "New interpretation," 459, note 126 above; Brooke, "Entrepreneurial action," 225–226, note 126 above.

129 Julia Black, "The role of risk in regulatory processes," in Robert Baldwin et al. (eds), *The Oxford Handbook of Regulation* (New York: Oxford University Press, 2010), pp. 302–348; Michael Power, *The Risk Management of Everything: Rethinking the Politics of Uncertainty* (London: Demos, 2004) (suggesting the pervasive regulatory preoccupation with reputational risk management is a means to escape accountability). See, e.g., UK Financial Services Authority, *Consultation Paper 142: Operational Risk Systems and Controls* (July 2002), available at www.bankofengland.co.uk/financialstability/fsc/Documents/FSAConsultationPaper142.pdf; US Office of Mgmt. & Budget (OBM) and US Office of Science and Technology Policy (OSTP) Memorandum for the Regulatory Working Group & Office of Sci. & Tech. Policy, Memorandum M-07-24, *Updated Principles for Risk Analysis* (September 19, 2007), available at www.whitehouse.gov/sites/default/files/omb/assets/omb/memoranda/fy2007/m07-24.pdf.

130 Jean-Baptiste Michel et al., "Quantitative analysis of culture using millions of digitized books" (2010) 331 *Science* 176–182 (frequency data based on Google Books n-gram viewer). The data are limited by the scope of books available through Google Books.

131 Paul Kelly, "The end of certainty," note 68 above

132 UK Financial Services Authority, *Reasonable Expectations: Regulation in a Non-Zero Failure World* (2003), available at www.fsa.gov.uk/pubs/other/regulation_non-zero.pdf.

133 Lobel, "The renew deal," 354, note 16 above.

134 See, e.g., Tom Baker, "Embracing risk, sharing responsibility" (2008) 56 *Drake L Rev* 561–570, at 562–563 (describing how risk-based thinking has led to, e.g., the shift from "defined benefit" to "defined contribution" employment based insurance, changes in US Social Security retirement benefits and social welfare benefits, or even lower health care insurance premia for "healthy workplaces," with a corresponding culture of control around health-related employee behavior.)

135 Michael Power, "Risk management of everything," note 129 above.

136 Michel Foucault, *The Order of Things: An Archaeology of the Human Sciences* (New York: Routledge,1966); Michel Foucault, *Discipline and Punish* (New York: Vintage Books, 1977); Michel Foucault, "The ethic of care for the self as a practice of freedom: an interview with Michel Foucault on 20 January 1984," in James Bernaur & David Rasmussen (eds), *The Final Foucault* (Cambridge: MIT Press, 1987), p. 11. In his later years, Foucault made more

room for human agency. The concept of micro-power and personal self-policing also played a role in feminist scholarship: See, e.g., Sandra Lee Bartky, "Foucault, femininity and the modernization of patriarchal power," in Sandra Lee Bartky (ed.), *Femininity and Domination: Studies in the Phenomenology of Oppression* (New York: Routledge, 1990).

137 See, e.g., Pierre Bourdieu, *Distinction: A Social Critique of the Judgment of Taste* (Cambridge: Harvard University Press, 1984). Steven Lukes, *Power: A Radical View*, 2nd edn., no. 1 (New York: MacMillan, 2005), p. 152 (traces the idea of intellectual hegemony from Gramsci back to Marx and Engels).

138 James N. Rosenau & Ernst-Otto Czempiel (eds), *Governance without Government: Order and Change in World Politics* (New York: Cambridge University Press, 1992).

139 James N. Rosenau, "Governance, order, and change in world politics," in James N. Rosenau & Ernst-Otto Czempiel (eds), *Governance without Government: Order and Change in World Politics* (New York: Cambridge University Press, 1992), p. 4. Colin Scott provides an insightful analysis of the linkages between Foucault's governmentality analysis, legal pluralism, and regulation in "Regulation in the age of governance," 154–156. See also Ronen Shamir, *The Colonies of Law: Colonialism, Zionism and Law in Early Mandate Palestine* (Cambridge: Cambridge University Press, 2000), p. 53 (suggesting that despite the enlightening way in which Foucault's work shifted "the analytic gaze" to less visible sites of power, his account of law was oversimplified and underestimated its importance to modern forms of power).

140 See also generally Teubner, above note 18 (addressing critical and postmodern theoretical challenges to law in compatible ways, though using the term "reflexive law" rather than governance).

141 Michael Moran, "Understanding the regulatory state" (2002) 32 *British J Pol Sci* 391–413, at 405.

142 Braithwaite, "Accountability and governance," 90, note 93 above.

143 See, e.g., Roberto Mangabeira Unger, "The critical legal studies movement" (1983) 96 *Harv L Rev* 561–675; Duncan Kennedy, "Legal education and the reproduction of hierarchy" (1982) 32 *J Legal Educ* 591–615.

144 See e.g., Catherine A. MacKinnon, *Feminism Unmodified: Discourses on Life and Law* (Cambridge: Harvard University Press, 1987); Nicola Lacey, "Feminist legal theory" (1989) 9 *Oxford J Legal Stud* 383–394; Judith Butler, *Gender Trouble: Feminism and the Subversion of Identity* (New York: Routledge, 1990); Martha Nussbaum, *Sex and Social Justice* (New York: Oxford University Press, 1998).

145 Richard Delgado, "When a story is just a story: does voice really matter?" (1990) 76 *Va L Rev* 95–111; Derrick A. Bell, "Who's afraid of critical race theory?" (1995) *U Ill L Rev* 893–910. But see Patricia J. Williams, *The Alchemy of Race and Rights* (Cambridge: Harvard University Press, 1992).

146 David Lodge, "Goodbye to all that," *The New York Review of Books* (May 27, 2004), available at www.nybooks.com/articles/archives/2004/may/27/goodbye-to-all-that/?pagination=false.

147 Michael C. Dorf & Charles F. Sabel, "A constitution of democratic experimentalism" (1998) 98 *Colum L Rev* 298–473; Cass R. Sunstein, *Free Markets and Social Justice* (New York: Oxford University Press, 1997), pp. 5, 7, 32–69, 271–297.

148   See, e.g., Stanley Fish, *Is there a Text in this Class?: The Authority of Interpretive Communities* (Cambridge: Harvard University Press, 1980). For a response, see Julia Black, "Talking about regulation" (1998) Pub L 77–98.

149   I am indebted to Carol Heimer for this point.

150   Gunningham, Kagan & Thornton, "Shades of green," 17, 41–74, note 100 above; also Daniel H. Cole & Peter Z. Grossman, "When is command-and-control efficient? Institution, technology, and the comparative efficiency of alternative regulatory regimes for environmental protection" (1999) 5 *Wisc L Rev* 887–938.

151   For a thoughtful early exposition see Christopher Stone, *Where the Law Ends: The Social Control of Corporate Behavior* (New York: Harper & Row, 1975). See also Richard B. Stewart, "Regulation and the crisis of legalisation in the United States," in Terence Daintith (ed.), *Law as an Instrument of Economic Policy: Comparative and Critical Approaches* (Berlin: de Gruyter, 1988), pp. 97–133 (arguing that regulatory efforts to address social issues, as opposed to purely economic ones, provoked litigation, which in turn made traditional forms of regulation in those areas more difficult and less effective).

152   The terminology is Susan Sturm's, from "Second generation employment discrimination: a structural approach" (2001) 101 *Colum L Rev* 458–568, but the concern traces its origins to the idea of substantive equality in radical feminism. See MacKinnon, "Feminism unmodified," 63–65, note 144 above.

153   Robert C. Ellickson, "Of Coase and cattle: dispute resolution among neighbors in Shasta County" (1986) 38 *Stan L Rev* 623–687; Lisa Bernstein, "Opting out of the legal system: extralegal contractual relations in the diamond industry" (1992) 21 *J Legal Stud* 115–157; Robert M. Cover, "Foreword: nomos and narrative" (1983) 97 *Harv L Rev* 4–69.

154   Tom R. Tyler, *Why People Obey the Law* (New Haven: Yale University Press, 1990).

155   In the UK, see Quentin Skinner, *Liberty Before Liberalism* (New York: Cambridge University Press, 1998).

156   See, e.g.,, Frank Michelman, "Law's republic" (1988) 97 *Yale LJ* 1493–1537; Phillip Pettit, *Republicanism: A Theory of Freedom and Government* (New York: Oxford University Press, 1997).

157   Mark Seidenfeld, "A civic republican justification for the bureaucratic state" (1992) 105 *Harv L Rev* 1511–1576; Michelman, "Law's republic," note 156 above.

158   Ayres & Braithwaite, "Responsive regulation," note 17 above. John Braithwaite has also coauthored with Phillip Pettit: see *Not Just Desserts: A Republican Theory of Criminal Justice* (New York: Oxford University Press, 1990)

159   In its "softest law" versions, governance operates without legal authority or perhaps even government in the classic sense. See, e.g., Colin Scott, "Private regulation of the public sector: a neglected facet of contemporary governance" (2002) 29 *JL & Soci* 56–76; Colin Scott, "Governing without law," note 92 above. On soft law, see Linda Senden, *Soft Law in European Community Law* (Oxford: Hart Publishing, 2004), p. 112 (defining soft law as "[r]ules of conduct that are laid down in instruments which have not been attributed legally binding force as such, but nevertheless may have certain (indirect) legal effects, and that are aimed at and may produce practical effects"); Abbott & Snidal, "Hard and soft law," 422, note 92 above ("'soft law' begins once legal arrangements are

weakened along one or more of the dimensions of obligation, precision, and delegation.").

160   The conversation about whether flexible regulation is "neoliberal" continues in Chapter 5; see also my definition of the term, adopted from Michèle Lamont and contained in the first footnote of this book.

161   See Flavio Romano, *Clinton and Blair: The Political Economy of the Third Way* (New York: Routledge, 2006), p. 3 (citing Blair, "The Third Way," note 84 above; William J. Clinton, "State of the Union Address," January 27, 1998, in *Congressional Record, V. 144, Pt. 1, January 27, 1998 to February 13 1998* (Washington, DC: United States Government Printing Office, 2003).

162   See, e.g., Julia Black, "Decentring regulation: understanding the role of regulation and self-regulation in a 'post-regulatory' world" (2001) 54 *Current Leg Prob* 103–146.

3   FOUR KEY PERSPECTIVES: FLEXIBLE REGULATION AND THE LINK TO INNOVATION

1   National Commission on the BP Deepwater Horizon Oil Spill and Offshore Drilling (ed.), *Deep Water: The Gulf Oil Disaster and the Future of Offshore Drilling* (Washington, DC: United States Government Printing, 2011) p. 122, available at www.gpo.gov/fdsys/pkg/GPO-OILCOMMISSION/pdf/GPO-OILCOMMISSION.pdf.

2   UK Financial Services Authority [FSA], *The Turner Review: A Regulatory Response to the Global Banking Crisis* (2009), at 49, available at www.fsa.gov.uk/pubs/other/turner_review.pdf.

3   As the Northern Rock debacle in the UK highlighted, the FSA was far from adequately staffed. The FSA acknowledged extraordinarily high turnover of FSA staff directly supervising the bank, inadequate numbers of staff, and very limited direct contact with bank executives among the reasons for its "unacceptable" regulatory performance. See UK Financial Services Authority Internal Audit Division, *The Supervision of Northern Rock: A Lessons Learned Review* (March 2008), available at www.fsa.gov.uk. Its Major Retail Groups Division was reduced by some twenty staff between 2004 and 2008, notwithstanding the division's responsibility for substantial and complex FSA priorities such as Basel and the Treating Customers Fairly initiative, in addition to its core firm risk-assessment work. The example of the SEC's Consolidated Supervised Entities program (CSE) is even more striking. Leaving aside that the program was *voluntary*, its Division of Trading and Markets had only seven staffers and no executive director, even though, from March 2007 onward, it had been charged with overseeing four otherwise-unregulated major broker-dealer firms, which together were the backbone of the American-based shadow banking industry, based on an alternative capital adequacy method. One of the effects of understaffing was that Trading and Markets staff had not completed any inspections of the division's subject firms in the eighteen months prior to the collapse of Bear Stearns in September 2008. The CSE program was terminated that month.

4 Sharon Gilad, "Juggling conflicting demands: the case of the UK Financial Ombudsman Service" (2009) 19 *J Pub Admin Res & Theory* 661–680; Julia Black, "The rise, fall and fate of principles based regulation" (2010) 17 *LSE Law Society and Economy Working Papers*, at 18–19, available at www.lse.ac.uk/collections/law/wps/wps.htm.

5 The program sought to produce genuine cultural change among firms that sold financial products to retail investors in the UK. It focused on what was perceived as a widespread culture of "mis-selling," or what in North America would be understood as registrants' failures to ensure the suitability of a product for an investor. Early in 2007, the FSA set March 2008 as the deadline by which firms should be able to demonstrate their capability to fully assess and measure their operations against TCF outcomes by means of adequate management information, and December 2008 as the date by which firms should be able to show that they were consistently treating their customers fairly. The FSA conducted industry-wide reviews around March 2008 and subsequently published a progress report suggesting that 87 percent of large and medium-size financial firms failed to pass this review. The final industry-wide TCF review, which was scheduled to take place around December 2008, was cancelled in November 2008 in light of the financial crisis. Sharon Gilad, "Institutionalizing Fairness in Financial Markets: Mission Impossible?" (2011) 5 *Reg & Gov* 309–332.

6 Some leading lights from the regulatory governance academy – prominently, Cass Sunstein and Jody Freeman – went on to serve in regulatory capacities with the US federal government or federal administrative agencies during the Obama Administration. Many other scholars in the fields of regulation and governance and financial regulation have and continue to testify before Congressional and Parliamentary subcommittees, provide expert opinions, be involved in influential think tanks and advocacy groups, and otherwise influence policy.

7 Eugene Bardach & Robert A. Kagan, *Going by the Book: The Problem of Regulatory Unreasonableness* (Philadelphia: Temple University Press, 1982).

8 See, e.g., Richard B. Stewart, "Administrative law in the twenty-first century" (2003) 78 *NYU L Rev* 437–460 at 446 ("It generally takes a very long time to formulate and adopt new regulations and a long time to implement them. Regulatory results often fall short of expectations at the same time that regulatory requirements grow ever more burdensome. In my view, these headaches are primarily due to excessive reliance on command-and-control methods of regulation"); Thomas O. McGarity, "Some thoughts on 'deossifying' the rulemaking process" (1992) 41 *Duke LJ* 1385–1462 at 1397 ("When rulemaking is aimed at advancing progressive social agendas, regulatees and their trade associations have fiercely resisted the rulemaking process, seeking to lard it up with procedural, structural, and analytical trappings that have the predictable effect of slowing down the agency").

9 Cass R. Sunstein, "Administrative substance" (1991) *Duke LJ* 607–646, at 627 (emphasis added).

10 Ibid., at 633.

11 Richard B. Stewart, "Environmental regulation and international competitiveness" (1993) 102 *Yale LJ* 2039–2106 at 2050.

12   Sarbanes-Oxley Act of 2002, Pub. L. No. 107–204, 116 Stat 745 (2003), codified at 15 USC §§ 7201; Dodd-Frank Wall Street Reform and Consumer Protection Act, Pub. L. No. 111–203, 124 Stat. 1376, codified at 12 USC 5301 (2010).

13   Richard B. Stewart, "Environmental regulation and international competitiveness" (1993) 102 *Yale LJ* 2039–2106, at 2089.

14   Lester M. Salamon & Odus V. Elliot, *The Tools of Government: A Guide to New Governance* (New York: Oxford University Press, 2002), p. 9 (emphasis in original) (Salamon recognizes that tools are political at p. 11).

15   See, e.g., Bronwen Morgan & Karen Yeung, *An Introduction to Law and Regulation: Text and Materials* (Cambridge University Press, 2007), pp. 79–113.

16   Stephen Breyer, *Regulation and its Reform* (Cambridge: Harvard University Press, 1982).

17   Other important scholarly works from the 1980s include Richard Stewart, "Regulation in a liberal state: the role of non-commodity values" (1983) 92 *Yale LJ* 1537–1590. In keeping with the historical story above, many were informed by the new economic analysis of law.

18   Ian Ayres & John Braithwaite, *Responsive Regulation: Transcending the Deregulatory Debate* (New York: Oxford University Press, 1992).

19   Ibid., at 19 ("Some corporate actors will only comply with the law if it is economically rational for them to do so; most corporate actors will comply with the law most of the time simply because it is the law; all corporate actors are bundles of contradictory commitments to values about economic rationality, law abidingness, and business responsibility").

20   Oliver Wendell Holmes, "The path of the law" (1897) 10 *Harv L Rev* 457, at 459 ("A man who cares nothing for an ethical rule which is believed and practiced by his neighbors is likely nevertheless to care a good deal to avoid being made to pay money, and will want to keep out of jail if he can").

21   Ayres & Braithwaite, "Responsive regulation," note 18 above; see also Eugene Bardach & Robert A. Kagan, *Going by the Book: The Problem of Regulatory Unreasonableness* (Philadelphia: Temple University Press, 1982).

22   Originally published in Robert Axelrod & William D. Hamilton, "The evolution of cooperation" (1981) 211 *Science* 1390–1396.

23   Ayres & Braithwaite, "Responsive regulation," note 18 above. Flexible regulation does not reject the use of regulatory floors and ceilings. In fact, it may incorporate regulatory ceilings or, more often, floors into its regulatory structure. See, e.g., William W. Buzbee, "Asymmetrical regulation: risk, preemption, and the floor/ceiling distinction" (2007) 82 *NYU L Rev* 1547–1619; See also Benjamin Sovacool, "The best of both worlds: environmental federalism and the need for federal action on renewable energy and climate change" (2008) 27 *Stan Envl LJ* 397–476.

24   Ayres & Braithwaite, "Responsive regulation," 101–116, note 18 above.

25   Ibid., at 56.

26   Ibid., at 97.

27   Ibid., at 18.

28   See, e.g., John Braithwaite, *Restorative Justice & Responsive Regulation* (Oxford: Oxford University Press, 2002), p. 133 (linking his restorative justice model with "other social movements against domination"); John Braithwaite,

"Relational republican regulation" (2013) 7 *Reg & Gov* 124–144 at 128 ("The essence of the republican ideal is that good policy is that which advances freedom as non-domination; deft checks and balances against arbitrary power are keys to republican freedom from domination"). For Braithwaite, the key republican work is likely Philip Pettit, *Republicanism: A Theory of Freedom and Government* (Oxford: Oxford University Press, 1997).

29   See, e.g., Saule T. Omarova, "Bankers, bureaucrats, and guardians: toward tripartism in financial services regulation" (2012) 37 *J Corp L* 621–674 (proposing the creation of an independent Public Interest Council to promote financial stability); Neil Gunningham & Darren Sinclair, *Leaders & Laggards: Next-Generation Environmental Regulation* (Sheffield: Greenleaf, 2002), pp. 157–188 (describing how the Victorian Environmental Protection Authority shifted from bipartism to tripartism as part of a broader change towards facilitative regulation); Kenneth W. Abbott & Duncan Snidal, "Taking responsive regulation transnational: strategies for international organizations" (2013) 7 *Reg & Gov* 95–113 (in transnational regulatory settings, intergovernmental organizations provide the "orchestration" needed to support and steer regulators and regulates, paralleling the benefits of domestic tripartism); Robert F. Weber, "New governance, financial regulation, and challenges to legitimacy: the example of the internal models approach to capital adequacy regulation" (2010) 62 *Admin L Rev* 783–869, at 863–867 (arguing the disclosure requirements in Basel II as incomplete tripartisim).

30   Ayres & Braithwaite, "Responsive regulation," 82, note 18 above (references omitted).

31   Ibid.

32   Chapter 1 discussed administrative rulemaking efforts in the context of the Dodd-Frank Act. Of course, we also remain concerned, especially in the US after its Supreme Court's decision in *Citizens United* v. *Federal Election Commission*, 558 US 310, 130 S. Ct. 876, 175 L. Ed. 2d 753 (2010), about industry and corporate influence in politics as a whole.

33   Ayres & Braithwaite, "Responsive regulation," 83, note 18 above.

34   Paul Kelly, *The End of Certainty: The Story of the 1980s* (St. Leonards: Allen & Unwin, 1992).

35   Eric W. Orts, "Reflexive environmental law" (1994) 89 *Nw U L Rev* 1227–1340.

36   See especially Gunther Teubner, "Substantive and reflexive elements in modern law" (1983) 17 *Law & Soc'y Rev* 239–285.

37   For more on this, see Bradley C. Karkkainen, "'New governance' in legal thought and in the world: some splitting as antidote to overzealous lumping" (2004) 89 *Minn L Rev* 471–497, at 481–484 (distinguishing between the more pragmatic American stream of New Governance and the more theoretical European versions, including especially Teubnerian reflexive law). Teubner's version of reflexive law does draw directly on work by two other American scholars, Philippe Nonet and Philip Selznick.

38   Teubner uses the term "social subsystems." For clarity I will refer as appropriate to institutions, organizations, or systems.

39   Teubner, "Substantive and reflexive elements," 280, note 36 above (references omitted).

40   Orts, note 35, above at 1312 ("the EMAS forthrightly attempts to use markets as well as morals to encourage environmentally responsible management. But

though the EMAS relies in part on markets for its success, the primary operative mechanism in the EMAS is not market based. Instead, the crux of the EMAS is a legal strategy of disclosure. The EMAS employs disclosure to make transparent to the public that participating businesses have in fact adopted effective environmental attitudes and to reward the companies that do so").

41 Ibid., at 1232.

42 Julia Black, *Rules and Regulators* (Oxford: Clarendon Press, 1997); Julia Black, "Regulatory conversations" (2002) 29 *JL & Soc'y* 163–196.

43 Neil Gunningham & Peter M. Grabosky, *Smart Regulation: Designing Environmental Policy* (New York: Oxford University Press, 1998).

44 Bronwen Morgan & Karen Yeung, *An Introduction to Law and Regulation: Text and Materials* (Cambridge University Press, 2007), p. 124.

45 See also, prominently, Breyer, "Regulation and its reform," note 16 above; Richard A. Posner, "Theories of economic regulation" (1974) 5 *Bell J of Econ & Mgmt Sci* 335–358.

46 See also Louis Kaplow, "Rules versus standards: an economic analysis" (1992) 42 *Duke LJ* 557–629.

47 Ultimately, they conclude that it is only safe to leave matters to self-regulation in situations where there exists a sense of a "community of shared fate" within which industry norms will make self-policing meaningful. See also Joseph V. Rees, *Hostages of Each Other: The Transformation of Nuclear Safety since Three Mile Island* (Chicago: University of Chicago Press, 1996).

48 Tom R. Tyler, *Why People Obey the Law* (New Haven: Yale University Press, 1990); John Braithwaite, *To Punish or Persuade: Enforcement of Coal Mine Safety* (Albany: State University of New York Press, 1985); Ayres & Braithwaite, "Responsive regulation," note 18 above.

49 Neil Gunningham & Darren Sinclair, *Leaders and Laggards: Next-Generation Environmental Regulation* (Sheffield: Greenleaf, 2002).

50 Neil Gunningham, Robert Kagan & Dorothy Thornton, *Shades of Green: Business, Regulation, and Environment* (Stanford: Stanford University Press, 2003).

51 The idea of networks of regulatory actors has been especially productive in the transnational context. See, e.g., Kenneth W. Abbott & Duncan Snidal, "Strengthening international regulation through transnational new governance: overcoming the orchestration deficit" (2009) 42 *Vanderbilt J Transnatl L* 501–578 (among their other works); and, Terence C. Halliday & Gregory Shaffer (eds), *Transnational Legal Orders* (New York: Cambridge University Press, 2015).

52 Several compendia, special journal volumes, and books investigate the features and boundaries of "new governance" as a general approach. See, e.g., Gráinne de Búrca & Joanne Scott, "Narrowing the gap? law and new approaches to governance in the European Union: introduction" (2007) 13 *Colum J Eur L* 513–764; Joanne Scott & David M. Trubek, "Mind the gap: law and new approaches to governance in the European Union" (2002) 8 *Eur L J* 1–18; Gráinne de Búrca, "New governance and experimentalism: an introduction" (2010) 2010 *Wis L Rev* 227–238; Gráinne de Búrca & Joanne Scott (eds), *Law and New Governance in the EU and the US* (Portland: Hart Publishing, 2006).

53 Orly Lobel, "The renew deal: the fall of regulation and the rise of governance in contemporary legal thought" (2004) 89 *Minn L Rev* 342–470 at 343. Along with "new paradigm," another metaphor that is evocative of the sea change that scholars perceived is that of generational change. See, e.g., Sturm, Susan, "Second generation employment discrimination: a structural approach" (2001) 101 *Colum L Rev* 458–568 at 460–461, 553–566; Dennis D. Hirsch, "Symposium introduction: second generation policy and the new economy" (2001–2002) 29 *Cap U L Rev* 1–20 at 5–15; Richard B. Stewart, "A new generation of environmental regulation" (2001–2002) 29 *Cap U L Rev* 21–182.

54 But see Bradley C. Karkkainen, "New governance," note 37, above at 481–489 (arguing that American new governance is not "soft law"); also Cristie L. Ford, "Principles-based securities regulation in the wake of the global financial crisis" (2010) 45 *McGill L Rev* 257–307 at 285–286.

55 Lobel, "The renew deal," 344–345, note 53 above.

56 Cary Coglianese & David Lazer, "Management-based regulation: prescribing private management to achieve public goals" (2003) 37 *Law & Soc'y Rev* 691–730.

57 In their level of detail, they are almost comparable to Malcolm Sparrow's description of what it takes to "pick important problems and fix them" within an enforcement agency: Malcolm K. Sparrow, *The Regulatory Craft: Controlling Risks, Solving Problems, and Managing Compliance* (Washington, DC: Brookings Institution Press, 2000), pp. 132–134. Another similar approach is called safety case regulation. A thoughtful treatment is Neil Gunningham, *Mine Safety: Law Regulation Policy* (Marrickville: Southwest Press, 2007), pp. 67–82.

58 Christine Parker, *The Open Corporation: Effective Self-Regulation and Democracy* (New York: Cambridge University Press, 2002). Bronwen Morgan has developed a somewhat different concept of "meta-regulation:" Bronwen Morgan, "The economization of politics: meta-regulation as a form of nonjudicial legality" (2003) 12 *Soc'y & Legal Stud* 489–523 at 490 (defining meta-regulation focusing on "the specific political conflict between 'social' and 'economic' goals in regulatory policy," and highlighting processes that are embedded in a systematic way in everyday policymaking to create a "general mechanism of governance").

59 Julia Black, Martyn Hopper & Christa Band, "Making a success of principles-based regulation" (2007) 1 *L & Fin Markets Rev* 191–206; Julia Black, "The rise, fall and fate of principles based regulation" (2010) LSE Law, Society and Economy Working Papers 17; Ford, "Principles-based securities regulation," note 54 above; Cristie L. Ford, "New governance, compliance, and principles-based securities regulation" (2008) 45 *Am Bus LJ* 1–60.

60 Neil Gunningham, "Environment law, regulation and governance: shifting architectures" (2009) 21 *J Envtl L* 179–212 at 190–191 (partially citing Parker, "Open corporation," note 58 above).

61 Parker, "Open corporation," 15, note 58 above.

62 Gráinne de Búrca, Robert O. Keohane & Charles Sabel, "New modes of pluralist global governance" (2013) 45 *NYU J Int'L L & Pol* 723–787 at 739.

63 Ibid., at 738.

64 Edward Rubin, "The myth of accountability and the anti-administrative impulse" (2005) 103 *Mich L Rev* 2073–2136, 2131–2134 (citing organizational theorists); see also Cary Coglianese & Evan Mendelson, "Meta-regulation and self-regulation,"

in Robert Baldwin et al. (eds), *The Oxford Handbook of Regulation* (New York: Oxford University Press, 2010), pp. 17, 30–32; Cary Coglianese, "The limits of performance-based regulation" (2017) 50 *U Mich JL* Reform (in press).

65 Explicitly acknowledging Roberto Unger's work but also the ways in which exper- imentalism aims to be more context-specific and concrete, the concept of "desta- bilization" is central to one of the most influential experimentalist law review articles: Charles F. Sabel & William H. Simon, "Destabilization rights: how pub- lic law litigation succeeds" (2004) 117 *Harv L Rev* 1015–1101.

66 See, e.g., Sabel & Simon, "Destabilization rights," note 65 above; Joanne Scott & Susan Sturm, "Courts as catalysts: re-thinking the judicial role in new gov- ernance" (2007) 13 *Colum J Eur L* 565–594; Kathleen G. Noonan, Charles F. Sabel & William H. Simon, "Legal accountability in the service-based Welfare State: lessons from child welfare reform" (2009) 34 *Law & Soc Inquiry* 523–568 at 536–537, 554–556.

67 de Búrca, Keohane & Sabel, "New modes," 781, note 62 above ("as a necessary condition for Experimentalist Governance that: *Governments are unable to formu- late a comprehensive set of rules and efficiently and effectively monitor compliance with them.* This condition will be met in uncertain and diverse environments, where it is difficult for central actors to foresee the local effects of rules, and where even effective rules are likely to be undermined by unpredictable changes" [emphasis in original]).

68 My own views on rules and principles can be found in part in Ford, "New gover- nance," note 59 above; and Ford, "Principles-based," 266–270, note 54 above.

69 A small selection of interesting work on this topic would include, e.g., Julia Black, "Regulatory conversations" (2002) 29 *JL & Soc'y* 163–196; Susan Silbey & Ruthanne Huising, "Governing the gap: forging safe science through relational regulation" (2011) 5 *Reg & Gov* 14–42; Frederick Schauer, "The convergence of rules and standards" (2003) 3 *NZ L Rev* 303–328; Robert Baldwin, "Why rules don't work" (1990) 53 *Mod L R* 321–337; Daniel A. Farber, "Taking slippage seri- ously: noncompliance and creative compliance in environmental law" (1999) 23 *Harv Envtl L Rev* 297–325.

4   FLEXIBLE REGULATION SCHOLARSHIP BLOSSOMS AND DIVERSIFIES: 1980–2012

1 David Levi-Faur, "'Big government' to 'big governance'?" in David Levi-Faur (ed.), *The Oxford Handbook of Governance* (New York: Oxford University Press, 2012), p. 3.

2 Experimentalism is one approach that is philosophically located within the prag- matic philosophical tradition, which for Dorf and Sabel assume [An] account of thought and action as problem solving in a world, familiar to our time, that is bereft of first principles and beset by unintended consequences, ambiguity, and difference. Thus, a central theme ... is the reciprocal determination of means and ends: ... the objectives presumed in the guiding understandings of theories, strategies, or ideals of justice are transformed in the light of the experience of their pursuit, and these transformations in turn redefine what counts as a means

to a guiding end. Pragmatism thus takes the pervasiveness of unintended consequences, understood most generally as the impossibility of defining first principles that survive the effort to realize them, as a constitutive feature of thought and action, and not as an unfortunate incident of modern political life. Michael C. Dorf & Charles F. Sabel, "A constitution of democratic experimentalism" (1998) 98 *Colum L Rev* 267–473.

3   See Appendix A, Methodology for more information. The qualitative coding questions are contained in Appendix B, and more information on the results is contained in Appendix C. This book chapter covers only a few of the findings that emerge from the qualitative study and the cluster analysis performed.

4   The breakdown is: administrative law (12 articles); governance, including local and transnational (8); legal and constitutional theory (7); general policy (5); government relations (4); government agencies (3); civil rights and antipoverty initiatives (2).

5   All three first articles were published in the Stanford Law Review. They were Howard Latin, "Ideal versus real regulatory efficiency: implementation of uniform standards and 'fine-tuning' regulatory reforms" (1985) 37 *Stan L Rev* 1267–1332; Bruce A. Ackerman and Richard B. Stewart, "Reforming environmental law" (1985) 37 *Stan L Rev* 1333–1365 (commenting on the Latin article); and Cass R. Sunstein, "Interest groups in American public law" (1985) 38 *Stan L Rev* 29–87.

6   The relatively small number of articles published after 2010 likely reflects the timing of data collection rather than a dearth of publications during that year. In calculating frequency of an article's citation, to even the playing field between older and newer articles, I counted only citations within five years of when an article was published. Since there is no way to know authoritatively which more recent articles will become the most heavily cited, however, there is a limit to the ability to compensate for the passage of time.

7   It also reflects the search terms used to create the database. Names of specific private sector innovations (e.g., financial innovations like CDOs, ABSs, etc.; or other specific innovations including new pollution mitigation technologies, new nanotechnologies, GMOs or genetic modification in health care regulation, and any number of other important innovations) were not used as search terms. Including the names of all potential innovations would have been practically unworkable, and would not have helped illuminate the relationship between flexible regulation and innovation that this book is concerned with. Note, however, that notwithstanding that no specific innovations were included in search terms, the financial innovation articles still discussed specific underlying private sector innovations in a way that other articles from environmental or health regulation, for example, did not. Notably, of the 9% of articles coded as "private sector innovations", not regulatory innovations, most still have a strong regulatory overlay. The difference is that they focus on private sector innovations first, with regulatory implications second, rather than focusing primarily on regulatory innovations as the other 91% of articles do, sometimes with private sector innovations of secondary interest. For example, the three most-cited of these 18 private innovation-focused articles, with fifteen or more cites each, are Wendy E. Wagner, "The triumph of technology based standards" (2000) *U Ill L Rev* 83–114; Jeffrey J.

Rachlinski, "Innovations in environmental policy: The psychology of global climate change" (2000) *U Ill L Rev* 299–319; and Susan Sturm, "Second generation employment discrimination: a structural approach" (2001) 101 *Colum L Rev* 458–568. Of the 18 articles, only two discuss private law (commercial or contract law) as functional alternatives to regulation; all the rest discuss private sector innovation as it relates to or interacts with formal regulatory regimes. Those two articles are omitted from Table 4.2 below, but the other 16 are included as relevant.

8 See, e.g., Susan Sturm, "The architecture of inclusion: advancing workplace equity in higher education" (2006) 29 *Harv JL & Gender* 247, at 249–334.

9 Another, more organic metaphor that evokes a somewhat different image – of neither private nor public forces setting the parameters for the other – is the "braiding" of public and private governance regimes. Ronald Gilson et al., "Contracting for innovation: vertical disintegration and interfirm collaboration" (2009) 109 *Colum L Rev* 431–502, at 489.

10 Note that the Glass-Steagall Act of 1933, along with separating commercial banking from securities, also prohibited banks from paying interest on demand deposits and imposed interest rate ceilings on other kinds of depository accounts. US federal law also prohibited federal banks from engaging in other lines of business including real estate ownership and insurance underwriting: R. Alton Gilbert, "Requiem for Regulation Q: What it did and why it passed away," Federal Reserve Bank of St. Louis, February 1986, available at research.stlouisfed.org/publications/review/86/02/Requiem_Feb1986.pdf; Saule T. Omarova, "The quiet metamorphosis: how derivatives changed the 'business of banking'" (2009) 63 *U Miami L Rev* 1041–1109, at 1049–1050.

11 The stages blur, overlap with and inform each other. As noted in this book's Introduction, regulation is often described as requiring three fundamental things: some capacity for standard-setting, some capacity for information-gathering, and some capacity for behavior modification. Literature identifying "stages of regulation" is relatively sparse but see Kenneth W. Abbott & Duncan Snidal, "The governance triangle: regulatory standards institutions and the shadow of the law," in Walter Mattli & Ngaire Woods (eds), *The Politics of Global Regulation* (Princeton: Princeton University Press, 2009), pp. 44, 46 (identifying five stages of regulatory activity: (1) agenda-setting, (2) negotiation of standards, (3) implementation, (4) monitoring, and (5) enforcement). In most flexible regulation scholarship, as in (non-captured) regulation generally, the initial agenda-setting stage remains with the state.

12 Andrew Flynn & Robert Baylis, "Pollution regulation and ecological modernization: the formulation and implementation of best available techniques not entailing excessive costs" (1996) 1 *Int Plan Stud* 311–329 (describing the origins of the term).

13 Ian Ayres & John Braithwaite, *Responsive Regulation: Transcending the Deregulatory Debate* (New York: Oxford University Press, 1992). Flexible regulation does not reject the use of regulatory floors and ceilings. In fact, it may incorporate regulatory ceilings or, more often, floors into its regulatory structure. See, e.g., William W. Buzbee, "Asymmetrical regulation: risk, preemption, and the floor/ceiling distinction" (2007) 82 *NYU L Rev* 1547–1619; Benjamin K. Sovacool, "The best of both worlds: environmental federalism and the need for

federal action on renewable energy and climate change" (2008) 27 *Stan Envl LJ* 397–476.

14 What we see in the literature is that flexibility is more likely to be recommended around areas where regulators must be nimble, or where private actors have access to information that regulators do not, or where involving private actors in the regulatory process is seen to produce important ancillary benefits such as fostering an endogenous "culture of compliance." Flexibility makes less sense where certainty and consistency is more important than perfect congruence, see Colin S. Diver, "Optimal precision of administrative rules" (1983) 93 *Yale LJ* 65–109; Cristie L. Ford, "Principles-based securities regulation in the wake of the global financial crisis" (2010) 45 *McGill L Rev* 257–307.

15 Lessig describes this leveraging power as a unique feature of law: "The new Chicago school" (1998) 27 *J Legal Stud* 661–691, at 666.

16 Adrienne Héritier & Dirk Lemkuhl, "The shadow of hierarchy and new modes of governance" (2008) 28 *J Pub Pol'y* 1–17; also Michael P. Vandenbergh, "The private life of public law" (2005) 105 *Colum L Rev* 2029–2096, at 2030.

17 Neil Gunningham, "Environment law, regulation and governance: shifting architectures" (2009) 21 *J Envtl L* 179–212 at 180–184. Other terms are "indirect regulation" or "regulation by proxy" – see Harold Seidman & Robert S. Gilmour, *Politics, Position, and Power: From the Positive to the Regulatory State* (New York: Oxford University Press, 1986) – or "third party government" – see Lester M. Salamon, *The Tools of Government: A Guide to New Governance* (New York: Oxford University Press, 2002).

18 The market-based articles with more than fifteen cites within the database are Troy A. Paredes, "On the decision to regulate hedge funds: the SEC's regulatory philosophy, style, and mission" (2006) *U Ill L Rev* 975–1036; Roberta Romano, "Empowering investors: a market approach to securities regulation" (1998) 107 *Yale LJ* 2359–2430; and James Salzman & J.B. Ruhl, "Currencies and the commodification of environmental law" (2000) 53 *Stan L Rev* 607–694 (this last identifying the limits of environmental trading markets to "value" non-fungible environmental assets).

19 Three-quarters of the articles in the "other" category describe regulatory innovations that transcend regulatory scales or jurisdiction, or reallocate responsibilities between either levels or branches of government. These articles generally have more to do with federalism or allocation of authority between existing regulators than they do with regulatory innovations, so they are excluded from Figure 5.2 below. E.g., the articles with more than fifteen cites in this category are Benedict Kingsbury, Nico Krisch & Richard B. Stewart, "The emergence of global administrative law" (2005) 68 *Law & Contemp Probs* 15–61 Nicholas Bagley & Richard L. Revesz, "Centralized oversight of the regulatory state" (2006) 106 *Colum L Rev* 1260–1329; David E. Adelman & Kirsten H. Engel, "Reorienting state climate change policies to induce technological change" (2008) 50 *Ariz L Rev* 835–878. One other article in the "other" category has more than fifteen cites but is an outlier in terms of topic: it is Cass R. Sunstein, "Cognition and cost-benefit analysis" (2000) 29 *J Leg Stud* 1059–1103.

20 See, e.g., Bradley Karkkainen, "Information as environmental regulation: TRI and performance benchmarking, precursor to a new paradigm?" (2001) 89 *Geo LJ*

257–370; or Daniel C. Esty, "Environmental protection in the information age" (2004) 79 *NYU L Rev* 115–211.

21 The proportions are as follows: "spanning public/private divide in new way, incorporating private standards or capacity, collaborating," n=66, or 37%; "other" as discussed above, and "new mandatory standards or top-down strategy – e.g., ex ante licensing, bright-line rules or certification requirements," each n=28, or 16%; "incentive-based regulatory design to align private actors' interests with public interests," n=21, 12%; "new information-forcing requirements," n=20, or 11%; "market forces," n=11 or 6%; and both "bringing in third parties as quasi-official regulatory surrogates e.g., monitors, auditors, certifiers" and "bringing in civil society or community e.g., name-and-shame or awards for industry leaders" at n=3 each, or 2% each.

22 I hesitate to make any quantitative claims about this scholarship given the difficulties in extricating private sector from public sector innovations in the literature. However, it is noteworthy that several articles in the database were: (a) written before the financial crisis, i.e., published in or before 2008, in which (b) privately-sector innovations, (c) in the financial sector were (d) thought to create winners and losers and (e) in which the "winners" were the financial innovators themselves, sometimes at considerable cost to others, (f) thereby raising concerns about the consequences for regulation or the adequacy of the existing regulatory regime. We do not see a similarly skepticism about innovation in the other subject areas, environmental and administrative law (which tend to be cited more within the database). The articles meeting the above criteria are Willa Gibson, "Are swap agreements securities or futures?: The inadequacies of applying the traditional regulatory approach to OTC derivatives transactions" (1999) 24 *J Corp L* 379–416 and Frank Partnoy, "The Siskel and Ebert of financial markets?: Two thumbs down for the credit rating agencies" (1999) 77 *Wash U L Q* 619–714 (with 9 cites each in the database); and with seven cites each: Henry T.C. Hu, "Swaps, the modern process of financial innovation and the vulnerability of a regulatory paradigm" (1989) 138 *U Pa L Rev* 333–435; Kimberly D. Krawiec, "Accounting for greed: unraveling the rogue trader mystery" (2000) 79 *Oregon L Rev* 301–338; Kathleen C. Engel & Patricia A. McCoy, "A tale of three markets: the law and economics of predatory lending" (2002) 80 *Texas L Rev* 1255–1381; and Arthur E Wilmarth Jr, "The transformation of the U.S. financial services industry, 1975–2000: competition, consolidation, and increased risks" (2002) *U Ill L Rev* 215–476. With six cites: Jerry W. Markham, "'Confederate bonds,' 'General Custer,' and the regulation of derivative financial instruments" (1994) 25 *Seton Hall L Rev* 1–73. The article in the dataset that was perhaps the most skeptical of innovation and the most emphatic about the need for continued forceful, fairly traditional regulation was also on the topic of financial regulation: it was Robert A. Prentice, "The inevitability of a strong SEC" (2006) 91 *Cornell L Rev* 775–839 (12 cites).

In addition, three pre-crisis articles focused on the need for regulatory reforms in response to the concerns arising from private sector financial innovation, without focusing to the same degree on the private innovation itself. They are William W. Bratton, "Does corporate law protect the interests of shareholders and other stakeholders? Enron and the dark side of shareholder value" (2002) 76 *Tulane L Rev* 1275–1361 (24 cites); Thomas Lee Hazen, "Disparate regulatory schemes for parallel activities: securities regulation, derivatives regulation, gambling, and insurance" (2005) 24 *Ann Rev Banking & Fin L* 375–441 (9 cites); and Kenneth A. Bamberger, "Regulation as delegation: private firms, decisionmaking, and accountability in the administrative state" (2006) 56 *Duke L J* 377–468 (9 cites). On the other hand, one early article recommended a regulatory change, integrating the SEC and the CFTC, but for the purpose of further spurring financial innovation: Thomas A. Russo & Marlisa Vinciguerra, "Financial innovation and uncertain regulation: selected issues regarding new product development" (1991) 69 *Texas L Rev* 1431–1538 (10 cites).

At the same time, it is also noteworthy that many of the financial articles in the database discussed the importance of increasing regulatory coordination across borders, including several articles that emphasized the value of competition between regulators. This latter emphasis was a noticeable contrast relative to some other fields (e.g., environmental regulation), where risks associated with regulatory arbitrage seem to have been more front-of-mind. Discussing cross-border regulation are: Ethiopis Tafara & Robert J. Peterson, "A blueprint for cross-border access to U.S. investors: a new international framework" (2007) 48 *Harv Intl L J* 31–68 (23 cites); Edward F. Greene, "Beyond borders: time to tear down the barriers to global investing" (2007) 48 *Harv Intl L J* 85–97 (response to article by Ethiopis Tafara and Robert J. Peterson above) (10 cites); and Eric J. Pan, "A European solution to the regulation of cross-border markets" (2007) 2 *Brooklyn J Corp, Fin & Comm L* 133–166 (7 cites). On the value of regulatory competition, including transnationally, are: Marcel Kahan & Ehud Kamar, "The myth of state competition in corporate law" (2002) 55 *Stan L Rev* 679–749 (13 cites); Christopher Brummer, "Stock exchanges and the new markets for securities laws" (2008) 75 *Chicago L Rev* 1435–1491 (11 cites); and Roberta Romano, "The need for competition in international securities regulation" (2001) 2 *Theor Inq L* 387–562 (7 cites).

23 These articles are more heavily cited within the database than the financial regulation articles discussed immediately above. Of the articles in the administrative law category which argue that on balance the innovation in question (always a regulatory innovation in these articles) has the potential to lift all boats, those with more than fifteen cites within the database are Jody Freeman, "Collaborative governance in the administrative state" (1997) 45 *UCLA L Rev* 1–98; Jody Freeman, "The Private Role in Public Governance" (2000) 75 *NYU L Rev* 543–675; Sunstein, "Cognition and cost-benefit analysis," note 19 above; Richard B. Stewart, "Administrative law in the twenty-first century" (2003) 78 *NYU L Rev* 437–460; Daniel C. Esty, "Good governance at the supranational scale globalizing administrative law" (2006) 115 *Yale LJ* 1490–1562; and Bagley & Revesz, "Centralized oversight," note 19 above. Other administrative law scholars expressed more concern about making flexible regulation work for all stakeholders – see, e.g., Mark Seidenfeld, "Empowering stakeholders limits on collaboration as the basis for flexible regulation" (2000) 41 *Wm & Mary L Rev* 411–501.

24 To be clear, the article of mine in the dataset, on financial regulation and published in 2008, falls in this category: Cristie L. Ford, "New governance, compliance, and principles-based securities regulation" (2008) 45 *Am Bus LJ* 1–60 (29 cites).

25 The articles are too many to list here, but articles coded as responding to new manufactured/human-created risk, which have more than fifteen cites within the database, are: Cass R. Sunstein, "Administrative substance" (1991) *Duke LJ* 607–646; Daniel C. Esty, "Revitalizing environmental federalism" (1996) 95 *Mich L Rev* 570–653; David Driesen, "Is emissions trading an economic incentive program?: replacing the command and control/economic incentive dichotomy" (1998) 55 *Wash & Lee L Rev* 289–350; Paul L. Joskow & Richard Schmalensee, "The political economy of market based environmental policy: the US acid rain program" (1998) 41 *J Law Econ* 37–84; Rena I. Steinzor, "Reinventing environmental regulation: the dangerous journey from command to self control" (1998) 22 *Harv Envtl L Rev* 103–202; Daniel Farber, "Taking slippage seriously: noncompliance and creative compliance in environmental law" (1999) 23 *Harv Envtl L Rev* 297–326; Daniel Farber, "Triangulating the future of reinvention: three emerging models of environmental protection" (2000) 2000 *U Ill L Rev* 61–82; Seidenfeld, "Empowering stakeholders," note 24 above; Wagner, "Technology based standards," note 7 above; Richard B. Stewart, "A new generation of environmental regulation" (2001–2002) 29 *Cap U L Rev* 21–182; William W. Buzbee, "Recognizing the regulatory commons: a theory of regulatory gaps" (2003) 89 *Iowa L Rev* 1–64; Bradley C. Karkkainen, "Adaptive ecosystem management and regulatory penalty defaults" (2003) 87 *Minn L Rev* 943–998; and Daniel C. Esty, "Good governance at the supranational scale globalizing administrative law" (2006) 115 *Yale LJ* 1490–562. Two additional articles in this category, which go to responding to human-created risk but in quite a different way, are Elena Kagan, "Presidential administration" (2001) 114 *Harv L Rev* 2245–2385; and Oren Bar-Gill & Elizabeth Warren, "Making credit safer" (2008) 157 *U Pa L Rev* 1–101.

26 Of the 21 articles in this category, four are specifically concerned with Project XL. They are Dennis D. Hirsch, "Bill and Al's XL-ent adventure: an analysis of the EPA's legal authority to implement the Clinton Administration's Project XL" (1998) 129 *U Ill L Rev* 129–172; Bradford C. Mank, "The Environmental Protection Agency's 's Project XL and other regulatory reform initiatives: the need for legislative authorization" (1998) 25 *Ecology LQ* 1–88; Dennis D. Hirsch, "Project XL and the special case: the EPA's untold success story" (2001) 26 *Colum J Envtl L* 219–258; Shi-Ling Hsu, "A game-theoretic approach to regulatory negotiation and a framework for empirical analysis" (2002) 26 *Harv Envtl L Rev* 33–108. Six other articles, all but one of which were published between 1999 and 2002, deal with other aspects of EPA regulation including toxic risk, the Clean Air Act and cap and trade initiatives (all focused on the policy initiative itself, rather than the underlying technology of creating tradable emissions permits). They are Howard Latin, "Good science, bad regulation, and toxic risk assessment" (1988) 5 *Yale J Reg* 89–148; Cass R. Sunstein, "Is the Clean Air Act unconstitutional?" (1999) 98 *Mich L Rev* 303–394; Rena I. Steinzor, "Devolution and the Public Health" (2000) 24 *Harv Envtl L Rev* 351–465; Bradley Karkkainen, "Information as environmental regulation: TRI and performance benchmarking, precursor to a new paradigm?" (2001) 89 *Geo LJ* 257–370; Byron Swift, "How environmental laws work: an analysis of the utility sector's response to regulation of nitrogen oxides and sulfur dioxide under the Clean Air Act" (2001) 14 *Tul Envtl LJ* 309–426; and Cass R. Sunstein, "The arithmetic of arsenic" (2002) 90 *Geo LJ* 2255–2310.

Two other articles are focused on regulatory regimes associated with climate change: they are David M. Driesen, "Free lunch or cheap fix?: The emissions trading idea and the climate change convention" (1998) 26 *BC Envtl Aff L Rev* 1–88; and David E. Adelman & Kirsten H. Engel, "Reorienting state climate change policies to induce technological change" (2008) 50 *Ariz L Rev* 835–878. Of the remaining articles, one is about public housing (Lisa T. Alexander, "Stakeholder participation in new governance: lessons from Chicago's public housing reform experiment" (2009) 16 *Geo J on Poverty L & Pol'y* 117–186); one is about financial regulation (Paredes, "Decision to regulate," note 18 above); and seven are primarily focused on administrative law or legal theory. They are: Thomas O. McGarity, "Some thoughts on 'deossifying' the rulemaking process" (1992) 41 *Duke LJ* 1385–1462; Robert L. Glicksman & Stephen B. Chapman, "Regulatory reform and (breach of) the contract with America: improving environmental policy or destroying environmental protection?" (1996) 5 *Kan JL & Pub Pol'y* 9–46; David L. Markell, "The role of deterrence-based enforcement in a 'reinvented' state/federal relationship: the divide between theory and reality" (2000) 24 *Harv Envtl L Rev* 1–114; Jody Freeman, "The contracting state" (2000) 28 *Fla St UL Rev* 155–214; J.B. Ruhl, "Regulation by adaptive management – is it possible?" (2005) 7 *Minnesota J L, Sci & Tech* 21–58; Buzbee, "Asymmetrical regulation," note 13 above; and David M. Trubek & Louise G. Trubek, "New governance & legal regulation: complementarity, rivalry, and transformation (Narrowing the gap? law and new approaches to governance in the European Union)" (2007) 13 *Colum J Euro L* 539–564.

27 The six articles in this category published between 2003 and 2005 are: Rob Frieden, "Adjusting the horizontal and vertical in telecommunications regulation: a comparison of the traditional and a new layered approach" (2003) 55 *Fed Comm LJ* 207–250; Daniel C. Esty, "Environmental protection in the information age" (2004) 79 *NYU L Rev* 115–211; E. Goodman, "Spectrum rights in the telecoms to come" (2004) 41 *San Diego L Rev* 269–404; Beth Simone Noveck, "The electronic revolution in rulemaking" (2004) 53 *Emory LJ* 433–518; R. Alex DuFour, "Voice over Internet protocol: ending uncertainty and promoting innovation through a regulatory framework" (2005) 13 *Comm Law Conspectus* 471–508; and Philip J. Weiser & Dale N. Hatfield, "Policing the spectrum commons" (2005) 74 *Fordham L Rev* 663–694. Of the four other articles in the category, three concern new financial products or technology and date from well before or well after this period. They are: Hu, "Swaps," note 22 above; Gibson, "Securities or futures," note 22 above; and Erik F. Gerding, "Code, crash, and open source: the outsourcing of financial regulation to risk models and the global financial crisis" (2009) 84 *Wash L Rev* 127–291. The final article is about nanotechnology: Jordan Paradise et al., "Evaluating oversight of human drugs and medical devices: a case study of the FDA and Implications for Nanobiotechnology" (2009) 37 *J L Med & Ethics* 598–624.

28 The six articles in this category published in 2007 or later Pan, "A European solution," note 22 above; Steven Schwarcz, "Systemic risk" (2008) 97 *Geo LJ* 197–250; Jill E. Fisch, "Top cop or regulatory flop? The SEC at 75" (2009) 95 *Va L Rev* 785–823; William K. Sjostrom Jr, "The AIG bailout" (2009) 66 *Wash & Lee L Rev* 943–991; Lucian A. Bebchuk & Holger Spamann, "Regulating bankers' pay"

(2010) 98 *Geo LJ* 247–288; and Charles Whitehead, "Reframing financial regulation" (2010) 90 *BU L Rev* 1–50. Of the others, four deal with the creation and operation of emissions trading permits. They are Robert W. Hahn & Gordon L. Hester, "Where did all the markets go? An analysis of EPA's emissions trading program" (1989) 6 *Yale J on Reg* 109–153; Richard Toshiyuki Drury et al., "Pollution trading and environmental injustice: Los Angeles' failed experiment in air quality policy" (1999) 9 *Duke Envtl L & Pol'y F* 231–290; James Salzman & J.B. Ruhl, "Currencies and the commodification of environmental law" (2000) 53 *Stan L Rev* 607–694; and Jonathan Remy Nash & Richard L. Revesz, "Markets and geography: designing marketable permit schemes to control local and regional pollutants" (2001) 28 *Ecology LQ* 569–663. The other three are earlier articles dealing with other financial innovations including Enron and Sarbanes-Oxley: they are Jerry W. Markham, "Confederate bonds," note 22 above; Jeffrey N. Gordon, "What Enron means for the Management and control of the modern business corporation: some initial reflections" (2002) 69 *U Chicago L Rev* 1233–1250; and Lawrence A. Cunningham, "The Sarbanes-Oxley yawn: heavy rhetoric, light reform (and it just might work)" (2003) 35 *Conn L Rev* 915–988.

29   The most-cited articles are set out in Appendix A. These five are Steinzor, "Reinventing environmental regulation," note 25 above; Karkkainen, "Information as environmental regulation," note 20 above; Stewart, "New generation of environmental regulation," note 25 above; Buzbee, "Asymmetrical regulation," note 13 above; and Schwarcz, "Systemic Risk," note 28 above.

30   Cary Coglianese, "Assessing consensus: the promise and performance of negotiated rulemaking" (1997) 46 *Duke LJ* 1255–1349; Freeman, "Collaborative governance," note 23 above; Michael C. Dorf & Charles F. Sabel, "A constitution of democratic experimentalism" (1998) 98 *Colum L Rev* 298–473; Sturm, "Second generation employment discrimination," note 7 above; and Kristen Engel, "Harnessing the benefits of dynamic federalism in environmental law" (2006) 56 *Emory LJ* 159–190.

31   Freeman, "Private role of public governance," note 23 above; and Cary Coglianese & David Lazer, "Management-based regulation: prescribing private management to achieve public goals" (2003) 37 *Law & Soc'y Rev* 691–730. Each of these articles also claims public benefit in its prescriptions; this records their primary emphasis only.

32   Orly Lobel, "The renew deal: the fall of regulation and the rise of governance in contemporary legal thought" (2004) 89 *Minn L Rev* 342–470; and Charles F. Sabel & William H. Simon, "Destabilization rights: how public law litigation succeeds" (2004) 117 *Harv L Rev* 1015–1101.

5   WHY FLEXIBLE REGULATION WAS NOT SIMPLY A MISGUIDED, NEOLIBERAL PROJECT

1   David Levi-Faur, "The global diffusion of regulatory capitalism" (2005) 598 *Annals Am Acad Pol & Soc Sci* 12–32, at 14.

2   On the relationship between regulation and the market see, e.g., ibid. (noting that "efficient markets do not exist outside the state"); see also generally Clifford D.

Shearing, "A constitutive conception of regulation," in John Braithwaite & Peter Grabosky (eds), *Business Regulation and Australia's Future* (Canberra: Australian Institute of Criminology, 1993), pp. 67–79 (challenging the myth of deregulation, Shearing proposes a "constitutive" conception of regulation and of markets. He notes that markets are not self-ordering, but are always and necessarily regulated through careful constitutive, and inevitably political, work – that is, through regulation).

3   Scott H. Jacobs, "The golden age of regulation" (2000) 7 *CEPMLP Internet Journal*, available at regulatoryreform.com/wp-content/uploads/2014/11/the_golden_age_of_regulation_scott_jacobs.pdf.

4   David Levi-Faur & Jacint Jordana, "The making of a new regulatory order" (2005) 598 *Annals Am Acad Pol & Soc Sci* 6–9, at 8.

5   Colin Diver, "The optimal precision of administrative rules" (1983) 93 *Yale L J* 65–109.

6   See, e.g., Niamh Moloney, "The legacy effects of the financial crisis on regulatory design in the EU," in Eilís Ferran et al. (eds), *The Regulatory Aftermath of the Global Financial Crisis* (Cambridge: Cambridge University Press, 2012), pp. 140–145.

7   Karl Polanyi, *The Great Transformation: the Political and Economic Origins of our Time* (Boston: Beacon Press, 1944).

8   Milton Friedman, *Capitalism and Freedom* (Chicago: University of Chicago Press, 1962).

9   Ronen Shamir, "Corporate social responsibility: towards a new market-embedded morality?" (2008) 9 *Theor Inq L* 371–394; similarly, see Mariana Pargendler, "The corporate governance obsession" (2015) Stanford Law and Economics Olin Working Paper No. 470; FGV Direito SP Research Paper Series n. 111, available at ssrn.com/abstract=2491088.

10 Ibid., at 378.

11 Ibid., at 373, 383. The state's expectation that corporations will act responsibly results in a similar commodification of socio-moral tasks, to the extent that there is a "business case" for corporate social responsibility. Ibid., at 391.

12 Ibid at 393–394.

13 Christine Parker, "The 'compliance' trap: the moral message in responsive regulatory enforcement" (2006) 40 *L & Soc'y Rev* 591–622, at 611–612.

14 See, e.g., Neil Gunningham, Robert A. Kagan & Dorothy Thornton, *Shades of Green: Business, Regulation, and Environment* (Stanford: Stanford University Press, 2003) (explaining the social license to operate); Christine Parker *The Open Corporation* (Cambridge: Cambridge University Press, 2002) (explaining "triple-loop learning"); Ian Ayres & John Braithwaite, *Responsive Regulation: Transcending the Deregulatory Debate* (New York: Oxford University Press, 1992) (explaining tripartism).

15 Jody Freeman, "The private role of public governance" (2000) 75 *NYU L Rev* 543–675, at 574.

16 See, e.g., Michael Moran, *The British Regulatory State: High Modernism and Hyper-Innovation* (New York: Oxford University Press, 2003).

17 See, e.g., Peter Aucoin, "Administrative reform in public management: paradigms, principles, paradoxes and pendulums" (1990) 3 *Governance* 115–137.

18 Kathleen G. Noonan, Charles F. Sabel & William H. Simon, "Legal account-ability in the service-based Welfare State: lessons from child welfare reform" (2009) 34 *Law & Soc Inquiry* 523–568.

19 Lisa T. Alexander, "Stakeholder participation in new governance: lessons from Chicago's public housing reform experiment" (2009) 16 *Geo J on Poverty L & Pol'y* 117–186 (sounding a skeptical note about new governance).

20 Michael C. Dorf & Charles F. Sabel, "Drug treatment courts and emergent experimentalist government" (2000) 53 *Vand L Rev* 831–884; Joanne Scott & Susan Sturm, "Courts as catalysts: re-thinking the judicial role in new governance" (2007) 13 *Colum J Eur L* 565–594.

21 See the historical discussion in Chapter 2.

22 See, e.g., James S. Liebman & Charles F. Sabel, "A public laboratory Dewey barely imagined: the emerging model of school governance and legal reform" (2003) 28 *NYU Rev L & Soc Change* 183–304, at 184; James S. Liebman & Charles F. Sabel, "The federal No Child Left Behind Act and the post-desegregation civil rights agenda" (2002) 81 *NC L Rev* 1703–1750, at 1713–1715.

23 Robert Vischer, "Subsidiarity as a principle of governance: beyond devolution" (2001) 35 *Ind L Rev* 103–142.

24 Judith Resnik, Joshua Civin & Joseph Frueh, "Ratifying Kyoto at the local level: sovereigntism, federalism, and Translocal Organizations of Government Actors (TOGAs)" (2008) 50 *Ariz L Rev* 709–786, at 768–769.

25 Amy J. Cohen, "Governance legalism: Hayek and Sabel on reasons and rules, organization and law" (2010) *Wis L Rev* 357–388, at 370–375. The discussion below is based on Cohen's article.

26 Friedrich von Hayek, *Road to Serfdom* (Chicago: University of Chicago Press, 1944).

27 Richard Epstein, *Simple Rules for a Complex World* (Cambridge: Harvard University Press, 1997).

28 See, e.g., Joshua Cohen & Charles Sabel, "Directly-deliberative polyarchy" (1997) 3 *Eur L J* 313–342.

29 See Peter Mascini, "Why was the enforcement pyramid so influential? and what price was paid?" (2013) 7 *Reg & Gov* 48–60; also John Braithwaite, "Relational republican regulation" (2013) 7 *Reg & Gov* 124–144 at 128.

30 Reportedly, this claim was made in jest at a festschrift in his honor in 2009. The joke did not make it into the publication that came out of the festschrift, however: Gralf-Peter Callies et al. (eds), *Soziologische Jurisprudenz: Festschrift Für Gunther Teubner Zum 65 Geuburtstag* (Boston: De Gruyter, 2009) pp. 465, 475–477.

31 On this point, I agree with Lawrence A. Cunningham, "A prescription to retire the rhetoric of principles-based systems in corporate law, securities regulation, and accounting" (2007) 60 *Vand L Rev* 1411–1493.

32 My own critiques of the ways in which financial regulatory practice fell badly short of flexible regulation theory can be found in Cristie L. Ford, "Principles-based securities regulation in the wake of the global financial crisis" (2010) 45 *McGill L Rev* 257–307; and in Cristie Ford, "New governance in the teeth of human frailty: lessons from financial regulation" (2010) *Wis L Rev* 441–489.

33 The similarity is superficial and inaccurate. See, e.g., Ford, "Principles-based securities regulation," 283–286, note 32 above.

34 See, e.g., Ayres & Braithwaite, "Responsive Regulation," note 14 above; Michael C. Dorf & Charles F. Sabel, "A constitution of democratic experimentalism" (1998) 98 *Colum L Rev* 267–473 at 281–289.

35 See also Cristie Ford, "Macro-and micro-level effects on responsive financial regulation" (2011) 44 *UBC L Rev* 589–626.

36 Mark Bevir & R.A.W. Rhodes, *Governance Stories* (New York: Routledge, 2006); see also Orly Lobel, "The renew deal: the fall of regulation and the rise of governance in contemporary legal thought" (2004) 89 *Minn L Rev* 342–470 (warning against the "illusion of information and transparency–that the information age, through its own mechanisms, can solve all problems"); Robert F. Weber, "New governance, financial regulation, and challenges to legitimacy: the example of the internal models approach to capital adequacy regulation" (2010) 62 *Admin L Rev* 783–869, at 851 (noting further that "the non-state actors with the best access to, and the greatest ability to process and present, information might be expected to exert disproportionate influence over the information-based policymaking process").

37 See generally Steve Tombs & David Whyte, "Transcending the deregulation debate? regulation, risk and the enforcement of health and law in the UK" (2013) 7 *Reg & Gov* 61–79, at 67 (discussing the Labour Government's approach to regulation in the United Kingdom in the late 1990s through the 2000s).

38 Julia Black, "Forms and paradoxes of principles-based regulation" (2008) 3 *Cap Mark L J* 425–457, at 430.

39 John Tiner, "Better regulation: objective or oxymoron," Remarks at the SII Annual Conference (May 9, 2006) available at www.fsa.gov.uk/pages/Library/Communication/Speeches/2006/0509_jt.shtml; see also Clive Briault, "Principles-based regulation – moving from theory to practice," Speech at the ABI 2007 Conference (May 10, 2007), available at www.fsa.gov.uk/pages/Library/Communication/Speeches/2007/0510_cb.shtml. The tone is reminiscent of the US Environmental Protection Agency's Project XL a decade earlier, which also built on (vaguely developed) flexible regulation ideas. Project XL (which stood for "eXcellence and Leadership") was billed as developing "cleaner, cheaper, and smarter" new solutions to environmental issues that also, somehow, ensured greater accountability to stakeholders. US Environmental Protection Agency, "Project XL" (October 2004), available at www.epa.gov/ProjectXL/intel/0998.htm.

40 Corporate entities' short-term horizons make the disconnect even starker: Lynne L. Dallas, "Short termism, the financial crisis, and corporate governance" (2012) 37 *J Corp L* 265–364.

41 To be clear, it is too convenient to simply blame implementation every time a theory goes awry. If a theory fails in practice, that failure is a lesson that may shine light on the theory itself. The financial crisis has certainly taught us a lot about ways in which flexible regulation can be "gamed:" I make that point in, e.g., Cristie Ford, "New governance," note 32 above. Given that I think that all regulatory structures are gameable and will be gamed, I do not think this is a fatal flaw. For this reason, while I agree with Tombs and Whyte when they argue that responsive regulatory practices have decreased enforcement and thereby weakened regulation, I would not go so far as to say, as they do, that responsive regulation "contains the seeds of its own perennial degradation." Tombs & Whyte, "Transcending," 62, note 37 above.

42   Among others see, e.g., Dan Awrey, "Regulating financial innovation: a more
      principles-based proposal?" (2011) 5 *Brook J Corp, Fin & Comm L* 273–315.

43   For example, key provisions of the Dodd-Frank Act, Pub. L. No. 111–203, 124 Stat.
      1376, codified at 12 USC § 5301 (2010) and associated rulemaking that would spe-
      cifically affect the scope of financial innovation include: (1) a proposed FDIC
      rule that would require financial institutions to retain more of the credit risk asso-
      ciated with securitization, and prohibit them from hedging or transferring that
      risk (s.15G of the Securities Exchange Act of 1934 Pub. L. 73–291, 48 Stat. 881,
      codified at 15 USC 78a (1934)); (2) the Volcker Rule, which would limit the extent
      to which firms engaged in banking activities could use depositors' funds to fund
      their own proprietary trading (s.619 of the Dodd-Frank Act, codified at 12 U.S.C.
      § 1851); (3) the Collins Amendments, which allow regulators to increase capital
      that firms must keep on hand for products and practices, including securitization
      and derivatives, that may be determined *in future* to be particularly risky (s.171 of
      the Dodd-Frank Act, codified at 12 USC 5371); (4) a requirement that credit rat-
      ing agencies disclose their ratings methodologies, including due diligence reports
      by third parties, to the SEC (s.932 of the Dodd-Frank Act); (5) SEC and CFTC
      rules that would require as a general rule that "swaps," which can be bought and
      sold as derivatives, must by cleared by a central clearinghouse and traded on an
      exchange (Title VII of Dodd-Frank, also known as the Wall Street Transparency
      and Accountability Act of 2010, Pub. L. 111–203, 124 Stat. 1641, codified at 15 USC
      8301). As they affect financial innovation, the first three rules above affect innova-
      tors' incentives: they try to ensure that innovators have more "skin in the game"
      when they innovate, and give regulators the ability to make future innovations
      costlier if they are riskier. The next two try to chip away at the opacity that charac-
      terizes these instruments, by requiring more disclosure and more standardization,
      so that each innovation can be compared more effectively and prices can be more
      discoverable. (That said, the rules still leave a lot of room for non-standardized
      derivatives to be traded in opaque markets.) The Dodd-Frank Act is, of course, a
      massive piece of statutory reform and several other provisions within it – notably
      its various conflict of interest provisions – are likely to affect the scope of possible
      financial innovation in more indirect ways. While they affect financial innovation
      less directly, efforts to designate financial institutions (or products, practices, or
      benchmarks in Canada) as systemically important and to subject them to higher
      regulatory standards are also crucial.

      The other major kind of legal reform in the years since the financial crisis is
      arguably more of the "have your cake and eat it too" variety, meaning efforts to
      maintain the benefits of unfettered private financial innovation while limiting a
      state's exposure to its downsides, as unilateral initiatives like "ring-fencing" try to
      do. The UK Financial Services (Banking Reform) Act 2013, the Financial Services
      and Markets Act 2000 (Ring-fenced Bodies and Core Activities) Order 2014, the
      Financial Services and Markets Act 2000 (Excluded Activities and Prohibitions)
      Order 2014, and the Financial Services and Markets Act 2000 (Banking Reform)
      (Pensions) Regulations 2015 (Requiring that by January 2019, banks with more
      than £ 25 billion insulate their retail banking operations from their wholesale,
      derivatives and speculative trading activities. This is a have-your-cake-and-eat-it-
      too initiative because it aims to keep investment banks and financial innovation

located in the City of London to the extent possible while ensuring that, in the event of default or crisis, the UK government can protect retail deposit holders without having to worry about the bank's other activities. Whether and how the 2016 Brexit vote will affect this timeline, or the approach generally, is unknown at the time of publication).

44 Thomas Eisenbach et al., "Supervising large, complex financial institutions: what do supervisors do?" (May 2015) *Federal Reserve Bank of New York Staff Reports* no. 729, at 12, 21–28, available at www.newyorkfed.org/research/staff_reports/sr729.pdf. Recently, the FRBNY has begun to move embedded on-site examiners back to central FRBNY offices. Ibid., at 18.

45 Julia Black, "Paradoxes & failures: 'new governance' techniques and the financial crisis" (2012) 75 *Mod L Rev* 1037–1063, at 1046, 1048, 1052.

46 Dan Awrey, "Complexity, innovation, and the regulation of modern financial markets" (2012) 2 *Harv Bus L Rev* 235–294.

47 Julia Black, "Paradoxes & failures," 1038, note 45 above. As noted previously, I prefer the term "bright-line" or "traditional" regulation to "command and control," because the latter had acquired such a pejorative valence by the 1990s, but the approach being discussed is the same.

6   REFOCUSING REGULATION AROUND THE CHALLENGE OF INNOVATION

1 Michael C. Dorf & Charles F. Sabel, "A constitution of democratic experimentalism" (1998) 98 *Colum L Rev* 267–473.

2 Christine Parker, *The Open Corporation: Effective Self-Regulation and Democracy* (New York: Cambridge University Press, 2002). The example of Basel II and its relationship to meta-regulation and some versions of principles-based regulation is discussed below.

3 Genealogically, through Charles Sabel in particular, we can trace a connection between innovation studies and regulatory studies. Sabel's 1980s-era work argued for "flexible specialization" in labor in late twentieth-century Western economies as a response to the Keynesian Welfare State's stalling. This work on the labor market drew on industrial sociology and political economy from the first Industrial Revolution, through what he described as "high technology cottage industry," in the process incorporating new thinking about how and why innovation develops. See Charles F. Sabel, *Work and Politics: the Division of Labor in Industry* (New York: Cambridge University Press, 1982); Michael J. Piore & Charles F. Sabel, *The Second Industrial Divide: Possibilities for Prosperity* (New York: Basic Books, 1984); also, in the first of what has turned out to be a long term scholarly collaboration, Charles F. Sabel & Jonathan Zeitlin " Historical alternatives to mass production: politics, markets and technology in nineteenth century industrialization" (1985) 108 *Past & Present* 133–176. Experimentalism's emphases on decentralized, pragmatic, on-the-ground learning and flexibility, forging links between private and public actors, and the possibility of transcending entrenched divides or loyalties are all already evident in this work. This is familiar ground for some innovation scholars too.

4   See, e.g., Maureen Farrell, "Bank execs shrug off Volcker Rule ... even Jamie Dimon," *Wall Street Journal*, January 16, 2014, available at blogs.wsj.com/moneybeat/2014/01/16/bank-execs-shrug-off-volcker-rule-even-jamie-dimon/.

5   See, e.g., Autorité des marchés financiers (AMF), "What are the priorities for financial markets?" (2011), at 2, 9 (suggesting that priorities concentrate on "socially beneficial" innovations); European Parliament, "Report on derivatives markets: future policy actions" (2010) A7-0187/2010, para. 9 (proposing to reduce the overall volume of derivatives trading); Lord Mandelson, "Address to the Labour Party Conference in Brighton UK," September 28, 2009 (arguing for "less financial engineering and a lot more real engineering").

6   Josh Lerner & Peter Tufano, "The consequences of financial innovation: a counterfactual research agenda," in Josh Lerner & Scott Stern (eds), *The Rate and Direction of Inventive Activity Revisited* (Chicago: University of Chicago Press, 2012), pp. 523–578.

7   See, e.g., "On the move," *The Economist*, April 16, 2016, available at www.economist.com/news/special-report/21696790-much-hangs-mobile-money-move.

8   A powerful critique of the existing banking options available to the poor in the United States is Mehrsa Baradaran, *How the Other Half Banks* (Cambridge: Harvard University Press, 2015); on student loans in the United States, see Joseph E. Stiglitz, "Student debt and the crushing of the American dream," *New York Times*, May 21, 2013, available at opinionator.blogs.nytimes.com/2013/05/12/student-debt-and-the-crushing-of-the-american-dream/?_r=0, subsequently reprinted in *The Great Divide: Unequal Societies and What We Can Do About Them* (New York: Norton and Company, 2015). Fintech startups that address these particular issues include, respectively, Bread and CommonBond. Other fintech companies aim to make financial planning and investment more affordable (e.g., Betterment, LearnVest, Personal Capital, Wealthfront) or to help consumers manage spending and control debt levels (e.g., Debitize, Moven).

9   E.g., Axial, Bond Street, Fundera, Lending Club (which provides peer-to-peer loans for individuals as well as businesses), OnDeck, Onevest.

10 E.g., Robinhood, Motif.

11 E.g., TransferWise, World First, WorldRemit.

12 E.g., Spare, Mission Markets.

13 Consider EquityZen, which allows private company shareholders to sell shares that would otherwise be illiquid. This has implications for corporate governance and corporate finance, as well as potentially for regulatory assumptions about how the exempt market operates.

14 See, e.g., Henry T.C. Hu & Bernard Black, "The new vote buying: empty voting and hidden (morphable) ownership" (2006) 61 *S Cal L Rev* 811–908; Ronald J. Gilson & Charles K. Whitehead, "Deconstructing equity: public ownership, agency costs, and complete financial market" (2008) 108 *Colum L Rev* 231–264; Tamar Frankel, "The new financial assets: separating ownership from control" (2010) 33 *Sea U L Rev* 931–964; Kathryn Judge, "Fragmentation nodes: a study in financial innovation, complexity, and systemic risk" (2012) 64 *Stan L Rev* 657–725, at 659, 676.

15 William W. Bratton & Adam J. Levitin, "Transactional genealogy of scandal: from Michael Milken to Enron to Goldman Sachs" (2013) 86 *S Cal L Rev* 783–868; *see*

also Zachary J. Gubler, "The financial innovation process: theory and application" (2011) 36 *Del J Corp L* 55–119 (describing financial innovation as a process of change that can make banks and markets substitutes and complements to each other).

16 See Financial Stability Board, *Global Shadow Banking Monitoring Report* (2014), available at www.financialstabilityboard.org/wp-content/uploads/r_141030.pdf (suggesting that the scale of growth in shadow banking has become a source of "systemic risk"; Arthur E. Wilmarth Jr, "The transformation of the U.S. financial services industry, 1975–2000: competition, consolidation, and increased risks" (2002) *U Ill L Rev* 215–476; Chris Brummer, "Disruptive technology and securities regulation" (2015) *Fordham L Rev* 977–1052, at 977, 1021.

17 Michael Lewis, *Flash Boys: A Wall Street Revolt* (New York: W.W. Norton & Company, 2014), pp. 37–38. High-frequency trading has also changed the nature of the market itself, by creating a wholly different kind of cushion of liquidity derived from transaction volume in and out of particular stocks over timeframes measured in milliseconds (or microseconds, or nanoseconds).

18 See, e.g., UK Houses of Parliament, Parliamentary Office of Science & Technology, "Financial technology (FinTech)" (2016) 525 Postnote, available at researchbriefings.files.parliament.uk/documents/POST-PN-0525/POST-PN-0525.pdf (describing potentially disruptive new applications of digital technology to financial services in the form of alternative financing arrangements, data analytics, new payment methods, and distributed ledger technology, which is the technology underlying bitcoin); Douglas W. Arner, Janos Nathan Barberis & Ross P. Buckley, "The evolution of FinTech: a new post-crisis paradigm?" (2015) University of Hong Kong Faculty of Law Research Paper No. 2015/047, available at papers.ssrn.com/sol3/papers.cfm?abstract_id=2676553 (describing financial technology as having evolved over three distinct eras, and counseling regulatory forbearance).

19 See, e.g., Financial Stability Board, Consultative Document (2nd) Assessment Methodologies for Identifying Non-Bank Non-Insurer Global Systematically Important Financial institutions (2015) available at www.financialstabilityboard.org/wp-content/uploads/2nd-Con-Doc-on-NB NI-G-SIFI-methodologies.pdf.

20 Ibid., at 2–3.

21 In the United States, designation of "systemically important financial institutions," or SIFIs, refers to banks with consolidated assets over $50 billion, which are automatically deemed systemically important and require no further designation; and non-bank financial companies that the Financial Stability Oversight Council, FSOC, has designated as systemically important: Dodd-Frank s. 113, FSOC Final Rule on Authority to Require Supervision and Regulation of Certain Non-bank Financial Companies, 12 C.F.R. Para 1310. In the UK, the Prudential Regulatory Authority, PRA, regulates significant financial institutions ("PRA-authorised persons"), with the goal of ensuring their business "is carried on in a way which avoids any adverse effect on the stability of the UK financial system," and minimizing the adverse effect that their failure could have on "the stability of the UK financial system." Financial Services Act 2012 ss. 2B(2), (3). Unlike the US, however, the Financial Policy Committee, housed in the Bank of England, also has a broader oversight role. Ibid., ss. 9C, 9G-9W. In the EU, which has quite a different system,

banks deemed significant under the Single Supervisory Mechanism (SSB) are supervised directly by the European Central Bank. The European Systemic Risk Board (ESRB) also plays an oversight role. It is less institution-oriented, though it is structurally linked to the ECB's institution-centered approach. See, inter alia, Regulation (EU) No. 1092/2010 of the European Parliament and of the Council of November 24, 2010 on European Union macro-prudential oversight of the financial system and establishing a European Systemic Risk Board, [2010] OJ L 331/1, art 16. For a comparison of regulatory approaches to systemic risk, see Cristie Ford, "Systemic risk regulation in comparative perspective" (2016), available at papers.ssrn.com/sol3/papers.cfm?abstract_id=2798419.

22 In keeping with what it sees as evolving learning on this front, the Canadian federal government, in its current statutory effort to regulate systemic risk in Canadian capital markets, designates systemically significant products, practices, and benchmarks – rather than institutions. See the proposed Capital Markets Stability Act, ss. 18–23, available at ccmr-ocrmc.ca/wp-content/uploads/cmsa-consultation-draft-revised-en.pdf; also Ford, "Systemic risk," ibid.

23 On regulatory, as opposed to private sector, innovation, see Julia Black, Martin Lodge & Mark Thatcher (eds), *Regulatory Innovation: A Comparative Analysis* (Northampton: Edward Elgar, 2005).

24 Ronald Wright *A Short History of Progress* (Toronto: Anansi Press, 2004). According to some scholars, it was the loss of big game through over-hunting that actually pushed humans to rely on other food sources. There is still considerable debate about the so-called "overkill hypothesis." For recent studies arguing for both sides of the debate, see Matheus Souza Lima-Ribeiro & José Alexandre Felizola Diniz-Filho, "American megafaunal extinctions and human arrival: improved evaluation using a meta-analytical approach" (2013) 299 *Quat Int'l* 38–52 (arguing humans were not responsible); Brigid S. Grund, Todd A. Surovell & S. Kathleen Lyons, "Range sizes and shifts of North American Pleistocene mammals are not consistent with a climatic explanation for extinction" (2012) 44 *World Arch* 43–55 (arguing humans were responsible). Yet, there seems to be abundant evidence that at least in island ecosystems, humans were primary drivers of extinctions either through direct hunting or indirect habitat expansion with the use of fire.

25 Niccolò Machiavelli, Harvey C. Mansfield (tran.), *The Prince*, 2nd edn. (Chicago: University of Chicago Press, 1998); Francis Bacon, "Of innovations," in Thomas Marby (ed.), *The Essays, or, Counsels, Civil and Moral, with a Table of the Colours of Good and Evil* (London: Parker, 1853).

26 Joseph Schumpeter, *Capitalism, Socialism and Democracy* (New York: Harper & Brothers, 1942). In a story that says something about how the innovation of innovation studies actually developed, Schumpeter was not even the first to develop a theory of innovation. Gabriel Tarde, a French sociologist, wrote about social change in the late 1800s in similar terms. Benoît Godin, "Innovation: the history of a category" (2008) Project on the Intellectual History of Innovation, Working Paper No. 1, at 2, 26–27. As well, like any developed academic field, innovation scholarship has its internal disputes. I can only hit the high points here, and the points most relevant to the regulatory scale of action. I make no attempt to be comprehensive.

27 At least sometimes, there does seem to be a cognizable "innovator's personality." Personality research on innovativeness and entrepreneurship does seem to suggest a meaningful relationship between entrepreneurial conduct and how those engaged in it score on what psychologists call the "Big 5 personality traits" – those broad personality indicators typically used to describe individual tendencies. The five factors are openness, conscientiousness, extraversion, agreeableness, and neuroticism. In particular, entrepreneurship and innovation seem linked to the personality trait of openness to experience. Hermann Brandstätter, "Personality aspects of entrepreneurship: a look at five meta-analyses" (2011) 51 *Personality & Individual Differences* 222–230; Alberto Marcati, Gianluigi Guido & Alessandro M. Peluso, "The role of SME entrepreneurs' innovativeness and personality in the adoption of innovations" (2008) 37 *Research Pol'y* 1579–1590. Openness is also linked to boundary-pushing more broadly. On the fact that risk-taking and boundary-pushing are rewarded in the financial industry, right up to the point where they are not, see Donald C. Langevoort, "Chasing the greased pig down Wall Street: A gatekeeper's guide to the psychology, culture, and ethics of financial risk taking" (2011) 96 *Cornell L Rev* 1209–1246.

28 Jan Fagerberg, "Innovation: a guide to the literature," in Jan Fagerberg, David C. Mowery & Richard R. Nelson (eds), *The Oxford Handbook of Innovation* (New York: Oxford University Press, 2005), pp. 1–26, at 1, 9–10.

29 Scholars who talk about innovation tend to draw a key distinction between "invention," as the first creation of an idea or good, and "innovation," which is the process of applying an invention in practice. Regulation, because it cares about practical application in the world of action, is primarily concerned with innovations, not inventions. This is even how patent law works. It is use, not invention, which allows someone to lay claim to a new thing.

30 Brett Frischmann & Mark Lemley, "Spillovers" (2007) 107 *Colum L Rev* 257–301, at 258.

31 Individual curiosity, and the pleasure that derives from exploration, has generated many inventions and innovations. Innovators can be and often are also pro-socially motivated, meaning they are inventing and innovating in an effort to meet the needs of others, including future generations. Interestingly, recent evidence suggests that innovators who are hedonically motivated (that is, "in it for fun" or driven by individual curiosity) tend to come up with more novel solutions, but pure hedonic motivation can also lead to fewer useful solutions. Hedonic motivation when combined with pro-social motivation can lead to solutions that are both useful and novel. See Ruth Maria Stock, Pedro Oliveira & Eric von Hippel, "Impacts of hedonic and utilitarian motives on the novelty and utility of user-developed innovations" (2013) MIT Sloan School of Management, Working Paper; Adam M. Grant & James W. Berry, "The necessity of others is the mother of invention: intrinsic and prosocial motivations, perspective taking, and creativity" (2011) 54 *Acad Mgmt J* 73–96.

32 See, e.g., William J. Baumol, *The Free-Market Innovation Machine: Analyzing the Growth Miracle of Capitalism* (Princeton: Princeton University Press, 2002).

33 In what seems like an exceptionally bold conceptual link, political economists Peter Hall and David Soskice have proposed that, as among varieties of capitalism, liberal market economies are more likely to produce radical innovations while

coordinated market economies are more likely to produce incremental innovations. Peter A. Hall & David Soskice, "An introduction to varieties of capitalism," in Peter A. Hall & David Soskice (eds), *Varieties of Capitalism: The Institutional Foundations of Comparative Advantage* (New York: Oxford University Press, 2001), pp. 38–44.

34 Kristine Bruland & David C. Mowery, "Innovation through time," in Jan Fagerberg, David C. Mowery & Richard R. Nelson (eds), *The Oxford Handbook of Innovation* (New York: Oxford University Press, 2005), pp. 349–379, at 350, 352–354.

35 For a review of this literature, see Joel Mokyr, "Editor's introduction: the new economic history and the industrial revolution," in Joel Mokyr (ed.), *The British Industrial Revolution: An Economic Perspective*, 2nd edn. (Boulder: Westview Press, 1999). See also Gregory Clark & David Jacks, "Coal and the Industrial Revolution, 1700–1869" (2007) 11 *Eur Rev Econ Hist* 39–72; Bruland & Mowery, "Innovation through time," 356–357, note 34 above; H. I. Dutton, *The Patent System and Inventive Activity During the Industrial Revolution, 1750–1852* (Dover: Manchester University Press, 1984). The relative importance of the patent system is contested: see Mokyr, "Editors introduction," 28–29.

36 Mokyr, "Editors introduction," 30–39, note 35 above.

37 Bruland & Mowery, "Innovation," 355, note 34 above; David Mitch, "The role of education and skill in the Industrial Revolution," in Joel Mokyr (ed.), *The British Industrial Revolution: An Economic Perspective*, 2nd edn. (Boulder: Westview Press, 1999), pp. 241–279.

38 William Lazonick, "The innovative firm," in Jan Fagerberg, David C. Mowery & Richard R. Nelson (eds), *The Oxford Handbook of Innovation* (New York: Oxford University Press, 2005), pp. 34–36; Josiah Wedgwood, who apprenticed with another ceramic maker in the Staffordshire Potteries industrial area, is an example. Once he founded his own ceramics firm he innovated in technical ways, such as developing a more accurate means of measuring kiln temperatures, but far more important were his managerial innovations. He effectively created the modern controlled and disciplined workforce through such changes as an assigned division of labor, use of an early time clock, and written rules for worker behavior. Neil McKendrick, "Josiah Wedgwood and factory discipline" (1961) 4 *Hist J* 30–55.

39 Joel Mokyr, "Editors introduction," 23–24, note 35 above. The importance of microinventions from collective learning, i.e., incremental innovations, as opposed to the individual inventor creating macroinventions, i.e., radical innovations, has been increasingly favored in the literature. See, e.g., Alessandro Nuvolari, "Collective invention during the British Industrial Revolution: the case of the Cornish pumping engine" (2004) 28 *Cambridge J Econ* 347–363. The distinction between incremental and radical innovations is relevant to regulation and is discussed in this book's next two chapters.

40 Mokyr, "Editors introduction," 36, note 35 above.

41 Stephen J. Kline & Nathan Rosenberg, "An overview of innovation," in Ralph Landau & Nathan Rosenberg (eds), *The Positive Sum Strategy: Harnessing Technology for Economic Growth* (Washington, DC: National Academy Press, 1986) cited in Jan Fagerberg, "Innovation: a guide," 8–9, note 28 above.

42 Charles Edquist, "Systems of innovation: perspectives and challenges," in Jan Fagerberg, David C. Mowery & Richard R. Nelson (eds), *The Oxford Handbook of Innovation* (New York: Oxford University Press, 2005), pp. 181–208, at 190–195.

43 Stephen J. Kline & Nathan Rosenberg, "An overview of innovation," in Ralph Landau & Nathan Rosenberg (eds), *The Positive Sum Strategy: Harnessing Technology for Economic Growth* (Washington, DC: National Academy Press, 1986), pp. 275–305, at 291.

44 Jared M. Diamond, *Guns, Germs, and Steel: The Fates of Human Societies* (New York: W.W. Norton & Company, 1997), p. 243.

45 Alice Lam, "Organizational innovation," in Jan Fagerberg, David C. Mowery & Richard R. Nelson (eds), *The Oxford Handbook of Innovation* (New York: Oxford University Press, 2005), pp. 115–147, at 117–122. For example, what Burns and Stalker described half a century ago as "mechanistic" structures, like stereotypical bureaucracies, may be more suitable for stable environments. "Organic" structures based on personal autonomy and engagement may be more suitable for dynamic environments: Tom Burns & G.M. Stalker, *The Management of Innovation*, 2nd ed. (London: Tavistock, 1966). The workplace has changed enormously in the intervening years but the general distinction, as perhaps describing the extreme ends of a spectrum, remains compelling.

46 Management gurus Peter Drucker is probably still the most influential of these writers, though he tended to talk "around" the concept of innovation itself. See, e.g., Peter Drucker, *Technology, Management and Society* (New York: Routledge, 1970). Others describing innovation-enhancing "firm culture" include Keld Laursen & Ammon Salter, "Open for innovation: the role of openness in explaining innovation performance among U.K. manufacturing firms" (2005) 27 *Strat Mgmt J* 131–150; Robert F. Hurley & G. Tomas M. Hult, "Innovation, market orientation, and organizational learning: an integration and empirical examination" (1998) 62 *J Marketing* 42–54. Some also suggest that flexible, organic, adapt and open "adhocracies" are better at fostering so-called "radical" innovations, whereas organizational communities based on embedded routines, team relationships and shared culture are relatively good at making incremental innovations and transferring tacit knowledge. The latter are sometimes called "J-form" (or Japan form) structures. Alice Lam, "Organizational innovation," in Jan Fagerberg, David C. Mowery & Richard R. Nelson (eds), *The Oxford Handbook of Innovation* (New York: Oxford University Press, 2005), pp. 127–132.

47 Jean-Philippe Vergne & Rodolphe Durand, "The missing link between the theory and empirics of path dependence: conceptual clarification, testability issue, and methodological implications" (2010) 47 *J Mgmt Stud* 736–759, at 741–744.

48 Mary Tripsas & Giovanni Gavetti, "Capabilities, cognition and inertia: evidence from digital imaging" (2000) 21 *Strat Mgmt J* 1147–1161.

49 Arch G. Woodside & Wim G. Biemans, "Modeling innovation, manufacturing, diffusion and adoption/rejection processes" (2005) 20 *J Bus & Industrial Marketing* 380–393.

50 Everett M. Rogers, *Diffusion of Innovations*, 4th edn. (New York: Free Press, 1995), pp. 143–147.

51 Clayton Christensen coined the term "disruptive" innovation. He describes multiple examples in which small, initially poor-quality and non-threatening changes

around the margin of an industry (like the incursion of staticky transistor radios into big stereo-makers' turf, or the incursion of low-grade steel mini-mills into US Steel's turf) over time can disrupt entire industries. Clayton M. Christensen, *The Innovator's Dilemma: When New Technologies Cause Great Firms to Fail* (Boston: Harvard Business School Press, 1997). The notion of "disruptive" innovation, while helpful, has become something of a cliché. It is not discussed in depth here because the model of incremental quality improvements made by outside disruptors is not the kind of development that really counts as a "financial innovation" in this book's terms.

52   Christopher Freeman & Luc Soete, *The Economics of Industrial Innovation*, 3rd edn. (MIT Press, 1997); see also Christopher Freeman, John Clark & Luc Soete, "Unemployment and technical innovation: a study of long waves and economic development" (1983) 17 *J Econ Issues* 803–808. Kenneth Arrow used the similar terms "non-drastic" and "drastic," though discussed the concepts strictly in terms of how it affected monopolies' incentives to innovate, see Kenneth J. Arrow, "Economic welfare and the allocation of resources for invention," in Richard Nelson (ed.), *The Rate and Direction of Inventive Activity: Economic and Social Factors* (Princeton: Princeton University Press, 1962).

53   Christopher Freeman & Francisco Louçã, *As Time Goes By: From the Industrial Revolutions to the Information Revolution* (Oxford: Oxford University Press, 2001).

54   Bengt-Åke Lundvall (ed.), *National Systems of Innovation: Towards a Theory of Innovation and Interactive Learning* (London: Anthem Press, 1992).

55   Bjørn T. Asheim & Meric S. Gertler, "The geography of innovation: regional innovation systems," in Jan Fagerberg, David C. Mowery & Richard R. Nelson (eds), *The Oxford Handbook of Innovation* (New York: Oxford University Press, 2005), pp. 291–317, at 292–294.

56   Ibid., at 297–298. Some also argue that highly talented workers prefer to live in regions that offer a particular kind of high quality of life (for example, diverse demographics and rich cultural offerings) – this is the so-called "New York phenomenon."

57   Franco Malerba, "Sectoral Systems: how and why innovation differs across sectors," in Jan Fagerberg, David C. Mowery & Richard R. Nelson (eds), *The Oxford Handbook of Innovation* (New York: Oxford University Press, 2005), pp. 280–406, at 382 (discussing the "Schumpeter Mark II sectors").

58   See, e.g., David Strang & John W. Meyer, "Institutional conditions for diffusion" (1993) 22 *Theory & Soc'y* 487–511. Network analysis is an enormous and growing field of study. This chapter aims to hit some of the high points but makes no claim to be comprehensive.

59   Virgile Chassagnon & Marilyne Audran, "The impact of interpersonal networks on the innovativeness of inventors: from theory to empirical evidence" (2011) 15 *Int'l J Inn Mgmt* 931–958; Emmanouil Tranos, "Networks in the innovation process," in Mandfred M. Fischer & Peter Nijkap (eds), *Handbook of Regional Science* (New York: Springer, 2013). Formal contractual relationships can be strong (such as equity ties, manufacturing ventures, research and development ventures), or weak (such as marketing and licensing agreements or training agreements). Informal ties include social networks, and professional communities that

provide opportunities to participate in educational programs, conferences, trade associations and the like.

60 Morten T. Hansen, "The search-transfer problem: the role of weak ties in sharing knowledge across organization subunits" (1999) 44 *Admin Sci Q* 82–111; Tim Rowley, Dean Behrens & David Krackhardt, "Redundant governance structures: an analysis of structural and relational embeddedness in the steel and semiconductor industries" (2000) 21 *Strat Mgmt J* 369–386 (suggesting that weak ties are more important in the semiconductor industry, which focuses on product innovation, while strong ties are more important in the steel industry, which focuses on complex and nuanced process innovation).

61 Brian Uzzi, "Social structure and competition in interfirm networks: the paradox of embeddedness" (1997) 42 *Admin Sci Q* 35–67.

62 Walter W. Powell & Stine Grodal, "Networks of innovators," in Jan Fagerberg, David C. Mowery & Richard R. Nelson (eds), *The Oxford Handbook of Innovation* (New York: Oxford University Press, 2005), pp. 56–85.

63 Victor Gilsing et al., "Network embeddedness and the exploration of novel technologies: technological distance, betweenness centrality and density" (2008) 37 *Research Pol'y* 1717–1312.

64 Jenny M. Lewis, Damon Alexander & Mark Considine, "Policy networks and innovation', in Stephen P. Osborne & Lewis Brown (eds), *Handbook of Innovation in Public Services* (Northampton: Edward Elgar, 2013), pp. 360–375.

65 Burt argues that "[t]he hole is a buffer, like an insulator in an electric circuit. As a result of the hole between them, the two contacts provide network benefits [to the hole-bridging entrepreneur] that are in some degree additive rather than overlapping." Ronald S. Burt, *Structural Holes: A Social Structure of Competition* (Cambridge: Harvard University Press, 1992), p. 18. The evidence for the benefits of structural holes is not uniform, and they seem more useful in searching for new information than in transferring complex knowledge. Powell & Grodal, "Networks of innovators," 68–69, note 62 above.

66 Rogers, "Diffusion of innovations," 204–251, note 50 above.

67 Melissa A. Schilling & Christina Fang, "When hubs forget, lie, and play favorites: interpersonal network structure, information distortion, and organizational learning" (2014) 35 *Strat Mgmt J* 974–994.

68 David Strang & John W. Meyer, "Institutional conditions for diffusion" (1993) 22 *Theory & Soc'y* 487–511, at 492–498.

69 Paul J. DiMaggio & Walter P. Powell, "The iron cage revisited: institutional isomorphism and collective rationality in organizational fields" (1983) 48 *Am Soc Rev* 147–160.

70 Writing in the context of newly industrializing countries, Kim and Nelson distinguish "duplicative imitation" from "creative imitation." Duplicative imitation does not change the technology, but it gives the innovator a competitive edge if it can produce the same good more cheaply. Counterfeit goods and knockoffs are in this category. Creative imitation or adaptation modifies the original innovation in some way and blurs the line between innovation and imitation. Linsu Kim & Richard R. Nelson, "Introduction," in *Technology, Learning, and Innovation: Experiences of Newly Industrializing Economies* (Cambridge: Cambridge University Press, 2000), pp. 4–5.

71   Fritz Redlich, "Innovation in business: a systematic presentation" (1951) 10 *Am J Econ & Soc* 285–291; Fagerberg, "Innovation: a guide," 8, note 28 above.

72   Christopher Freeman, Luc Soete & John Clark, *Unemployment and Technical Innovation: A Study of Long Waves and Economic Development* (London: F. Pinter, 1982), p. 65.

73   William L. Silber, "Innovation, competition and new contract design in futures market" (1981) 1 *J Futures Mkts* 123–155, at 125.

74   Nicola Cetorelli & Stavros Peristiani, "The role of banks in asset securitization" (2012) FRBNY Economic Policy Review, at 54, available at www.newyorkfed.org/medialibrary/media/research/epr/12v18n2/1207peri.pdf.

75   According to Harvey Rosenblum, Executive Vice President of the Federal Reserve Bank of Dallas, the percentage of banking assets held by the five largest US banks has more than tripled, starting from just 17% in 1970 and reaching 52% in 2005. Harvey Rosenblum, "Choosing the road to prosperity: why we must end too big to fail – now" (2012) *Annual Report 2011, Federal Reserve Bank of Dallas*. In absolute terms, US banks have grown increasingly larger over time but they have also grown larger relative to the banking industry because the number of banks has declined overall. David C. Wheelock, "Too big to fail: the pros and cons of breaking up big banks," (2012) *The Regional Economist* 10–11. While the US banking industry is less concentrated than banking systems in other industrialized countries, for example in Canada where the top five banks hold a jaw-dropping 86% of banking assets, the US derivatives market is dominated by a small group of large financial institutions. Globally, US derivatives markets represent one third of the total market for derivatives. Further, four banks (JP Morgan Chase, Citibank, Bank of America, and Goldman Sachs) represent 93% of the total banking industry notional amounts. International Monetary Fund, "IMF Country Report No. 15/89: United States" (2015), available at www.imf.org/external/pubs/ft/scr/2015/cr1589.pdf; Claudio A. Eggert, "A strategy analysis of the 'Big Five'" Canadian banks," available at dtpr.lib.athabascau.ca/action/download.php?filename=mba-12/open/eggertclaudioProject.pdf.

76   E.g., Anastasia Nesvetailova points out that throughout the 2002–2007 credit boom, the same banks that had created complex CDOs were also the buyers of those CDOs. In 2004, 32% of the risky slices of CDOs were bought by other CDOs, by 2007 that number grew to 67%. At the end of the credit boom, almost half of all CDOs sponsored by Merrill Lynch had bought large portions of other Merrill Lynch CDOs. Anastasia Nesvetailova, "Shadow banking and the political economy of financial innovation" (2015), available at web.isanet.org/Web/Conferences/FLACSO-ISA%20BuenosAires%202014/Archive/2e2d3609-f464-45aa-84e9-56179ea86542.pdf.

77   Peter Tufano, "Financial innovation and first mover advantages" (1989) 25 *J Fin Econ* 213–240.

78   Geoffrey G. Bell, "Clusters, networks, and firm innovativeness" (2005) 26 *Strat Mgmt J* 287–295, at 292.

79   Interestingly, according to Farhi and Cintra, "London and New York together dominated the issue of shares and bonus, the foreign exchange market, and the transactions in the market for over-the-counter derivatives. In 2007 London accounted for 42.5% of world issues of foreign exchange and interest rate

derivatives and New York, 24%. As to credit derivatives the US market share was 40% in 2006 and London, 37% (after reaching 51% in 2002)." Maryse Farhi & Marcos Antonio Macedo Cintra, "The financial crisis and the global shadow banking system" (2009) 5 *Revue de la régulation*, available at regulation.revues. org/7473.

80 Historically, financial innovations were considered difficult if not impossible to patent. Peter Tufano, "Financial innovation," in G.M. Constantinides, M. Harris & R. Stulz (eds), *Handbook of the Economies of Finance* (Amsterdam: Elsevier, 2003) at 330. Following *State Street Bank* v. *Signature Financial*, 149 F 3d 1368, 47 USPQ 2d (BNA) 1596 (Fed. Cir. 1998) in the US, however, the number of financial patents issued in that country has grown steadily. Increased patenting does not necessarily imply that firms are developing more innovations; they could also be engaging in patenting for other reasons including being able to sell patent rights to others, or patenting defensively. Megan M. La Belle & Heidi Mandanis Schooner, "Big banks and business method patents" (2014) 16 *U PA J Bus L* 431–495, at 449; Joshua Lerner, "Where does State Street lead? A first look at financial patents, 1971 to 2000" (2002) 57 *J Finance* 901–930.

81 Thorsten Beck, Tao Chen, Chen Lin & Frank Song, "Financial innovation: The bright and the dark sides," *Vox EU*, October 2, 2012, available at voxeu.org/article/financial-innovation-good-and-bad.

82 US Department of the Treasury, Office of Financial Research, available at www.financialresearch.gov.

83 Luis E. Lopez & Edward B. Roberts, "First-mover advantages in regimes of weak appropriability: the case of financial services innovations" (2002) 55 *J Bus Res* 997–1005.

84 J.O. Matthews has argued that a self-reinforcing cycle exists between market share and innovation, which also has the effect of hindering innovation by smaller firms: J.O. Matthews, *Struggle and survival on Wall Street: The Economics of Competition Among Securities Firms* (New York: Oxford University Press, 1994), cited in Tufano, "First mover advantages," note 77 above.

85 The Turner Review pointed out that as often as not, financial innovation in the years leading up to the financial crisis was undertaken for the purpose of extracting rents and avoiding regulation, not improving products or markets. UK Financial Services Authority [FSA], *The Turner Review: A Regulatory Response to the Global Banking Crisis* (2009), at 49, available at www.fsa.gov.uk/pubs/other/turner_review.pdf. As Martin Wolf has also pointed out, "an enormous part of what banks did in the early part of this decade – the off-balance-sheet vehicles, the derivatives and the 'shadow banking system' itself – was to find a way round regulation." Martin Wolf, "Reform of regulation has to start by altering incentives," *Financial Times* (London), June 23, 2009, at para 11.

86 See also Cristie Ford, "New governance, compliance and principles based securities regulation" (2008) 45 *Am Bus LJ* 1–60, at 47–50.

87 See, e.g., Chris Brummer, "Disruptive Technology and Securities Regulation" 84 *Fordham L Rev* 977 (2015) (describing how particular regulatory moves, like the SEC's Rule 144A in 1994 or Regulation NMS in 2007, unexpectedly rearranged markets and altered the business models of the very intermediaries – exchanges, broker-dealers and the like – they were intending to regulate).

88 See also Saule T. Omarova, "The quiet metamorphosis: how derivatives changed the 'business of banking'" (2009) 63 *U Miami L Rev* 1041–1110 (describing the change in the business of banking over time and its relationship to regulatory changes).

89 As Ethiopis Tafara has pointed out, "where regulated firms face competition from either an unregulated sector (e.g., hedge funds) or foreign competitors facing lower regulatory costs, it leads to pressures on regulators to curtail domestic oversight." Ethiopis Tafara, "Foreword," in Eilís Ferran et al., *The Regulatory Aftermath of the Global Financial Crisis* (Cambridge: Cambridge University Press, 2012) at xvii.

90 Lawrence G. Baxter, "Adaptive regulation in the amoral bazaar" (2011) 128 *SA LJ* 253–272, at 267.

91 With regard to swaps, the difficulty for regulators was categorizing them into the existing categories of futures, securities, or loans. Their categorical ambiguity allowed swaps to go unregulated for many years. For a history of the interplay between derivatives and their regulatory treatment in the last decades of the twentieth century, see Frank Partnoy, "The shifting contours of global derivatives regulation" (2001) 22 *U Pa J Int'l Econ* 421–495; on swaps in particular, see Russell J. Funk & Daniel Hirschman, "Derivatives and deregulation: financial innovation and the demise of Glass-Steagall" (2014) 59 *Admin Sci Q* 669–704.

92 Financial options are financial derivatives, meaning that their value is derived from the value of some underlying asset. An option is a contract that gives its holder the option (or the obligation, but not both) to either buy or sell a particular underlying security, at some predetermined future date, at a predetermined price. Whether an option is worth exercising at the time it comes due will depend on the price of the underlying asset at that future time. It will only be worth exercising if the option price for the underlying security is better for the option-holder than the open market price that the option-holder could otherwise get. Since it is impossible to know in advance what the future price of the underlying security will be, it is difficult to price options at the time when the initial options contract is signed. Black-Scholes drew on earlier mathematical inventions, such as the Capital Asset Pricing model, and it was further improved upon by later mathematical work, notably by Robert Merton: see especially Robert C. Merton, "Theory of rational option pricing" (1973) 4 *Bell J Econ & Mgmt Sci* 141–183; Robert C. Merton, "Option pricing when underlying stock returns are discontinuous" (1976) 3 *J Fin Econ* 125–144.

93 Lynn A. Stout, "Why the law hates speculators: regulation and private ordering in the market for OTC derivatives" (1999) 48 *Duke LJ* 701–786.

94 The Black-Scholes model applies to European-style options, which are exercisable only at maturity. The model calculates the premium on an option to determine its theoretical price. The model has essentially two parts: first, the expected benefit from an outright current purchase of the asset; and second, the current value of paying the exercise price at the option's maturity. The present value of the option is the difference of those two parts. The inputs are the current price of the underlying asset, the option strike price, the amount of time until expiration, the implied volatility, and the risk-free interest rate.

Actual volatility is an unobservable input, so implied volatility is inferred based on options that have been traded or price fluctuations in the underlying asset. In determining volatility, the model moved from using historical prices, to using historical price volatility, which made it more predictive.

95   (The contract would still discount for the time value of money.) Fischer Black & Myron Scholes, "The pricing of options and corporate liabilities" (1973) 81 *J Pol Econ* 637–655.

96   Robert C. Merton, R.V. Simons & A.D. Wilkie, "Influence of mathematical models in finance on practice: past, present and future" (1994) 347 *Phil Trans Phys Sci Eng* 451–463, at 454.

97   Donald A. MacKenzie, *An Engine, Not a Camera: How Financial Models Shape Markets* (Cambridge: MIT Press, 2006) p. 158.

98   Anna Gelpern & Erik F. Gerding, "Inside safe assets" (2016) 33 *Yale J on Reg* 363.

99   Michael Lewis, "Flash boys," 244, note 17 above.

100 In a similar vein, Iris Chiu has proposed that we think about the effects of financial innovation along three lines: identifying what the change is (e.g., identifying new channels for meeting financial needs, new intermediaries, or newly-identified financial needs); trying to determine its substitutive potential (e.g., to what extent financial end-users are migrating to a new technology); and trying to determine its structural impact (e.g., the extent to which a new technology can undermine regulatory assumptions or frameworks). Iris H.-Y. Chiu, "The disruptive implications of fintech – policy themes for financial regulators," presented at the Digital Currencies and Financial Conference, Centre for Law, Economics and Society (July 27–28, 2016), at 9–11, available at papers.ssrn.com/sol3/papers.cfm?abstract_id=2812667.

101 John Braithwaite, "Restorative justice for banks through negative financing" (2009) 49 *Brit J Criminol* 439–450, at 446.

102 William Redmond, "Financial innovation, diffusion, and instability" (2013) 47 *J Econ Issues* 525–531, at 526. Marvin B. Lieberman & Shigeru Asaba, "Why do firms imitate each other" (2006) 31 *Acad Manag Rev* 366–385; Lopez & Roberts, "First-mover advantages," 1003, note 83 above.

103 Tufano, "First mover advantages," note 77 above; Lopez & Roberts, ibid., at 997–1005.

104 Ibid., at 1003 (considering the adoption of pension funds, credit and debit cards in Costa Rica).

105 Phil Molyneux & Nidal Shamroukh, "Diffusion of financial innovations: the case of junk bonds and note issuance facilities" (1996) 28 *J Money, Cred & Banking* 502–522, at 519.

106 One study found that among innovators in the financial services industry, 44.7% innovate more than once a year and 31.6% innovate once a year: Guy Gellatly & Valerie Peters, "Understanding the Innovation Process: Innovation in Dynamic Service Industries" (1999) Statistics Canada Working Paper No. 127.

107 Ben S. Bernanke, "The global savings glut and the current US current account deficit," Remarks at the Sandridge Lecture Virginia Association of Economics (March 10, 2005), available at www.federalreserve.gov/boarddocs/speeches/2005/200503102/.

108 In economics, goods such as these, where consumers cannot independently assess their quality even after the fact, are sometimes referred to as "credence goods." See, e.g., Winand Emons, "Credence goods and fraudulent experts" (1997) 28 *Rand J Econ* 107–119.

109 Redmond, "Financial innovation," 526, note 102 above; Michael Haliassos, *Financial Innovation: Too Much or Too Little?* (Cambridge: MIT Press, 2013).

110 Marvin B. Lieberman & Shigeru Asaba, "Why do firms imitate each other" (2006) 31 *Acad Manag Rev* 366–385.

111 We return to this proposal in Chapter 7 but see, e.g., Saule T. Omarova, "License to deal: mandatory approval of complex financial products" (2012) 90 *Wash U L Rev* 63–140; Eric A. Posner & E. Glen Weyl, "An FDA for financial innovation: applying the insurable interest doctrine to 21st Century financial markets" (2015) 107 *Nw U L Rev* 1307–1358.

112 This may be the case in Canada at present with regard to what are commonly known as mutual funds, or investment funds. Investment funds that are sold by securities dealers are subject to extensive disclosure requirements, while functionally identical products can be sold as insurance products and subject to a much lower regulatory burden. See generally David Johnston, Kathleen Rockwell & Cristie Ford, *Securities Regulation in Canada* 5th edn. (Markham: LexisNexis 2014), chapter 16.

113 See, e.g., Carol A. Heimer, "Disarticulated responsiveness: the theory and practice of responsive regulation in multi-layered systems" (2011) 44 *UBC L Rev* 663–693; Donald C. Langevoort, "Global securities regulation after the financial crisis" (2010) 13 *J Econ L* 799–815; Partnoy, "Shifting contours," note 91 above; Michael W. Taylor, *Twin Peaks' Revisited… a Second Chance for Regulatory Reform* (London: Centre for the Study of Financial Innovation, 2009), pp. 26 (talking about the internal tension within the UK FSA between its prudential functions and its consumer protection functions as a reason for breaking the agency apart).

114 Erik Gerding, *Law, Bubbles, and Financial Regulation* (New York: Routledge, 2014).

115 Braithwaite, "Restorative justice," 446, note 101 above.

7 SEISMIC INNOVATION: THE RADICAL STEP CHANGE
AS REGULATORY OPPORTUNITY

1 "In place of safety nets," *The Economist*, April 20, 2011, available at www .economist.com/node/18586658.

2 Christopher Freeman, "The economics of technical change," in Daniele Archibugi & Jonathan Michie (eds), *Trade, Growth and Technical Change* (New York: Cambridge University Press, 1998), pp. 16–54, 31.

3 Ibid., at 31.

4 Jonathan Downar et al., "A multimodal cortical network for the detection of changes in the sensory environment" (2000) 3 *Nat Neurosci* 277–283 at 277 ("changes in the sensory environment, especially abrupt changes, tend to draw attention involuntarily. A sensory element undergoing a change also inserts

itself preferentially into awareness. For example, a hiker might not notice the constant sound of birds chirping unless they were to stop abruptly, at which point the hiker would become aware of both the birds and the sudden absence of noise.").

5   E.g., Michael L. Tushman & Philip Anderson, "Technological discontinuities and organizational environments" (1986) 31 *Admin Sci Q* 439–465; Philip Anderson & Michael L. Tushman, "Technological discontinuities and dominant designs: a cyclical model of technological change" (1990) 35 *Admin Sci Q* 604–633.

6   Both the terms "radical" and "seismic" also correspond to the high-growth phase of the famous technology life cycle "S-curve," in which a new technology moves from research and development, through a steep ascent curve in growth as it is taken up – the radical or seismic component – followed by a mature phase where product adoption is high but growth has flattened, and finally by decline (or diffusion). The image is idealized and real life is more complex (in fact there tend to be multiple overlapping S-curves with combined effects across time), but it accurately depicts our experience of technology take-up in a general sense.

7   Elen Stokes has developed thoughtful treatments of the active ways in which regulatory framing influences how we see empirical phenomena: Elen Stokes, "Regulating nanotechnologies: sizing up the options" (2009) 29 *Leg Stud* 281–304; Elen Stokes, "Regulatory domain and regulatory dexterity: critiquing the UK governance of 'fracking'" (2016) 79 *Modern L Rev* 961–986; see also Bart Nooteboom, *Learning and Innovation in Organizations and Economies* (New York: Oxford University Press, 2000), p. 2 (problematizing the word "radical").

8   Considering the radicalness of an innovation in retrospect is also vulnerable to all kinds of cognitive errors, including hindsight bias and the tendency to see more recent events as more significant. Even experts evaluating the radicalness of innovations retrospectively tend to discount the impact of older innovations in favor of newer ones. Alina B. Sorescu, Rajesh K. Chandy & Jaideep C. Prabhu, "Sources and financial consequences of radical innovation: insights from pharmaceuticals" (2003) 67 *J Marketing* 82–102, at 83. We discuss hindsight bias further in the next chapter.

9   See, e.g., Simon Sebag Montefiore writing about the 1995 collapse of Barings Bank, as cited in Anthony Giddens, "Risk and responsibility" (1999) 62 *Mod L Rev* 1–10, at 1, 2; Gillian Tett, *Fool's Gold* (London: Abacus, 2010), p. 6 ("The J.P. Morgan derivatives team was engaged in the banking equivalent of space travel").

10 Sorescu, Chandy & Prabhu, "Insights from pharmaceuticals", 85–93, note 8 above; John Bessant & Tim Venables (eds), *Introduction* in *Creating Wealth from Knowledge: Meeting the Innovation Challenge* (Northampton: Edward Elgar, 2008), pp. 1–16, 3. Another factor, essential in many industries, though not in finance, has been publicly funded basic research at universities.

11 Natasa Bilkic, Thomas Gries & Wim Naudé, "The radical innovation investment decision refined" (2013) IZA, Discussion Paper No. 7338, at 3.

12 Peter Tufano, "Financial innovation and first mover advantages" (1989) 25 *J Fin Econ* 213–40.

13 While an earlier assumption commonly made in innovation studies was that dominant market players were less likely to be innovative – this is the so-called "incumbent's curse" – it turns out that this is not always the case. See, e.g., Rajesh

K. Chandy & Gerard J. Tellis, "The incumbent's curse? Incumbency, size, and radical product innovation" (2000) 64 *J Marketing* 1–17.

14 Sorescu, Chandy & Prabhu, "Insights from pharmaceuticals," 94, note 8 above.

15 Lisa Schöler, Bernd Skiera & Gerard J. Tellis, "Stock market returns to financial innovations before and during the financial crisis in the United States and Europe" (2014) 31 *J Prod Innov Manag* 973–986 at 982; Paul K. Chaney, Timothy M. Devinney, & Russel S. Winer, "The impact of new product introductions on the market value of firms" (1991) 64 *J Bus* 573–610; E.J. Kleinschmidt & R.G. Cooper, "The impact of product innovativeness on performance" (1991) 8 *J Prod Innov Manag* 240–251.

16 Alfred D. Chandler, *The Visible Hand: The Managerial Revolution in American Business* (Cambridge: Belknap Press, 1977), pp. 90–92.

17 Ibid., at 92–94.

18 John F. Stover, *American Railroads*, 2nd edn. (Chicago: University of Chicago Press, 1977), pp. 61–85.

19 Ibid., at 97–110; Peter Tufano, "Business failure, judicial intervention, and financial innovation: restructuring U.S. railroads in the Nineteenth Century" (1997) 71 *Bus Hist Rev* 1–40, at 2–3.

20 Stover, "American railroads," 125–126, note 18 above.

21 The discussion in this section is drawn from Tufano, "Business failure," note 19 above.

22 Ian Ayres & Robert Gertner, "Filling gaps in incomplete contracts: an economic theory of default rules" (1989) 99 *Yale LJ* 87–130, at 91–93.

23 Tufano, "Business failure," 35, note 19 above.

24 Ibid., at 36.

25 See, e.g., Thomas K. McCraw, *Prophets of Regulation: Charles Francis Adams, Louis D. Brandeis, James M. Landis, Alfred E. Kahn* (Cambridge: Belknap Press, 1984), pp. 57–79.

26 To be clear, the ICC's interventions in the market, in the form of price regulation in particular, probably benefited the railroads at least as much as it benefited the public (if not more). These are Welfare State efforts in the sense that they take a top-down, direct, rigid form. Not all Welfare State-era directive regulation was associated with stabilization, redistribution efforts, or the provision of public benefits.

27 The information in this section is drawn from the National Commission on the BP Deepwater Horizon Oil Spill and Offshore Drilling (ed.), *Deep Water: The Gulf Oil Disaster and the Future of Offshore Drilling* (United States Government Printing: Washington, DC, 2011) p. 122, available at www.gpo.gov/fdsys/pkg/GPO-OILCOMMISSION/pdf/GPO-OILCOMMISSION.pdf. Important developments (and large oil spills) in other parts of the world are not discussed here, and there is no claim that developments in the Gulf of Mexico are broadly representative. The point is to try to illustrate the idea that some innovations can be defensibly described as seismic, at a scale that is relevant to a regulator's bailiwick, even if the same phenomenon may look different when evaluated at a different scale.

28 Outer Continental Shelf Deep Water Royalty Relief Act, Title III Pub. L. 104–158 (1995), codified at 43 USC §§ 1337.

29 National Commission, "Deep-water," 31, note 27 above [citations omitted].

30 Ibid., at vii.

31 US Securities and Exchange Commission, *Performance and Accountability Report* (2008), available at www.sec.gov/about/secpar/secpar2008.pdf; Patricia A. McCoy, Andrey D. Pavlov & Susan M. Wachter, "Systemic risk through securitization: the result of deregulation and regulatory failure" (2009) 41 *Conn L R* 1327–1377; Steven L. Schwarcz, "Distorting legal principles" (2010) 35 *J Corp L* 697–727. Maryse Farhi & Marcos Antonio Macedo Cintra, "The financial crisis and the global shadow banking system" (2009) 5 *Revue de la regulation* (The primary innovative actors before the financial crisis were large, regulated investment banks, but a significant amount of innovative activity came from the shadow banking system, including intermediaries such as SIVs, hedge funds and other institutional investors).

32 Lynn A. Stout, "Why the law hates speculators: regulation and private ordering in the market for OTC derivatives" (1999) 48 *Duke LJ* 701–786; Lynn A. Stout, "Derivatives and the legal origin of the 2008 credit crisis" (2011) 1 *Harv Bus L Rev* 13–23.

33 Vinod Kothari, *Credit Derivatives and Structured Credit Trading* (Singapore: John Wiley & Sons, 2008); John Biggins & Colin Scott, "Public-private relations in a transnational private regulatory regime: ISDA, the state and OTC derivatives market reform" (2012) 12 *European Business Organization Law Review* 309–346; Annelise Riles, *Collateral Knowledge: Legal Reasoning in the Global Financial Markets* (Chicago: University of Chicago Press, 2011); Chris Brummer, "Disruptive technology and securities regulation" (2015) *Fordham L Rev* 977–1052. Experimentalists, citing to Dewey, adopt this position as well: see, e.g., Charles F. Sabel & William H. Simon, "Minimalism and experimentalism in the administrative state" (2011–2012) 100 *Geol LJ* 53–94, at 88 ("Experimentalism co-opts the paradox of standardization: By imposing uniformity along a few dimensions, we permit more variations on others"). The original ISDA Master Agreement was introduced in 1985. It has been fine-tuned several times in the years since.

34 See, e.g., Monica Billio et al., "Econometric measures of connectedness and systemic risk in the finance and insurance sectors" (2012) 104 *J Fin Econ* 535–559, at 549 (using network analysis to demonstrate the increasing interconnectedness between the largest global financial institutions between 1994 and 2008).

35 Andrew G. Haldane & Robert M. May, "Systemic risk in banking ecosystem" (2011) 469 *Nature* 351–355.

36 Hyun-Song Shin & Tobias Adrian, "The changing nature of financial intermediation and the financial crisis of 2007–2009" (2010) 2 *Ann Rev Econ* 603–618, at 606.

37 Frank Knight, *Risk, Uncertainty and Profit* (New York: Houghton Mifflin Company, 1921).

38 Ibid.; also Geoffrey T.F. Brooke, "Uncertainty, profit and entrepreneurial action: Frank Knight's contribution reconsidered" (2010) 32 *J Hist Econ Thought* 221–235, at 222; Richard N. Langlois & Metin M. Cosgel, "Frank Knight on risk, uncertainty and the firm: a new interpretation" (1993) 31 *Econ Inquiry* 456–465, at 459.

39 "World Economic Forum has observed, Rethinking financial innovation: reducing negative outcomes while retaining the benefits," (2012) at 7; see also Andrew Haldane, Simon Brennon & Vasilieos Madouros, "What is the contribution

of the financial sector: miracle or mirage?" in *The Future of Finance: The LSE Report* (The London School of Economics and Political Science, 2010), pp. 87–120, 106.

40   See, e.g., the companies listed in the roadmap in Chapter 9 of this book. Not all fintech aims to disrupt the industry. Some see existing financial institutions as clients. See Stephane Dubois, "Silicon Alley and Silicon Valley jostle for the fintech crown," *Xignite*, March 28, 2015, available at resources. xignite.com/h/i/90435027-guest-article-silicon-alley-and-silicon-valley-jostle-for-the-fintech-crown-news (putting EidoSearch, Estimize, and Standard Treasury in that category, in which Xignite itself, of which Dubois is the CEO, also sits). Large US financial institutions are also investing heavily in fintech: see, e.g., Sofia, "FinTech buyers club: who invests in FinTech start-ups?" *Let's Talk Payments*, February 9, 2016, available at letstalkpayments.com/fintech-buyers-club-who-invests-in-fintech-startups.

41   Robert C. Merton, "Financial innovation and the management and regulation of financial instruments" (1995) 19 *J Banking & Fin* 461–481, at 468–469.

42   James C. Scott, *Seeing Like a State: How Certain Schemes to Improve the Human Condition Have Failed* (New York: Vail Ballou Press, 1998); Michael Moran, *The British Regulatory State: High Modernism and Hyper-Innovation* (New York: Oxford University Press, 2003).

43   Diane Vaughan, "Autonomy, interdependence, and social control: NASA and the Space Shuttle Challenger" (1990) 35 *Admin Sci Q* 225–257, at 255 [citations omitted].

44   Bryan D. Jones & Frank R. Baumgartner, *The Politics of Attention: How Government Prioritizes Problems* (Chicago: University of Chicago Press, 2005), p. 6 (discussing the image shift of nuclear power as "atoms for progress" in the 1950's but "environmental danger, workplace safety, and fear of nuclear proliferation" in the 1960's).

45   William Starbuck & Frances J. Milliken, "Challenger: changing the odds until something breaks," in William Starbuck, *Organizational Realities: Studies in Strategizing and Organizing* (New York: Oxford University Press 2006), pp. 233–256, at 254.

46   The point applies at the macro-level too. As Joseph Rouse has said about Thomas Kuhn's concept of the paradigm shift, which shares interesting conceptual common ground with the notion of radical innovation: in retrospect, historical judgment may discern sharp breaks and crucial turning points, but these almost inevitably blur when looked at closely or without hindsight. Revolution is likewise a matter of retrospective interpretation. Whether a new development amounts to a revolution rather than an articulation of a prevailing paradigm depends on how one interprets that paradigm; some interpretations would make the shift more dramatic than others. Joseph Rouse, "Kuhn's philosophy of scientific practice," in Thomas Nickles (ed.), *Thomas Kuhn* (New York: Cambridge University Press, 2003), pp. 101–121, at 113.

47   For a thoughtful alternative argument, however, see Frank Partnoy, "The right way to regulate from behind" (2013) 18 *NC Banking Inst* 113 (arguing that because regulation will inevitably be "behind" the private sector, which makes *ex ante*

regulation ineffective, more robust and principles-based *ex post* enforcement is preferable in responding to financial innovation).

48 Fiona Haines, *The Paradox of Regulation: What Regulation Can Achieve and What it Cannot* (Northampton: Edward Elgar, 2011), p. 134 (describing regulation used to manage political risk).

49 Roberta Romano, "The Sarbanes-Oxley Act and the making of quack corporate governance" (2005) 114 *Yale LJ* 1521–1611.

50 Lawrence G. Baxter, "Betting big: value, caution and accountability in an era of large banks and complex finance" (2012) 31 *Rev Banking & Fin L* 765–879, at 844.

51 Saule Omarova & Adam Feibelman, "Risks, rules, and institutions: a process for reforming financial regulation" (2009) 39 *U Mem L Rev* 881–930; Lawrence A. Cunningham & David Zaring, "The three or four approaches to financial regulation: a cautionary analysis against exuberance in crisis response" (2009) 78 *Geo Wash L Rev* 39–113.

52 Bradley C. Karkkainen, "Information as environmental regulation: TRI and performance benchmarking, precursor to a new paradigm?" (2001) 89 *Geo LJ* 257–370.

53 Sharon Gilad, "It runs in the family: meta-regulation and its siblings" (2010) 4 *Reg & Gov* 485–506, at 488; Cristie Ford, "Principles-based securities regulation in the wake of the global financial crisis" (2010) 45 *McGill L Rev* 257–307, at 288–293.

54 World Economic Forum, *Rethinking Financial Innovation: Reducing Negative Outcomes while Retaining the Benefits* (2012), p. 7, available at www3.weforum.org/docs/WEF_FS_RethinkingFinancialInnovation_Report_2012.pdf.

55 J. Wang, "Offshore safety-case approach and formal safety assessment of ships'"(2002) 33 *J Safety Res* 81–115.

56 T.P. Kelly & J.A. McDermid, "A systematic approach to safety-case maintenance'"(2001) 71 *Reliability Engineering and System Safety* 271–284 (describing the problems that sedimentary innovation may present for updating safety-cases, which do not apply as much to seismic innovations).

57 For a thoughtful treatment, see Neil Gunningham, *Mine Safety: Law Regulation Policy* (Marrickville: Southwest Press, 2007), pp. 67–82.

58 See also Cristie Ford, "Principles-based securities regulation in the wake of the global financial crisis" (2010) 45 *McGill L Rev* 257, at 288–293.

59 See Cristie Ford, "Prospects for scalability: relationships and uncertainty in responsive regulation" (2013) 7 *Regulation & Governance* 14–29, at 21–23; John Braithwaite (2009) "Restorative justice for banks through negative financing" (2009) 49 *Brit J Criminol* 439–450, at 439–450.

60 "In place of safety nets," note 1 above; but see Saule T. Omarova, "Wall Street as a community of fate" (2011) 159 *U Pa L Rev* 411–492, at 447–449. In the deepwater drilling context, proposals have been advanced to help internalize all the social costs of a spill. See, e.g., Mark A. Cohen et al., "Deepwater drilling: law, policy, and economics of firm organization and safety" (2011) 64 *Vand L Rev* 1853–1916 (recommending, *inter alia*, raising the liability cap to the worst-case scenario social costs, which are many multiples larger). Systemic risk is of a different

order again, even while efforts to force financial institutions to internalize all their social costs have merit.

61 See, e.g., Carol A. Heimer, "Disarticulated responsiveness: the theory and practice of responsive regulation in multi-layered systems" (2011) 44 *UBC L Rev* 663–693, at 675–676 (describing drug companies complaining that FDA approval takes an increasingly long time).

62 Geoffrey R.D. Underhill, *Reforming Global Finance: Coping better with the Pitfalls of Financial Innovation and Market-based Supervision*, PEGGED Policy Paper (2011), at 19–20.

63 Lawrence G. Baxter, "Betting big: value, caution and accountability in an era of large banks and complex finance" (2012) 31 *Rev Banking & Fin L* 765–879, at 872–873. In 2013, the UK newspaper the *Guardian* enlisted several individuals to consider the Precautionary Principle too. See, e.g., Andy Stirling, "Why the precautionary principle matters," *Guardian*, July 8, 2013, available at www.guardian.co.uk/science/political-science/2013/jul/08/precautionary-principle-science-policy; Tracey Brown, "The precautionary principle is a blunt instrument," *Guardian*, July 9, 2013, available at www.guardian.co.uk/science/political-science/2013/jul/09/precautionary-principle-blunt-instrument.

64 Omarova, "License to deal: mandatory approval of complex financial products" (2012) 90 *Wash U L Rev* 63–140, at 66.

65 Eric A. Posner & E. Glen Weyl, "An FDA for financial innovation: applying the insurable interest doctrine to 21st Century financial markets" (2015) 107 *Nw U L Rev* 1307–1058.

66 Omarova, "License to deal," 67, note 64 above.

67 Daniel P. Carpenter, "Protection without capture: product approval by a politically responsive, learning regulator" (2004) 98 *Am Pol Sci Rev* 613–631 (speaking about pharmaceutical, not financial, licensing).

8 SEDIMENTARY INNOVATION: RESPONDING TO INCREMENTAL CHANGE

1 Christopher Freeman, "The economics of technical change," in Daniele Archibugi & Jonathan Michie (eds), *Trade, Growth and Technical Change* (New York: Cambridge University Press, 1998), pp. 16–54, at 32.

2 Brian Barrett, "The biggest mistake people made about the iPad," *Gizmodo*, March 9, 2012, available at gizmodo.com/5891895/the-biggest-mistake-people-made-about-the-ipad.

3 Or consider the fascinating story of the shipping container: Marc Levinson, *The Box: How the Shipping Container Made the World Smaller and the World Economy Bigger* (Princeton: Princeton University Press, 2006).

4 Bruce Campbell, "The Lac-Mégantic disaster: where does the buck stop?," Canadian Centre for Policy Alternatives, October 23, 2013, available at www.policyalternatives.ca/publications/commentary/lac-m%C3%A9gantic-where-does-buck-stop. See also Transportation Safety Board of Canada, "Railway Investigation Report R13D0054" (2014).

5 Campbell, "Lac-Mégantic disaster," note 4 above.

6   Bruce Campbell *Willful Blindness? Regulatory Failures Behind the Lac-Mégantic Disaster* (Canadian Centre for Policy Alternatives, 2014), p. 8.

7   Ibid.

8   Tim Shufelt, "After the Lac-Mégantic disaster," *Canadian Business*, July 12, 2013, available at www.canadianbusiness.com/companies-and-industries/after-the-lac-megantic-disaster/.

9   Gillian Flaccus, "Officials want hold on oil trains after derailment," *Statesman Journal*, June 16, 2016, available at www.statesmanjournal.com/story/news/2016/06/16/oregon-officials-want-hold-oil-trains-derailment/86018886/. There were no injuries but the derailment forced evacuations in a nearby town and caused an oil spill into the river.

10 Ralph Vartabedian, "Why are so many oil trains crashing? Track problems may be to blame," *Los Angeles Times*, October 7, 2015, available at www.latimes.com/nation/la-na-crude-train-safety-20151007-story.html.

    In Oregon, trains carrying exclusively crude began running along this section of the Columbia river in 2014 (Flaccus, "Hold on oil trains," note 9 above).

11 Ibid.

12 Charles Perrow, *Normal Accidents: Living with High Risk Technologies* (New York: Basic Books, 1984).

13 Actually, if a frog were placed in gradually heating water, it would try to escape as the temperature rose. See Karl S. Kruszelnicki, "Frog fable brought to boil," *Conservation Magazine*, March 3, 2011, available at conservationmagazine.org/2011/03/frog-fable-brought-to-boil/.

14 *New State Ice Co. v. Liebmann*, 285 US 262, 56 (1932) (Brandeis J. dissenting).

15 See, e.g., Charles Sabel & Michael Dorf, "A constitution of democratic experimentalism" (1998) 98 *Colum L Rev* 298–473, at 267–473; James S. Liebman & Charles F. Sabel, "A public laboratory Dewey barely imagined: the emerging model of school governance and legal reform" (2003) 28 *NYU Rev L & Soc Change* 183–304. The idea of laboratories for democracy appears quite frequently in the flexible regulation literature as it is reflected in the database described in Chapter 4 above. In banking law, see also Arthur E. Wilmarth Jr, "The expansion of state bank powers, the federal response, and the case for preserving the dual banking system" (1990) 58 *Fordham L Rev* 1133–1256, at 1155–1156. Other articles from the database that discuss the "laboratories for democracy" concept in some depth, in generally though not unequivocally positive terms, and which were cited within the database more than fifteen times are Daniel C. Esty, "Revitalizing environmental federalism" (1996) 95 *Mich L Rev* 570–653; Orly Lobel, "The renew deal: the fall of regulation and the rise of governance in contemporary legal thought" (2004) 89 *Minn L Rev* 342–470; Kristen Engel, "Harnessing the benefits of dynamic federalism in environmental law" (2006) 56 *Emory LJ* 159–190; William W. Buzbee, "Asymmetrical regulation: risk, preemption, and the floor/ceiling distinction" (2007) 82 *NYU L Rev* 1547–1619; and, David E. Adelman & Kirsten H. Engel, "Adaptive federalism: the case against reallocating environmental regulatory authority" (2008) 92 *Minn L Rev* 1796–1850. Volume 50 Issue 3 of the *Arizona Law Review* also contains several papers compiled from a February 2008 conference entitled, "Constitutional Structures of Government Conference: Federalism and Climate Change," in which the

idea was examined. Other scholars are more skeptical. See, e.g., Ann Carlson, "Iterative federalism and climate change" (2009) 103 *Nw UL Rev* 1097; and David A. Super, "Laboratories of Destitution: Democratic Experimentalism and the Failure of Antipoverty Law" 157 *U Pa L Rev* 541 (2008) (with 13 and 9 cites respectively).

16 See, e.g., Australian Securities and Investment Commission, "16-185MR ASIC consults on a regulatory sandbox licensing exemption," available at http://asic .gov.au/about-asic/media-centre/find-a-media-release/2016-releases/16-185mr-asic-consults-on-a-regulatory-sandbox-licensing-exemption/; Ontario Securities Commission, OSC Launchpad, available at www.osc.gov.on.ca/en/osclaunchpad .htm; Singapore: Monetary Authority of Singapore, *FinTech Regulatory Sandbox Guidelines* (2016), available at www.mas.gov.sg/News-and-Publications/ Consultation-Paper/2016/Consultation-Paper-on-FinTech-Regulatory-Sandbox-Guidelines.aspx; UK Financial Conduct Authority, "Regulatory sandbox," available at www.the-fca.org.uk/firms/project-innovate-innovation-hub/ regulatory-sandbox.

17 Arthur E. Wilmarth Jr, "The OCC's preemption rules exceed the agency's authority and present a serious threat to the dual banking system and consumer protection" (2004) 23 *Ann Rev Banking & Fin L* 225–364, at 259 [citations omitted].

18 Wilmarth, "OCC's preemption rules," 259–226 [citations omitted], note 17 above. Wilmarth attributes the increase in competition to a competitive imbalance between state and federally chartered banks, which prior to 1980 had been more evenly matched. See also Arthur E. Wilmarth Jr, "Transformation of the U.S. financial services industry, 1975–2000: competition, consolidation, and increased risks" (2002) *U Ill L Rev* 215–476, at 441. Sometimes, private sector innovation can also force the hand of a regulator, or (as Wilmarth notes above) can help identify regulatory champions for an innovation not because it is in the public interest, but because it is in the regulator's competitive interest vis-à-vis other regulators. This is one account of the repeal of the Glass-Steagall Act (GSA), which restricted commercial banks from participating in the securities industry. Glass-Steagall was formally repealed via the Financial Services Modernization Act of 1999, better known as the Gramm-Leach-Bliley Act (GLBA). The $70 billion merger between Citicorp, Inc. and Travelers Group Inc., which violated certain provisions of the GSA and the Bank Holding Company Act of 1956, had already been announced before the GLBA's initial draft was even approved (though it did not become legal under after the GLBA had been implemented). The biography of Sandy Weill, former chief executive and chairman of Citicorp, outlines the strategy employed by Weill and Citicorp Chairman John S. Reed, to force the repeal of the GSA. See Academy of Achievement, "Sanford Weill Biography – Academic of Achievement," available at www.achievement.org/ autodoc/page/weiobio-1.

19 Saule T. Omarova, "The quiet metamorphosis: how derivatives changed the 'business of banking'" (2009) 63 *U Miami L Rev* 1041–1110, at 1044–1045 [citations omitted].

20 Moreover, the availability of 30-year mortgages in the US has been connected to the ability to securitize those assets in the markets. Richard Green & Susan Wachter, "The American mortgage in historical and international context" (2005)

19 *J Econ Perspect* 93–114; also Tobias Adrian & Hyun Song Shin, "Liquidity and leverage" (2010) 19 *J Financ Intermed* 418–437.

21 Claude Lévi-Strauss, *The Savage Mind* (Paris: Librairie Plon, 1962), p. 11.

22 Ewald Engelen et al., "Reconceptualizing financial innovation: frame, conjecture and bricolage" (2010) 39 *Econ & Soc'y* 33–63, at 54.

23 Ibid., at 53–56.

24 Arguably, relative to radical innovation, sedimentary innovation could be more amenable to rent-seeking as well – another function served by long chains of transactions in which intermediaries are involved at each step. Radical innovative contexts may be characterized by too much uncertainty to allow participants to identify or take advantage of interstitial rent-seeking opportunities. Once there is more collective experience with a particular innovation, however, there may be more incentive to tweak it in marginal ways, or add another layer of parties or detail, in ways that might capture particular benefits.

25 Robert C. Merton, "Financial innovation and economic performance" (1992) 4 *Bank Am J Appl Corp Finance* 12–22, at 19.

26 Post-crisis systemic risk regulation does in fact focus more on systemically important financial institutions (SIFIs, or, globally, G-SIFIS): see, e.g., Basel Committee on Banking Supervision, "Globally systemically important banks: assessment methodology and the additional loss absorbency requirement" (2011), *Bank for International Settlements*, available at www.bis.org/publ/bcbs207.pdf.

27 Stacey Schreft, "Map gives clearer picture of pathways that affect financial stability," US Department of the Treasury, Office of Financial Research, July 14, 2016, available at financialresearch.gov/from-the-management-team/2016/07/14/map-gives-clearer-picture-of-pathways/ (describing contagion, funding, and collateral network maps developed in recent OFR papers).

28 Sheri Markose, Simone Giansanteb & Ali Rais Shagaghi, "Too interconnected to fail' financial network of US CDS market: topological fragility and systemic risk'"(2012) 83 *Journal of Economic Behavior & Organization* 627–646.

29 Mark P. Hampton & John Christensen, "Offshore pariahs? Small island economies, tax havens, and the re-configuration of global finance" (2002) 30 *World Dev't* 1657–1673.

30 Eun-Ju Lee & Jinkook Lee, "Haven't adopted electronic financial services yet? The acceptance and diffusion of electronic banking technologies" (2002) 11 *J Fin Couns & Planning* 49–61.

31 Donald Mackenzie, "Long-term capital management and the sociology of arbitrage" (2003) 32 *Econ & Soc'y* 349–380, at 352.

32 Ibid.

33 Wolf Wagner, "The homogenization of the financial system and financial crises" (2008) 17 *J Financ Intermed* 330–356; Kartik Anand et al., "A network model of financial system resilience" (2013) 85 *J Econ Behav & Org'n* 219–235.

34 Boaventura de Sousa Santos, "Law: a map of misreading. Toward a post-modern conception of law" (1987) 14 *JL & Soc'y* 279–302; see also Cristie Ford, "Prospects for scalability: relationships and uncertainty in responsive regulation'"(2013) 7 *Reg & Gov* 14–29 (applying de Sousa Santos's framework to responsive regulation).

35 Roger Lee et al., "The remit of financial geography – before and after the crisis'"(2009) 9 *J Econ Geog* 723–747, at 731 [citations omitted].

36   Ibid., at 732.

37   Current Affairs, BBC Radio 4 broadcast, March 19, 2009, available at news.bbc. co.uk/nol/shared/spl/hi/programmes/analysis/transcripts/19_03_09.txt (As quoted in Lee, "Remit of financial geography," 742, note 35 above).

38   Engelen puts it more colorfully, and perhaps more cynically, than most:

   In the absence of a general system of property rights in financial innovation, novelty and rapid upscaling are critical because doing the same thing year after year brings in imitators and encourages commodification, which reduces first-mover high profits for the institution and high bonuses for the individual. While newness in itself is no guarantee of success, novelty matters within each conjuncture. This incidentally also limits collective memory and respect for older, established members among intermediary groups. More exactly, what matters is scalable differentiation because the high margins on financial innovation are generally taken early in the product cycle. In a world where profit arithmetically equals margins times volume, the intermediaries of the financial sector (just like big pharmaceutical firms) need not have striking originality but can instead pursue differentiation and mass sales through a succession of blockbusters. The last conjuncture's blockbuster was securitization in the wholesale markets which spawned umpteen differentiations that could be scaled up, generating large volume and fees, above all because they connected with retail feedstock from mass saving and borrowing. Ewald Engelen et al., "Reconceptualizing financial innovation: frame, conjuncture and bricolage" (2010) 39 *Econ & Soc'y* 33–63.

39   Peter Haiss, "Bank herding and incentive systems as catalysts for the financial crisis" (2010) 7 *IUP J Behav Fin* 30–58 (arguing that herding behavior provoked by common incentive systems between banks may have been one of the causes of the financial crisis).

40   John Maynard Keynes, "The consequences to the banks of the collapse of money values," in *Essays in Persuasion* (London: MacMillan and Co., 1931), p. 168.

41   Michiyo Nakamoto & David Weighton, "Citigroup chief stays bullish on buyouts," *Financial Times*, July 9, 2007, available at www.ft.com/cms/s/0/80e2987a-2e50-11dc-821c-0000779fd2ac.html#axzz30ZjjRf3M.

42   Amos Tversky & Daniel Kahneman, "Judgement under uncertainty: heuristics and biases" (1974) 185 *Science* 1124–1231.

43   Shane Frederick, George Loewenstein & Ted O'Donoghue, "Time discounting and time preference: a critical review" (2002) 40 *J Econ Lit* 351–401.

44   Raymond S. Nickerson, "Confirmation bias: a ubiquitous phenomenon in many guises" (1998) 2 *Rev Gen Psych* 175–220.

45   Lennart Sjöberg, "Factors in risk perception" (2002) 20 *Risk Anal* 1–12; Tversky & Kahneman, "Judgement under uncertainty," note 42 above.

46   John Allen Paulos, *Innumeracy: Mathematical Illiteracy and its Consequences* (New York: Hill & Wang, 1988).

47   E.g., Daniel J. Simons, Steven L Franconeri & Rebecca L Reimer, "Change blindness in the absence of a visual disruption" (2000) 29 *Perception* 1143–1154; Philip M. Groves & Richard F. Thompson, "Habituation: a dual-process theory" (1970) 77 *Psych Rev* 419–450.

48   James E. Ferrell Jr, "Signaling motifs and Weber's law" (2009) 36 *Molecular Cell* 724–727.

49 M. V. Rajeev Gowda, "Heuristics, biases and the regulation of risk" (1999) 32 *Policy Sci* 59–78, at 62–63.

50 For a review on bounded rationality, see Gerd Gigerenzer & Reinhard Selten (eds), *Bounded Rationality: The Adaptive Toolkit* (Cambridge: MIT Press, 2002). Frank Knight was also an early pioneer in exploring how people make decisions in with limited information: see Tim Rakow, "Risk, uncertainty and prophet: the psychological insights of Frank H. Knight" (2010) 5 *Judgment and Decision Making* 458–466.

51 Paul Slovic et al., "Risk as analysis and risk as feelings: some thoughts about affect, reason, risk, and rationality" (2004) 24 *Risk Anal* 311–322.

52 William Saletan, "Nuclear overreactors," *Slate*, March 14, 2011, available at www .slate.com/articles/health_and_science/human_nature/2011/03/nuclear_ overreactors.html.

53 Paul Slovic, "Perception of risk" (1987) 236 *Science* 280–285.

54 George F. Loewenstein et al., "Risk as feelings" (2001) 127 *Psych Bull* 267–286, at 267–286.

55 Ibid., at 275–278.

56 William Samuelson & Richard Zeckhauser, "Status quo bias in decision making" (1988) 1 *J Risk Uncertainty* 7–59. This can partly be explained by the endowment effect and risk aversion: better the devil you know. Daniel Kahneman, Jack L. Knetsch & Richard H. Thaler, "Anomalies: the endowment effect, loss aversion, and status quo bias" (1991) 5 *J Econ Perspect* 193–206. Emotions seem to play a role as well: Antoinette Nicolle et al., "A regret-induced status quo bias" (2011) 31 *The Journal of Neuroscience* 3320–3327.

57 See William McChesney Martin, Chairman of the Federal Reserve from 1951 to 1970, in a speech to the New York Group of the Investment Bankers Association of America: "In the field of monetary and credit policy, precautionary action to prevent inflationary excesses is bound to have onerous effects – if it did not it would be ineffective and futile. Those who have the task of making such policy don't expect you to applaud. The Federal Reserve, as one writer put it, after the recent increase in the discount rate, is in the position of the chaperone who has ordered the punch bowl removed just when the party was really warming up." William McChesney Martin, Speech (October 19, 1955), available at fraser.stlou-isfed.org/docs/historical/martin/martin55_1019.pdf.

58 Donald C. Langevoort, "Getting (too) comfortable: In-house lawyers, enterprise risk, and the financial crisis" (2012) *Wis L Rev* 495–519, at 511–512.

59 Scott A. Hawkins & Reid Hastie, "Hindsight: biased judgments of past events after the outcomes are known" (1990) 107 *Psych Bull* 311–327.

60 Gowda, "Heuristics," 63, note 49 above.

61 Thomas S. Kuhn, *The Structure of Scientific Revolutions* (Chicago: University of Chicago Press, 1962).

62 Tim Bartley, "Transnational governance as the layering of rules: intersection of public and private standards" (2011) 12 *Theoretical Inq L* 517–542.

63 Ibid., at 541.

64 Carol A. Heimer, "Disarticulated responsiveness: the theory and practice of responsive regulation in multi-layered systems" (2011) 44 *UBC L Rev* 663–693, at 666–671.

65 Jeffrey Friedman & Wladimir Kraus, *Engineering the Financial Crisis* (Philadelphia: University of Pennsylvania Press, 2011), p. 2.

66 Bankruptcy Abuse Prevention and Consumer Protection Act of 2005, Pub.L. 109–108, 119 Stat. 23, codified in various sections of 11 USC.

67 Stephen J. Lubben, "The Bankruptcy Code without safe harbors" (2010) 84 *Am Bankr LJ* 123–144, at 138–140.

68 Ibid.

69 Mark J. Roe, "The derivatives market's payment priorities as financial crisis accelerator" (2011) 63 *Stan L Rev* 539–590.

70 Erik F. Gerding, "Credit derivatives, leverage, and financial regulation's missing macroeconomic dimension" (2011) 8 *Berkeley Bus LJ* 29–73.

71 UK Financial Services Authority, Internal Audit Division, *The Supervision of Northern Rock: A Lessons Learned Review* (2008), available at www.fsa.gov .uk.pubs/other/nr_report.pdf.

72 US Securities and Exchange Commission, *SEC's Oversight of Bear Stearns and Related Entities: The Consolidated Supervised Entity Program*, Report No. 446-A (2008), p. 81, available at www.sec.gov/about/oig/audit/2008/446-a.pdf.

73 Ian Ayres & John Braithwaite, *Responsive Regulation: Transcending the Deregulatory Debate* (New York: Oxford University Press, 1992).

74 Gordon's main point is that cost/benefit analyses done *ex ante* regulation can never accurately reflect the actual cost/benefit balance *ex post*. Jeffrey N. Gordon, "The empty call for benefit-cost analysis in financial regulation" (2014) 43 *J Legal Stud* 351–378.

75 Ibid., at 374.

76 Julia Black & Robert Baldwin, "When risk-based regulation aims low: approaches and challenges" (2012) 6 *Reg & Gov* 2–22, at 2.

77 Kenneth W. Abbot & Duncan Snidal, "Taking responsive regulation transnational: strategies for international organizations" (2013) 7 *Reg & Gov* 95–113; Andrew William (Andy) Mullineux, "Financial innovation and social welfare" (2010) 18 *J Fin Reg & Compl* 243–256, at 248–249.

78 Mullineux, "Financial innovation," 248–249, note 77 above.

79 Haiss, "Bank herding," note 39 above.

80 Annelise Riles has examined how collateral contracts did exactly that: Riles, *Collateral Knowledge: Legal Reasoning in the Global Financial Market* (Chicago: University of Chicago Press, 2011).

81 Kathryn Judge, "Interbank discipline" (2013) 60 *UCLA L Rev* 1262–1323.

82 The OFR's mission is to "promote financial stability by delivering high-quality financial data, standards and analysis for the Financial Stability Oversight Council and public" by "Improving the scope, quality, and accessibility of financial data; Assessing and monitoring threats to financial stability; Developing tools for risk measurement and monitoring that reach across the financial system; Conducting applied and fundamental research on the stability of the financial system; and Conducting studies and providing advice on the impact of policies designed to improve resilience in the financial system". Office of Financial Research, *2015 Annual Report to Congress*, preface, available at financialresearch.gov/annual-reports/files/office-of-financial-research-annual-report-2015.pdf.

83 Charles Whitehead, "The Goldilocks approach: financial risk and staged regulation" (2012) 97 *Cornell L Rev* 1267–1308, at 1273.

84 Brett McDonnell & Daniel Schwarcz, "Regulatory contrarians" (2010) 89 *NC L Rev* 1629–1666. Models include the ombudsman contrarian, consumer representative contrarian, investigative contrarian, and research contrarian.

85 E.g., Basel Committee on Banking Supervision, "Global systematically important banks: assessing methodology and the additional loss absorbency requirement" (2011), *Bank for International Supervision*, available at www.bis.org/publ/bcbs207.pdf.

86 Steven L. Schwarcz, "Regulating complexity in financial markets" (2009) 87 *Wash UL Rev* 211–269.

9   INNOVATION-READY REGULATION: LEARNING TO SEE FINANCIAL INNOVATION

1 Allen Buchanan, Tony Cole & Robert O. Keohane, "Justice in the diffusion of innovation" (2011) 19 *J Polit Phil* 306–332, at 309–311.

2 Anuja Utz & Carl Dahlman, "Promoting inclusive innovation," in Mark A. Dutz (ed.), *Unleashing India's Innovation: Toward Sustainable and Inclusive Growth* (Washington, DC: World Bank, 2007), pp. 105–128, at 106; B. Bowonder, "Impact analysis of the green revolution in India" (1979) 15 *Technol Forecast Soc Change* 297–313, at 312.

3 See, e.g., Magdalena Ramada-Sarasola, "Can mobile money systems have a measurable impact on local development" (2012) *Innovation & Research Multiplier and Social Trade Organization for the International Development Research Centre*, available at papers.ssrn.com/sol3/papers.cfm?abstract_id=2061526; cf. Peter Senker, "A dynamic perspective on technology, economic inequality and development," in Sally Wyatt et al. (eds), *Technology and In/Equality: Questioning the Information Society* (New York: Routledge, 2000), pp. 197–218, at 214.

4 Susan E. Cozzens & Raphael Kaplinsky, "Innovation, poverty and inequality: cause, coincidence, or co-evolution?" in Beng-Ake Lundvall et al. (eds), *Handbook of Innovation Systems and Developing Countries* (Northampton: Edward Elgar, 2009), pp. 57–82, at 60.

5 Soete argues that "destructive creations" share common motivational features: short-termism, opportunities for free-riding, and dependency on networks in which the major source for innovation is trying to game the regulatory framework (p. 135). His examples are unsustainable, innovation-led consumerism, and financial innovation (Luc Soete, "Is innovation always good?" in Jan Fagerberg et al. (eds), *Innovation Studies: Evolution & Future Challenges* (Oxford: Oxford University Press, 2013), pp. 134–146).

6 For a summary of the scholarly debate on whether financial innovation is a net positive for society, see Peter Tufano, "Financial innovation," in G.M. Constantinides, M. Harris & R. Stulz (eds), *Handbook of the Economics of Finance* (Amsterdam: Elsevier, 2003), pp. 307–335, at 307–337, 327–329.

7   Michael Haliassos (ed.), *Financial Innovation: Too Much or Too Little?* (Cambridge: MIT Press, 2013), pp. xi–xii. Consistent with this book's argument, Haliassos argues that "the basic link between financial innovation and crisis has to do with the nature and pace at which innovation proceeds, the use of new financial products by users and providers, and the mechanisms available for monitoring and regulating such use." (p. xv).

8   Donald MacKenzie, *An Engine, Not a Camera: How Financial Models Shape Markets* (Cambridge: MIT Press, 2006).

9   A compatible proposal in this vein is Allen Buchanan, Tony Cole & Robert O. Keohane, "Justice in the diffusion of innovation" (2011) 19 *J Pol Philos* 306–332, proposing the creation of a new global institution, the Global Institute for Justice in Innovation, as a method for ameliorating the relationship between innovation and justice/equality. According to the authors, GIJI would be an international organization "designed to construct and implement a set of rules and policies governing the diffusion of innovations, on the basis of a sound set of principles. It would operate under conditions of accountability, according to rule-governed procedures, and would seek gradually to inculcate norms that specified appropriate behavior with respect to the diffusion of innovations." ibid., at 314. Cf. Theo Papaioannou, "Technological innovation, global justice and politics of development" (2011) 11 *Prog Dev Stud* 321–338, at 332 (expressing skepticism that developed countries would support the initiative).

10   James C. Scott, *Seeing Like a State: How Certain Schemes to Improve the Human Condition Have Failed* (New Haven: Yale University Press, 1998), p. 8.

11   On this point, see also K. Sabeel Rahman, *Democracy Against Domination* (New York: Oxford University Press, 2016), p. 145 et seq.

12   At the SEC: www.sec.gov/investorad; in Canada, the Ontario Securities Commission has formed such a body: www.osc.gov.on.ca/en/Investors_advisory-panel_index.htm.

13   See also, e.g., Louise Brown & Stephen P. Osborne, "Risk and innovation: towards a framework for risk governance in public services" (2013) 15 *Public Manag Rev* 186–208 (proposing a "negotiated risk governance" model that would incorporate transparent, public, broadly participatory negotiations about the potential costs and benefits of innovation).

14   Andreas Georg Scherer & Emilio Marti, "The normative foundation of finance: how misunderstanding the role of financial theories distorts the way we think about the responsibility of financial economists" (2011) IOU Working Paper No. 108; also Emilio Marti & Andreas Georg Scherer, "Financial regulation and social welfare: the critical contribution of management theory" (2016) 41 *Acad Manag Rev* 298–323. They rely on Habermas, but the ideas are also consistent, as is much of Habermas himself, with the civic republican underpinnings of flexible regulation.

APPENDIX A: METHODOLOGY

1   My initial hope was to include articles from JSTOR (which spans many social science fields plus some law), and publications from leading thinktanks. Ultimately

I was limited to LexisNexis because it was the only source that allowed for a sophisticated search query.

2 I included articles that had the term "innovation" in the same paragraph as any of "new governance," "new institutionalism," "contractual governance," "reflexive law," "reflexive regulation," "experimentalism," "responsive regulation," "responsive law," or "command-and-control." I also included articles in which the term "innovation" appeared close to regulatory reform, design, architecture, tool kit, or tool box. I also included articles in which "innovation" appeared close to the term "regulation," which itself was very close to any of the terms "instrument," "compliance," "analysis," "flexible," "technique," "strategy," "tactic," "practice," "mechanism," "recognition," "program," or "foster." Finally, I included articles in which "innovation" appeared in a paragraph with "governance," but among those excluded articles that mentioned "corporate governance" too frequently. I also excluded articles that mentioned the terms "antitrust" or "family law" too frequently in their main text, since these articles generally had an entirely different focus.

3 The k-means approach analysis finds the solution (i.e., groupings) that minimizes the variance *within* clusters while maximizing the variance *between* clusters. It is exploratory and data-driven, rather than qualitatively determined.

Select Bibliography

GOVERNMENT REPORTS AND SOURCES

United Kingdom

Blair, Tony, *The Third Way: New Politics for the New Century* (Fabian Society, 1998).

Tiner, John, "Better regulation: objective or oxymoron," Remarks at the SII Annual Conference, May 9, 2006, available at www.fsa.gov.uk/pages/Library/Communication/Speeches/2006/0509_jt.shtml.

UK Financial Services Authority, *The Turner Review: A Regulatory Response to the Global Banking Crisis* (2009), available at www.fsa.gov.uk/pubs/other/turner_review.pdf.

UK Financial Services Authority Internal Audit Division, *The Supervision of Northern Rock: A Lessons Learned Review* (March 2008), available at www.fca.org.uk/publication/corporate/fsa-nr-report.pdf.

UK Houses of Parliament, Parliamentary Office of Science & Technology, "Financial technology (FinTech)" (2016) 525 Postnote, available at researchbriefings.files.parliament.uk/documents/POST-PN-0525/POST-PN-0525.pdf.

United States

"Memorandum From the President on Alternative Approaches to Regulation to the Heads of Executive Departments and Agencies," June 13, 1980, *Public Papers of the Presidents of the United States, Jimmy Carter, 1980–1981, Book 2: May 24 to September 26, 1980*.

Clinton, William J., "State of the Union Address," January 27, 1998, in *Congressional Record, V. 144, Pt. 1, January 27, 1998 to February 13 1998* (Washington, DC: United States Government Printing Office, 2003).

Financial Accounting Standards Board: *Proposal: Principles-based Approach to U.S. Standard Setting* (2005), available at www.fasb.org/project/principles-based_approach_project.shtml.

The Financial Crisis Inquiry Commission, *Final Report of the National Commission on the Causes of the Financial and Economic Crisis in the United States* (2011), available at www.gpo.gov/fdsys/pkg/GPO-FCIC/pdf/GPO-FCIC.pdf.

US Securities and Exchange Commission, *Study Pursuant to Section 108(d) of the Sarbanes-Oxley Act of 2002 on the Adoption by the United States Financial Reporting System of a Principles-Based Accounting System* (2003), available at www.sec.gov/news/studies/principlesbasedstand.htm.

National Commission on the BP Deepwater Horizon Oil Spill and Offshore Drilling, *Deep Water: The Gulf Oil Disaster and the Future of Offshore Drilling* (Washington, DC: United States Government Printing, 2011), available at www.gpo.gov/fdsys/pkg/GPO-OILCOMMISSION/pdf/GPO-OILCOMMISSION.pdf.

International

Basel Committee on Banking Supervision, Bank for International Settlements, "Basel II: international convergence of capital measurement and capital standards: a revised framework" (2004), available at www.bis.org/publ/bcbs107.htm.

Basel Committee on Banking Supervision, Bank for International Settlements, "Revised Pillar 3 disclosure requirements" (2015), available at www.bis.org/bcbs/publ/d309.htm.

Financial Stability Board, *Global Shadow Banking Monitoring Report* (2014), available at www.financialstabilityboard.org/wp-content/uploads/r_141030.pdf.

Secondary Sources

Aaron, Henry J., *Politics and the Professors: The Great Society in Perspective* (Washington, DC: Brookings Institution, 1978).

Abernathy, Nell, Mike Konczal & Kathryn Milani (eds), *Untamed: How to Check Corporate, Financial, and Monopoly Power* (New York: Roosevelt Institute, 2016).

Adrian, Tobias & Hyun Song Shin, "Liquidity and leverage" (2010) 19 *J Financ Intermed* 418–437.

Anand, Kartik et al., "A network model of financial system resilience" (2013) 85 *J Econ Behav & Org'n* 219–235.

Arner, Douglas W., Jànos Barberis & Ross P. Buckley, "The evolution of fintech: a new post-crisis paradigm?" (2015) University of Hong Kong Faculty of Law, Research Paper No. 2015/047, available at ssrn.com/abstract=2676553.

Aucoin, Peter, "Administrative reform in public management: paradigms, principles, paradoxes and pendulums" (1990) 3 *Governance* 115–137.

Awrey, Dan, "Complexity, innovation, and the regulation of modern financial markets" (2012) 2 *Harv Bus L Rev* 235–294.

"Toward a supply-side theory of financial innovation" (2013) 42(2) *J Comp Econ* 401–419.

Ayres, Ian & John Braithwaite, *Responsive Regulation: Transcending the Deregulatory Debate* (New York: Oxford University Press, 1992).

Baker, Tom, "Embracing risk, sharing responsibility" (2008) 56 *Drake L Rev* 561–570.

Bamberger, Kenneth A., "Technologies of compliance: risk and regulation in a digital age" (2010) 88 *Tex L Rev* 669–739.

Bartley, Tim, "Global production and the puzzle of rules," in Hilary E. Kahn (ed.), *Framing the Global: Entry Points for Research* (Bloomington: Indiana University Press, 2014), pp. 229–252.

"Transnational governance as the layering of rules: intersections of public and private standards" (2011) 12 *Theoretical Inq L* 517–542.

Baumgartner, Frank R. & Bryan D. Jones, *Agendas and Instability in American Politics*, 2nd edn. (Chicago: University of Chicago Press, 2009).

Baxter, Lawrence G., "Adaptive regulation in the amoral bazaar" (2011) 128 *SA LJ* 253–272.

Bell, Geoffrey G., "Clusters, networks, and firm innovativeness" (2005) 26 *Strat Mgmt J* 287–295.

Bernstein, Peter L., *Against the Gods: The Remarkable Story of Risk* (New York: John Wiley & Sons, 1998).

Bevir, Mark & R.A.W. Rhodes, *Governance Stories* (New York: Routledge, 2006).

Black, Fischer & Myron Scholes, "The pricing of options and corporate liabilities" (1973) 81 *J Pol Econ* 637–655.

Black, Julia, "Paradoxes & failures: 'new governance' techniques and the financial crisis" (2012) 75 *Mod L Rev* 1037–1063.

Rules and Regulators (Oxford: Clarendon Press, 1997).

"The rise, fall and fate of principles based regulation" (2010) LSE Law, Society and Economy Working Papers 17.

"What is regulatory innovation?" and "Tomorrow's worlds: frameworks for understanding regulatory innovation," in Julia Black, Martin Lodge & Mark Thatcher (eds), *Regulatory Innovation: A Comparative Analysis* (Northampton: Edward Elgar, 2005), pp. 1–44.

Braithwaite, John, "The essence of responsive regulation" (2011) 44 *UBC L Rev* 475–520.

Bratton, William W., "Enron, Sarbanes-Oxley and accounting: rules versus principles versus rents" (2003) 48 *Vill L Rev* 1023–1056.

Bratton, William W. & Adam J. Levitin, "A transactional genealogy of scandal: from Michael Milken to Enron to Goldman Sachs" (2013) 86 *S Cal L Rev* 783–868.

Breyer, Stephen, *Regulation and its Reform* (Cambridge: Harvard University Press, 1982).

Brummer, Christopher, "Disruptive technology and securities regulation" (2015) *Fordham L Rev* 977–1052.

Buchanan, Allen, Tony Cole & Robert O Keohane, "Justice in the Diffusion of Innovation" (2011) 19 *J Polit Phil* 306–332.

Carpenter, Daniel & David A. Moss (eds), *Preventing Regulatory Capture: Special Interest Influence and How to Limit It* (New York: Cambridge University Press, 2014)

Chiu, Iris H.-Y., "The disruptive implications of fintech – policy themes for financial regulators," presented at the Digital Currencies and Financial Conference, Centre for Law, Economics and Society (July 27–28, 2016), available at papers. ssrn.com/sol3/papers.cfm?abstract_id=2812667.

Coglianese, Cary, "The limits of performance-based regulation" (2017) 50 *U Mich JL Reform* (in press)

Coglianese, Cary & David Lazer, "Management-based regulation: prescribing private management to achieve public goals" (2003) 37 *Law & Soc'y Rev* 691–730.

Cohen, Amy J., "Governance legalism: Hayek and Sabel on reasons and rules, organization and law" (2010) *Wis L Rev* 357–388.

Dallas, Lynne L., "Short termism, the financial crisis, and corporate governance" (2012) 37 *J Corp L* 265–364.

de Búrca, Gráinne, "New governance and experimentalism: an introduction" (2010) *Wis L Rev* 227–238.

de Búrca, Gráinne, Robert O. Keohane & Charles Sabel, "New modes of pluralist global governance" (2013) 45 *NYU J Int'L L & Pol* 723–787.

de Sousa Santos, Boaventura, "Law: a map of misreading. Toward a post-modern conception of law" (1987) 14 *JL & Soc'y* 279–302.

Desmond, Matthew, "Is democratic regulation of high finance possible?" (2013) 649 *Annals Am Acad Polit & Soc Sci* 180–184.

DiMaggio, Paul J. & Walter P., "The iron cage revisited: institutional isomorphism and collective rationality in organizational fields" (1983) 48 *Am Soc Rev* 147–160.

Diver, Colin, "The optimal precision of administrative rules" (1983) 93 *Yale LJ* 65–109.

Dorf, Michael C. & Charles F. Sabel, "A constitution of democratic experimentalism" (1998) 98 *Colum L Rev* 267–473.

Engelen, Ewald et al., "Reconceptualizing financial innovation: frame, conjuncture and bricolage" (2010) 39 *Econ & Soc'y* 33–63.

Esping-Andersen, Gøsta, "After the golden age: welfare state dilemmas in a global economy," in Gøsta Esping-Anderson (ed.), *Welfare States in Transition: National Adaptations in Global Economies* (London: Sage, 1996),, pp. 1–31.

Fagerberg, Jan, "Innovation: a guide to the literature," in Jan Fagerberg, David C. Mowery & Richard R. Nelson (eds), *The Oxford Handbook of Innovation* (New York: Oxford University Press, 2005), pp. 1–26.

Ford, Cristie, "New governance in the teeth of human frailty: lessons from financial regulation" (2010) *Wis L Rev* 441–489.

Ford, Cristie L., "Principles-based securities regulation in the wake of the global financial crisis" (2010) 45 *McGill L Rev* 257–307.

Ford, Cristie, "Systemic risk regulation in comparative perspective" (2016), available at papers.ssrn.com/sol3/papers.cfm?abstract_id=2798419.

Frankel, Tamar, "The new financial assets: separating ownership from control" (2010) 33 *Sea U L Rev* 931–964.

Freeman, Christopher & Luc Soete, *The Economics of Industrial Innovation*, 3rd edn. (MIT Press, 1997).

Friedman, Jeffrey & Wladimir Kraus, *Engineering the Financial Crisis* (Philadelphia: University of Pennsylvania Press, 2011).

Frischmann, Brett & Mark Lemley, "Spillovers" (2007) 107 *Colum L Rev* 257–301.

Funk, Russell J. & Daniel Hirschman, "Derivatives and deregulation: financial innovation and the demise of Glass-Steagall" (2014) 59 *Admin Sci Q* 669–704.

Gelpern, Anna & Erik F. Gerding, "Inside safe assets" (2016) 33 *Yale J on Reg* 363.

Gerding, Erik F., *Law, Bubbles, and Financial Regulation* (New York: Routledge, 2014).

Giddens, Anthony, "Risk and responsibility" (1999) 62 *Mod L Rev* 1–10.

Gilson Ronald J. & Charles K. Whitehead, "Deconstructing equity: public ownership, agency costs, and complete financial market" (2008) 108 *Colum L Rev* 231–264.

Glendon, Mary Ann, *Rights Talk: The Impoverishment of Political Discourse* (New York: Free Press, 1991).

Godin, Benoît, "Innovation: the history of a category" (2008) Project on the Intellectual History of Innovation, Working Paper No. 1.

Gordon, Jeffrey N., "The empty call for benefit-cost analysis in financial regulation" (2014) 43 *J Legal Stud* 351–378.

Gowda, M.V. Rajeev, "Heuristics, biases and the regulation of risk" (1999) 32 *Policy Sci* 59–78.

Grewal, David Singh & Jedediah Purdy, "Introduction: law and neoliberalism" (2014) 77 *L & Contemp Probs* 1–23.

Gubler, Zachary J., "The financial innovation process: theory and application" (2011) 36 *Del J Corp L* 55–119.

Gunningham, Neil, "Environment law, regulation and governance: shifting architectures" (2009) 21 *J Envtl L* 179–212.

Gunningham, Neil & Peter M. Grabosky, *Smart Regulation: Designing Environmental Policy* (New York: Oxford University Press, 1998).

Gunningham, Neil, Robert A. Kagan & Dorothy Thornton, *Shades of Green: Business, Regulation, and Environment* (Stanford: Stanford University Press, 2003).

Haines, Fiona, *The Paradox of Regulation: What Regulation Can Achieve and What it Cannot* (Northampton: Edward Elgar, 2011).

Haldane, Andrew G. & Robert M. May, "Systemic risk in banking ecosystem" (2011) 469 *Nature* 351–355.

Haliassos, Michael, "Financial Innovation and Economic Crisis: An Introduction," in Michael Haliassos, *Financial Innovation: Too Much or Too Little?* (Cambridge: MIT Press, 2013), Vii-xxii.

Hazen, Thomas Lee, "Disparate regulatory schemes for parallel activities: securities regulation, derivatives regulation, gambling, and insurance" (2005) 24 *Ann Rev Banking & Fin L* 375.

Heimer, Carol A., "Disarticulated responsiveness: the theory and practice of responsive regulation in multi-layered systems" (2011) 44 *UBC L Rev* 663–693.

Hu, Henry T.C., "Swaps, the modern process of financial innovation and the vulnerability of a regulatory paradigm" (1989) 138 *U Pa L Rev* 333–435.

Hu, Henry T.C. & Bernard S. Black, "The new vote buying: empty voting and hidden (morphable) ownership" (2006) 79 *S Cal L Rev* 811–908.

Judge, Kathryn, "Fragmentation nodes: a study in financial innovation, complexity, and systemic risk" (2012) 64 *Stan L Rev* 657–725.

Karkkainen, Bradley C., "'New governance' in legal thought and in the world: some splitting as antidote to overzealous lumping" (2004) 89 *Minn L Rev* 471–497.

Knight, Frank H., *Risk, Uncertainty and Profit* (New York: Houghton Mifflin Company, 1921).

Krawiec, Kimberly D., "Don't 'screw Joe the plummer': the sausage-making of financial reform" (2013) 55 *Ariz L R* 53–103.

Krippner, Greta R., *Capitalizing on Crisis: The Political Origins of the Rise of Finance* (Cambridge: Harvard University Press, 2011).

La Belle, Megan M. & Heidi Mandanis Schooner, "Big banks and business method patents" (2014) 16 *U Pa J Bus L* 431–495.

Lamont, Michèle, "Toward a comparative sociology of valuation and evaluation" (2012) 38 *Ann Rev Sociol* 201–221.

Langevoort, Donald C., "Global securities regulation after the financial crisis" (2010) 13 *J Econ L* 799–815.

"Chasing the greased pig down Wall Street: a gatekeeper's guide to the psychology, culture, and ethics of financial risk taking" (2011) 96 *Cornell L Rev* 1209–1246.

Selling hope, Selling Risk: Corporations, Wall Street, and the Dilemmas of Investor Protection (New York: Oxford University Press, 2016).

Lazonick, William, "The innovative firm," in Jan Fagerberg, David C. Mowery & Richard R. Nelson (eds), *The Oxford Handbook of Innovation* (New York: Oxford University Press, 2005).

Lee, Roger et al., "The remit of financial geography – before and after the crisis" (2009) 9 *J Econ Geog* 723–747.

Lerner, Josh & Peter Tufano, "The consequences of financial innovation: a counterfactual research agenda," in Josh Lerner & Scott Stern (eds), *The Rate and Direction of Inventive Activity Revisited* (Chicago: University of Chicago Press, 2012), pp. 523–578.

Lessig, Lawrence, "The new Chicago school" (1998) 27 *J Legal Stud* 661–691.

Levi-Faur, David, "The global diffusion of regulatory capitalism" (2005) 598 *Annals Am Acad Polit & Soc Sci* 12–32.

Levinson, Marc, *The Box: How the Shipping Container Made the World Smaller and the World Economy Bigger* (Princeton: Princeton University Press, 2006).

Lewis, Michael, *Flash Boys: A Wall Street Revolt* (New York: W.W. Norton & Company, 2014).

Lindblom, Charles E., "The science of 'muddling through'" (1959) 19 *Publ Admin Rev* 79–88.

Lobel, Orly, "The renew deal: the fall of regulation and the rise of governance in contemporary legal thought" (2004) 89 *Minn L Rev* 342–470.

Mackenzie, Donald, "Long-term capital management and the sociology of arbitrage" (2003) 32 *Econ & Soc'y* 349–380.

Majone, Giandomenico, "Regulation and its modes," in Jeremy Richardson (ed.), *Regulating Europe* (London: Routledge, 2002), pp. 9–27.

Markose, Sheri, Simone Giansanteb & Ali Rais Shagaghi, "'Too interconnected to fail' financial network of US CDS market: topological fragility and systemic risk" (2012) 83 *J Econ Behav & Org'n* 627–646.

McCoy, Patricia A., Andrey D. Pavlov & Susan M. Wachter, "Systemic risk through securitization: the result of deregulation and regulatory failure" (2009) 41 *Conn L R* 1327–1377.

McCraw, Thomas K., *Prophets of Regulation: Charles Francis Adams, Louis D. Brandeis, James M. Landis, Alfred E. Kahn* (Cambridge: Belknap Press, 1984).

McDonnell, Brett & Daniel Schwarcz, "Regulatory contrarians" (2010) 89 *NC L Rev* 1629–1666.

Merton, Robert C., "Financial innovation and economic performance" (1992) 4 *Bank Am J Appl Corp Finance* 12–22.

"Option pricing when underlying stock returns are discontinuous" (1976) 3 *J Fin Econ* 125–144.

"Theory of rational option pricing" (1973) 4 *Bell J Econ & Mgmt Sci* 141–183.

Michelman, Frank, "Law's republic" (1988) 97 *Yale LJ* 1493–1537.

Miller, Merton H., "Financial innovation: the last twenty years and the next" (1986) 21 *J Financ Quant Anal* 459–471.

Moloney, Niamh, "The legacy effects of the financial crisis on regulatory design in the EU," in Eilís Ferran et al., *The Regulatory Aftermath of the Global Financial Crisis* (New York: Cambridge University Press, 2012), pp. 111–202.

Moran, Michael, *The British Regulatory State: High Modernism and Hyper-Innovation* (New York: Oxford University Press, 2003).

Morgan, Bronwen & Karen Yeung, *An Introduction to Law and Regulation: Text and Materials* (Cambridge: Cambridge University Press, 2007),pp. 79–113.

Ogus, Anthony I., *Regulation: Legal Form and Economic Theory* (New York: Oxford University Press, 2004).

Omarova, Saule T., "License to deal: mandatory approval of complex financial products" (2012) 90 *Wash U L Rev* 63–140.

"The quiet metamorphosis: how derivatives changed the 'business of banking'" (2009) 63 *U Miami L Rev* 1041–1110.

Omarova, Saule T. & Robert C. Hockett, "The Finance Franchise" (2017 Forthcoming) 102 *Cornell L Rev*; (2016) Cornell Legal Studies Research Paper No. 16–29.

Orts, Eric W., "Reflexive environmental law" (1994) 89 *Nw U L Rev* 1227–1340.

Osborne, David & Ted Gaebler, *Reinventing Government: How the Entrepreneurial Spirit is Transforming the Public Sector* (Reading: Addison-Wesley Publishing Company, 1992).

Ostrom, Elinor, *Governing the Commons: The Evolution of Institutions for Collective Action* (New York: Cambridge University Press, 1990).

Parker, Christine, "Meta-regulation: the regulation of self-regulation," in *The Open Corporation: Effective Self-Regulation and Democracy* (New York: Cambridge University Press, 2002).

"The 'compliance' trap: the moral message in responsive regulatory enforcement" (2006) 40 *L & Soc'y Rev* 591–622.

The Open Corporation: Effective Self-Regulation and Democracy (New York: Cambridge University Press, 2002).

Partnoy, Frank, *Infectious Greed: how deceit and risk corrupted the financial markets* (London: Profile, 2003).

"The shifting contours of global derivatives regulation" (2001) 22 *U Pa J Int'l Econ* 421–495.

"The Siskel and Ebert of financial markets?: two thumbs down for the credit rating agencies" (1999) 77 *Wash U L Q* 619–714.

Perrow, Charles, *Normal Accidents: living with high risk technologies* (New York: Basic Books, 1984).

Pettit, Phillip, *Republicanism: A Theory of Freedom and Government* (New York: Oxford University Press, 1997).

Piketty, Thomas & Arthur Goldhammer, *Capital in the Twenty-First Century* (Cambridge: Harvard University Press, 2014).

Polanyi, Karl, *The Great Transformation: the Political and Economic Origins of our Time* (Boston: Beacon Press, 1944).

Posner, Eric & E. Glen Weyl, "An FDA for financial innovation: applying the insurable interest doctrine to 21st Century financial markets" (2015) 107 *Nw U L Rev* 1307–1358.

Power, Michael, *The Audit Society: Rituals of Verification* (New York: Oxford University Press, 1997).

The Risk Management of Everything: Rethinking the Politics of Uncertainty (London: Demos, 2004).

Prentice, Robert A., "The inevitability of a strong SEC" (2006) 91 *Cornell L Rev* 775–840.

Rahman, K. Sabeel, *Democracy Against Domination* (New York: Oxford University Press, 2016).

Redmond, William, "Financial innovation, diffusion, and instability" (2013) 47 *J Econ Issues* 525–531.

Reich, Charles A., "The new property" (1964) 73 *Yale LJ* 733–787.

Riles, Annelise, *Collateral Knowledge: Legal Reasoning in the Global Financial Markets* (Chicago: University of Chicago Press, 2011).

Roe, Mark J., "The derivatives market's payment priorities as financial crisis accelerator" (2011) 63 *Stan L Rev* 539–590.

Rogers, Everett M., *Diffusion of Innovations*, 4th edn. (New York: Free Press, 1995).

Sabel, Charles F. & William H. Simon, "Destabilization rights: how public law litigation succeeds" (2004) 117 *Harv L Rev* 1015–1101.

"Minimalism and experimentalism in the administrative state" (2011–2012) 100 *Geo LJ* 53–94.

Scherer, Andreas G. & Emilio Marti, "Financial Regulation and Social Welfare: The Critical Contribution of Management Theory" (2016) 41(2) *Acad Manage Rev* 298–323.

Schwarcz, Steven L., "Regulating complexity in financial markets" (2009) 87 *Wash UL Rev* 211–269.

"Systemic risk" (2008) 97 *Geo LJ* 197–250.

Scott, Colin, "Regulation in the age of governance: the rise of the post-regulatory state," in Jacint Jordana and David Levi-Faur (eds), *The Politics of Regulation: Institutions and Regulatory Reforms for the Age of Governance* (Cheltenham: Edward Elgar Publishing, 2004), pp. 145–174.

Scott, James C., *Seeing Like a State: How Certain Schemes to Improve the Human Condition Have Failed* (New Haven: Yale University Press, 1998).

Shamir, Ronen, "Corporate social responsibility: towards a new market-embedded morality?" (2008) 9 *Theoretical Inq L* 371–394.

Shin, Hyun Song & Tobias Adrian, "The changing nature of financial intermediation and the financial crisis of 2007–2009" (2010) 2 *Ann Rev Econ* 603–618.

Short, Jodi L., "The paranoid style in regulatory reform" (2012) 63 *Hastings LJ* 633–694.

Silbey, Susan & Ruthanne Huising, "Governing the gap: forging safe science through relational regulation" (2011) 5 *Reg & Gov* 14–42.

Simon, William H., "Optimization and its discontents in regulatory design: bank regulation as an example" (2009) 4 *Reg & Gov* 3–21.

Skinner, Quentin, *Liberty Before Liberalism* (New York: Cambridge University Press, 1998).

Sparrow, Malcolm K., *The Regulatory Craft: Controlling Risks, Solving Problems and Managing Compliance* (Washington, DC: Brookings Institution Press, 2000).

Stewart, Richard B., "Administrative law in the twenty-first century" (2003) 78 *NYU L Rev* 437–460.

Stout, Lynn A., "Derivatives and the legal origin of the 2008 credit crisis" (2011) 1 *Harv Bus L Rev* 13–23.

Sturm, Susan, "Second generation employment discrimination: a structural approach" (2001) 101 *Colum L Rev* 458–568.

Sunstein, Cass R., *After The Rights Revolution: Reconceiving the Regulatory State* (Cambridge: Harvard University Press, 1993).

Tett, Gillian, *Fool's Gold* (London: Abacus, 2010).

Teubner, Gunther, "Substantive and reflexive elements of modern law" (1983) 17 *Law & Soc'y Rev* 239–285.

Tufano, Peter, "Financial innovation," in G.M. Constantinides, M. Harris & R. Stulz (eds), *Handbook of the Economics of Finance* (Amsterdam: Elsevier, 2003), pp. 307–335.

"Financial innovation and first mover advantages" (1989) 25 *J Financ Econ* 213–240.

Tushnet, Mark, "Reflections on democratic experimentalism in the progressive tradition" (2012) 9 *Contempo Prag'm* 255–261.

Tversky, Amos & Daniel Kahneman, "Judgement under uncertainty: heuristics and biases" (1974) 185 *Science* 1124–1131.

Tyler, Tom R., *Why People Obey the Law* (New Haven: Yale University Press, 1990).

Vandenbergh, Michael P., "The private life of public law" (2005) 105 *Colum L Rev* 2029–2096.

Vaughan, Diane, "Autonomy, interdependence, and social control: NASA and the Space Shuttle Challenger" (1990) 35 *Admin Sci Q* 225–257.

Veljanovski, Cento, "Economic approaches to regulation," in Robert Baldwin et al. (eds), *The Oxford Handbook of Regulation* (New York: Oxford University Press, 2010), pp. 17–38.

Whitehead, Charles, "Reframing financial regulation" (2010) 90 *BU L Rev* 1–50.

Wilmarth Arthur E. Jr, "The transformation of the U.S. financial services industry, 1975–2000: competition, consolidation, and increased risks" (2002) *U Ill L Rev* 215–476.

Yeung, Karen, "The regulatory state," in Robert Baldwin et al. (eds), *The Oxford Handbook of Regulation* (New York: Oxford University Press, 2010), pp. 64–85.

Index